Reading
From Process
to Practice

THE COL

Reading
From Process
to Practice

Edited by

L. John Chapman and Pam Czerniewska
for the Reading Diploma Course Team
at the Open University

London and Henley
Routledge & Kegan Paul
in association with
The Open University Press

First published in 1978
by Routledge & Kegan Paul Ltd
39 Store Street,
London WC1E 7DD and
Broadway House,
Newtown Road,
Henley-on-Thames,
Oxon RG9 1EN
Photoset in 10 on 11 Times by
Kelly and Wright, Bradford-on-Avon, Wiltshire
and printed in Great Britain by
Lowe & Brydone Ltd,
Thetford, Norfolk

British Library Cataloguing in Publication Data

Reading.

1. Reading
I. Chapman, John   II. Czerniewska, Pam
III. Open University
428'.4   LB1050

ISBN 0-7100-0055-3
ISBN 0-7100-0064-2 Pbk

Contents

vi *Contents*

Acknowledgments

The Open University and the publishers would like to thank the following for permission to reproduce copyright material. All possible care has been taken to trace ownership of the selections included and to make full acknowledgment for their use.

Reading
1.1 © Unesco, 1977.
1.2, 7.1 Copyright © 1976 by the National Council of Teachers of English. Reprinted by permission of the publisher and the authors.
1.3, 2.3 and 2.5 Copyright © 1970, 1977, 1977 by President and Fellows of Harvard College.
1.4, 2.2, 2.6, 3.4, 5.3 and 7.2 Reprinted with permission of the authors and the International Reading Association.
2.1 Copyright © 1967 by McGraw-Hill Inc. Used with permission of McGraw-Hill Book Company.
2.4 By permission of Donald Moyle and the UKRA, 1974.
3.1 By permission of Routledge & Kegan Paul Ltd, 1971.
3.2 and 6.2 © Unesco, 1973.
3.3 Reprinted from *Interchange*, volume 5, no. 4—a Journal of Educational Studies published quarterly by The Ontario Institute for Studies in Education, by permission of Rebecca Barr.
4.1 By permission of the editor, *Reading Research Quarterly*, 1974–5.
4.2 and 5.1 By permission of Ward Lock Educational, 1970, 1977.
4.3 By permission of the editor, *Forum*, 1974.
4.4 Copyright © Pluto Press 1977. Reprinted with permission.
5.2 By permission of NFER Publishing Company Ltd, 1975.
6.1 By permission of Michael Marland, 1977.
6.3 © The Open University, 1978.

Introduction

The nature of the reading process and the ways of teaching reading have been the subject of much debate. Countless books, papers, articles, schemes and items of equipment have grown out of such argument, each representing and defending different definitions of what is involved in the development of reading. This collection of articles will not clear the confusion by stating yet another 'right way' to teach reading. Rather it is a *selection* of papers about reading which reflect current, often contradictory, trends and perspectives.

Our aim is to provide teachers with a reasoned base from which to participate in the debate on reading, as it affects them directly. This Reader will have achieved little if it fails to contribute to the teacher's work in the classroom. A teacher's involvement with the issues of current concern may be, and should be, reflected in his or her planning and classroom practice.

Section 1 Looking at Literacy

The teacher of reading is involved, whether this is consciously realised or not, in the development of a literate society. And every teacher, therefore, needs to determine what level of literacy is demanded by society, what role he or she should take in achieving the desired standard of literacy, and what the implications of literacy are in a world context.

The Unesco report (1.1) presents a world view of literacy. Too often we limit our thoughts to the relatively small proportion of illiterates in our own country and fail to see it in its international context.

The problems facing developing nations are also facing industrialised nations. Literacy, as the report points out, is 'inextricably intertwined with other aspects of national development . . . [and] . . . national development as a whole is bound up with the world context'. Literacy is not a by-product of social and economic development—it is a component of that development. Literacy can help people to function more effectively in a changing environment and ideally will enable the individual to change the environment so that it functions more effectively.

Literacy programmes instituted in different countries have taken and are taking different approaches to the problem: for example the involvement of voluntary non-governmental organisations, which underlines the importance of seeing literacy not as a condition imposed on people but as a consequence of active participation within society. Perhaps we can learn from the attempts of other countries to provide an adequate 'literacy environment'.

Who are the 'illiterates' and how do we define them? At what point do we decide that illiteracy ends and literacy begins? Robert

Hillerich (1.2) addresses these questions. An illiterate, he finds, 'may mean anything from one who has *no* formal schooling to one who has attended four years or less, to one who is unable to read or write at a level necessary to perform successfully in his social position.' Literacy, he points out, is not something one either has or has not got: 'Any definition of literacy must recognize this quality as a continuum, representing all degrees of development.'

An educational definition—i.e. in terms of grades completed or skills mastered—is shown to be inadequate in that educationally defined mastery may bear only minimal relation to the language proficiency needed in coping with environmental demands. From a sociological/economic viewpoint the literacy needs of individuals vary greatly, and any definition must recognise the needs of the individual to engage effectively and to act with responsible participation.

Such a broadened definition excludes assessment based on a 'reading-level type'; assessment must, rather, be flexible to fit both purpose and population.

Two points emerge from this article:

> to what extent has the educational system considered the literacy requirements of adult living, and built these into the reading curriculum?

and

> to what extent are Hillerich's concluding remarks merely optimistic hopes rather than operational goals?

The Unesco report and Hillerich's paper take for granted that literacy is a necessary condition for the development of society.

But there are other views about literacy which need to be voiced alongside these. Neil Postman (1.3) challenges the promotion of literacy as 'a major force for political conservatism'. His major tenet is that 'to teach reading, or even to promote vigorously the teaching of reading, is to take a definite political position on how people should behave and on what they ought to value.' The printed word, for Postman, is a medium which leads to 'political and social stasis'. While schools limit themselves to the written media, he contends, education works against change and fails to generate new patterns of behaviour.

Whether or not you agree with the stand taken by Postman, it is worth asking yourself how well you can answer his final questions:

> What is reading good for? What is it better or worse than? What are my motives in promoting it? And the ultimate political question of all, 'Whose side am I on?'

One response to these questions is made by Frank Smith (1.4). He argues that Postman's view of the printed medium as the cause of educational disenchantment and failure is ill founded. The 'malaise' of schools is not that they teach reading but *how* they teach it. Adverse effects of reading, such as suggested by Postman, are the consequence of the way reading is taught. Reading, or in fact any subject, will produce 'mental stultification' if schools do not aim for independent exercise of thought . . . 'The price of literacy need not be the reader's free will and intelligence'.

Both Postman's and Smith's articles are highly polemical but the arguments cannot be easily discounted. Without deciding what are our motives for fostering reading skills, and how best we can promote literacy, we may find that, as Smith suggests, 'ignorance is clustered in our educational institutions.'

Taken together, the papers in this section provide insights into the problem of literacy—its meaning, its definitions, and hence the battlegrounds on which the teaching of reading takes place.

1. 1 Literacy in the world: shortcomings, achievements and tendencies

Unesco

World literacy: 1965–1975

I *The quantitative aspects of the problem*

An overall view of the situation. The number of illiterates has always been difficult to calculate. Partly because figures are not always reliable, and also because where illiteracy rates are high they are either unobtainable or incomplete. Even when obtainable, they are often incomparable, because 'illiteracy' is defined differently in different places. Nevertheless in as far as general estimations have been made, figures available at the beginning of the last quarter of the 20th century show that the world is still far from reaching universal literacy. Although the percentage of illiteracy had steadily fallen from 44.3% in 1950 to 39.3% in 1960 and 34.2% in 1970, the total number of adult illiterates in the world had risen and is now approximately 800,000,000. This increase in absolute terms of the illiteracy population must be imputed to the population explosion, and inadequate as well as misdirected educational provision.

In 1970 Africa and the Arab States still had the largest percentage of illiteracy in their adult populations, followed by Asia—then Latin America. All four regions decreased their illiteracy rate by between 7 and 9% between 1960 and 1970. But whereas in 1970 this left a rate of illiteracy in Latin America of about 24%, both in Africa and the Arab States it was still over 70% and in Asia just under 50%.

Source: Unesco, 'Literacy in the world since the 1966 Teheran Conference: shortcomings, achievements, tendencies', International Symposium for Literacy, Persepolis, 1975.

Illiteracy has a close correlation with poverty. In the twenty-five least developed countries, where the per capita product is less than $100 a year, illiteracy rates are over 80%. It should be said also that countries with the highest illiteracy rates tend also to have higher population growth rates. Further, the proportion of women illiterates is steadily growing. In 1960, 58% of illiterates were women; by 1970 this had risen to 60%. In those ten years the number of illiterate men rose by 8 millions and that of illiterate women by 40 millions.

The proportionate number of illiterates living in rural areas is also much higher than in urban areas. Even though much progress has been made in the provision of primary school education in the last few decades, many children still do not enter formal primary schools, and many others drop out before completion. For example statistics given for enrolment ratios in the twenty-five least developed countries indicate that if trends observed in the last two decades were to continue to 1985, less than 30% of the children aged 6–11 would be in school by end of the period. Thus new generations of illiterates continue to join the adult population. As a result, illiteracy is growing on the world scale.

II *The qualitative aspects of the problem*

The limiting factors. Many governments in Africa, Latin America and Asia have taken realistic and imaginative steps to overcome illiteracy. In certain countries, through the dynamic mobilization of their resources, illiteracy has been virtually completely eradicated; others, due to apathy, negligence (even when resources have been available) and other causes have failed to tackle their problem with serious intent. Further, the developed countries have not given the eradication of illiteracy a high priority in their bilateral or multilateral aid programmes.

But the problem has still greater dimension—illiteracy is caught in a vicious circle: not only is it a source of inequalities but it is simultaneously the product of other inequalities in a society (e.g. political, social and economic). Centuries of colonial rule held back the right of people to their own self-determination. Existing social structures in some countries do not favour equality of opportunity; education has often been misdirected, with undue emphasis on the training of elites and the adoption of standards inappropriate for the participation of the general population, and even reforms have led to new structures thus favouring elites. Social/economic situations still exist in which literacy is not required (subsistence farming, barter trading systems, etc.). Some indigenous cultures have been absorbed by foreign influences, often leading to cultural alienation. In many countries land reforms and attempts at income redistribution have not yet been undertaken. These and many other factors have inhibited both the provision of literacy programmes and the motivation of potential learners.

Yet even in situations where literacy programmes do exist, many obstacles hinder progress and efficient planning. These include lack of human and material resources; social structures which place the illiterate majority at a disadvantage; an unrealistic content to literacy materials; bad communications; lack of transport facilities; scattered population groups; multiple language situations; problems of choice of language for instruction; lack of written material; lack of trained teachers. But perhaps the most important of all is 'the lack of literacy environment', i.e. the social structures and facilities geared to the uses of literacy.

Major facts of literacy action in the last ten years

III *Policies and structures*

Planning. Many countries have taken far-reaching steps in the field of literacy planning. Due to profound differences in national structures, these steps varied very widely; but the aim of many of them was to introduce more rigorous programming and to establish medium-term objectives. Some Arab countries, for example, have set themselves the goal of total literacy, within certain age-limits, in the space of ten years (fifteen in other cases). In Burma, the Philippines, Madagascar and Tanzania, government decrees and related regulations provide for systematic literacy campaigns. Brazil envisages to reduce the percentage of adult illiteracy to less than 10% for 1980; in Iran, the fourth five-year development plan (1967–72) aimed at a 30% reduction in the illiteracy rate.

Recently two major industrial countries announced national programmes for their adult illiterate population, which ran into millions because it is not only in developing countries that illiteracy is a problem. Furthermore, these programmes are not considered as emergency programmes, but long-term programmes, as the provision and content of existing formal primary education is not expected to overcome the problem of a substantial number of drop-outs who form the core of the semi-literate population.

Legislation. Some countries have taken legislative action in favour of literacy: for example, Argentina, Brazil, Chile, Dominican Republic, Ecuador, Haiti, Paraguay, Chad, Madagascar, Togo, Indonesia and Iran, where decrees giving priority to literacy programmes were adopted. In Libya, Iraq, the Arab Republic of Yemen, Syria, Sudan, CAR and Mali, laws have been promulgated making it compulsory for illiterate adults to attend courses. Elsewhere, in Guatemala, Venezuela, the Congo Republic and the Arab Republic of Egypt, for example, the aim of new legislation was to generalize the system under which enterprises invest a part of their profits in literacy programmes for their personnel. In El Salvador and Ecuador, in Ethiopia and Somalia, recent laws required literate adults to assist in the education of their illiterate compatriots.

Other laws and decrees aimed at the reform of administrative structures in the light of the demands of literacy development. Thus new national literacy services have been created in the Congo Republic, Dahomey, Ethiopia, Korea and Mauritania. In Indonesia, Madagascar, Mauritius, Argentina, Paraguay and the Arab Republic of Egypt existing institutions have been reorganized, while many countries have set up entirely new regional, provincial or municipal structures for literacy.

Administration. Various countries have approached the literacy work as an endeavour of a multiple character, vesting, therefore, the responsibility of the literacy action in more than one governmental department; for example, as in Colombia, Burma, Nepal, Gabon and Senegal. In others—India, Thailand, Ivory Coast and Mali—national literacy committees representing a very wide selection of competent organs have had the explicit tasks of advising the government in defining the national policy. In Algeria, the Arab Republic of Egypt, Iraq and Tunisia, these committees included also spokesmen for political parties, social associations or trade unions and co-operatives.

Often, literacy work has been placed under a variety of authorities, thus in Afghanistan, for example, there have been programmes running concurrently under the authority of the Ministry of Education, of the Department of Rural Development of the Ministry of the Interior, of the Welfare Society (for women only) and of the Army. In Latin America private undertakings operated many literacy programmes in conjunction with vocational training centres of an autonomous character. In certain African countries bodies responsible for literacy work have been placed under the authority of a Minister other than the Minister of Education, such as the Minister of Community Development in Zambia, the Prime Minister in Jamaica, the Ministry of Co-operatives and Social Services in Kenya and the Minister of Local Administration in Swaziland.

A new organizational approach. The Mobral system, which started its activities in 1967 in Brazil, in its massive tackling of the illiteracy problem, has developed and applied innovative organizational and managerial patterns, so different from those of traditional public administration. The main features of Mobral's strategy, by which it seems that it has been possible to overcome some of the difficulties arising from the mass approach, have been the following:

(a) the illiteracy problem is approached on a massive scale, but its eradication is attempted by progressive operational targets, different for each state of the Union. Six states should have reached the targets in 1975, three should reach them in 1976, four in 1977, nine in 1978;

(b) the programmes operate at four levels: central, regional, State and municipal; the first three levels have a directional character, the fourth has the responsibility for execution; this decentralization reduces Mobral's administrative machinery, strengthens local institutions, and makes easier the adjustment of the programme to local conditions;

(c) the clear, but not rigid, priorities which have been established: (i) to attack illiteracy first in urban areas, and (ii) to direct the literacy action to the 15–35-year age group preferably;

(d) the special nature of its administration; the Executive Secretary, in fact, is assisted by Advisory Bodies on Organization, Methods, Supervision and Planning, as well as by five Management Divisions: those of Pedagogical Activities, Mobilization, Research and Training, Finance and Supporting Activities.

New institutions. It should be said that a fair number of new institutions have been established recently at national and regional levels, in several countries, with the aim of providing technical orientation and assistance in literacy research, planning, organization, training, implementation and evaluation. Among the regional bodies, one may mention the Regional Council for Adult Education and Literacy in Africa (CREAA), which has its headquarters in Lomé, Togo; this Council has the aim of promoting and co-ordinating literacy work in the nations of the West African region; the Society for the Promotion of Adult Literacy in Africa, Nairobi, Kenya (AFROLIT); the African Adult Education Association (AAEA) at the Ahmadu Bello University in Nigeria; the Arab States Literacy Organization (ARLO) in Cairo, Arab Republic of Egypt; the Asian-South Pacific Bureau of Adult Education (ASPBAE) in Sydney, Australia, and the very recent International Adult Education Council in Toronto, Canada.

Among national bodies: the National Centre for Adult Education and Training in Iran which was established by the

Iranian government, with Unesco co-operation, for carrying out methodological research and studies on problems concerning adult education and literacy; the Regional Centre for Adult Education (CREA) in Caracas, Venezuela, and the National Institute for Functional Literacy and Applied Linguistics (INAFLA) in Bamako, Mali.

Finally, many university schools of education, in the Americas as well as in Africa, Asia and Europe, have sponsored literacy studies or organized courses in literacy, as, for example, the University of Ibadan in Nigeria, the University of Dar es Salaam in Tanzania, the University of Teheran in Iran, the University of Reading in Britain, Indiana University in the USA and Nice University in France. Courses in literacy have also been included in teacher-training colleges' curricula, as in the Central African Republic (CAR), Chad and Liberia.

The NGOs' contribution. The years 1965–75 have seen a continuing participation of non-governmental organizations in literacy activities throughout the world. Women's organizations, youth committees, students' teams, co-operatives, trade unions, groups of social action, voluntary agencies, individual leaders have provided a large contribution to literacy by launching and carrying out local activities, as well as by organizing national or local meetings, by holding motivational discussions and lectures, by planning and conducting researches and studies, and by training cadres and agents who had to take part in field operations.

A growing contribution to literacy has also been made by religious bodies: Koranic, Buddhist, Christian. Indeed in many countries the first alphabets were developed by religious teachers, the first written manuscripts were religious texts, the first books to be translated and written were often religious books, the first schools were established by religious ministers, and the first purpose of literacy was conceived as religious teaching. We now find many religious leaders regarding literacy not only as an instrument of moral teaching and spiritual development, but also, in a wider context, as a factor in social and economic progress.

The co-ordination among the various non-governmental organizations is provided by their International Federations having consultative status with Unesco. Among the most active are found the following: the World Labour Confederation; the International Women's Council; the World Federation of the Democratic Women's Associations; Caritas International; International Council of Cinema and T.V.; World Alliance of Young Men's Christian Associations; World Young Women's Christian

Association; Associated Country-women of the World; World Association of Girl Guides and Girl Scouts.

The NGOs' initiatives often have shown limited objectives and ephemeral duration, but they have revealed the presence of a wealth of intellectual and educational resources at local level. It has now been recognized that to overcome illiteracy in a country a widespread capillary programme is needed. This type of programme cannot be effective if it is not founded on the authentic energy of the local groups. But their activities require co-ordination and technical advice from a permanent government institution. This co-ordination between governmental structures and private groups should take different configurations, according to the nature of the existing inter-relationships between the two levels, which varies from country to country.

IV *Participatory approaches*

Too often in the past, literacy action took the form of campaigns offered to illiterates without their involvement. An innovative change has been seen in the last few years. The illiterates themselves have no longer been addressed as passive receivers of knowledge and skills, but have been called upon, in some cases, to take an active role in the process of their own education. Literacy has represented for them a bridge toward participation in the civic, economic and social life of their local community and national society. This drive toward participation has been developed in different ways and directed towards objectives having different natures and levels according to the political conditions of each given country.

Literacy as enhancement of popular participation in social, economic and political life. Like the USSR and Cuba in the past, several countries (Algeria; Brazil, Colombia, Guatemala, Mexico, Jamaica, Peru; Burma, China, Indonesia, Thailand, Vietnam; Cameroon, Ethiopia, Guinea, Somalia, Tanzania and Zambia among others) have launched mass campaigns. Results in some countries have been good, in others fair, in some, disappointing.

The cases which seem to us to be of interest are those showing how literacy dissemination may enhance popular participation in the social, economic and political life of a country.

In China, for example, in 1949 more than 80% of the population were illiterate. According to recent information, the literate population is now 75%, while approximately 80% of children of school age benefit from educational programmes. This was achieved by utilizing the energy potential of the people, by involving them in their own process of education, by decentralizing the literacy administration to local communes, by giving the teachers working in the countryside a higher status and the label of honour.

Tanzania's approach has been rurally oriented and agriculturally based. 'Development' has been considered as the process increasing the capacities and well-being of the average citizen and therefore education as the way to meet family and community needs, rather than providing the nation with high level manpower. For this reason, literacy in Tanzania has been and is an integral part of a basic adult education approach based on community activities. The Tanzanian post-literacy follow-up experience has also been very relevant as, for example, it has been applied in the '1973 Mass Health Education Campaign'.

Somalia: during two years, starting from March 1973, students and teachers were mobilized and sent to the peripheral quarters of the capital, to the coastal towns, to the villages of the interior and along the paths of the bush, to carry out literacy work, to teach reading and writing to the herdsmen, the craftsmen and the farmers. This concentrated effort should make it possible to lower the illiteracy rate from 90 to 20%. An important feature of the Somali literacy campaign has been its efficient motivational phase which started in 1972 immediately after the adoption of the Latin alphabet for the Somali language, one year before the beginning of literacy activities, through the radio and newspapers and the traditional ways of communication in the countryside. The slógan was 'A school at the foot of each tree'. The campaign was organized and directed by a co-ordinating committee composed of five ministers: education, health, zootechniques, transport and planning.

In Peru, within the framework of the educational reform which advocates decentralized structures such as educational nuclei and local community councils, an important literacy campaign has recently been launched. It is called 'Operación Alfabetización Integral' and its main characteristics are:

(a) to have as primary objectives those of giving to the learner a new consciousness of his or her social and historic conditions and of calling for his or her active participation in the educational process;

(b) to have a programme which continues after the literacy courses with appropriate follow-up operations;

(c) to have curricula oriented to the life and work exigencies of the learners;

(d) to be based on a decentralized educational approach supported and guided by local social groups;

(e) to address its activities in priority in favour of the socially and economically more deprived sectors of the national society.

Literacy as part of national development projects. Measuring the ground covered in the last ten years, it emerges clearly that a better understanding has been achieved of illiteracy as a feature of underdevelopment. This understanding has led the responsible authorities to link the problems of literacy to those of development.

In the light of the recommendations of the 1965 Teheran Conference, literacy has been increasingly recognized as a contributing factor to social changes because it provides individuals with the knowledge and skills needed to become the real agents of these changes.

It has been realized, in fact, that by adding functional literacy as a component of a developmental action, required skills, general efficiency and ability to function more effectively in a changing environment are enhanced.

The majority of the most recent literacy activities have been linked to national development priorities and their curricula geared to life and functional skills.

We can witness today a multitude of attempts to link together literacy and socio-economic development. In Gabon, Niger, Upper Volta, Iraq and Pakistan, for example, literacy work has been combined with campaigns for rural development. In Algeria and Tunisia literacy work became a feature of agricultural and industrial development projects. Considering the many aspects of development, there are several in which literacy work has played a particularly vital role in many countries of the world, such as, among others, in Africa: Ghana, Mali, Nigeria, Kenya, Zambia; in Asia: India, Indonesia, Malaysia, Pakistan; in Latin America: Colombia, Ecuador, Guatemala, Mexico, Panama, Venezuela.

Literacy for the assumption of socio-political responsibilities. Several literacy programmes launched in various countries of Latin America, as well as in other continents, have been improved by the ideas of the Brazilian educator, Paolo Freire, and by his practical experiences carried out years ago in Brazil and Chile. His educational philosophy is based on the principle that the illiterate adult is a person able to create 'culture' and that his culture, being of great value, should be taken as the starting point of an educational process leading him towards the awakening of his self-awareness (concientização) in relation to others and to his entire environment. Freire took a critical position vis-à-vis the traditional education structures and methods, calling this education the banking system, where the teacher's role is to withdraw selected concepts from the bank of knowledge and deposit them in the heads of adults. He advocated the establishment of a dialogue between the participants in the educational process, one of whom is acting as 'co-ordinator' and not as teacher. The 'co-ordinator' helps the adults to analyse the real situation in which they are living and, with the support of *generative words*, starts their process of mastering reading and writing skills, meanwhile the reflection on the illiterates' reality progressively liberates them from the feeling of powerlessness. The Freire theory and practices have had, and continue to have, a wide influence on adult literacy in Latin America as well as in other parts of the world.

The participation of the local traditional institutions to literacy work. There has been, during the recent past, at national and international levels, a growing acceptance of the idea that literacy programmes will be more effective if they are planned from the bottom and are built on community self-determination.

Indeed, we do not find many examples showing the implementation of participatory processes from the bottom, but among the few recent practical experiences which have tried to translate this idea into reality, without doubt the most valuable have been those where traditional institutions have been actively associated from the beginning with the literacy work, as happened in certain areas of Peru, Madagascar, Mali, Tanzania and the Philippines. The Tanzanian case is particularly interesting; its participatory approach was based on a local popular institution, the Ujamaa Village, a small democratically-managed rural unit which assumed in fact direct responsibility for planning and implementing literacy activities, greatly contributing to the success of the national literacy effort.

V *Methods and materials*

Literacy as an instrument for life skills development. Literacy has been made more responsive to country needs and individual aspirations. The dichotomy between traditional and functional literacy has been greatly reduced. It could be said that at present, almost everywhere, literacy programmes, curricula and materials are no longer centred on pure sound-symbol analyses or on mechanical fixation processes. Literacy appears not to be accepted as an end in itself, as viable in its own right; on the contrary, it can be affirmed that it is presently generally part of a basic education process. The analysis of the most recent literacy experiences in the world shows that it has been almost always integrated, alternatively, and in various levels and degrees, into the following components: civic education, family planning, family health, sanitation, nutrition, child care, improvement of housing, training in pre-vocational and vocational skills, etc. Therefore, the very process of learning to read and write has been made an opportunity for acquiring information that can immediately be used to improve living standards, an instrument for life-skills development, mastery of the environment, training for work, increased productivity, greater participation in civil life and better understanding of the surrounding world. This has involved relevant conceptual and methodological implications, such as that of the diversification of the programmes. Many countries, in fact, have adapted the contents of their literacy programmes as well as the terms of their operational approaches to the different situations, both quantitative and qualitative, in which literacy actions were considered relevant and necessary.

The press for new literates. Increased evidence in the past years of relapses into illiteracy on the part of former participants in adult literacy classes has emphasized the need for post-literacy activities, encouraging the retention of literacy and other skills and knowledge learnt in literacy programmes, and making possible continuing acquisition of more knowledge. For this reason the majority of literacy projects produced and distributed reading materials for new literates, following and improving the procedures adopted in the past. But what seems to be a special feature of these last years is the proliferation and the permanence of a new press specifically addressed to new literates. These periodicals bring news and information, which help readers to improve their health, agriculture, general living conditions, raising at the same time their civic consciousness. By opening their columns to the people, on several occasions a dialogue between governments and country-dwellers has started.

In spite of the many problems caused by the lack of financial resources, the lack of printing facilities, of paper and of distribution systems, more than thirty countries in these last years have been able to produce and distribute periodicals and newspapers especially designed for new literates, often in local languages.

Increased use of mass media in support of literacy. In a considerable number of countries mass media are increasingly being used to combat illiteracy. Radio programmes in support of literacy efforts seem to have increased steadily over the last ten years—perhaps because of the rapid increase in the number of radios. In the middle 1960s only ten developing countries were using either radio or television in combating illiteracy; by 1971, according to a survey made by Unesco of radio and TV in literacy work, the number using radio had increased to twenty-three, while twelve countries (with some overlap) reported using television for this purpose.

Some fourteen Latin American countries have experimented with literacy education by radio through organized listening groups. ACPO (Acción Cultural Popular) in Colombia pioneered in this field and now has a network of transmitters and a publishing programme that reaches some 20,000 listening groups.

In 1971, twenty African countries were using radio, radiovision or television for mass education, and radio clubs and listening groups play an important role in Niger, Ivory Coast, Ghana, Togo, Nigeria, Senegal, and the Congo Republic. The Arab Republic of Egypt conducts a steady 6-day-a-week literacy campaign by radio reaching more than a million illiterates. Some countries, Jamaica for instance, have begun experimentation with closed-circuit television for literacy teaching.

Interesting experiments utilizing radio cassettes for literacy are at present being carried out in the Arab Republic of Egypt under the sponsorship of ASFEC. The Mobral utilized radio broadcasts as support to its literacy training programmes, reaching approximately 100,000 teachers.

Some proponents of mass media for literacy education consider it a means of potential breakthrough to wipe out illiteracy. The costs of developing, perfecting and generating this methodology are recognized; but in proportion to the numbers that can be reached, these costs are not considered exorbitant, particularly when a network of broadcasting stations already exists.

Other reasons advanced in favour of radio programmes are the penetration of the transistor into rural areas and the possibility of cumulative action day after day. Many projects are exploring ways of getting feedback and of involving listeners in programme evaluation and development. This is an excellent trend to maximize the educational impact of the media.

Literacy and vernacular tongues. In the last decade a strong impetus has been given to the rehabilitation of mother and vernacular tongues in literacy, versus the adoption of the language inherited from the colonizing country.

Literacy in a foreign language has been the pattern for many past programmes, but the inefficiency of imparting literacy in a language which, in certain cases, 80% of the participants did not speak, determined some countries to choose as the medium of instruction for literacy their vernacular tongue.

In Mali, for example, literacy courses were conducted in Mande, Bambara, Peul, Tamasheq and Senghoy. In Togo, Niger and Burundi literacy texts are prepared in different local languages. In Somalia, thanks to the transcription of the national language in Latin characters, a mass campaign of unparalleled impact was organized. In India, the functional literacy material was translated from Hindi into nine regional languages: Bengali, Gujurati, Kannada, Malayalam, Marathi, Oriya, Punjabi, Tamil and Telugu. Zambia used seven languages for instructional purposes. Peru adopted in some of its regions a bilingual attempt at literacy education starting from vernacular Quechua and going into Spanish. Mother tongue literacy programmes have also been established in Papua New Guinea, in Mexico and in Vietnam.

Thanks to these experiences there is today in several countries, particularly in Africa, a growing acceptance of the idea that in a multilingual situation the vernacular tongue is to be adopted for literacy instruction, because: (a) the forms and knowledge of the values of a culture are better learnt and transmitted in mother tongues; (b) the attitudes of the learners towards the language of instruction often influence their desire and motivation to learn; (c) from a pedagogical point of view the teaching of the first literacy skills in the learner's mother tongue is preferable since it permits an adequacy between the contents and the forms of teaching with the logical structures and the mental processes of the learners, and avoids psychological shocks. Finally, it should be said on this theme that the choice of a language for literacy is not purely a linguistic problem but often it is emotionally cultural and always political.

Research and evaluation. For nearly a century, a vast and growing volume of educational research has been concentrated upon child development and the teaching in schools and universities. This research has been largely confined to the wealthier and more highly industrialized countries. In the recent past the attention of research workers turned to the needs of adults in developing countries, and especially to the two-fifths or more of the world's adult population who remain illiterate. Three broad types of research activity were conducted in the adult literacy field. The first, fundamental research, included long-term investigations designed to test hypotheses and establish general conclusions and to lay a foundation of knowledge on which practice can be built. The second type, action research, included systematic, but generally short-term, studies carried out by the operational staff of a project, or by research workers assigned to it. The third type, evaluation, measured the achievements of a programme or activity against its defined operational objectives.

In the last ten years, inspired by the Experimental World Literacy Programme, within and outside its framework, hundreds of research projects in literacy and in related fields such as linguistics and economics have been carried out in almost all the countries of the world. Sometimes these projects have received the support of foreign universities and research institutes as well as of international organizations, but the majority of them have been carried out autonomously, by national specialists, working often in teams, within the framework of national evaluation councils or units, established ad hoc, as was the case in Algeria, Ecuador, Ghana, India, etc.

VI *Personnel and training*

New approaches to selecting personnel. The school-teacher, usually at primary level, remains the keystone of most adult literacy programmes; in defence of this practice it is often pointed out that school-teachers are already respected members of the community, that they have been trained in teaching methods, and that they have access to teaching facilities (a schoolroom, blackboard, etc.). On the negative side, it is indicated that they can only teach after school hours or during vacations, that for them adult learners are a secondary responsibility, and that they are used to teaching children and may find it difficult to treat adult learners as adults. But many of the countries where illiteracy is most prevalent lacked trained cadres to assume teaching and administrative posts and provide back-up services in literacy programmes. The task of finding new literacy personnel has posed major challenges in the period under review.

Many countries such as Mali and Tanzania used non-professionals in national literacy programmes—people who were neither teachers nor specialists in any component of the adult literacy programmes. Such persons were usually called 'volunteers'; sometimes they were paid, but more often they were not.

In some countries members of the armed forces have been in charge of teaching literacy: in Iran, for example, soldiers who have received four months' instruction in teaching methods were sent to remote villages as literacy teachers, while in Israel girl soldiers with training as teachers spent thirty to forty hours a week teaching anyone who wanted to become literate, at hours suited to the learners' schedules.

Students often served as volunteer teachers. Zambia reported that almost every secondary school and teacher-training college in the country had a literacy club. In addition to organizing literacy classes, raising money to buy books and other materials, and helping to construct shelters or classrooms, club members also taught. In Cuba many of the young men and women who took part as very young students in the 1961 mass literacy campaign then worked in educational institutions; their contact with rural illiterates and their experience during the literacy campaign were decisive factors in their choice of a career.

Youth service organizations also provide literacy teachers. In Madagascar, young men joining the Malagasy Civic Service opted for teaching literacy as part of the national development effort; similarly in Indonesia and several other countries.

In Iran and India progressive farmers, with no pedagogical background or teaching experience, have conducted literacy courses with success; and in Tanzania natural leaders of the Ujamaa Villages have effectively complemented the work of young trained teachers.

New approaches to training personnel. The acceptance in recent years of the idea that to teach illiterate or semi-literate adults successfully requires special training even for qualified school-teachers, and the spread of projects and programmes engaging no professional personnel as literacy teachers and supervisors, has created a need for adequate and innovative procedures. In this respect a consensus has been reached on the fact that the emphasis should be shifted from pre-service training to in-service training and refresher courses, as well as from supervision to pedagogical counselling. To attain this objective new retraining procedures have been established, carefully designed semi-programmed materials have been produced, multi-media schemes have been launched, radio programmes adopting micro-teaching techniques have been broadcast and 'echoed' concentric training services have been organized. One of the most interesting and successful innovations in training has been considered to be the operational field seminar.

The operational field seminars are intensive training exercises, developed in actual working situations. They are meant not only for teachers or educational agents but are also addressed to professional cadres from different backgrounds and disciplines who are involved in literacy programmes.

The participants train themselves for three to four weeks within the framework of a project already in operation, or recently started, which is located either within their own country or in a foreign country. There, *in an actual working context*, with the assistance of the host team they participate in a performance-based experience which at the same time will be a part of the on-going literacy process. Their involvement will be confined to a segment of the curriculum and to a fraction of the educational calendar, but will be global because it will cover phases both prior to their arrival and subsequent to their departure from the given zone.

In practice they will first contact a small group from the target population of the project and study their physical, economic and social environment. They will then identify some of the problems of the group, determine the remedial operations needed for solving them and devise curricular units based upon the knowledge and skills needed. Finally, they will introduce these units to the teachers, advise them on their use, supervise their transfer and evaluate their impact.

Operational field seminars have been systematically tried out since 1970; in the beginning within the framework of the World Experimental Literacy Programme, and thereafter directly sponsored by national institutions. During the years 1971–4 approximately fifty operational field seminars have been carried out in different countries of Latin America, Asia and Africa.

The contribution of international co-operation

VII *Illiteracy and the literate world*

A sharpening awareness. How has the literate world—and particularly the industrialized nations—reacted to the problem of illiteracy over the last ten years? Incontestably, there has been a sharpening awareness on the part of policy-makers, opinion-shapers and academics. Eminent leaders, including many heads of state, have spoken for the eradication of illiteracy and expressed their desire to support action to achieve this objective. Newspapers, radio and television have given copious attention to the problem, both as it affects the Third World and as it has been rediscovered in the population of industrialized countries.

Economists, anthropologists, linguists and sociologists—in addition of course to educationists—have come to take a greater interest in illiteracy, thus reflecting its interdisciplinary ramifications. Indeed, it would seem that the increasingly interdisciplinary approach to the problem of illiteracy has led, in at least some settings, to an enrichment and what might be called the 'humanization' of the image held of the illiterate.

Illiterates have often been perceived in the past as limited in their individual capacities and marginal to their society. They were described as being without education and without educational motivation, as well as without scientific and technical dimensions, full of superstition and even backward and primitive. Their illiteracy was considered as an effect more than a cause of their marginal condition.

One of the most valuable changes of these recent years has then been the progressive understanding and recognition of the fact that illiterates are not empty bottles to be filled, but persons possessing clear logical structures, strong working experiences and expertise, a great sense of individual and social responsibility, not to mention highly developed aesthetic expressions as revealed by their traditional poetry, music and folk arts; in short, a complex heritage of creative qualities, social values and unlimited potential abilities for action.

This consciousness gradually being acquired by the literate minority, of the spiritual and intellectual values possessed by the large, poor, masses of illiterates may represent for many national societies an incentive for a leap forward toward a cultural, social and economic renaissance.

Persisting doubts. In addition to the sharpening awareness of the problem of illiteracy, and the broadening of certain literates' image of the illiterate, doubts persist in the minds of at least some observers about the literate world's views and intentions regarding illiterates. Solemn proclamations have not always been followed, in a reasonable lapse of time, by concrete action. Where action has occurred, it has sometimes seemed in the interest more of the literate élites—nationally and internationally—than of the illiterate masses.

It also seems that, whatever the positive aims of opinion-shapers, the man in the street of many industrial countries tends to remain immune to the problem of illiteracy—and of development in general. Speeches by eminent personalities, newspaper and magazine articles, radio and TV programmes, as well as other efforts in the media field, do not seem to have made long strides toward overcoming the ignorance, indifference or insensitivity of many common citizens of industrialized countries. Still less effect seems to have been had by generally limited and experimental attempts to introduce issues such as underdevelopment and literacy into the curricula of formal education institutions of those countries, although such out-of-school groups as co-operatives, trade unions and youth groups have increasingly tried to focus members' attention on these issues.

It must be stressed, of course, that these doubts do not refer solely—or even chiefly—to illiteracy. Other human problems, such as malnutrition and poverty in general, have not reached the more favoured sectors of humanity with sufficient force to move them (in both senses of the word). Thence stems the gap between declarations of intention and the scope of concrete action.

VIII *Unesco action: past and future*

The experimental world literacy programme. The launching in 1966 of the World Programme represented one of the major responses of the international community—and particularly Unesco and UNDP—to the problem of illiteracy in the Third World. Following a series of contacts and missions reaching no fewer than fifty-two Member States, it was agreed to undertake Experimental Literacy Projects in thirteen countries: i.e. Algeria, Afghanistan, Ecuador, Ethiopia, Guinea, India, Iran, Madagascar, Mali, Sudan, Syria, Tanzania and Venezuela.

The main pilot projects of the programme fell into two categories: (a) projects implemented by national governments and Unesco (although Unesco was the sole executing agency, these sometimes received technical assistance from one or more of the other United Nations Specialized Agencies, such as FAO, ILO and WHO); and (b) agricultural development programmes implemented by FAO with a Unesco literacy component.

The majority of these pilot projects—those in Algeria, Ecuador, Ethiopia, Guinea, Iran, Madagascar, Mali, the Sudan and Tanzania—belonged to the first category. In the second category were the projects in Afghanistan, where a functional literacy component was integrated into a government/FAO agricultural credit and co-operative programme; in India, where a functional literacy component was part and parcel of a government/FAO programme for the production of high-yield varieties of food crops; and in Syria, where Unesco is providing the functional literacy component in a government/FAO agricultural-development project. UNDP financed the international aspect of most of these projects.

The thirteenth, the functional literacy pilot project in Venezuela, was conducted exclusively with national resources and only the evaluation component was financed by the United Nations system.

The dual objective of the Programme was *both* to test and demonstrate the economic and social returns of literacy—i.e. literacy's pre-investment role with regard to development—*and* (in the words of the 13th Session of Unesco's General Conference in 1964) 'to pave the way for the eventual execution of a world campaign . . .'

The testing and demonstration function of the Programme, although encountering greater obstacles than originally expected, has yielded a harvest of interesting information about how—and how not—to undertake literacy work. Among many other lessons, the Programme's results suggest that: (a) the needs and aspirations of illiterate individuals and groups should be taken into account in the identification of literacy objectives; (b) curricula should be functional in terms of a broad range of political, social, cultural and economic knowledge and skills of use to new literates; (c) teaching methods should be as varied and as active as possible, giving stress to 'learning by doing'; (d) international aid can complement—but should not attempt to replace—national initiative, both intellectual and material; and (e) the idea of follow-up must be replaced, where substantial numbers of new literates appear on the scene in largely illiterate countries, with the notion of building the infrastructure for a literate and continuously self-educating society.

The EWLP's second objective—to pave the way for a possible world campaign against illiteracy—does not seem to have been achieved. The very complexity of literacy work, particularly when it is linked to development, was clearly underlined by the Experimental Programme. The need for more flexible forms of international co-operation was also pointed out. These and other problems make the achievement of universal world literacy likely to be a more arduous and longer-term task than was thought a decade ago.

Other international efforts. Partly in connection with the Experimental World Literacy Programme, and also in the framework of its longer-term action in this field, Unesco has launched and/or aided a number of international efforts that have enabled the Secretariat to play a role—as stimulator, accumulator and disseminator of experiences—in the world at large.

In the ten years since the Teheran Conference, numerous meetings organized by Unesco, as well as by governmental or non-governmental bodies, have taken place, certain of them international, others regional or national, contributing to mutual knowledge or experiences and to stimulating the awareness of responsible authorities, technicians and the general public. The regional conferences of Ministers of Education of the developing world, convened by Unesco in this period, stressed the importance of literacy work. The Third International Conference on Adult Education (Tokyo, 1972) also dealt with literacy. One of its general conclusions points out that 'The eradication of illiteracy is a key factor in development. Literacy is a cornerstone of adult education.

But it is a means to an end, not an end in itself.' Furthermore, the 18th Session of the General Conference of Unesco included the 'intensification of the struggle against illiteracy' among the priority goals the Organization should achieve in the coming years.

The celebration, each year since 1967, of International Literacy Day on 8 September has provided a unique opportunity to mobilize human and economic resources in support of adult literacy.

Other relevant incentives to the literacy cause have been the Mohammad Reza Pahlavi Prize made possible by the gift of HIM the Shahinshah of Iran, which is awarded annually on International Literacy Day to an individual or institution for meritorious work in adult literacy, and the Nadezhda K. Krupskaya Literacy Prize made possible by an offer in 1969 by the government of the USSR is awarded annually to reward outstanding work in the fight against illiteracy.

Created in 1966, the International Consultative Liaison Committee for Literacy met four times between June 1967 and December 1973. Among numerous other subjects, the Committee's deliberations covered the following: (a) Problems of Experimental World Literacy Programme; (b) Literacy and Human Rights; (c) Needs and Prospects of Literacy in the Second Development Decade; (d) Improvement and Normalization of Literacy Data; (e) Ways and Means of International Co-operation; and (f) Possible Creation of an International Foundation for Literacy.

Having worked in their respective regions for a number of years before the EWLP, the adult education regional centres in Latin America (CREFAL) and the Arab States (ASFEC) were encouraged to furnish training, documentation and technical assistance more sharply focused on functional literacy during the life of the EWLP. Beginning in 1968, the International Institute of Adult Literacy Methods (located in Teheran) embarked on a world-wide information service which it is expected to supplement with research and training activities in the near future.

Unesco, on one hand, and regional and national agencies and specialists on the other, have been able to improve the exchange of literacy-related ideas, information and skills as a result of these various efforts. On balance, this effort has had undeniable positive results in terms of quickening the diffusion of information and upgrading the cadre of national personnels. It should be clear that these international efforts were and continue to be geared to enhancing national initiatives, and were and are not intended to replace such initiatives in achieving tangible achievements in the field.

Guidelines for future Unesco action in support of literacy. It is to be stressed that, as the Director-General of Unesco told the 59th Session of ECOSOC (July 1975), 'victory over illiteracy can only come from the political resolve of the government of the country concerned. There is clear evidence that whenever a government has tackled the problem because it was a precondition of other social changes, the results have been favourable.'

Just as literacy is inextricably intertwined with other aspects of national development, moreover, so national development as a whole is bound up with the world context in which the developing countries find themselves. As has been pointed out, the map of world illiteracy coincides closely with the map of world poverty, particularly rural poverty. It is increasingly recognized that illiteracy and poverty are not interlinked in some inevitable 'vicious circle' but are an integral part of the prevailing economic (and social and even political) world order. In the long run, then, literacy will probably be achieved massively only in the framework of an evolution toward a new world order. The acceleration of such an evolution is one of the major tasks with which governments have entrusted the United Nations system as the world enters the last quarter of the twentieth century.

Within the framework (and assuming the acceleration) of such an evolution, what may be the specific role of Unesco in the field of literacy? Without pre-judging the results of the 19th Session of the General Conference, it does seem possible to point to certain guidelines for short- and medium-term Unesco action in this sphere. Emerging from analysis of the results of the Experimental World Literacy Programme and from other sources (e.g. new trends in international co-operation generally), these guidelines may be sketched here in terms of certain new principles, approaches and procedures.

The overriding principle guiding future work is that international efforts, whether intellectual or material, must not substitute themselves for national thought and action. Development can be autonomous and sustained only if the countries concerned rely first and foremost on themselves for ideas and resources. External aid can only 'top up' national efforts. Thus, international co-operation should increasingly attempt to devise diversified approaches to meet varying needs defined nationally. Intellectual and material dependence should increasingly give way to inter-dependency, this being the substance of true (rather than rhetorical) partnership.

In the application of these principles, new approaches to international co-operation will have to be devised. In particular, international (exogenous) help should strive to bolster internally generated (endogenous) action and innovation in the design, implementation and evaluation of literacy work. International co-operation should, for example, encourage the creation or extension of national education-related industries for producing paper, books, teaching equipment, etc., rather than finance the import of such articles. Care should be taken to ensure that external aid does not compete with existing or potential national production. Moreover, the provision of aid from the 'centre' to the 'periphery' should increasingly be replaced with more truly multilateral co-operation. That is, considerable work should be done to enhance literacy-related exchanges of people, information and ideas among developing countries, as well as between them and industrialized nations. Means and literacy methods developed in virtually any country may be a potential contribution to literacy work in virtually any other, whatever its state of development.

This new approach would require, in turn, a revision of prevailing (albeit now evolving) aid procedures. Since literacy and post-literacy work are long-term efforts, international bodies should make commitments for periods of several years. Long-term commitments should not, however, make for still more rigid forms of aid than those existing today. On the contrary, greater flexibility should be sought so as to adapt the kinds of aid to diverse national needs. Short-term consultant services may often be more useful than long-term expert posts. It should also become possible, replacing the donor-beneficiary relationship with true partnership, to use multilateral aid to finance local fellowships and the salaries of national specialists, etc. In brief, emphasis should be placed on national will and effort, but it will also be necessary to provide sufficient agile and timely expressions of international solidarity, in whose concertation Unesco will have an essential role to play.

IX *Conclusions*

The pith of the world's experience in the struggle against illiteracy over the last ten years may be summarized as follows:

(a) Although the percentage of illiterates among adults in the world has fallen, their absolute numbers has continued to grow. Illiteracy has affected particularly women and rural people in the developing countries. These patterns are not different from those experienced by the world, prior to the 1965 Teheran Conference. However, some developing countries, thanks to the combined effect of their more efficient school system and of their intense literacy work, did achieve a considerable reduction of the absolute number of their illiterates. It is agreeable to notice here that the number of countries in which illiteracy tends to be confined only to older age groups is steadily increasing.

(b) These ten years have led to an increased conviction on the part of governments, international agencies and others concerned that illiteracy is a feature of the underdevelopment and that literacy work ought to be inextricably linked with the many aspects of development as well as inscribed into national global policies and programmes.

(c) The intensified efforts made to achieve literacy in the last ten years, although encountering numerous obstacles, have provided the world community with a 'corpus' of innovative experiences in institutional structures, approaches and methods. Thus, it can be affirmed that mankind possesses now a sufficient knowledge of literacy strategies and methodologies by which it will be possible to overcome illiteracy any time other determinant factors, such as political will and capacity of mobilizing human and financial resources, are available.

(d) The Experimental World Literacy Programme has been particularly rich in lessons; it has represented, indeed, a source of inspiration to those responsible for literacy work by indicating to them the most effective ways of linking literacy with development, obtaining active participation of the adults in their social changes, preparing educational materials centred on problems of the milieu, training actively personnel of different types and levels and considering literacy as an integral part of lifelong education.

(e) In recent years, it has become more widely accepted that although literacy work should remain a primarily national endeavour, international co-operation of increasingly innovative kinds will be necessary to enhance (but not replace) nationally generated solutions to nationally identified problems.

(f) Finally, it should be said that, in spite of the achievements of these last ten years, the gulf which separates the developed countries and those in the course of development has become deeper, and the disparity between the modest means available and the immense needs to be met has become sharper. In other words, these ten years have yielded great hopes, but have also shown the permanence of serious anxieties.

1. 2 Toward an assessable definition of literacy

Robert L. Hillerich

Between wars and other political/economic crises, concern for literacy has been one of the pressing world problems of this century. One is tempted, initially, to say that like motherhood and flag, literacy is an unequivocally accepted goal of the literate for the non-literate. Such a statement, however, would be a gross oversimplification, if not a blatant lie, for several reasons.

First, the term *literate* has no universally accepted definition. It may refer to degrees of proficiency with print, ranging from the formation of a personal signature to the interpretation of a written passage; or it may reflect no proficiency at all, representing nothing more than a duration of time spent in a building called 'school.'

Second, if literacy is associated with proficiency in communication/thinking skills, acceptance of its desirability varies in terms of political/philosophical positions. Here one is faced with varying values, varying views of the worth of the individual versus the group. Here one faces the question, 'To what extent should the individual be developed?' Should he be educated only to the extent that he becomes an economic contributor and self-supporting agent within the existing structure? Or should he be developed to the extent that he becomes an independent thinker who may contribute to—or even cause—a change in the status quo?

It is the purpose of this paper to examine existing definitions of literacy in an effort to arrive at a definition of literacy which can lead to the assessment of its attainment in a population.

The need for clarification of 'literacy'

One of the most significant contributions in the efforts to clarify

Source: *English Journal*, 65, 1976, pp. 50–5.

and to awaken interest in the need for literacy was the Unesco monograph, *The Teaching of Reading and Writing* (Gray, 1956). At that time, nearly twenty years ago, the author pointed out the lack of agreement on a definition of literacy. Even the goals of literacy were not agreed upon (p. 18):

> At one extreme is the traditional attitude that ability to read and write is of first importance . . .
> At the opposite extreme, some believe that efforts to teach reading and writing have little if any place . . . in helping individuals and groups meet many of their immediate problems . . .
> A third point of view assumes that the spread of literacy and the effort to solve . . . problems are so closely interrelated that each can be achieved best through a coordinated approach.

This analysis could well have been written today! In fact, it was well represented at the Harvard symposium (Harvard, 1970), where expressed views ranged from Laubach's job-oriented reading instruction to Harman's 'education for freedom.'

While lack of an agreed-upon definition makes available literacy data imprecise at best, the problem of illiteracy—by any definition—is apparent. Almost 50% of the world population has been classed as illiterate in Unesco studies (Unesco, 1965). Whether or not progress has been made in the effort toward greater literacy depends upon one's view: Harman (1970) reported Unesco figures which indicated that the percentage of illiterates decreased but absolute numbers increased between 1950 and 1960, with the pattern continuing through 1970.

What is this 'illiteracy' that lies behind the figures? It may mean anything from one who has *no* formal schooling, to one who has attended four years or less, to one who is unable to read or write at a level necessary to perform successfully in his social position.

Figure 1.2.1

Implicit in any definition of literacy is the ability to communicate. The priority placed on communication in printed form—reading and writing—varies from low, in the case of Stanley

(1972), to the high priorities of reading people such as Southgate (1972). It seems that unless one is to construe his own original definition, 'literacy' must at least *include* the dictionary definition, the 'ability to read and write.' However, such a definition obviously raises more questions than it answers, especially if one is concerned with measurement: reading and writing to what extent? with what quality? as measured by what instruments or procedures?

Further, implied in such a statement is the view that one either 'has' the ability or does not 'have it,' that one is either 'literate' or 'illiterate.' Such an artificial dichotomy is unrealistic in any definition; one cannot assume that there is some magic point at which an individual suddenly moves from 'illiteracy' to 'literacy.' Any definition of literacy must recognize this quality as a continuum, representing all degrees of development.

At the risk of an artificial separation of a different kind, I will explore the definition of literacy from two viewpoints: the *educational* and the *sociological/economic*. The separation is artificial in that both have as ultimate general goals the improved functioning of the individual in his society. They are quite different, however, in their philosophical bases and in their measurement implications.

Literacy: an educational view

Many of the existing standards of literacy are defined in terms of years of schooling completed. If a given number of years in school is accepted as the basis for literacy, one needs merely to pick the grade level that will be used as the criterion. That decision may be made in terms of the number of illiterates one wants to claim—the higher the grade designated for literacy, obviously the more 'illiterates' identified. Or the designated grade may be chosen on the basis of some assumed 'necessary' level for adult success.

In practice, grade designations have varied: Unesco set the completion of grade 4 as the criterion for literacy; the U.S. Census Bureau, grade 5; the U.S. Army, grade 5; and the U.S. Office of Education, grades 4 to 8.

Obviously, defining literacy in terms of years of schooling has an advantage: It is easy to assess. Unfortunately, it also has little validity from *any* viewpoint.

If years in school is taken to represent some degree of skill attainment, this assumption is invalid, Grade levels in elementary school tend to reflect age more than they do achievement: An individual in fifth grade may be reading at a preprimer level or at a college level. As a case in point, Harman (1970) reported a study in the Woodlawn area of Chicago where 95.4% of the subjects were 'literate' in that they had completed grade 5; but on the basis of a reading achievement test, 50.7% were 'functionally illiterate.'

If a specific grade-level-completed is designated in the belief that it assures adult reading success, it is based on an unproven assumption, and the designation of grade 4—or even grade 5—is certainly open to serious question. Spache (1970) criticized the grade 4 criterion as representing no assurance of future success, referencing the fact that Britain was dropping the 11 + exams because of their lack of predictive value.

Further evidence of the lack of relationship between the grade-level criterion and success was offered by Fisher and Brown (1971). With 9,000 subjects, the investigators studied the effectiveness of remedial training designed to raise the educational level of these men to grade 5 or higher. When the investigators compared success in the remedial program with success on the job, they found little difference between those who had been successful in the program and those who had not.

Finally, the completion of fourth or fifth grade, even if it did reflect a commensurate reading level, is questionable as an adequate level for the successful performance of most adult reading tasks. And merely to raise the level to grade 8, for example (Boulmetis, 1973), seems only to dodge the issue. Moreover, the arbitrary designation of a grade level again exemplifies false dichotomizing.

One educational method of viewing literacy is to accept it as involving the communication skills and then to enumerate, in order of complexity, the continuum of these skills. An abbreviated sampling is shown in Figure 1.2.1.

Not shown on this continuum is the psychological progression that must underlie the sequence: Achievement grows out of values, which themselves must grow out of awareness. In other words, the individual first becomes aware of each subsequent step, then develops values for it, obtains that skill, and uses the skill.

The continuum must recognize all degrees of skill, from the inability to communicate at all, to facility in many languages. It also must recognize the three-year-old, for example, as he functions at the level of oral communication appropriate to him on the continuum. In essence, the diagram contains the values—and the limitations—of the United Kingdom Reading Association's definition of literacy as 'the mastery of our native language in all its aspects, as a means of communication' (Southgate, 1972).

This definition recognizes listening and speaking along with reading and writing as criteria for literacy. On the other hand, it suggests 'mastery' as if that were a point on the continuum to be achieved, as if it were a pass-fail criterion. That point, however, is not defined, anymore than I have attempted to label it on the continuum.

Is it really necessary to place a point on the continuum, to say that above this point is 'literacy,' below is 'illiteracy'? As I have already suggested, that point would be, by its very nature, arbitrary. Further, we seem to be moving from use of the term 'illiteracy' to the recognition of various stages of 'literacy.' At the root of any concern in the area of literacy is a desire—whether based on altruistic, political, or economic motives—for enabling the individual to cope better with his or her environment. Such being the case, no arbitrary point of proficiency will fit all individuals. The fact of this statement was demonstrated by Sticht (1972) in a study of 1,600 army personnel in four job classifications: cook, vehicle repairman, supply clerk, armor crewman. The men were evaluated through an objective test of job knowledge, a four-to-five-hour job simulation sampling, and a supervisor's rating. The investigators found that the level of reading necessary for success varied with the job. For example, a low grade level of reading skill was adequate for cooks; grade 14 was necessary for supply clerks.

This recognition of variation in reading skill needs should come as no great surprise; nor should its implications be news. The professor of linguistics, abruptly shifted into a chemical engineering position, would not be any more successful than would the Australian Aboriginal suddenly moved into the lowest secretarial position. (Of course, this is not to imply that either could not be successful with appropriate educational re-training.)

All this fails to settle the issues, however, of *what is literacy* and what is *satisfactory* literacy. To attempt to answer these questions, considerations from the sociological/economic view must be brought to the continuum.

Literacy: a sociological/economic view

Over the past half century there has evolved a concept of 'functional literacy.' This concept was well-defined—albeit non-behaviorally—in a 1956 Unesco monograph (Gray, 1956, p. 24):

> . . . a person is functionally literate when he has acquired the knowledge and skills in reading and writing which enable him to engage effectively in all those activities in which literacy is normally assumed in his culture or group.

A slightly broader—and less intelligible—interpretation of this definition was adopted by Unesco in 1962 (Stanley, 1972, p. 382):

A person is literate when he has acquired the essential knowledges and skills which enable him to engage in all those activities in which literacy is required for effective functioning in his group and community and whose attainments in reading, writing and arithmetic make it possible for him to continue to use these skills towards his own and the community's development and for active participation in the life of his country.

This later Unesco definition is not basically different from what one can read into the much more concise statement by the Conference on Strategies for Generating a National 'Right to Read' Adult Movement: literacy is 'the ability to read, write and compute with the functional competence needed for meeting the requirements of adult living' (Harman, 1970, p. 228).

Such definitions recognize the varying literacy needs of individuals within and among groups. Furthermore, these definitions provide for the special sub-groups of society: there is a literacy in music, in math, in medicine, in computer language, and so on.

Of course the definitions still leave open the specific question necessary for any assessment: What *are* these 'knowledges and skills'? In terms of the definition, however, the implication is that the function of literacy is to enable the individual to cope better in his society. Presumably this coping will contribute to the individual's person and social productivity.

Often in recent years this goal of functional literacy has led to specific job-related training in reading and writing, as exemplified by Laubach (Harvard, 1970) or Nasution (1972). In the latter case, Nigerian programs in reading and writing were entirely work-oriented, with enrollees involved in their development. The result was intended to lead to increased economic productivity, a benefit to the individual and to the state.

On the other hand, such work-oriented literacy programs have come in for criticism. Freire (1972) and Stanley (1972), for example, see such programs as a means whereby the 'haves' control the 'have-nots.' Learning to read at a functional level increases economic productivity, but it does not awaken the individual to the possibility of changing his circumstances, of seeing a better life. Stanley sharply criticizes specific job-oriented definitions of literacy as technicist, as indicating that 'you are literate if you can obey our orders when they are written down.'

Stanley (1972, p. 400) defines literacy as:

. . . the minimal capacity both to understand the moral implications of and to act upon the demands of competence for what a particular society defines as responsible participation of the person-as-agent in nature, society, and other persons.

The stress here is on 'responsible participation of the person-as-agent' as opposed to the person as merely part of society.

It is not pertinent in this paper to debate whether a society will—or even should—plan an educational program that leads to its own downfall. What is important is the fact that the sociological definitions, from Gray to Stanley, can be applied to the literacy continuum: It may be from the needs of the individual 'to engage effectively' or from his need to act with 'responsible participation' that the quality of his literacy can be assessed on the continuum and his needs-discrepancy determined.

From any view except that of ease of assessing, literacy can not be defined as a point on the continuum, applicable to all: It cannot be defined purely from the educational viewpoint. I suggest bringing the educational and the sociological viewpoints together to generate the following definition:

> Literacy is that demonstrated competence in communication skills which enables the individual to function, appropriate to his age, independently in his society and with a potential for movement in that society.

This definition departs from others in allowing for the recognition of children as 'literate.' Further, it recognizes the need for potentiality if the individual is to survive in changing societies. It is consistent with other definitions in its implications that one must communicate in the culture in which he finds himself. Finally, it recognizes the need for independence in the use of communication skills; as demonstrated in follow-up reports on literacy programs (Gray, 1956), unless the individual reaches a level of independence in his skills, he does not use them and those skills deteriorate.

Some thoughts on the assessment of literacy

In moving from a grade-completed or a reading-level criterion of literacy, we find assessment a more honest but much more difficult task. No longer can a pass-fail instrument be developed at the level of decision and applied like a knife to divide the 'literate' from the 'illiterate.'

On the other hand, an assessment need not measure everything; some facets can be limited. The fact that 'communication skills' are included in the definitions does not automatically require that all the communication skills be assessed. Unless the intent is to assess pre-school children, oral skills (barring physical deficits) can be assumed to be as well developed—usually better developed—as reading/writing skills. In fact, the accepted measure of the disabled reader's potential is that level at which he can listen to and comprehend printed material.

With this in mind, two avenues to assessment seem clear: (1) information can be collected on the entire communication skills continuum from all age groups, or (2) certain age groups can be assessed through the application of identified sample tasks appropriate to those age groups.

In the first type of information collecting, an assessment would enable the identification of the current level of literacy development of a sample age group or of a sample geographic area. While the assessment could be done through pencil and paper testing, adults should have tests developed at their interest level if an accurate measure is expected (Boulmetis, 1973; Jackson 1972).

If the assessment is to be related to a specific group, tasks need to be developed related to the activities engaged in by that group. For example, if the group is of school age, the appropriate tasks would seem to be a sampling of the activities in which these individuals engage—mostly school tasks. On the other hand, if the group is an adult group, the tasks need to be relevant to their interests.

The development of appropriate tasks for the assessment of adults raises many questions, in view of the fact that different positions require different degrees of literacy. A beginning—but again back to a very basic 'functional literacy'—is the work of Educational Testing Service on criterion referenced items developed from analyses of the basic reading needs of adults in our society (Boulmetis, 1973; Jackson, 1972).

Such an effort must be undertaken carefully; the pitfalls are numerous, as pointed out in criticisms of the Harris Literacy Study of 1970 (Caughran, 1972). The Harris study used too limited a class of sample items (five facsimile forms to be completed). In addition, the facsimiles were not equivalent in difficulty to the original forms. Hence, the study is of doubtful value.

To move beyond this kind of assessment of the 'functional literacy' of adults would require an analysis of the language skills required for the many situations in which an adult might find himself in our society. Such an analysis could have the negative influence of implying a particular job 'slotting' if not used carefully.

There is still the possibility, however, that such precision in determining position-related reading-skill needs is not necessary. While more research is still needed on this point, there is some evidence to support a generalized reading skill. As reported, Fisher (1971) found that success in remedial reading programs at the adult level had little correlation with success on the job. Important to remember here is the reading achievement of the sample, a very narrow range at the lower level. In contrast, Sticht (1972) dealt with a much broader range of reading achievements. He reported that the California Achievement Test and the Armed Forces Qualification Test correlated best of all measures, including supervisor's ratings, with job performance.

In this paper I have explored definitions of *literacy* with a thought toward its possible assessment. Typical grade-standard definitions have been rejected, as have purely job-related functional definitions. Proposed is a definition which recognizes literacy as a continuum on which an individual may find himself; this continuum of 'degrees of literacy' replaces the arbitrary 'literacy/ illiteracy' dichotomy. The individual's level of literacy is appropriate if, for his age, he can function effectively and independently in his society and if he retains a capability for movement in that society.

Such a definition does not prescribe a specific kind of assessment, in that the nature of the assessment should vary with the purpose and population to be assessed. The definition does, however, preclude a grade-standard or a purely reading-level type of criterion for the determination of 'literacy.'

The consideration of literacy as a continuum deliberately avoids setting a level too high for achievement or too low for satisfaction. Furthermore, it recognizes a necessary progression in literacy, never better expressed than by Dorothy Jones, in her response to a criticism of job-oriented literacy training (Harvard, 1970, p. 273):

> . . . I don't want to see all my people getting to be custodians in the Bank of America or anywhere else. . . . But at the same time I've got to remember, looking at the history of my people, that we couldn't start sitting in for the right to eat at some greasy spoon in Mississippi until first we had gotten the right to survive. We had to get to the point where most of us were not starving to death before we could begin to think of the other issues. And I think there's a parallel here. If we can get everybody at least to basic literacy, these people will then begin to have access to some of the books I read when I was a hungry kid during the depression, and begin to get an idea of what's possible. If I had never been able to read those books I might even have been content to stay where I was because that's all I knew. I would not be willing to accept janitorial work as a final goal. I am willing to accept it as a first step.

References

Boulmetis, John (1973) 'Cognitive evaluation in ABE', *Adult Leadership*, September, 108–9.
Caughran, Alex M. and John A. Lindlof (1972) 'Should the "Survival Literacy Study" Survive?', *Journal of Reading*, March, 429–35.

Education Centre Library (1962) 'A Special Report on Illiteracy', Toronto, Board of Education, June.

Fisher, Allan H. Jr. and George H. Brown (1971) 'Army "New Standards" Personnel: Effect of Remedial Literacy Training on Performance in Military Service', ED 056-272, April.

Freire, Paulo (1972) *Pedagogy of the Oppressed*, N.Y., Herder & Herder; also Penguin Books.

Gray, William S. (1956) *The Teaching of Reading and Writing*, Chicago, Unesco and Scott Foresman.

Harman, David (1970) 'Literacy: an overview', *Harvard Educational Review*, May, 226–43.

Harvard Educational Review (1970) 'Illiteracy in America: a symposium', *Harvard Educational Review*, May, 264–76.

Jackson, Rex (1972) 'The Development of a Collection of Adult Tasks for Assessment of Literacy', paper presented at American Educational Research Association, Chicago, 4 April, ED 061–023.

Nasution, Amir (1972) 'Functional-Literacy: A Method of Vocational Training for Farmers-Workers', International Literacy Day, ED 065–776.

Southgate, Vera (ed.) (1972) *Literacy at all Levels* (proceedings of the Annual Study Conference of the United Kingdom Reading Association, Manchester, 1971), Ward Lock.

Spache, George D. (1970) 'The Research and Development Program on Reading', National Reading Conference, December, ED 050–892.

Stanley, Manfred (1972) 'Literacy: the crisis of a conventional wisdom', *School Review*, May, 373–408.

Sticht, Thomas G. *et al*. (1972) 'Project REALISTIC: determination of adult functional literacy skill levels', *Reading Research Quarterly*, spring, 424–65.

Unesco (1965) *Statistics of Illiteracy*, Paris, Unesco.

1. 3 The politics of reading

Neil Postman

Teachers of reading comprise a most sinister political group, whose continued presence and strength are more a cause for alarm than celebration. I offer this thought as a defensible proposition, all the more worthy of consideration because so few people will take it seriously.

My argument rests in a fundamental and, I think, unassailable assumption about education: namely, that all educational practices are profoundly political in the sense that they are designed to produce one sort of human being rather than another—which is to say, an educational system always proceeds from some model of what a human being *ought* to be like. In the broadest sense, a political ideology is a conglomerate of systems for promoting certain modes of thinking and behavior. And there is no system I can think of that more directly tries to do this than the schools. There is not one thing that is done to, for, with, or against a student in school that is not rooted in a political bias, ideology, or notion. This includes everything from the arrangement of seats in a classroom, to the rituals practiced in the auditorium, to the textbooks used in lessons, to the dress required of both teachers and students, to the tests given, to the subjects that are taught, and most emphatically, to the intellectual skills that are promoted. And what is called reading, it seems to me, just about heads the list. For to teach reading, or even to promote vigorously the teaching of reading, is to take a definite political position on how people should behave and on what they ought to value. Now, teachers, I have found, respond in one of three ways to such an assertion. Some of them deny it. Some of them concede it but without guilt or

Source: *Harvard Educational Review*, 4(2), 1970, pp. 244–52.

defensiveness of any kind. And some of them don't know what it means. I want to address myself to the latter, because in responding to them I can include all the arguments I would use in dealing with the others.

In asserting that the teaching of reading is essentially a political enterprise, the most obvious question I am asking is, 'What is reading good for?' When I ask this question of reading teachers, I am supplied with a wide range of answers. Those who take the low ground will usually say that skill in reading is necessary in order for a youngster to do well in school. The elementary teacher is preparing the youngster for the junior high teacher, who prepares him for the senior high teacher, who, in turn, prepares him for the college teacher, and so on. Now, this answer is true but hardly satisfactory. In fact, it amounts to a description of the *rules* of the school game but says nothing about the purpose of these rules. So, when teachers are pushed a little further, they sometimes answer that the school system, at all levels, makes reading skill a precondition to success because unless one can read well, he is denied access to gainful and interesting employment as an adult. This answer raises at least a half-dozen political questions, and most interesting of which is whether or not one's childhood education ought to be concerned with one's future employment. I am aware that most people take it as axiomatic that the schooling process should prepare youth for a tranquil entry into our economy, but this is a political view that I think deserves some challenge. For instance, when one considers that the second most common cause of death among adolescents in the US is suicide, or that more people are hospitalized for mental illness than all other illnesses combined, or that one out of every twenty-two murders in the United States is committed by a parent against his own child, or that more than half of all high school students have already taken habit-forming, hallucinogenic, or potentially addictive narcotics, or that by the end of this year, there will be more than one-million school drop-outs around, one can easily prepare a case which insists that the schooling process be designed for purposes other than vocational training. If it is legitimate at all for schools to claim a concern for the adult life of students, then why not pervasive and compulsory programs in mental health, sex, or marriage and the family? Besides, the number of jobs that require reading skill much beyond what teachers call a 'fifth-grade level' is probably quite small and scarcely justifies the massive, compulsory, unrelenting reading programs that characterize most schools.

But most reading teachers would probably deny that their major purpose is to prepare students to satisfy far-off vocational requirements. Instead, they would take the high ground and insist that the basic purpose of reading instruction is to open the student's mind to the wonders and riches of the written word, to give him access to great fiction and poetry, to permit him to function as an informed citizen, to have him experience the sheer pleasure of reading. Now, this is a satisfactory answer indeed but, in my opinion, it is almost totally untrue.

And to the extent that it is true, it is true in a way quite different from anything one might expect. For instance, it is probably true that in a highly complex society, one cannot be governed unless he can read forms, regulations, notices, catalogues, road signs, and the like. Thus, some minimal reading skill is necessary if you are to be a 'good citizen,' but 'good citizen' here means one who can follow the instructions of those who govern him. If you cannot read, you cannot be an obedient citizen. You are also a good citizen if you are an enthusiastic consumer. And so, some minimal reading competence is required if you are going to develop a keen interest in all the products that it is necessary for you to buy. If you do not read, you will be a relatively poor market. In order to be a good and loyal citizen, it is also necessary for you to believe in the myths and superstitions of your society. Therefore, a certain minimal reading skill is needed so that you can learn what these are, or have them reinforced. Imagine what would happen in a school if a Social Studies text were introduced that described the growth of American civilization as being characterized by four major developments: (1) insurrection against a legally constituted government, in order to achieve a political identity; (2) genocide against the indigenous population, in order to get land; (3) keeping human beings as slaves, in order to achieve an economic base; and (4) the importation of 'coolie' labor, in order to build the railroads. Whether this view of American history is true or not is beside the point. It is at least as true or false as the conventional view *and* it would scarcely be allowed to appear unchallenged in a school-book intended for youth. What I am saying here is that an important function of the teaching of reading is to make students accessible to political and historical myth. It is entirely possible that the main reason middle-class whites are so concerned to get lower-class blacks to read is that blacks will remain relatively inaccessible to standard-brand beliefs unless and until they are minimally literate. It just may be too dangerous, politically, for any substantial minority of our population *not* to believe that our flags are sacred, our history is noble, our government is representative, our laws are just, and our institutions are viable. A reading public is a responsible public, by which is meant that it believes most or all of these superstitions, and which is probably why we still have literacy test for voting.

One of the standard beliefs about the reading process is that it is more or less neutral. Reading, the argument goes, is just a skill. What people read is their own business, and the reading teacher merely helps to increase a student's options. If one wants to read about America, one may read De Toqueville or *The Daily News*; if one wants to read literature, one may go to Melville or Jacqueline Susann. In theory, this argument is compelling. In practice, it is pure romantic nonsense. The *New York Daily News* is the most widely read newspaper in America. Most of our students will go to the grave not having read, of their own choosing, a paragraph of De Toqueville or Thoreau or John Stuart Mill or, if you exclude the Gettysburg Address, even Abraham Lincoln. As between Jacqueline Susann and Herman Melville—well, the less said, the better. To put it bluntly, among every 100 students who learn to read, my guess is that no more than one will employ the process towards any of the lofty goals which are customarily held before us. The rest will use the process to increase their knowledge of trivia, to maintain themselves at a relatively low level of emotional maturity, and to keep themselves simplistically uninformed about the social and political turmoil around them.

Now, there are teachers who feel that, even if what I say is true, the point is nonetheless irrelevant. After all, they say, the world is not perfect. If people do not have enough time to read deeply, if people do not have sensibilities refined enough to read great literature, if people do not have interests broad enough to be stimulated by the unfamiliar, the fault is not in our symbols, but in ourselves. But there is a point of view that proposes that the 'fault,' in fact, *does* lie in our symbols. Marshall McLuhan is saying that each medium of comunication contains a unique metaphysic—that each medium makes special kinds of claims on our senses, and therefore, on our behavior. McLuhan himself tells us that he is by no means the first person to have noticed this. Socrates took a very dim view of the written word, on the grounds that it diminishes man's capacity to memorize, and that it forces one to follow an argument rather than to participate in it. He also objected to the fact that once something has been written down, it may easily come to the attention of persons for whom it was not intended. One can well imagine what Socrates would think about wire-tapping and other electronic bugging devices. St Ambrose, a prolific book writer and reader, once complained to St Jerome, another prolific writer and reader, that whatever else its virtues, reading was the most anti-social behavior yet devised by man. Other people have made observations about the effects of communications media on the psychology of a culture, but it is quite remarkable how little has been said about this subject. Most criticism of print, or any other medium, has dealt with the content of the medium; and it is only in recent years that we have begun to understand that each medium, *by its very structure*, makes us do things with our bodies, our senses, and our minds that in the long run are probably more important than any other messages communicated by the medium.

Now that it is coming to an end, we are just beginning to wonder about the powerful biases forced upon us by the Age of the Printed Word. McLuhan is telling us that print is a 'hot' medium, by which he means that it induces passivity and anesthetizes almost all our senses except the visual. He is also telling us that electronic media, like the LP record and television, are reordering our entire sensorium, restoring some of our sleeping senses, and, in the process, making all of us seek more active participation in life. I think McLuhan is wrong in connecting the *causes* of passivity and activity so directly to the structure of media. I find it sufficient to say that whenever a new medium—a new communications technology—enters a culture, *no matter what its structure*, it gives us a new way of experiencing the world, and consequently, releases tremendous energies and causes people to seek new ways of organizing their institutions. When Gutenberg announced that he could manufacture books, as he put it, 'without the help of reed, stylus, or pen but by wondrous agreement, proportion, and harmony of punches and types,' he could scarcely imagine that he was about to become the most important political and social revolutionary of the Second Millenium. And yet, that is what happened. Four hundred and fifty years ago, the printed word, far from being a medium that induced passivity, generated cataclysmic change. From the time Martin Luther posted his theses in 1517, the printing press disseminated the most controversial, inflammatory, and wrenching ideas imaginable. The Protestant Reformation would probably not have occurred if not for the printing press. The development of both capitalism and nationalism were obviously linked to the printing press. So were new literary forms, such as the novel and the essay. So were new conceptions of education, such as written examinations. And, of course, so was the concept of scientific methodology, whose ground rules were established by Descartes in his *Discourse on Reason*. Even today in recently illiterate cultures, such as Cuba, print is a medium capable of generating intense involvement, radicalism, artistic innovation, and institutional upheaval. But in those countries where the printed word has been pre-eminent for over 400 years, print retains very few of these capabilities. Print is not dead, it's just old—and old technologies do not generate new patterns of behavior. For us, print is the technology of convention. We have accommodated our senses to it. We have routinized and even ritualized our responses to it. We have devoted our institutions, which are now venerable, to its service. By maintaining the printed word as the keystone of education, we are therefore opting for political and social stasis.

It is 126 years since Professor Morse transmitted a message electronically for the first time in the history of the planet. Surely it is not too soon for educators to give serious thought to the message he sent: 'What hath God wrought?' We are very far from knowing the answers to that question, but we do know that electronic media have released unprecedented energies. It's worth saying that the gurus of the peace movement—Bob Dylan, Pete Seeger, Joan Baez, Phil Ochs, for instance—were known to their constituency mostly as voices on LP records. It's worth saying that Viet Nam, being our first television war, is also the most unpopular war in our history. It's worth saying that Lyndon Johnson was the first president ever to have resigned because of a 'credibility gap.' It's worth saying that it is now commonplace for post-TV college sophomores to usurp the authority of college presidents and for young parish priests to instruct their bishops in the way of *both* man and God. And it's also worth saying that black people, after 350 years of bondage, want their freedom—now. Post-television blacks are, indeed, our true *now* generation.

Electronic media are predictably working to unloose disruptive social and political ideas, along with new forms of sensibility and expression. Whether this is being achieved by the structure of the media, or by their content, or by some combination of both, we cannot be sure. But like Gutenberg's infernal machine of 450 years ago, the electric plug is causing all hell to break loose. Meanwhile, the schools are still pushing the old technology; and, in fact, pushing it with almost hysterical vigor. Everyone's going to learn to read, even if we have to kill them to do it. It is as if the schools were the last bastion of the old culture, and if it has to go, why let's take as many down with us as we can.

For instance, the schools are still the principal source of the idea that literacy is equated with intelligence. Why, the schools even promote the idea that *spelling* is related to intelligence! Of course, if any of this were true, reading teachers would be the smartest people around. One doesn't mean to be unkind, but if that indeed is the case, no one has noticed it. In any event, it is an outrage that children who do not read well, or at all, are treated as if they are stupid. It is also masochistic, since the number of non-readers will obviously continue to increase and, thereby, the schools will condemn themselves, by their own definition of intelligence, to an increasing number of stupid children. In this way, we will soon have remedial reading-readiness classes, along with remedial classes for those not yet ready for their remedial reading-readiness class.

The schools are also still promoting the idea that literacy is the richest source of aesthetic experience. This, in the face of the fact that kids are spending a billion dollars a year to buy LP records and see films. The schools are still promoting the idea that the main source of wisdom is to be found in libraries, from which most schools, incidentally, carefully exclude the most interesting books. The schools are still promoting the idea that the non-literate person is somehow not fully human, an idea that will surely endear us to the non-literate peoples of the world. (It is similar to the idea that salvation is obtainable only through Christianity—which is to say, it is untrue, bigoted, reactionary, and based on untenable premises, to boot.)

Worst of all, the schools are using these ideas to keep non-conforming youth—blacks, the politically disaffected, and the economically disadvantaged, among others—in their place. By tasking this tack, the schools have become a major force for political conservatism at a time when everything else in the culture screams for rapid reorientation and change.

What would happen if our schools took the drastic political step of trying to make the new technology the keystone of education? The thought will seem less romantic if you remember that the start of the Third Millenium is only thirty-one years away. No one knows, of course, what would happen, but I'd like to make a few guesses. In the first place, the physical environment would be entirely different from what it is now. The school would look something like an electric circus—arranged to accommodate TV cameras and monitors, film projectors, computers, audio and video tape machines, radio, and photographic and stereophonic equipment. As he is now provided with textbooks, each student would be provided with his own still-camera, 8 mm camera, and tape cassette. The school library would contain books, of course, but at least as many films, records, videotapes, audio-tapes, and computer programs. The major effort of the school would be to assist students in achieving what has been called 'multi-media literacy.' Therefore, speaking, film-making, picture-taking, televising, computer-programming, listening, perhaps even music playing, drawing, and dancing would be completely acceptable means of expressing intellectual interest and competence. They would certainly be given weight at least equal to reading and writing.

Since intelligence would be defined in a new way, a student's ability to create an idea would be at least as important as his ability to classify and remember the ideas of others. New evaluation procedures would come into being, and standardized tests—the final, desperate refuge of the print-bound bureaucrat—would disappear. Entirely new methods of instruction would evolve. In fact, schools might abandon the notion of teacher instruction altogether. Whatever disciplines lent themselves to packaged, lineal, and segmented presentation would be offered through a computerized and individualized program. And students could choose from a wide variety of such programs whatever they wished to learn about. This means, among other things, that teachers would have to stop acting like teachers and find something useful to do, like, for instance, helping young people to resolve some of their more wrenching emotional problems.

In fact, a school that put electric circuitry at its center would have to be prepared for some serious damage to all of its bureaucratic and hierarchical arrangements. Keep in mind that hierarchies derive their authority from the notion of unequal access to information. Those at the top have access to more information than those at the bottom. That is in fact why they are at the top and the others at the bottom. But today those who are at the bottom of the school hierarchy, namely, the students, have access to at least as much information about most subjects as those at the top. At present, the only way those at the top can maintain control over them is by carefully discriminating against what the students know—that is, by labeling what the students know as unimportant. But suppose cinematography was made a 'major' subject instead of English literature? Suppose chemotherapy was made a 'major' subject? or space technology? or ecology? or mass communication? or popular music? or photography? or race relations? or urban life? Even an elementary school might then find itself in a situation where the faculty were at the bottom and its students at the top. Certainly, it would be hard to know who are the teachers and who the learners.

And then perhaps a school would become a place where *everybody*, including the adults, is trying to learn something. Such a school would obviously be problem-centered, *and* future-centered, *and* change-centered; and, as such, would be an instrument of cultural and political radicalism. In the process we might find that our youth would also learn to read without pain and with a degree of success and economy not presently known.

I want to close on this thought: teachers of reading represent an important political pressure group. They may not agree with me that they are a sinister political group. But I should think that they would want to ask at least a few questions *before* turning to consider the *techniques* of teaching reading. These questions would be: What is reading good for? What is it better or worse than? What are my motives in promoting it? And the ultimate political question of all, 'Whose side am I on?'

1. 4 The politics of ignorance
Frank Smith

In 'The Politics of Reading' Postman suggests that schools should relinquish their concern with written language literacy—which he thinks is 'political'—especially since a poor job is made of reading instruction and since electronic communications technology has made written language obsolete. While I shall briefly argue that Postman's pronouncements are ill-founded, my major purpose will be to place the issue of literacy within a far more general context.

Postman addresses himself to a *symptom* of the malaise that afflicts our schools, not to the cause. His electronic panacea would aggravate the complaint rather than cure it. I see only one political issue in education—and only one educational issue in politics—an issue that for want of a better word can be called *ignorance*. The question is not whether teachers should try to inculcate reading—or any other skill—in students, but the extent to which they should be permitted to contaminate children with the most contagious of social diseases, mental stultification.

Children do not arrive at school ignorant, though they may arrive illiterate. Whether or not they leave school illiterate, they frequently leave it ignorant, which is the state in which the more 'successful' of them may enter universities and other institutions of higher ignorance, some in due course to return to the classroom and spread the infection to another generation of children.

The ignorance explosion

First, some criterial attributes of ignorance. Ignorance is not a

Source: Sister R. Winklejohann (ed.), *The Politics of Reading*, Newark, Del., International Reading Association, 1973, pp. 43–55.

matter of not knowing, but of not knowing that you don't know or mistakenly believing that you do know, or that at least some expert somewhere does know. Ignorance is not so much not knowing an answer as not knowing the question, not being able ιo think when thinking is required. Ignorance is a blind dependence that someone else will be able to tell you what to do.

There is far more ignorance in the world today than ever before. Contemporary man finds himself in many more situations in which he believes he has or expects to be given solutions that in fact are non-existent or constitute more complex problems. Where once there was uncertainty about how to organize the economy of a feudal demesne, in today's megalopoli we are totally ignorant about making life bearable or even possible. Once we wrestled with the problem of winning local wars; today we have no idea how to survive peace. Limited transportation was once an unavoidable inconvenience; today the automobile chokes us. In place of occasional famine we eat foods essentially devoid of nourishment. Once we knew no better than to allow sewage to befoul the streets. Today we have invented so many kinds of artificial excrement that neither the oceans nor the air around us can accommodate it. Schools were once unsure about the best use of slate, a modest ignorance which contemporary technology has expanded through an incredible range of electronic gadgetry. The intelligence of the world is boggling under the brunt of what is incautiously called 'information'—a proliferation of negative entropy that makes it just about impossible to separate the true from the false, the real from the fantastic, the relevant from the rubbish. Our environment is clogged with nonsense.

But while ignorance abounds, it is by no means uniformly distributed. Ignorance is directly related to what you need to know, or to what you presume to know. The villager may not be able to direct the tourist to the nearest roadhouse, but it is not the villager who is lost. The doctor is ignorant, not the patient. And as I have already asserted, children do not come to school ignorant. The majority arrive, God help them, ready, willing, and able to learn. They have already resolved intellectual problems of astounding complexity—should we pause to think about it—ranging from mastering a language to organizing a coherent theory of the world around them, including their own place in it. They are adept at making sense of the world, at relating what is new to what they know already. They can cope.

Long before infants acquire control of their bladders they demonstrate an intellectual awareness, flexibility, and responsiveness that is the very antithesis of ignorance. Children can think long before they come to school. The first time most children meet nonsense in their lives is in the classroom (some basal reading systems pride themselves on the fact that their content is meaningless). Learning is not meaningful to many kids in school, any more than teaching is meaningful to many teachers. The first lesson that many children learn is 'Don't think, do as I tell you,' just as the teachers themselves have been taught 'Don't think, someone else will tell you what to do' (the concept of 'leadership'). But I am getting ahead of my argument.

As I was saying, ignorance is not distributed equally in this world. It is relative to the situation you are in, a function of your aspirations and expectations. In particular, ignorance is clustered in our educational institutions.

Ignorance in education

Two kinds of ignorance may be distinguished in education and conveniently labelled soft- and hard-core. Soft-core ignorance, which tends to be found in schools, is the ignorance of those who feel they need to be told what to do. Many teachers are trained to be ignorant, to rely on the opinions of experts or 'superiors' rather than on their own judgment. The questions I am asked after lectures to teachers (on the topic of reading) are always eminently *practical*—how should reading be taught, which method is best, and what should be done about a real-life child of eight who has the devastating misfortune to read like a statistically fictitious child of six? Teachers do not ask the right kind of question—instead of asking what they should *do*, which can never be answered with the generality they expect, they should ask what they need to *know* in order to decide for themselves. (It is a monument to the efficiency of the brainwashing that teachers receive during their training that they are practically immune to insult on the topic of their own intellectual capacity. The only time teachers express surprise or disbelief is when it is suggested that their own experience and intuition might be as good a guide for action as the dogma of some expert.)

Soft-core ignorance is not restricted to teachers. It is reflected at all levels of education in the pathetic faith that electronic technology will provide the answers to all problems (instead of creating more problems). A senior officer of the International Reading Association recently waxed lyrical regarding his board's joint exploration with the Boeing Aerospace Group of 'the possible applications of space-age telecommunications technology to help eradicate world illiteracy'—as if space engineers must be privy to some cabalistic knowledge about teaching reading. Man may not have got to the moon before the age of computers and systems analysis, but kids have been learning to read for centuries. Every method of teaching reading ever devised has worked with some children (which only goes to prove how adaptable children are). We do not need to find something different to do in the future, but rather to discover what we have been doing right in the past. We talk as if it was a miracle that any child ever learns to read. But if we think about the facility with which most 'illiterates' learned to talk, it might appear more remarkable that educators are able to arrange an environment in which so many children consistently fail to learn to read.

Soft-core ignorance, then, is the expectation that someone else can be relied upon to solve your practical problems and save you the trouble of thinking. Hard-core ignorance, on the other hand, is the belief that you know the answers to all problems and can do the thinking for other people. And hard-core ignorance is concentrated at the upper levels of our educational hierarchy (I use the term in its literal sense of a priesthood), notably in the universities.

In my experience, the promiscuity with which teachers are willing to be seduced by some overqualified outsider is exceeded only by the avidity with which academics from a range of totally irrelevant disciplines have their intellectual way with teachers. Nowhere is ignorance of the reading process more pronounced than among the linguists, psychologists, systems analysts, and brain surgeons who are prepared to tell reading teachers how to teach reading. The degree of PhD, it often seems to me, is a license to practice ignorance. (I am not prejudiced. Some of my best friends are ignoramuses, though I wouldn't want my daughter to marry one.)

Some specifics of educational ignorance

After such generalities, I shall now talk briefly about ignorance with respect to reading, reading instruction, electronic instructional technology, and the role of schools, all of which will give an opportunity to make at least a few points relevant to the Postman article.

Reading is a highly obscure topic closely surrounded by a dense fog of pedagogical mystique and mythology. Learning to read is frequently confused with reading instruction—the vast majority of books on 'reading' or the psychology thereof are thinly disguised tracts of instructional dogma. It is a typical teacher's error to confuse what is done in school with what a child learns. The most that can be said for any method of reading instruction that succeeds—and, as I have said, all methods succeed with some children—is that somebody must be doing something right. More dangerous are the widespread beliefs that a child will not learn unless told exactly what to do—which is obviously and fortunately false, because no one knows enough about reading to tell a child what to do—and that there must be something wrong with a child who does not learn to read.

There is a good deal to say about the reading process that I have no space to elaborate upon here, although I have tried to do so elsewhere. I shall list just a few points to give a flavor of them, and hopefully whet an appetite or two: reading is not primarily decoding to sound, nor do the eyes play a primary role in reading. Reading by 'phonics' is demonstrably impossible (ask any computer). Reading places an impossible burden upon the visual system and upon memory unless the reader is able to read fast, without an undue concern for literal accuracy, and with comprehension as immediate as it is for spoken language. Memorization interferes with comprehension, and so do 'comprehension tests.' Children learn to read by reading, and the sensible teacher makes reading easy and interesting, not difficult and boring.

I shall make four blanket assertions that may raise a good many hackles but that I regard as easily defensible—the fact that they are widely ignored and even suppressed in education would be a prime argument for the prosecution if I were trying to convict schools of criminal ignorance: A child does not need to be very intelligent to learn to read. A child does not need to be very mature to learn to read. A child does not need to come from a socially or economically superior home, or to have literate parents, in order to learn to read. A child does not need to wait to get to school to learn to read.

Most teachers of reading *know* the preceding statements are true, even if they are not familiar with the published sources—Durkin, Fowler, Moore, Torrey. But in any case, if you think intelligence, maturity, 'experience,' and skilled adult supervision are necessary for learning to read, how do you think an infant learns the much more complex skills of spoken language? As many parents in North America are discovering, a child has a reading problem only if he is still unable to read when he gets to school.

In short, all the evidence indicates that it is not so much inadequacy on the part of children that makes learning to read such a hassle as the way in which we expect them to learn—through instructional procedures that systematically deprive them of relevant practice and necessary information. The more difficulty a child experiences in learning to read, the less reading and the more nonsense drills we typically arrange for him to do.

Rather than pausing to reflect upon where the fault really lies, however, it is becoming fashionable these days to respond with a whatthehell, what's the need for children to learn to read in any case attitude. Postman, for example, suggests that written language has lost all utility as a medium of communication. Nevertheless, he entrusts his own messages to print and obviously expects someone to read them. He asserts that 'an important function of teaching reading is to make students accessible to political and historical myth,' without noting that reading might also provide grounds for rejecting such myth. One inestimable advantage of writing is that it forces the writer to make *statements* which can then be examined, analyzed, and even evaluated. Criticism is inherently a literary mode. It may be true—though I would dispute it—that written language appeals more to reason than to the emotions, but is this an argument against reading (any more than the opposite is an argument for or against electronic media)?

The fact that relatively few people may currently take advantage of reading seems to me irrelevant. It is almost certainly a consequence of the way reading is taught. There is information and knowledge and pleasure in print—not just in novels, but in newspapers, magazines, comics, programs, menus, directories, scripts, scenarios, letters, notices, and graffiti. Even Postman would include books in his brave new resource centers, despite his uncertainty about who might read them. He even suggests that being able to read might somehow be degrading, that it makes the individual a tool of his government, or of any bureaucrat. But is illiteracy any better? Once again, I think he confuses the reading process with the consequences of the way we teach reading. The price of literacy need not be the reader's free will and intelligence.

Postman further argues that written language has been misused and worn out, that the world is full of written garbage. But people need not read everything that has been written—one advantage of being able to read is that you can be selective. It may be true that reprints of Postman's paper will help to clutter thousands of useless filing cabinets, never to be looked at again. But one of the more dubious benefits of the electronic revolution is that neither the spoken word nor the visual gesture will remain biodegradable in the future. Students armed with cassette recorders and video cameras will record every cough and scratch. If ever there were media that inundated themselves the moment they were created, it was audio and video taping, open invitations to capture the trivial for posterity. One advantage of old fashioned manual media like writing and painting is that they require *effort*; squirting a video camera at 'life' is an indiscriminate way of being creative.

It is a fallacy to assume that anything written language can do video tape can do better. There is good and bad grammar in film just as in written language, and there is at least as much ignorance about film. It is fallacious to believe that either film or television gives more information than writing. *Different media do not convey the same information about the same event*, but offer different perspectives. This is a most important point that I cannot pursue here, though I highly recommend several chapters in the 1974 NSSE Yearbook on media and symbols.[2]

All media are selective—you take your choice whether you see an event through the eye of the writer or of the cameraman. One beauty of written language is the manner in which it is selective. We tend to overlook how much information words give us about context, about what is said 'between the lines.' Words give more information than pictures because they can take so much account of what the reader already knows. When I view a documentary, I need a spoken or written commentary to tell me what I should be looking at and how to relate it to what I know.

Any notion that film provides a particularly veridical or unadulterated image of 'life' or 'experience' is naive—where does the 'creativity' come in? Reading about a good meal does not reduce hunger, but neither does a picture of it. Movies do not automatically enhance our experience, whether of the Vietnam conflict or of sex. A competent writer may give a reasonable impression of what it is like to eat a gourmet meal, suffer a napalm attack, or make love, while an incompetent movie producer might do little more than illustrate the movements involved. (Will electronic exercises teach children that the art of any medium is to use the receiver's imagination?) Vietnam was the world's most televised war, but 'bringing it into the living room' did not seem to end it any sooner. Could the fact that there was little written literature on Vietnam—as opposed to 'factual reporting'—have anything to do with the way the war was tolerated, regardless of demonstrations, which were themselves televised into visual tedium?

Postman himself admits that nobody knows what the consequence would be of turning schools into electric circuses. Nor does he mention that the experiment has already been tried to a certain extent and has failed. During the past decade most new and many old facilities in schools and universities were decked out with audiovisual novelty, much of it never used and now being taken out. And just as much ignorance is being displayed in dismantling the electronic sideshows as was involved in their establishment. Hard-core ignorance is not exclusive to written language experts.

While not arguing that reading is a substitute for electronic media, I deny the opposite. I am certainly not 'anti-media,' though I reject any assertion of blind faith in the virtue of any medium, including writing. Electronic illiteracy is as debasing as the inability to read—and infinitely more probable given the present level of ignorance in education. I am not even arguing that schools should continue trying to teach reading, simply that reading cannot be replaced by television and the tape recorder. I might prefer to argue that literacy in any medium is too precious to leave to our schools and to political propagandists.

As Postman implies, we have scarcely any idea today of what schools are for. We do not know what we should do in schools. We do not even understand what we are doing in schools. Ignorance abounds. Not only do we not understand why hundreds of thousands of children fail to learn to read each year, we have no idea what happens with the hundreds of thousands of children who succeed. Practically everything we try to teach in educational institutions we teach ineptly. If we succeed at all, it can be reasonably predicted that the student will not want to practice what he has learned or will do so reluctantly. And there is absolutely no evidence that we will do any better if we encourage our students to film and tape record everything in sight.

Don't talk about master teachers, love of learning, respect for knowledge, or academic integrity—these are more than exceptions within the modern system; they are freaks, aberrations. Schools are training institutions, managed by teachers who are themselves taught in training institutions, and the entire perverse and misbegotten process is founded on the premise that no one should actually think. *That* is the political issue.

The prime concern of schools is getting through the day. Schools are not concerned with literacy, nor with creativity, nor with intelligence, except as items in tests or in end-of-term reports. Superintendents and trustees are concerned with buildings, budgets, and enrollment projections. Principals are concerned with pacification, keeping the lid on, and maintaining stability. And teachers are concerned with discipline and control; how could they be otherwise, since thinking is an individual activity that produces unmanageable oddballs, whether in the classroom or in the staffroom? At every level there is one concern; it involves neither 'learning' nor the child—it is good administration. I know there are exceptions, but the discussion is not about exceptions, nor can most school systems tolerate them.

Schools make a poor job of teaching reading, suggests Postman, so why not release teachers from that burden and entrust them instead with something important, something 'relevant,' like 'helping young people to resolve some of their more wrenching emotional problems'? One can only wonder how anyone could think it is only literacy that schools can foul up. Will teachers be good for anything except distributing popcorn if we make them ushers in an electric circus?

The alternative to ignorance

The opposite of ignorance is not knowledge, which is either a dead end or a route to new ignorance. The opposite of ignorance is understanding—an active verb—achieved only through awareness and thought. And awareness and thought are not faculties that you acquire from experts or skills that can be taught in schools. Rather they are aspects of human nature that are inherent in all children—until they are drilled out of them by a process that is called socialization.

The opposite of ignorance is keeping the mind alive, always considering alternatives, never shutting the system down. It is remembering that every question might be put differently, that authority is not necessarily right, and that superficial glibness (including this paper and Postman's) is not necessarily erudition. The opposite of ignorance is never to rest content doing something you do not understand.

I am not arguing for the unattainable. Being told what to do is a good short run solution in an emergency situation, such as changing a tire or floating off the roof in a flood. But education should not be an emergency situation, and even if no one is really sure of what is going on in the classroom, at least the question could be mutually examined by those who are most involved, the child and the teacher.

I am not proposing that the printed word should remain the keystone of education, an extreme as radical as Postman's nomination of electronic media as a substitute. I would much prefer not to make a big issue of reading instruction, or of anything else. In fact I would suggest that we forget about 'teaching' for a while, or at least have a moratorium on the topic, and instead think a little about how schools might be reorganized as places where children and adults collaboratively or independently learn, a situation that would guarantee the exercise of thought. A prime focus for initial study might be how the acquisition of literacy in written language and electronic media might help the individual, teacher, or child to resist the blandishments and misinformation that daily assault all our senses. But there is much ignorance for us to think our way out of in these topics.

Let me go out even further on my self-appointed limb. Children do not learn by instruction, they learn by example, and they learn by making sense of what are essentially meaningful situations. Remember, children have been learning since birth. A child learns when he hears his mother talking to him or to a neighbor. He learns when his father lets him take a chance with a hammer and nails. He learns when he finds it necessary to check the price of sports equipment in a catalog. Always he learns in order to make sense of something, and especially when there is an example, a model, to be copied. Even when he learns to loot stores, sniff glue, or mug cripples, he does so by example and because it makes sense in his environment. If thinking or asking questions paid off, and if some good models were around, a child might even spend a few years at school doing just that—thinking and asking questions.

Encouraging people to think would be an enormously political issue. It is not one that currently occupies much of the attention of politicians, nor is it a dominant question in schools. In educational psychology, thinking is usually equated with problem solving, concept formation, and excursions to the nearest museum. The alternative to ignorance would be revolutionary in more than one sense of the word. It might even enable us to start asking the right sorts of questions about education.

Eradicating ignorance might also put a lot of experts out of business. What will be the use of having all of the right answers, even electronic ones, if people are going to start asking different kinds of questions and, worse still, to start educating their children to do the same?

Personal postscript

Someone is bound to ask how ignorant this paper is, or I am. My answer depends on how the question is put. If it is boorish, I shall say that the question itself is ignorant. But otherwise, I readily admit there is a great deal I do not know (which by my definition is not ignorance, of course), and for the rest, I try to keep an open mind.

References

1 Frank Smith, *Understanding Reading*, N.Y., Holt, Rinehart & Winston, 1971; and *Psycholinguistics and Reading*, Holt, Rinehart & Winston, 1973.
2 David R. Olson (ed.), *Media and Symbols: The Forms of Expression, Communication, and Education* (73rd Yearbook of the National Society for the Study of Education), University of Chicago Press, 1974.

Section 2 The Reading Process

The aim of this section is to look at various views of the nature of the reading process. The articles have been chosen not because they are representative of the available 'models' of reading but because implicit in each article is the view that the concept we have of reading strongly influences the way reading is taught.

The opening article by Ruth Strang (2.1) begins by looking at the reasons why reading is important—the way in which reading is significant for individuals at personal, social, national levels:

> In all nations an awareness has developed of the importance of worldwide literacy as a means of promoting individual welfare, social progress, and international understanding.

Readers might compare Strang's assessment of literacy with the views expressed in Section 1 of this volume.

The article goes on to look at the different ways of approaching the nature of reading. To view reading as merely word identification is to deny its value for personal fulfilment. The use one makes of reading largely determines what is read, why it is read, and how it is read.

The model of reading developed in the paper emphasises the need to fit the teaching of reading to the individual's cognitive and personal development. Reading does not begin and end with the learning of decoding skills, but continues throughout life. The reader at all ages is learning how to achieve desired reading outcomes. As the learner becomes more proficient, so he is able to draw new insights and respond more meaningfully to the printed page. Strang analyses the teaching of reading under four headings: product, process, prerequisites and procedures. The product of reading includes both word recognition and comprehension of the message, and these will require the processes of sensory impression, perception, conceptualisation and interpretation. Many factors determine the ability to read, and most factors are interdependent. The abilities to see, speak and listen are obviously important, but such factors as values and motivation need equal consideration for determining reading success or failure. Strang emphasises the need to see teaching procedures as a complex situation involving the interplay of teacher, pupil and materials.

Finally, Strang looks at the different modes of language: speaking, writing, listening and reading and the way in which the language 'arts' should be integrated—'all the aspects of language help[ing] to form the individual's developing personality.'

The general overview of the reading process presented by Strang goes beyond the initial stages of learning to read. However, it is the primary reading skills which have received most attention from psychologists, linguists and educationalists. The articles 2.2—2.5 look at ways of analysing what is involved in the reading task during the initial stages.

John Carroll (2.2) begins his analysis of the reading process by looking at the skills of the adult reader. He views the skilled reader as a decoder—someone who identifies unfamiliar words by recognising 'elements of it . . . that give him reasonably good cues as to how the word should be pronounced.' The reading material 'somehow merges together in such a way as to build up in your mind an impression of a meaningful message'. By first analysing the skills of the adult reader, Carroll determines the list of component skills to be learnt by the beginner reader. Each component, he believes, must be learnt and practised, and differences in reading practice result not from *what* should be taught but from the *order* in which they are taught. And the order will be determined not only by the teacher's view of reading but also by the aptitudes and inclinations the child brings to the task.

(Readers of this article might consider in what order they would teach the eight components listed by Carroll; on what grounds they would advocate that order; and whether they would modify the order to suit the needs of different children.)

Frank Smith (2.3) would not accept Carroll's assumption that decoding skills are prerequisites for learning to read. Smith argues that the non-reader does not need to learn to recognise the elements of the written word in order to read; rather, 'fluency with the alphabet', for example, 'comes with being a competent reader' (cf. Carroll's second component skill). Smith contends that because competent readers can recognise the elements in the reading task this does not imply that recognition of the elements leads to competent reading.

Children, Smith believes, must have two fundamental insights before they can learn to read: (i) that print is meaningful and (ii) that written language is different from speech. (Compare his arguments with Carroll's seventh component.) In support of his first antecedent for reading—meaningful print—Smith points out that:

> Children will not learn by trying to relate letters to sounds, partly because the task does not make sense to them and partly because written language does not work that way . . . It is . . . the sense of the text, if the text has any sense, that enables readers to use spelling-to-sound correspondences effectively.

And in defence of the second necessary insight for reading—that print is different from speech—Smith points out the different constraints placed on speech and writing and therefore the need for learners to realise the different expectancies to be found in the printed form. Adults too often assume that we speak as we write (and vice versa) and thus fail to notice the features of the written form which will confront the non-reader.

Smith's review of reading material leads him to believe that instructional practices may thwart the learning of these insights: 'Children who can make sense of instruction should learn to read; children confronted by nonsense are bound to fail.'

Certainly one agrees with Smith that much 'nonsense' confronts the learner. But the views of Carroll and Smith are not necessarily mutually exclusive. It is possible to teach reading skills (as outlined by Carroll) within the context of meaningful material.

John Downing's short article (2.4) takes up points made in the preceding articles in his discussion of problems posed by seemingly conflicting research results. For example, some researchers have found that visual discrimination abilities are not necessarily related to reading ability. And it has been found that it is easier to learn to read in two alphabets than it is in one. Such findings seem to conflict with adult notions of the reading process. Downing suggests that these paradoxes arise because we often fail to take into account 'the special ways in which children think and talk about reading and language.' Thus 'reading research may have been overconcerned with the external aspects of reading . . . at the expense of neglecting the "underlying more central processes"'. Viewing certain reading skills, e.g. letter-name knowledge, as a symptom of the child's conceptual growth corrects the emphasis of some teaching to consider only the skills to be mastered, without consideration of how the instructional material fits the child.

The first four articles (2.1—2.4) concern themselves largely with establishing the principles of reading teaching based on different views of the process. Kenneth and Yetta Goodman (2.5) investigate the reading process in a slightly different way. Instead of looking at what the skilled reader does (Carroll 2.2) or at the demands of written material (Smith 2.3), the Goodmans look at the errors or 'miscues' made by pupils and draw inferences about the skills the child brings to the task. Reading aloud, they contend, 'not only is a form of linguistic performance but also provides a powerful means of examining process and underlying competence.'

Miscue analysis has been growing in importance as a diagnostic tool for teachers and the explanation of this technique indicates the uses to which it can be put. Analysing the oral reading miscues and the way the child retells what was read 'provide an opportunity for the researcher or teacher to gain insight into how concepts and language are actively used and developed in reading.' The description and examples of one pupil's miscues and retellings demonstrate how the child actively participates in reading, bringing to the task expectations based on her own language experience. Reading involves, perhaps above all, prediction and construction of meaning.

The analysis of language into its abstract component parts—sounds, words and sentences—misses out the central component of language: that it is meaningful. As the Goodmans demonstrate, miscues provide a window on reading and other language processes.

The final article of this section, by Robert Ruddell (2.6), looks specifically at language acquisition and reading. In recent years major emphasis has been given to the linguistic skills involved in reading. Methods of teaching, such as language-experience approaches, strive to relate reading to the child's acquired oral language and to build on his or her linguistic knowledge. Ruddell's article provides a useful review of child language studies. He points to the language abilities the child brings to school but notes that 'substantial growth in structural and lexical language components must occur in the elementary school years.' Consideration is needed not only of linguistic maturity but also of such factors as the child's dialect and the language used in the home. The reading teacher needs to take into account the individual differences in language development and language use so that reading materials can be found which are compatible with the child's abilities.

2. 1 The nature of reading

Ruth Strang

Importance of reading

Reading proficiency is the royal road to knowledge; it is essential to the success in all academic subjects. In modern life, learning depends largely upon one's ability to interpret the printed page accurately and fully. A junior high school youngster summed it up in this way: 'You could list hundreds of reasons why being a good reader is important, but I guess I'd put it this way. Reading is the key to learning and personal enjoyment.' Another said, 'Reading to me is a way I can find out as much or as little as I choose to know or learn about something. And the more reading, the more learning.' Dr James Conant called reading the keystone of the arch of education. In 1964, Francis Keppel, United States Commissioner of Education, stated the value of reading still more broadly: 'Every examination of the problems of our schools, of poverty; every question raised by troubled parents about our schools, every learning disorder seems to show some association with reading difficulty' (Keppel, 1964, p. 8). The introduction to the report of the Carnegie Conference of Reading Experts (1962, p. 1) included this statement: 'Reading is the most important subject to be learned by children; a child will learn little else in today's world if he does not first learn to read properly . . .'

Personal values

Reading involves the whole personality, promising countless personal and social values. Reading is an entrance into almost all

Source: Ruth Strang *et al.*, *The Improvement of Reading*, N.Y., McGraw-Hill, 4th edn, 1967, pp. 4–39 (abridged).

vocations. Even routine mechanical work in a factory demands the reading of some material, such as basic rules, safety signs, and changes in regulations. Since many industrial accidents have been traced to employees' failure to read and comprehend signs and directions relating to safety, some firms now require that their personnel have at least a fourth-grade level of reading ability. The skilled trades require considerably more reading for the best quality of work and the integration of new practices.

In all the professions, of course, one must read a great deal after graduation, as well as during the preparation period, to keep pace with new developments. A lawyer considered that 'the ability to read well—to skim through an article, pick out important ideas in a paragraph, and make deductions from passages—is the most important single factor in a successful law practice.'

The best administrators and teachers demonstrate in their own lives the value of efficient reading; with pride in their work, they pursue a systematic course of professional reading. Lawyers, engineers, and physicians claim that reading is essential: one is successful only if he keeps up-to-date. For some professions, such as library work, writing, and bibliographical research work, extensive reading is so obviously a requisite that nothing further needs to be said.

Reading is a most rewarding use of the expanded leisure that comes as a result of automation. Given increasingly larger amounts of time and more opportunities to buy or borrow books, people should be educated to read at least one hour a day. 'Reading may be one of life's inexhaustible pleasures and blessings,' Walter de la Mare said. At its best, recreational reading affords more than mere entertainment. The reader has time to reflect on the ideas he meets and give play to the imagination.

Reading often relieves emotional tensions and gives insight into personal problems. Frequently the right book will fill the psychological need at a critical moment when the radio or television programs may be anything but agreeable to a mood.

Reading provides experience through which the individual may expand his horizons; identify, extend, and intensify his interests; and gain deeper understandings of himself, of other human beings, and of the world.

Reading organizes experience; it relates ideas from many sources.

Reading is a path to new experiences. Using his own firsthand experiences as a point of departure, the reader reaches out to those of an author and transcends the limitations of time and space. As Stevenson said, 'Reading takes us out of our country and ourselves.'

Reading is a creative act. As the writer creates a structure of thought, so the reader, re-creating the pattern of words, discovers for himself the essence of the author's idea.

Social values

But the value of reading in today's highly skilled democracy quickly over-reaches the purely personal and merges into social values. In fact, the general attitude toward reading is largely pragmatic, seeing it as an avenue to financial and social statuses. For its best welfare, society needs its members to have a minimum of education. As surveys show, non- or poor readers become the delinquent, the unemployed, or the misfit in a society which progresses to the extent that its mental resources do.

In general, reading disability severely restricts the adolescent's development. According to Krugman (1956), mental hygiene and reading underlie all teaching in schools and have the most pervasive influence on the student's success in school and adjustment in living. 'A reading disability or severe retardation in reading has the same profound influence on educational growth as a severe emotional involvement. Both limit successful functioning, cause feelings of inadequacy and frustration, bring about disturbed relationships, influence outlook on life, and result in a variety of undesirable behavior manifestations.'

The relation of reading disability to premature school leaving has been definitely established. Many students drop out of high school because of reading inability. Penty (1956) obtained clear evidence from data in the Battle Creek, Michigan, school system that the preponderance of early school leavers stood in the lowest quarter with respect to reading ability; only 14.5 per cent of those in the highest quarter left school before completing the senior year. More than three times as many poor readers as good readers left school; the peak of dropouts occurred in the tenth grade. Further study showed that a very large percentage of the poor readers who left, as well as of the poor readers who remained in school, had potential reading ability. With proper instruction they could have improved.

Three years after leaving school, young people of average intelligence made comments of this kind:

> I just didn't care for school except I liked Foods and Typing. I sometimes had difficulty in understanding English. I had no interest in reading whatsoever. I could read and read and get nothing out of it. I couldn't remember what I read either. I could have enjoyed school more if I had had help in reading. That is what put me behind.

> I didn't think that I was getting any place in school. I was working

part-time and wanted to work full-time. I had trouble reading and understanding assignments. I couldn't remember what I read and didn't like to recite, as I wasn't sure of myself.

Repeated academic failures caused by reading inability gave rise to feelings of inferiority and frustration: 'I didn't like to go to classes and be around other kids who seemed to learn easier than I did' (Penty, 1956).

Many other studies have shown that reading retardation is a frequent reason for giving up. The average dropout is retarded in reading two years or more.

Failure in reading may cause emotional disturbances. Even in the first grade, children who learned to read early showed self-confidence; those who did not make satisfactory progress felt anxious and insecure. One child said, 'I tried to read in the first grade. I tried a little while and then I just quit.' Another said, 'Teachers didn't do nothin' to help. They just asked me to read and when I couldn't they asked someone else.'

The child who fails to read may feel his family's disapproval. One child said wistfully, 'I wish my parents knew how I felt.' According to one study, the parents of severely retarded high school readers are more likely to use derogatory words and phrases in describing their children and more likely to disparage their abilities than are the parents of good readers.

Many statements of juvenile court judges and statistics of correctional institutions have pointed up the relationship between reading disability and delinquency. Judges have noted that as many as 50 per cent of the juvenile delinquents brought before the courts have severe reading disabilities. At one time approximately 30 per cent of the delinquent boys, aged twelve to fifteen, in the New York Training School for Boys were reading below second-grade level. To fail to recognize, diagnose, and correct these difficulties will result in the failure of any correctional program to rehabilitate a large proportion of delinquent and emotionally disturbed boys.

Reading retardation often produces a chain of consequences: inability to do the assignments and take part in the class discussion leads to feelings of inferiority, hopelessness, or hostility, which in turn bring about truancy, association with experienced delinquents, and delinquent acts. The final link is usually a court sentence. In each step of this sequence the individual's image of himself deteriorates. An adult in a penal institution vividly described how failure in reading affected his self-concept and his subsequent behavior: 'I couldn't read what they wanted me to in school, so after a while I got to thinking I was always going to be like this, and I didn't care. So I never did try to learn, 'cause I pictured me as an adult not reading, and that was OK.'

Wider imports

Such testimonials signal trouble for any country, affluent or poor. For despite the educational opportunities and wealth of this nation, 2.2 per cent of persons aged fourteen or over in the United States in 1959, according to census figures, March 1959, had not attained functional literacy; the percentages for individual states vary enormously. Draft figures reveal that thousands of men who are otherwise eligible for service cannot meet the Army's minimum educational standards. A much larger number either lack adequate comprehension of what they read or habitually distort it to conform to their prejudices.

Democracy cannot succeed when people are ignorant and cannot or will not think for themselves. If citizens fail to become cognizant of the implications of historical trends, fail to discriminate fact from opinion, or fail to detect and resist propaganda, both they and their nation are open to exploitation and manipulation.

Reading has international significance; recent figures indicate the magnitude of the problem. Half of the people of the world are completely illiterate and hardly a third have attained functional literacy, i.e., the level of reading that is normally expected of a child after four years of schooling. However, there is hope. According to Gray (1956, p. 1), interest in reading has never been so keen or so worldwide in scope as it is at the present time. In all nations an awareness has developed of the importance of worldwide literacy as a means of promoting individual welfare, social progress, and international understanding. [. . .]

Various views of reading

There are many misconceptions of reading. To some people, words are merely a supplement to pictures, an adjunct to television. To others, reading is a passive process—'expecting the book to come to you,' as one student said. Many people have been persuaded that reading is synonymous with word calling: if you can pronounce the words correctly, you are reading—even though you have no idea what the author said.

Reading is more than seeing words clearly, more than pronouncing printed words correctly, more than recognizing the meaning of isolated words. Reading requires you to think, feel, and imagine. Effective reading is purposeful. The use one makes of his reading largely determines what he reads, why he reads, and how he reads.

The teacher's overall concept of reading strongly influences his methods of diagnosing reading difficulty and of teaching reading.

If he thinks of reading primarily as a visual task, he will be concerned with the correction of visual defects and the provision of legible reading material. If reading to him is word recognition, he will drill on the basic sight vocabulary and word recognition skills. If he thinks reading is merely reproducing what the author says, he will direct the student's attention to the literal meaning of the passage and check his comprehension of it. If he views reading as a thinking process, he will be concerned with the reader's skill in making interpretations and generalizations, in drawing inferences and conclusions. If he thinks of reading as contributing to personal development and social welfare, he will provide his students with reading material that will help them develop sound values and that will have some application to their lives and to the modern world.

As a result of his historical approach to research into the causes of reading disability, Douglass (1963, p. 5) wrote that 'little attention has been directed toward developing an understanding of the nature of the reading process—of building a theoretical framework to help us comprehend the complex nature of what we call "reading".' If the process is not understood, the methods will be inadequate.

Reading and child development

Reading as an integral part of the child's development has implications for his personal and social development as well as for his mental growth.

The child-development theory of reading has been presented in different ways by Burton (1956), Olson (1959), and Russell (1961). Essentially, this theory shows how various aspects of the child's development—his physical growth, his language development, his general mental development, and his social development—are related to and contribute to his development in reading. It in turn induces growth in the other areas. These relationships may be expressed schematically as shown.

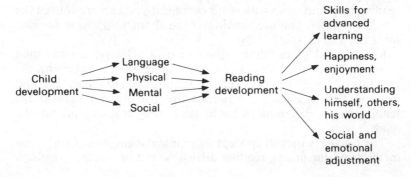

According to Olson, reading is part of a more or less predetermined pattern of growth which will emerge under favorable conditions. The child may be stimulated for a short time to exceed his natural rate of development, but special instruction, motivation, or medication will produce only a temporary spurt. The child quickly resumes his original growth pattern. At first glance, this point of view seems to discount the value of remedial work. However, if this work removes certain factors at home, or at school that have been interfering with the child's reading development and provides him with instruction and practice that were neglected in his earlier years, it may promote permanent growth that is in line with his true developmental trend. Sometimes this growth takes place without special instruction. Olson tells the story of two brothers, both of whom were late in starting to grow. Once started, however, they made pronounced gains in reading, one with and one without remedial instruction.

The implication of this example is that a child will grow in reading ability at his own natural pace regardless of any attempted training which is premature. A part of the child-development theory, this principle of pacing is operating when any procedure permits the child to progress at his own inherent rate of growth.

Such a method encourages wide individual differences within the classroom where they already exist to a complex degree. In one eighth grade, some pupils had a third-grade reading ability; others had comprehension at the college level. A teacher in such a situation has no easy complete solution; he must do the best he can through highly individualized instruction.

Adolescent development depends upon all that has gone before. Past hopes and fears, as well as future aspirations and apprehensions, help to determine how the adolescent responds to the positive and negative influences of the present. The poor reader as he gets older is increasingly handicapped by his inability to read because his lack inhibits his achievement in every subject and dims his chances of going to college. He realizes that many desirable occupations will be closed to him. In peer groups of the more able readers, he feels 'different.' Such alienation may affect his reading performance. Peer status is related to reading achievement (Porterfield and Schlicting, 1961).

Certain patterns of physical growth—especially accelerated or delayed growth—present special problems and more or less influence reading progress. Boys whose growth spurt comes early have an advantage: they can achieve a success in sports that helps to build up their self-esteem while boys maturing slowly miss this chance for prestige. With girls, accelerated growth is a social disadvantage. As one tall girl said, 'If you're taller than boys, it's bad enough, but if you're brighter, it's fatal.'

Other physiological changes and disabilities of the adolescent may give rise to feelings of self-consciousness or inferiority that frequently color attitudes toward achievement including reading. A youngster who is in the grip of emotional conflicts over any of the major adolescent problems may find himself unable to concentrate on books.

As Ephron (1953) has pointed out, fears enter into many reading problems—fears about schoolwork, fears of real or imagined inadequacies, anxiety about mistakes, fears of failure in hetero-sexual adjustment, fears connected with family relationships. The fearful individual may daydream or withdraw and be unable to concentrate. Or, resenting authority, he may resort to vandalism. Such conduct may depress the student's reading achievement or aggravate reading difficulties. The implications for a program of reading may overwhelm a teacher because he is the axis around which reading proficiency develops. But if the teacher is knowledgeable about the importance of reading and continually evaluates his views and techniques of reading, there need be no dismay.

A structured view of the teaching of reading

The first step in mastering a subject is to get a sense of its structure and perceive its relationships. Students have found it helpful to view the teaching of reading under four main headings: product, process, prerequisites, and procedures. Each of these becomes clear when described with adequate detail.

Product or goals

This heading includes the main reading competencies, or skills, and goals that students will achieve. Among these are:

A vocabulary of basic words that recur frequently, plus a constantly increasing repertory of words that a reader recognizes on sight. The lists grow in number and meanings through wide reading.

Word recognition skills—ability to pronounce and recognize the meaning of unfamiliar words. To do this the student may use a combination of (1) configuration clues—recognizing the word by its overall shape; (2) context clues—getting the meaning from the sentences in which the word is used; (3) phonics; (4) analysis of word structure; and (5) use of the dictionary.

Comprehension on three levels. The first level requires the student to derive literal meaning from sequential words and their grammatical relations to each other (the syntax) in sentences, paragraphs, and chapters. This ability to weave words together, giving each its proper weight and understanding the accumulation of significance in successive sentence structures, is what Edgar Dale called 'reading the lines.' Not merely parroting the author's words, the student must translate the author's thoughts into his own words. To achieve full comprehension, the reader must know not only the semantic and structural meaning but he must have had some experience related to the author's ideas.

One possible way of exacting the literal meaning of a paragraph is for the reader to hold in mind the content of the first sentence, while recognizing and relating the subsequent words and noting their sequence and relative importance. The reader then notes repeated key words, main ideas and supporting details. He follows the author's argument. In reading a short story he is alert to discover the theme, the climax, and the resolution. In reading an article, he watches for the author's generalizations and conclusions. In fiction, he visualizes the characters, the setting, and the events. All of these efforts help the reader to understand fully what the author is saying. Yet it is possible 'to read the lines' without getting their full value.

To go beyond the literal meaning of a passage—to 'read between the lines'—the mature reader recognizes the author's intent and purpose, interprets his thought, passes judgment on his statements, searches for and interprets clues to character and plot, distinguishes between fact and opinion, and separates his own ideas from those of the author. In interpreting, he appraises the sources of the author, taking into account their competence and authority. This level of comprehension also requires the reader to recognize and interpret many literary devices such as metaphors and irony.

The third level, 'reading beyond the lines,' involves deriving implications, speculating about consequences, and drawing generalizations not stated by the author. On this level the reader may arrange the author's ideas into new patterns, extending their scope or fusing them with ideas that he himself has gained from reading or from experience. By means of both analysis and synthesis, the reader gains a new insight or a higher level of understanding that enables him to reflect on the significance of the ideas. In this rewarding type of reading, he brings initiative, originality, and thought to bear on the literal meaning of the printed page.

Reacting and acting. This is still another dimension of reading. As one reads, he has feelings, mild or intense. He likes or dislikes the point of view of the selection, agrees or disagrees with it, finds it disturbing or reassuring. These emotional reactions interweave themselves with the cognitive process of reading so that not only does the reader get ideas—ideas get him.

Style also arouses some emotional response in the reader. A piece of writing may evoke pleasure in the author's felicity of expression, appreciation of the mode of characterization, and it may delight or exalt. Or it may bore, annoy, alarm, anger or provoke.

If students read creatively, they involve themselves in the book or article, empathizing with a fictional or a real character as he fights and suffers. Some degree of emotional involvement in the book or article is basic to creative reading (Hester, 1959).

Great books or poems may be a source of self-revelation—they stimulate the reader to explore himself and his world, for 'different minds have found different things in them' (Richards, 1942, pp. 11–12). Such works have met the emotional needs of many kinds of people. Students read them for the sake of the things their words—if understood—can do for them. But understanding these works, of course, is not making them mean something the reader knows and approves of already, nor is it detecting their limitations. It is using them to stretch his mind as they have stretched the minds of so many different readers through the centuries (Richards, 1942, p. 15). The reader not only reacts but moves to new acts—to learn about the nature of the world and of man; to enjoy leisure hours; to communicate ideas to others through speaking or writing; to secure information for solving problems; or to discover how to make and do things. Students may use reading as a springboard for creative activities—writing, dramatization, drawing, or painting.

The end result of reading is personal and social progression because it produces desirable changes in points of view, attitudes, feelings, and behavior. 'Growth *through* reading is the ultimate goal of instruction, while growth *in* reading is the means to that end' (Artley, 1959). [. . .]

Oral reading. Prior to 1900 reading aloud was widely practiced in American schools. After 1900, it began to decrease in popularity (Spache, 1963, ch. 11).

In an excellent summary of the arguments for and against oral reading, Spache (1963, ch. 11) recognized the value of oral reading in diagnosing difficulties in word recognition skills, in reinforcing the visual image of the word in beginning reading, and in appreciating literature. Oral reading, through intonation, stress, and rhythm, gives additional clues to meaning that silent reading does not give. While admitting possible interference with silent reading from overemphasis on oral reading, Spache does not consider this serious if 'oral reading is balanced by an adequate amount of practice in silent reading from the very beginning of instruction' (1963, p. 194). Edfeldt's study (1960), using electromyographic methods of determining the extent of inner vocalization during silent reading, demonstrated that some degree of inner or silent speech is present in all silent reading, but is not necessarily detrimental to good silent reading, though it may result in a slower rate of silent reading among some individuals.

As a tool of communication, oral reading is being used increasingly by parents and by teachers and other professional people, especially those engaged in radio and television programs. Reading aloud is a possible method for use in adult education for democracy. The conclusion is that oral reading has a definite place in the reading program.

If oral reading is to take its rightful place in the total reading program, it must be properly taught. Its purpose in different situations should be recognized. The reader prepares carefully for his performance. The audience should be attentive and constructive in their comments. The harmful effects of round-the-room reading, formerly so common, in slowing down and boring the good reader and embarrassing the poor reader should deter any teacher from using this method. [. . .]

Since oral reading, with its attention to pronunciation and voice quality, may inhibit concentration on the meaning of what is being read (Lloyd, 1965), students should read the text silently before reading aloud, to grasp the ideas and feelings intended by the author. Understanding underlies the ability to convey meaning to the audience. To do this the oral reader must not only have mastered word recognition and comprehension skills but also the skills of oral expression—phrasing, stress, intonation, inflection, pitch, and rate. If material which the pupil can read with understanding is selected, oral errors will usually not be a problem. Dialogs, stories with a great deal of conversation, and simple plays are excellent materials for oral reading. If a pupil is intent on getting the meaning, to call attention to errors is annoying and unnecessary. It may lead him to become so preoccupied with articulation that he loses sight of the meaning altogether. His attention is divided between the mechanical process of articulation of the words and the thought process of getting the meaning. When a pupil pronounces each word separately with pauses between words, a break in thought is indicated; he loses the thought of the sentence. [. . .]

Process

The psychological process of reading includes all that goes on between intake—the stimulus of the printed word—and output—

the reader's response in thought, spoken or written words, or action. Response may take the form of a mental image, a principle, or a new way of looking at something. It may be an answer to a question, a written summary, a drawing of a character or scene, or a motor response to a direction.

Visual reception. The reader must first get a clear visual impression on the retina of the eye, or rather a series of visual impressions as his eyes move across the line of print. The nervous impulses thus aroused are transmitted to the visual centers of the brain where they are 'decoded' and their meaning is recognized. The words have now been perceived.

Perception. This is a cognitive process by which visual impressions become meaningful in the light of the individual's past experience and present needs. It involves understanding, comprehending, organizing. 'To perceive is to know' (Garner, 1966). Perception of the meaning of printed words usually involves more than visual perception and discrimination, auditory perception and discrimination, and sound-symbol associations. The quality of one's perception is affected by the nature of the situation or set that exists at the moment, by the degree to which it occupies one's attention, by the ideas one has already acquired concerning it, and by one's needs, expectations, and personality (Russell, 1965). Perception is an active process. It is part of a larger pattern. It is also the first step in a sequence that leads to further abstraction and then to generalization.

Individuals differ in their perceptual styles (Robinson, 1964). Usually the more able learners and the better readers see words as wholes. Generally the poor readers perceive word fragments and tend to be preoccupied with unimportant details. Able readers recognize familiar syllables and words almost as quickly as individual letters and take in phrases and short sentences as readily as single words. According to Hollingsworth's (1928) theory of reading as clue reduction, efficient readers require fewer clues than do poor readers in order to recognize words or phrases.

Conceptualization. When perceptions are grouped into larger patterns that embrace classes or categories, conceptualization occurs. It contributes further to abstract thinking and generalization.

There is a reciprocal relation between perception and conceptualization. Concepts screen or filter impressions as they come into the mind. Thus the individual avoids dealing with a bewildering diversity of separate impressions. Perceptions are synthesized into concepts; concepts aid in the interpretation and organization of perceptions. This is possible because each perception leaves a trace or impression on the nervous system.

Conceptual ability and reading proficiency have a positive relation. Children of normal intelligence who fail in reading in the upper primary grades are often deficient in the ability to form concepts.

Research has clarified the first stages of the reading process— sensory impression, perception, conceptualization. What happens next is still a psychological no-man's-land.

Higher levels of association. It has been hypothesized that at the higher levels of association there are patterns, schema, or circuits—interrelated memory subsystems. As these are activated simultaneously, they become larger and better organized. Factual content will not be retained long unless it becomes integrated. As the interconnections of these memory systems are improved, the individual gains increased ability to interpret what he reads. For the word-by-word reader, each association occurs separately, rather than in a larger memory pattern. It is easy to see why the 'whole perceiver' has an advantage over the 'part perceiver.' Memory is not simply storing away impressions; it is retrieving what is relevant when it is needed. Thus the way a thing is learned helps to determine how it is applied.

Dr William S. Gray (1960, p. 9) describes the following steps in a mature reader's associative processes:

1 He recognizes the author's meaning.
2 He uses his previous knowledge to evaluate the soundness of the author's ideas, to reach valid conclusions, and to gain new insights and interests.
3 His feelings also enter into his decisions to accept or reject the ideas read.
4 He uses these enlarged patterns of associations in his further reading and thinking.

Questions as to the actual process in the mind of a person are waiting for research. How does the individual feel when he is confronted with a printed page? What incentive does he have for getting meaning from it? Why does he put forth much—or little—effort? How do his eyes and his mind actually work as he attempts to get the meaning? What use will he make of the knowledge he has assimilated? Questions like this can only be explored by study of the reading process.

Prerequisites

Certain prerequisites underlie both product and process. That is, the individual must possess distinct physical, mental, linguistic, personality, and environmental advantages if he is to realize his reading potential. Their presence or absence makes it either easy or difficult for a teacher to be successful in teaching reading.

Visual factors. In order to distinguish letter and word forms, the child must receive a clear visual impression of them. In clear vision, both eyes act together and their binocular acuity at reading distance is basic to reading efficiency. Most primary children are farsighted because visual acuity tends to develop gradually over several years. A kindergarten child generally cannot read print that is smaller than 24 point, i.e., ⅜ inch in height.

Visual clarity increases further as the eyes acquire ability to adjust to distance accommodation and convergence (Robinson and Huelsman, 1953). To receive a clear image of the printed word, the eyes must focus on or converge on it. Children under four years of age usually lack this ability. However, most children have acquired it by the age of five. Eames (1961) found no five-year-old child, in his study of 899 children, who scored below the minimum of binocular accommodation which he considered essential for reading. Girls were superior to boys; suburban children, to urban. Gifted children tend to be visually as well as intellectually a little more mature than average, with ordinary children reaching the peak of their power of convergence at fourteen or fifteen. [. . .]

The reader must not only focus on words and distinguish them from the background, but he must fuse the separate images from each eye into a single clear image. Otherwise the words blur. This neuromuscular skill basic to word discrimination is primary to reading (Spache and Tillman, 1962).

Among eye defects associated with poor reading is muscular imbalance which prevents the eyeballs from rotating into the best position for a clear unblurred image. When the eyeballs turn too far inward (*esophoria*) or too far outward (*exophoria*), it is a strain to fuse the images from the two eyes. Orthoptic training—special exercises for the eye muscles—has been helpful in correcting this difficulty.

Farsightedness, or *hyperopia*, is more likely to be associated with reading retardation than nearsightedness, or *myopia*. However, the percentage of the nearsighted increases among children past the age of nine. After studying a group of high school seniors, Jenkins (1953) reported that the best students, on the average, had better near vision, and the poorer students had better far vision. Farsightedness occurred in 12 per cent of Eames's unselected children and in 43 per cent of the reading failures (Eames, 1951). Astigmatism can be another source of reading difficulty.

A less well-known eye defect, *aniseikonia*, which brings about ocular images unequal in size or shape and thus inhibits fusion, may cause either ocular or general fatigue. By interfering with the peripheral view of the line of print, it may also decrease the span of recognition.

Another defect, *aniseidominance*, is seeing an image as brighter and nearer with one eye than the other. The effects are similar to those of aniseikonia.

From a study based on 3,500 cases, aged five to seventeen, including reading failures and unselected school children, Eames (1951) summarized the various kinds of inefficient vision. One class of eye defects includes the serious cases resulting from neurological disorders and disease which only ophthalmologists can help. Another kind, closely related to the first, is defects which may be corrected by eye exercises, glasses, or surgery. Both kinds of eye defects may diminish sharpness and clarity of vision. Finally, even the kind not reducing the normal range may give children trouble in learning to read and may cause older students fatigue and discomfort. Although studies such as Eames's establish types of subnormal vision, evidence about the relation between reading performance and eye defects is inconsistent. There are several explanations:

First of all, individuals vary in their sensitivity; a small defect that does not bother one person may block another in his efforts to read (Eames, 1951, p. 4).

Second, some individuals are more highly motivated than others; they learn to read despite visual defects. Or a student may rise above the limitations of his visual handicap during a test but not for longer periods of study.

Again, certain visual factors that are closely related to reading may not yet have been completely defined; existing instruments may not measure them.

Most studies have considered only separate factors rather than patterns or syndromes of visual defects.

A certain amount of eye uncoordination may be 'the effect rather than the cause of poor reading' (Vernon, 1957, p. 121).

Since any visual defect may cause discomfort and disinclination to read, any study of reading problems should include a visual screening test.

Although visual difficulties may hinder a student in learning to read, correction of them does not in itself ensure success. There still remains the task of teaching him to read.

Hearing and speech. Children who lack auditory acuity cannot imitate the speech they hear, and speech is the avenue to reading. Some children whose auditory acuity is intact still cannot perceive as words the sounds they hear. Still others lack auditory discrimination—ability to distinguish various language sounds. This capacity is a vital prerequisite to the development of oral communication and also to success in reading (Wepman, 1955). Boys are more often handicapped than girls in practicing phonic analysis that is based on auditory discrimination.

Physiological prerequisites. Malnutrition may lower a child's energy level. Endocrine disturbances may make a child either lethargic or overactive, interfering indirectly but seriously with his learning to read. Stresses and strains that alter the chemistry of the body and affect the synaptic transmission may lower the speed with which an individual reads familiar words or recognizes unfamiliar words (Smith and Carrigan, 1959). [. . .]

Intact neurological organization and functioning. This is another prerequisite to learning to read. Vernon concluded her summary of research with the statement that 'the relationship to reading disability of incomplete lateralization and cerebral dominance is extremely obscure' (Vernon, 1957, p. 155). Similarly, more recent neurological and psychological research recognizes (1) the difficulty of diagnosing neurological disorganization, (2) the importance of early diagnosis, and (3) the importance of focusing on what the child can do successfully rather than on his disturbances.

Mental prerequisites. Though it is known that a certain level of intelligence is necessary for success in learning to read, this level has not been precisely determined. It has often been stated that a mental age of six and one-half is requisite for beginning reading instruction, but many studies are challenging this figure. Results indicate that children with lower mental ages can be taught to read by means of special instruction and special materials—e.g., the Initial Teaching Alphabet (i.t.a.), the electric typewriter (with an adult responding as the child strikes the keys), and the Denver kindergarten program. The child's language experience, auditory and visual perception, and overall development are more significant for this purpose than his mental age. In fact, even a high mental age does not ensure success in beginning reading when the child lacks readiness in other important respects.

Evidence is accumulating that it is not a waste of time to teach reading to adolescents with individual intelligence quotients as low as 50. One boy with an IQ of 52 learned to read signs, directions, and other simple, practical material that he needed to master for a job. If a mentally retarded child is reading about as well as his intelligence permits, he should not be considered a remedial reading case.

There is need to experiment with various teaching methods designed expressly for students possessing various degrees of mental ability. Since there is always the possibility that the test results do not represent the individual's true potential mental ability, it seems wise, as P. E. Vernon suggested in a comment made to the author, to give each student the best possible instruction under favorable conditions and see how he responds to it.

Reading and intelligence, as measured, have so much in common that one would expect a high correlation between reading tests and tests of general mental ability. Actually, correlations of 0.50 to 0.80 are often reported between scores on group intelligence tests and scores on reading tests. The relation between word knowledge and general intelligence is especially close. Since group intelligence tests demand so much reading ability, it is easy to see how they may mismeasure the mental ability of poor readers and to understand why the group intelligence test should not be used to predict growth in reading.

Group intelligence tests that yield both a verbal and a quantitative score give a little more information than do those that yield a single score. The correlation between reading scores and quantitative-intelligence-test scores is much lower than that between reading scores and verbal-intelligence-test scores. With elementary school children tested by the California Test of Mental Maturity, the correlations were as follows (Strang, 1943):

Language factors with Thorndike–McCall Reading Test	0.824
Nonlanguage factors with Thorndike–McCall Reading Test	0.557

With ninth-grade pupils, the correlations of the California Test of Mental Maturity were as follows (Tinker, 1963):

Language factors with Iowa Silent Reading Tests	0.685 ± 041
Nonlanguage factors with Iowa Silent Reading Tests	0.356 ± 068
Language factors with Traxler Silent Reading Test	0.753 ± 034
Nonlanguage factors with Traxler Silent Reading Test	0.357 ± 068

With the same age group, using different intelligence tests, Hage and Stroud (1959) likewise found that reading comprehension and reading rate correlated more highly with verbal than with nonverbal intelligence scores. Verbal-intelligence-test scores are affected more than nonverbal scores by reading proficiency.

With college students there were equally large discrepancies between the correlations of their quantitative comprehension scores on the Iowa Silent Reading Tests and their linguistic and quantitative scores on both the American Council on Education Psychological Examination for College Freshmen and the California Test of Mental Maturity (McCaul, 1949; Wheeler and Wheeler, 1949). As might be expected, group-intelligence-test scores correlate more highly with tests of reading comprehension than with tests of reading rate.

Even the individual Stanford–Binet test, which has been widely used to estimate reading potential, tends to underestimate the intelligence of poor readers, because it includes so many items that require knowledge and use of words (Bond and Fay, 1950).

The Wechsler individual intelligence tests have the advantage of yielding both a verbal and a nonverbal score. The assumption has been made that when the nonverbal IQ is significantly higher than the verbal, the individual's reading can be improved up to the level of the nonverbal score. This is often, but not necessarily, true; children usually have higher nonverbal than verbal IQs on the Wechsler Intelligence Scale for Children (WISC). Moreover, several students who make the same intelligence-test score may differ, because of many internal and external factors, in their ability to acquire various reading skills.

Retarded readers have shown distinctive scoring patterns on the WISC. They tend to score low on the subtests of Information and Arithmetic and relatively low on Digit Span and Coding. On Picture Arrangement, Block Design, Picture Completion and Object Assembly, they often score relatively high. However, different groups of retarded readers, such as bilinguals and unilinguals, have shown different profiles, bilinguals being low on Information, Comprehension, Vocabulary, and Digit-span subtests, and relatively high in Picture Completion, Picture Arrangement, Block Design, Object Assembly, and Coding. They were significantly higher than the unilinguals in the subtests of Coding and Arithmetic, and significantly lower on Information and Vocabulary (Ekwall, 1966, pp. 147–52). Profiles also vary with the reading tests used and still more in individual cases. Bearing in mind these characteristic patterns, teachers can study individual profiles to observe deviations that may have special significance. These profiles indicate patterns of strength and weakness in the individual's mental functioning. Each high or low point represents some mental process involved in reading or basic to reading ability that may possibly be improved by practice and instruction.

Linguistic prerequisites. Linguists regard listening and speaking as prerequisites to reading. One must associate the letters with the sounds of the spoken words for which they are the visual symbols. The stories that children dictate to be written down by the teacher present only one unknown—the printed form; the sounds of their own words are already familiar to them. 'Word sense' and ability to recognize words in isolation as well as words in context are linguistic prerequisites to reading.

Linguists also emphasize, as a part of reading for meaning, an understanding of sentence structure, the source of syntax of English sentences. Meanings, they maintain, come not only from semantics of class words such as nouns, verbs, adjectives, and adverbs but also from structural signals such as word order and position. These items add another layer of meaning to a sequence of words, which becomes an integral part of the meaning. For example, the sentence. 'The man killed the dog,' has one meaning; but if the two nouns exchange positions so that the sentence reads 'The dog killed the man,' obviously the meaning is strikingly different even though no words have been added or omitted. It is operations like these which the linguists say are pertinent to reading. Meaning comes from constructions within constructions within a sentence rather than from strings of words. To unlock the full meaning of a sentence or passage, the child must have the vocabulary, comprehend the syntax, and possess the necessary experiences referred to in the content.

Personality and emotional prerequisites. Research based on paper-and-pencil personality tests has repeatedly failed to find a significant relationship between personality and reading achievement. Projective techniques, however, have uncovered some common personality patterns among severely retarded readers. The emotional difficulties associated with reading have been studied more extensively than the emotional strengths.

Value system, motivation, and self-concept. These three are inter-related. They may be the intangibles that account for the 24 per cent of the variance not accounted for by all the forty to fifty factors measured in Holmes and Singer's substrata studies (1964). The desire to read is the resultant of present needs, past experiences, and future hopes.

For the little child, desire for the approval of his teacher and his parents is a strong motivation. However, intrinsic interest in the content is a more stable long-run motivation. For the retarded teen-ager, a specific need sometimes awakens a desire to read better. He may need to pass the Army tests or to fill out an application blank for a part-time job or a driver's license.

In the words of one adolescent, needs like these have spurred previously indifferent teen-agers 'to get down to work on this reading business.' When asked why they wanted to read better, several slow learners gave these reasons: 'so no one will laugh at me,' 'so as not to be stupid,' 'so no one will cheat me.'

The most persistent and pervasive influence is the individual's self-concept and self-ideal. The self-concept may be predictive of reading improvement. It also affects, and is affected by, reading improvement. On the primary level, children's self-concepts were, in general, more predictive of reading achievement than their scores on the Detroit Beginning First-Grade Intelligence Test given near the end of the kindergarten year (Wattenberg and Clifford, 1964). On all age levels, the self-concept seems to be an important factor in achievement. Brookover (1964) found that seventh-grade pupils who had a positive attitude toward their ability in a given subject were high achievers in that subject. Their self-concepts were more accurate predictors than other established general estimates of ability. A student's self-concept also affects his motivation.

Many children and adolescents seem indifferent to school learning. Of these pupils teachers often say, 'They're just not interested in reading.' They do not read voluntarily; they show no enthusiasm for reading in class. Yet one of the teacher's most important tasks is to develop in his pupils a love of reading. What motivates students to read wisely and well?

To understand any instance of motivated behavior, teachers need to know what is stimulating the individual, what responses he has made to such patterns of stimulation, what consequences those responses had, and what deprivations he has experienced (Hall, 1961). A certain degree of anxiety is basic to learning; relieving anxiety becomes a goal. The individual is also motivated to maintain an equilibrium in body functioning; he tries to correct any imbalances, whether physiological or psychological.

Many psychologists have believed that basic motivations are formed during childhood and that it is therefore difficult to change the motivations of adults. However, some evidence is accumulating to show that adult motivations can be changed by education.

Motivations may be arranged in a hierarchy, starting with the most temporary, extrinsic, and superficial, and proceeding to the most lasting, pervasive, and deep-seated:

Stars, teacher's marks, and other extrinsic rewards.

Praise and blame. The effect of these incentives varies widely. Praise may stimulate one student but lessen the effort of another. Praise given by a loved and respected person will stimulate, whereas praise given by a person disliked will often have the opposite effect. Lavish, indiscriminate praise soon loses its value. Some individuals respond better to blame than to praise. In other cases, ignoring the person may be as effective as either praising or blaming. Neither praise nor blame is of much significance unless the student understands *why* his performance was good or poor.

Success. Usually success leads to further success just as failure breeds more failure. The child's desire for mastery and achievement is thwarted when he fails in such a socially important activity as reading. After successful reading experiences, the individual tends to raise his level of aspiration. However, the goal must be attainable, and the individual must see that he is making progress toward it. He also needs to understand the process by which he arrived at his correct responses and the reasons for his mistakes. If the teacher goes over a test paper with the students, either individually or in class, they will see why they made certain mistakes and learn how to avoid them in the future.

Increased competence. The satisfaction that comes from increased competence is motivating. For beginners, just knowing how to read is motivating. In other words, skill in reading is in itself a motivating force and a prerequisite to interest in reading. Teachers should never discount the motivating value of knowledge and skill. Since reading depends on skill in using abstract symbols, the child who has difficulty in dealing with abstractions becomes discouraged and may soon develop a general indifference toward reading.

Curiosity. This is a prime motivation for reading at any age. Unless suppressed, curiosity persists throughout life and frequently turns a person to reading, which offers wide opportunities to satisfy his mood of inquiry. In a study where intelligence was kept constant, children who were rated by their teachers as having a high degree of curiosity tended to sense the meaning of sentences more accurately than did those whose curiosity was rated as low (Maw and Maw, 1962).

Self-realization. Perhaps the most basic motivation of all is the deep-seated desire to develop one's potentialities, to do what one is best fitted to do, to function as well as one is capable of functioning. Reading can lead to self-realization or self-actualization. While the individual may be motivated by his observed disparity between his self-ideal and his present achievement, too wide a disparity may cause several types of maladjustment. This is especially true of an individual who feels he must achieve goals that have been imposed upon him by his parents or his peer group. Students may be motivated to improve their reading by such long-range goals as admission to an Ivy League college or preparation for a certain vocation. Their more immediate and specific goals include getting an 'A' on the next spelling test or obtaining information for a group report.

Faith may be a motivation in some remedial cases—faith in a new method, faith in a machine, faith in a new approach to their reading problem. Just being given a special individual attention sometimes motivates a student to make a marked improvement.

Environmental prerequisites. Many environmental conditions are conducive to success in reading. Of primary importance are the preschool prereading experiences that give children a foundation for reading instruction. All language learning stems from a combination of firsthand experiences and the learned or vicarious experiences that are acquired through reading. Parent–child relationships and parental attitudes toward reading have a strong influence on the child's self-concept and his attitudes toward reading. Time to read and access to suitable reading materials are important in building reading interest.

On the older age level, Wylie (1963) found that junior high school students from lower socioeconomic backgrounds tended to doubt their ability to do college work; they said they did not want to go to college, even if they had the ability. But she also found that these negative attitudes were not equally strong in all students at this socioeconomic level. From a more carefully controlled study, Lovell and Woolsey (1964) concluded that the factors responsible for failure in reading, or for very poor reading, operate in all social classes.

How persuasive is the undefined influence of the mass media of communication? To what degree do they elevate reading tastes? To what degree do they lower the standards of people who might otherwise read more mature material? The heavy content of violence in certain TV programs and some paperbacks may serve as a safety valve for some persons but stimulate unruly impulses in others. In her annual summaries of research in reading published in the *Reading Teacher* (1964, 1965), Helen Robinson has analyzed the content of current books, magazines, and newspapers; estimated the amount of time that persons of all ages spend in passively watching television, as compared with the time they spend in reading; and discussed other sociological substrata factors.

Procedures for teaching

Teaching procedures develop out of an understanding of (1) the product—what the learner can do when he has achieved the objectives; (2) the prerequisites he brings to the learning situation; and (3) the mental processes he employs. The teaching–learning process may be represented by the diagram.

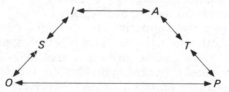

The individual. The focus is on *O*—the individual, whom psychologists often refer to as the *organism*. His physical condition, his mental abilities, his skills, his knowledge, and his need and desire to read—any or all of these items mentioned so far may make him more or less responsive to the teacher's instruction. His immediate intent or mind-set toward the reading situation governs his concentration and partly determines how much effort he puts forth. It influences his selection of books or parts of books and what he looks for. He sees relations, recognizes important ideas, and skips irrelevant details. On the other hand, his intent or mood may blind him to certain words, cause him to misinterpret some words, or give overpotency to others.

The situation. After the student, *O*, the next concern is the classroom or *stimulus situation, S*, over which the teacher has most control. The reading material is the focus, with both format and content important. Thick books with few open spaces for resting the eyes and mind often repel older children who lack proficiency in reading. Books densely packed with facts dissatisfy even the superior readers who must struggle in organizing the material to select key sentences and words from crowded pages.

The stimulus situation also includes the setting in which the reading is done—physical conditions, pupil–teacher relations, peer relations, parent–child relations. Although the relation between classroom illumination and reading efficiency remains somewhat ambiguous, there are wide individual differences in reading proficiency under varied conditions of lighting. All parts of the classroom or library where students continually read must provide good illumination.

To be conducive to reading, a classroom should be relatively quiet and orderly, the teacher planning activities to motivate reading and encourage and reward individual interests. Anxieties must not be intense, for learning takes place best in a secure, friendly, inspiring environment.

Students learn to adopt behavior that is rewarded or reinforced. The more quickly the reward follows the correct response, the better. Rats running in a maze showed a marked drop in errors when rewarded and a sharp increase in errors after the reward was withdrawn. Pigeons did not learn when the reward was deferred until the end result had been achieved; they learned rapidly when any move in the right direction brought them food. The Skinner reading machines, based on a highly specific analysis of learning, utilize this principle. Punishment may cause the child to continue an undesirable response which, if ignored, might have disappeared quickly. How different this theory is from the practice of too many teachers. Instead of reinforcing correct reading with a smile, a nod, a word of approval, they tend to say nothing until the student makes an error. Then they pounce upon him.

But the student who is absorbed in his reading needs no extrinsic reward; the fascinating content of the book is enough.

Instruction-application. Instruction and application (*I* and *A* in the diagram) should form a single continuous process. A teacher needs to show, not just tell, students how to recognize and remember new words; how to read a sentence, a paragraph, a chapter; how to interpret a poem or a story; how to read critically and creatively. He should go through the process with the students as many times as they need in order to learn it thoroughly. From then on the students should apply the procedure regularly in their independent reading. For example, in learning how to find and interpret clues to character, motives, and plot, first the teacher and his students find and discuss clues in several stories. Then the students read a story at home and report to the class their interpretation, supporting it with clues. Eventually the students will use this technique automatically whenever they read independently. It will greatly increase the enjoyment they gain from literature.

Reading material presented in different ways brings different results, even with the same individuals. A given method will not get the same results a second time if any part of the situation is different.

Trace or memory. The fifth symbol of the teaching-learning diagram is *T*, referring to the *trace* or impressions of previous experiences left on the nervous system. It is on this imprint of previous learning that proficiency in reading depends. If associations between words and their meanings are strengthened by success and satisfactions, additional knowledge and skills are more readily retained. The insecure or discouraged student has a special need to see results—a growing pile of cards containing words that he can recognize at sight, a graph showing an upcurve in speed or comprehension, a recently written or tape-recorded summary that is clearly superior to one he made last month.

Students differ widely in ability to retain what they have read. In one experiment (Dietz and Jones, 1931) pupils in grades 7 to 9 were given three factual passages to be read at their own rates. They were tested on comprehension and memory immediately after the reading; the test was repeated one day, fourteen days, thirty days, and one hundred days later. Factors which influence memory are three:

Familiar material is more easily remembered than new or strange material. One's memory of the ideas he gains in reading is more permanent if the words are anchored in his experience. Everyone has wells of meaning into which he dips when he is confronted with an unfamiliar word.

Second, the length of time intervening influences trace. The rate of forgetting is rapid at first, then slows. There is a positive correlation between an individual's immediate memory and his delayed memory.

The third is meaningfulness of the material. The initial forgetting for factual material is less abrupt than for nonsense syllables. With meaningful material, the point of complete forgetting is not approximated even after 100 days.

The child should use his information from reading at once because use reinforces retention. In general, retention is best when the student, engaging his mind actively, has sufficient time to register an impression, to associate new ideas with past experience and then to enjoy the knowledge.

Perception of the reading situation. P refers to the reader's *perception* of the reading situation—whether he perceives reading negatively as drudgery and a source of anxiety or hopefully as a source of satisfaction. The trace that is left, with its accompanying feeling tone, affects the individual's approach to the next reading. Once, after a class had enjoyed reading and discussing a ghost story, they looked forward eagerly to the next period. They asked, 'Are we going to have another story'; But instead, they were given an article on cultured pearls. They greeted the teacher the next day without enthusiasm, and asked, 'Are we going to have another *lesson*?'

It makes a great difference in the students' expectancy, readiness, and response whether they approach a reading task with boredom, dislike, anxiety, fear, and feelings of inferiority, or with enthusiasm, confidence, and interest. The student may perceive the new situation as pleasurable or threatening, as 'something in which he will succeed' or as 'something in which he will fail' (Strang, 1948, p. 68).

Basic to all teaching procedures is the attempt to make sure that each pupil has a reason for wanting to read and an expectation that pleasure and satisfaction will result. If these conditions prevail, the child will develop his own way of learning. He will learn to identify methods that bring good results and will be able to apply them appropriately. It is the role of the teacher to share his knowledge of effective learning methods with his pupils and to create, so far as possible, conditions conducive to learning.

Relation of reading to other language skills

Reading occupies a special place in the complex of language skills whose other components are listening, speaking, writing, and spelling. Reading seems to weave in and out among them all; it presupposes many abilities from the outset and some developed along the way, and at the same time it paves the way for still higher linguistic achievement.

Speech is primary. The child listens to his mother's words and comprehends some of them before he begins to speak, an event that usually occurs during the second year of life. The language learned in infancy has deep emotional roots. In bilingual children the teachers disrupt these roots when they forbid them to speak their native language at school. By giving children opportunities to think about what they hear and to verbalize their thoughts, teachers aid children to develop language skills basic for reading.

Listening

Both listening and reading are means of receiving communication. Both require the interpretation of symbols, heard in one instance, seen in the other. Both require skills such as interpreting the main idea, perceiving relationships, recognizing sequence of ideas, sensing the mood and intent of the speaker or writer, and organizing and evaluating his ideas. A person who can do all this while listening should be able to read content of similar difficulty.

According to Duker (1966), who pointedly summarizes the relationship between reading and listening abilities, visual presentation, as in reading, has been found to be more effective than auditory presentation with persons of higher intelligence and reading ability. The difficulty of the material also affects the relation between listening comprehension and reading comprehension. Easy material may be comprehended equally well through listening or reading. If the material is difficult, students of high scholastic aptitude and reading ability comprehend more efficiently by reading than by listening. Auditory methods seem to be preferred when content is personal or intimate; reading, when 'close discrimination and critical judgment are called for' (Berg, 1955, p. 55). However, King (1959) found no significant differences between boys' and girls' responses to auditory as compared with visual presentation of test material.

Fortunately the teacher need not choose, but can derive the most efficient comprehension through a combination of visual and auditory devices. One will reinforce the other.

Individuals vary greatly in their relative ability to comprehend by listening and by reading. Those who have auditory defects may find reading a better avenue of learning; visual defects may increase the relative listening efficiency of others. Practice also makes a difference: the person who has had more practice in listening than in reading is likely to be more proficient in auditory than in visual skills, and vice versa. Unless the individual is known to have had much more practice in one skill than the other, a higher competence in listening than in reading indicates an undeveloped reading potential.

It is difficult to say which of these communication arts is the more important. On the average, elementary school children are expected to listen two and one-half hours daily, or 57.5 per cent of their class time. Adults spend, on the average, much more time—42 per cent according to one estimate—in listening than in any other communication activity. Since television has increased the percentage of children's listening time, listening instruction in the curriculum is receiving more attention. By the time children have completed the sixth or seventh grade, their reading comprehension tends to surpass their listening comprehension. Of course, they do receive continuous instruction in reading but scarcely any in listening.

To date, the results of research on the effectiveness of brief periods of systematic instruction in listening have been inconclusive. Two investigators reported improved listening comprehension as a result of improved reading comprehension, while two others found no significant transfer. However, direct instruction in listening has been shown to be superior to indirect or incidental instruction.

There is an art in listening; a science, too. It is a language skill deserving more research. The attitude is important—the listener must expect to hear something of interest or value. He can get ready to listen by thinking about the topic: What does he already know about it? What does he want to know? How does it relate to his life?

He must listen for the main ideas and the facts or illustrations to support them. He has to catch ideas on the fly, weighing emotionally charged words and ignoring distractions.

After catching a significant point of a speech, the listener can annex it to his other ideas if the speaker's delivery is slow enough. And as soon as possible, the listener should review what he has learned from the speech by talking about it. Like reading with its method of Survey Q3R, listening has a formula: TQLR—Tune in, Question, Listen, Review.

Can one read or study efficiently while listening to the radio? This is a much disputed question between parents and children. Students differ in their opinions about the effect of having the radio turned on while they are studying. Some claim that it increases their reading efficiency; others admit that it distracts their attention. Though one experiment gave evidence that high school pupils studied more effectively when a musical radio program was turned on in study hall, this effect may have been obtained under the stimulus of a novel situation; it might not hold day in and day out. Fendrick (1937) concluded, from a more carefully controlled experiment with two groups of sixty college students, that music played while students were studying probably decreased their efficiency and that it affected the more intelligent students more seriously than it did those of lower mental ability. Loss in efficiency is greatest when noise begins. After a while students tend to ignore it. At that stage silence becomes a distraction. Thus the radio, because of its variety, is likely to be more distracting than a continued noise such as monotonous hammering.

There are, of course, individual differences in the degree to which listening to the radio interferes with comprehension in reading. Some persons can concentrate in spite of distracting music, conversation, and noise. Some may even work more intensely because of the distraction. However, in the long run, resisting distraction is nerve-racking; it tends to leave a person tired and irritable.

Television presents additional problems (Parker, 1963). Some high school pupils insisted that they could study while watching television. When asked how they did it, they said they did their studying during the commercials! Such remarks indicate the need for more information about the effects on reading efficiency of listening to the radio and watching television. Incidentally, there would be value in knowing the relative effects on reading of such activities as seeing motion pictures, going on excursions, participating in discussions, and engaging in handiwork or creative artwork.

Speaking

Some people talk more than they listen; many talk more than they read. Studies have shown that people spend 75 per cent of their communicative effort in speaking and listening, as compared with 25 per cent in writing and reading (Carney, 1964). Pronouncing the words on a page aloud is the usual bridge from listening to reading for meaning. Some linguists say it is the only bridge. They define reading as the process by which printed words are translated into spoken words and then endowed with the meanings that are already associated with the spoken words.

Facility in oral expression is a prerequisite to success in beginning reading. For beginning readers the easiest words to learn are those that are in their speaking vocabulary, arranged in their own sentence patterns, and that have personal significance for them. As the child grows older, his reading vocabulary tends to exceed his speaking vocabulary—he understands more words as he reads than he uses in speaking.

In general, there is a reciprocal relation between speaking and reading. Not being aware of the structure of the English language blurs the relationship between words and phrases. Effective speech makes reading more accurate. Conversely, efficient reading enriches oral communication.

Oral reading depends on many of the same processes that are involved in effective speech. Children who make speech errors such as 'jest' for 'just,' or 'wha cha doin'' for 'what are you doing' tend to develop sound-letter associations that are difficult to correct. Many of the boners reported by teachers seem to arise from faulty perception and pronunciation of words (*Bigger and Better Boners*, 1952):

> Acumen is the white of an egg.
> In mathematics Persia gave us the dismal system.
> The clown in *As You Like It* was named Touchdown.

The relation of faulty oral expression and speech defects to silent-reading ability is less clear. Research on this relationship is inconclusive. The most favorable effects on silent-reading achievement have been obtained by a combined language arts program that included speech improvement lessons, instruction in attentive listening and observation, techniques of self-expression, practice in speech sound discrimination, and practice in speech production, choral speaking, and discussion (Jones, 1951).

There is usually a high incidence of functional speech problems among children referred for remedial reading. Many poor readers with defective articulation have problems of auditory discrimination. The sounds difficult to discriminate are often the sounds difficult to articulate. For these cases, speech therapy plus reading therapy given to pupils with functional speech defects has improved reading skills.

Writing

Receiving through reading the thought that an author wishes to convey and transmitting that thought to others by speaking or writing are the intake and output ends of the communication continuum. Many schools and colleges are giving more attention to measuring students' ability to take in ideas than to communicate them. Since the objective-type silent-reading tests so widely used afford little practice in reading to communicate, more valuable is the unstructured or creative-response type of test that calls for a written response (Strang, 1953).

Whatever improves a student's oral language helps him to improve his writing. Understanding of the structure of English sentences contributes to both his writing and his reading. Practice in interpreting the literature he reads gives him a feeling for style, which might be expected to influence his writing more than a formal study of grammar. However, Wyatt (1962) did not find a definite relationship of extensive reading to certain writing skills of selected sixth-grade pupils.

Proficiency in reading, writing, and speaking develops all skills concomitantly; one language art reinforces the other. Because speech starts sooner than the other two, writing as well as reading may be more affected by speech difficulties than vice versa. The teaching of effective writing should not be isolated in English classes but should become a part of science, social studies, art, and music programs.

Spelling

Spelling is a part of the constellation of language arts. It is related to word recognition, grasp of meaning, vocabulary, and comprehension (Horn and Ashbaugh, 1950). Spelling is concerned with significant units of speech sound (*phonemes*) as each is represented by a letter or a combination of letters (*graphemes*), and as they are put together in words or parts of words (*morphemes*). In spelling, the student recalls the symbols for various sounds (*encoding*). He thinks of individual letters and may get a visual image of the whole word. In reading, the process is reversed. The child associates the printed symbol with the sound of the word and its associated meaning (*decoding*). The good reader does not pay attention to each individual letter (Freyberg, 1964; Hanna and Hanna, 1965).

Students tend to be either good or poor in both reading and spelling. Correlations are almost as high as those between reading and group-intelligence-test scores (Morrison and Perry, 1951; Waldman and Triggs, 1958). Improvement in reading often leads to better spelling. It does not follow, however, that deficiencies in reading or vocabulary necessarily cause poor spelling.

Improvement in spelling is often a by-product of wide reading and varied learning activities in each subject field. A spelling text that had a broad language approach and gave the student many opportunities to write words produced spelling achievement as high as that produced by a narrower phonetic approach (Hahn, 1964). None of the methods used in the Cedar Rapids, Iowa, schools was 'consistently superior to the others' (Reid, 1966). Teachers should feel free to develop any method or combination of methods which they can use successfully with their students. Pupils gain a sense of spelling power as they are helped to group similar elements. For example, having learned the *ing* cluster, they can spell this ending in many words such as *playing* and *eating* (Strickland, 1963).

Since writing almost always demands correct spelling, students should learn to spell the words they need to write. Some spelling lists are constructed on this basis.

Handwriting is related to spelling: poor handwriting may further confuse inaccurate visual word images. Directing children's attention to the correct spelling of words that they have misspelled is a better way of making them aware of their errors than by checking or underlining their misspelled words.

Integration of the communication arts

The communication arts should be closely integrated, one growing out of another. Paying careful attention to a television program may enable a student to make an effective oral or written report. A student composition that concerns something of real interest to a student may make excellent reading material for the whole class. Holbrook (1964) gives many examples of ways in which this kind of writing was produced by pupils in his slow-learning class. The dramatization of dialogs (Turner, 1964) gives practice in both reading and speech. A poem, article, or essay often serves as a springboard for creative writing. As students listen to good literature and read good books, they acquire a feeling for the style and rhythm of English speech, essentials for effective writing. Thus one avenue of communication contributes to the others. And all the aspects of language help to form the individual's developing personality. It is through expression that the individual discovers himself and achieves self-realization.

References

Artley, A. Sterl (1959) 'But—skills are not enough', *Education*, 79, 542.

Berg, Paul (1955) 'Reading in relation to listening', *Evaluating College Reading Programs* (4th Yearbook of the Southwest Reading Conference), Fort Worth, Texas, Texas Christian University Press, pp. 52–60.

Bigger and Better Boners (1952) New York, Viking Press.

Bond, Guy L. and Fay, Leo C. (1950) 'A comparison of the performance of good and poor readers on the individual items of the Stanford–Binet Scale, Forms L and M', *Journal of Educational Research*, 43, 475–9.

Brookover, Wilbur B., Thomas, Shailer and Paterson, Ann (1964) 'Self-concept of ability and school achievement', *Sociology of Education*, 37, 271–8.

Burton, William H. (1956) *Reading in Child Development*, Indianapolis, Bobbs-Merrill.

Carnegie Corporation of New York Quarterly (1962), 10.

Carney, John J. Jr. (1964) 'Anyone who writes well can speak well', *Improving College and University Teaching*, 12, 209–11.

Dietz, Alfred G. and Jones, George E. (1931) 'Factual memory of secondary school pupils for a short article which they read a single time', *Journal of Educational Psychology*, 22, 586–98; 667–76.

Douglass, Malcolm P. (1963) 'A point of view about reading', *Claremont Reading Conference* (Twenty-seventh Yearbook), Claremont, Calif., Claremont Graduate School and University Center.

Duker, Sam (1966) *Listening Readings*, N.Y., Scarecrow Press.

Eames, Thomas H. (1951) 'Visual handicaps to reading', *Journal of Education*, 141, 2–35.

Eames, Thomas H. (1961) 'Accommodation in school children: aged five, six, seven, and eight years', *American Journal of Ophthalmology*, 51, 1255–7.

Edfeldt, Ake W. (1960) *Silent Speech and Silent Reading*, University of Chicago Press.

Ekwall, Eldon E. (1966) 'The Use of WISC Subtest Profiles in the Diagnosis of Reading Difficulties', unpublished doctoral dissertation, Tucson, University of Arizona.

Ephron, Beulah (1953) *Emotional Difficulties in Reading: a Psychological Approach to Study Problems*, N.Y., Julian Press.

Fendrick, Paul (1937) 'The influence of music distraction upon reading efficiency', *Journal of Educational Research*, 31, 264–71.

Freyberg, P. S. (1964) 'A comparison of two approaches to the teaching of spelling', *British Journal of Educational Psychology*, 34, 178–86.

Garner, W. R. (1966) 'To perceive is to know', *American Psychologist*, 21, 11–19.

Gray, William S. (1957) *The Teaching of Reading: an International View* (The Burton Lecture, 1956), Harvard University Press.

Gray, William S. (1960) *The Major Aspects of Reading* (Supplementary Educational Monographs, no. 90), University of Chicago Press, pp. 8–24.

Hage, Dean S. and Stroud, James B. (1959) 'Reading proficiency and intelligence scores: verbal and nonverbal', *Journal of Educational Research*, 52, 258–62.

Hahn, William P. (1964) 'Phonics: a boon to spelling?', *Elementary School Journal*, 64, 383–6.

Hall, John F. (1961) *Psychology of Motivation*, Philadelphia, Lippincott.

Hanna, Paul R. and Hanna, Jean S. (1965) 'The teaching of spelling', *National Elementary Principal*, 45, 19–28.

Hester, Kathleen B. (1959) 'Creative reading: a neglected area', *Education*, 79, 537–41.

Holbrook, David (1964) *English for the Rejected*, Cambridge University Press.

Hollingsworth, Harry L. (1928) *Psychology, Its Facts and Principles*, N.Y., Appleton-Century-Crofts.

Holmes, Jack A. and Singer, Harry (1964) 'Theoretical models and trends toward more basic research in reading', *Review of Educational Research*, 34, 131–3.

Horn, Ernest and Ashbaugh, Ernest J. (1950) *Spelling We Use, Grades 2–8*, Philadelphia, Lippincott.

Jenkins, Nora Congdon (1953) 'Visual performance and scholastic success', *School Review*, 61, 544–7.

Jones, N. V. (1951) 'The effect of speech training on silent reading achievement', *Journal of Speech and Hearing Disorders*, 16, 258–63.

Keppel, Francis (1964) 'Research: education's neglected hope', *Journal of Reading*, 8, 3–9.

King, W. H. (1959) 'An experimental investigation into the relative merits of listening and reading comprehension for boys and girls of primary school age', *British Journal of Educational Psychology*, 29, 42–9.

Krugman, Morris (1956) 'Reading failure and mental health', *Journal of the National Association of Women Deans and Counselors*, 20, 10.

Lloyd, Bruce A. (1965) 'The chimera of oral reading', *Education*, 86, 106–8.

Lovell, K. and Woolsey, M. E. (1964) 'Reading disability, non-verbal reasoning, and social class', *Educational Research*, 6, 226–9.

McCaul, Robert L. (1949) 'The effects of attitudes upon reading interpretation', *Journal of Educational Psychology*, 40, 230–8.

Maw, Wallace T. and Maw, Ethel W. (1962) 'Children's curiosity as an aspect of reading comprehension', *The Reading Teacher*, 15, 239.

Morrison, Ida E. and Perry, Ida F. (1951) 'Spelling and reading relationships with incidence of retardation and acceleration', *Journal of Educational Research*, 52, 222–7.

Olson, Willard C. (1959) *Child Development*, Boston, D. C. Heath, pp. 141–90.

Parker, Edwin R. (1963) 'The effects of television on public library circulation', *Public Opinion Quarterly*, 27, 578–89.

Penty, Ruth (1956) *Reading Ability and High School Dropouts*, Teachers College Press, Teachers College, Columbia University.

Porterfield, O. U. and Schlicting, H. F. (1961) 'Peer status and reading achievement', *Journal of Educational Research*, 54, 291–7.

Reid, Hall C. (1966) 'Evaluating five methods of teaching spelling—second and third grades', *Instructor*, 75, 77, 82–3.

Richards, Ivor A. (1942) *How to Read a Page*, N.Y., Norton.

Robinson, Helen M. (1964) 'Perceptual and conceptual style related to reading', in J. Allen Figurel (ed.), *Improvement of Reading through Classroom Practice*, Newark, Del., International Reading Association Conference Proceedings, 9, 26–8.

Robinson, Helen M. and Huelsman, Charles B. Jr. (1953) 'Visual efficiency and progress in learning to read', in Helen M. Robinson (ed.), *Clinical Studies in Reading II* (Supplementary Educational Monographs, no. 77), University of Chicago Press, p. 41.

Russell, David H. (1961) *Children Learn to Read*, Boston, Ginn, 69–96.

Russell, David H. (1965) 'Research on the process of thinking with some applications to reading', *Elementary English*, 42, 370–8.

Smith, Donald E. P. and Carrigan, Patricia M. (1959) *The Nature of Reading Disability*, N.Y., Harcourt Brace & World.

Spache, George D. (1963) *Toward Better Reading*, Champaign, Ill., Garrard Press.

Spache, George D. and Tillman, Chester E. (1962) 'A comparison of the visual profiles of retarded and nonretarded readers', *Journal of Developmental Reading*, 5, 101–9.

Strang, Ruth (1943) 'Relationship between certain aspects of intelligence and certain aspects of reading', *Educational and Psychological Measurement*, 3, 355–9.

Strang, Ruth (1948) 'The contribution of the psychology of reading to international cooperation', *School and Society*, 67, 65–8.

Strang, Ruth (1953) 'What is communicated?', *Educational Forum*, 18, 15–19.

Strickland, Ruth (1963) 'Implication of research in linguistics for elementary teaching', *Elementary English*, 40, 168–71.

Tinker, Miles A. (1963) 'Legibility of print for children in the upper grades', *American Journal of Optometry and Archives of American Academy of Optometry*, 40, 614–21.

Turner, Richard H. (1964) *When People Talk on the Telephone, Books A & B*, Teachers College Press, Teachers College, Columbia University.

Vernon, M. D. (1957) *Backwardness in Reading: a Study of Its Nature and Origin*, Cambridge University Press.

Waldman, John and Triggs, Francis Oralind (1958) 'The measurement of word attack skills', *Elementary English*, 35, 459–63.

Wattenberg, William W. and Clifford, Clare (1964) 'Relation of self-concepts to beginning achievement in reading', *Child Development*, 35, 461–7.

Wepman, Joseph M. (1955) 'Nature of effective speech in oral reading', in Helen M. Robinson (ed.), *Oral Aspects of Reading* (Supplementary Educational Monographs, no. 82), University of Chicago Press, pp. 30–5.

Wheeler, Lester H. and Wheeler, Viola D. (1949) 'The relationship between reading ability and intelligence among university freshmen', *Journal of Educational Psychology*, 40, 230–8.

Wyatt, Nita M. (1962) 'Research in creative writing', *Educational Leadership*, 19, 307–10.

Wylie, Ruth C. (1963) 'Children's estimates of their school work ability, as a function of sex, race, and socioeconomic level', *Journal of Personality*, 31, 203–24.

2. 2 The nature of the reading process

John B. Carroll

As you silently read this very paragraph, what are you doing? If you are a skilled reader and are attending carefully to what this paragraph is trying to say, you will notice the following. First, what are your eyes doing? Moving together in a swift and well-coordinated way, your eyes are making a series of fixations, jumping from place to place on the page of print. The jumps are exceedingly rapid; you see little while your eyes are jumping. What is important are the fixations, when your eyes come to rest. Most of these fixations are actually on or close to the line of print, but unless you are reading quite slowly you cannot easily predict or control where your eyes will fixate. The fixations are usually quite short in duration; each one will last about one-quarter of a second on the average.

Usually the fixations progress from left to right along the first line of print, then back to the beginning of the next line and again from left to right across the line, and so on. For the average adult reader there will be about two fixations per inch of ordinary type like this. Some of these fixations may be very brief, amounting to minor adjustments in order to bring the print better into view. During most of the fixations, you receive an impression of a certain amount of printed material; that is, you instantaneously perceive and recognize one or more words, perhaps up to four or five in some cases. You are more likely to recognize the words that are in the immediate area of fixation; words outside this immediate area may be less well recognized, but some of them have been

Source: H. Singer and R. B. Ruddell (eds), *Theoretical Models and Processes of Reading*, Newark, Del., International Reading Association, 1970, pp. 8–18.

recognized in a previous fixation, and others may be more clearly recognized in a future fixation. Some of the words may never be clearly recognized, but you apprehend enough of the stimulus to fill them in from the general drift of what you are reading.

Let us just think about this process of instantaneous word recognition. Most of the words you see are words you have seen many times before; even though in actuality they may be relatively rare, they are familiar enough to you to permit 'instantaneous' recognition. Of course recognition is not really instantaneous; it takes a certain amount of time. Experiments in which words are exposed very briefly show that common words can be recognized quite accurately in less than one-tenth of a second; even words that are quite rare can be recognized with at least 50 percent accuracy in exposures of about one-fifth of a second. During the average fixation lasting one-quarter of a second it is often possible to take in several words. The point is that most words are recognized extremely rapidly. If you are a skilled reader you do not have to stop to figure out the pronunciation of a familiar word from its spelling; you are hardly conscious of the spelling at all. Still less do you attend to the particular phonetic values of the letters; in reading the word *women* it would scarcely occur to you to note that the 'o' in the first syllable stands for a sound that rhymes with /i/ in *whim*. The printed word *women* is a gestalt-like total stimulus that immediately calls to mind the spoken word that corresponds to it—or if not the spoken word itself, some underlying response which is also made when the word is spoken. As a skilled reader, you can consider yourself lucky to have a large 'sight' vocabulary.

The actual process by which we recognize words is not well understood, simply because the whole process of 'pattern perception,' as it is called, is one of the most mysterious problems in psychology. How, for example, do we recognize a table, a goblet, or a flagpole for what it is, regardless of the angle of regard? Nevertheless, it is a simple fact that we *can* learn to recognize words even though the words may be printed in different typefaces or written in different cursive styles, and in different sizes. Now even though word recognition is rapid, it obviously depends to a large extent on cues from the letters composing the word. There is little confusion among such highly similar items as *cob, rob, mob*, and *nob* even in fast single exposures. We do know that in recognizing longer words, the letters standing at the beginning and end are more critical than letters in the middle, for in fast exposures these middle letters can sometimes be altered or replaced without this being noticed by the reader. In ordinary reading we frequently fail to notice words that contain printer's errors. But there is little evidence to support the idea that a mature reader recognizes words merely by their outlines or general shape. It is unlikely that if you see the shape ⌐ you will recognize the word *dog*; you might just as well think it to be *day* or *dug*. Beginning readers sometimes use mere shape cues in trying to recognize words, but they will be overwhelmed with confusion if they depend solely on such cues apart from the recognition of the letters themselves. In the mature reader the process of rapid word recognition seems to depend upon his ability to integrate the information provided by the separate letters composing the word, some letters being more critical as cues than others. Because the recognizability of a word is apparently correlated rather highly with its frequency of use, word perception seems to be a skill that depends upon large amounts of practice and exposure.

Suppose, however, that the skilled reader comes to a word that he has never seen before, like *dossal, cunctation*, or *latescent*, or an unfamiliar proper name like *Vukmanovich* or *Sbarra*. Though the skilled reader can hardly be said to 'recognize' a word he has never seen before, he nevertheless recognizes elements of it—letters and patterns of letters that give him reasonably good cues as to how the word should be pronounced. *Dossal* may be recognized as similar to *fossil* and pronounced to rhyme with it, the first letter cuing the /f/ sound. *Cunctation* may give a little more difficulty but be recognized as somewhat similar to *punctuation* and at the same time a *mutation*; by following the total pattern of cues the reader may be able to infer the correct pronunciation. *Latescent* will probably be recognized not as a compound of *late* and *scent*, but as a member of a family of words like *quiescent, fluorescent*, etc. Somewhat the same principles apply to the reading of foreign proper names; even if he is not familiar with the foreign language involved, the skilled reader will be sensitive to the possible values of the letters and letter-combinations in the name, and come up with a reasonable pronunciation.

It should be noted that thus far we have been speaking of the recognition of words as particular combinations of letters. Actually, in English there are numerous instances of homographs —words that are pronounced in different ways depending on their use. The word 'read' is an interesting example: in the context *to read* it rhymes with *bead*, but in the context *to have read*, it rhymes with *bed*. The skilled reader instantaneously interprets the word in its proper 'reading' or pronunciation depending upon the context—i.e., the surrounding words and their meanings.

This takes us, in fact, to the next stage of our analysis of the reading process. As you take in material recognized in the succession of rapid fixations that is characteristic of skilled reading, it somehow merges together in such a way as to build up in your mind an impression of a meaningful message—a message that is in many ways analogous to the message you would apprehend if someone read the paragraph aloud to you, with all its proper inflections and accents. Some people report that as they read they can 'hear' (in the form of internal auditory images) the message as it might be spoken; at least they report that they 'hear' snatches of such a message. Other readers feel that they apprehend a meaning from the printed message directly—that is, without the intervention of any auditory images. In slow readers, or even in skilled readers reading very difficult material, one may notice slight articulatory movements that suggest that the reader is trying to pronounce the words subvocally.

The process of scanning a paragraph for a meaningful message does not, of course, always run smoothly. As one reads, there may be momentary lapses of attention (which can be due to lack of interest, distractions, or even stimulation from the content itself), or of comprehension (which can be due to the difficulty of the material, poor writing, or other conditions). The process of comprehension seems to have some influence on the movements of the eyes: when the reader fails to attend or comprehend, his eyes may 'regress,' moving back to fixate on a portion of the material already scanned. Difficulties in recognizing particular words may cause the eyes to dwell on or around a particular point in the text longer than the usual amount of time. There are large differences among individuals in all the reading processes we have mentioned. Some readers can read with markedly fewer fixations per line; some read with an abnormally higher number of fixations per line and exhibit many more regressions than normal. Few individuals have the same pattern of eye movements, even when they read at approximately the same speed. Obviously, there are wide individual differences in rate and accuracy of comprehension.

The *essential* skill in reading is getting meaning from a printed or written message. In many ways this is similar to getting meaning from a *spoken* message, but there are differences, because the cues are different. Spoken messages contain cues that are not evident in printed messages, and conversely. In either case, understanding language is itself a tremendous feat, when one thinks about it. When you get the meaning of a verbal message, you have not only recognized the words themselves; you have interpreted the words in their particular grammatical functions, and you have somehow apprehended the general grammatical patterning of each sentence. You have unconsciously recognized what words or phrases constitute the subjects and predicates of the sentence, what words or phrases modify those subjects or predicates, and so on. In addition, you have given a 'semantic' interpretation of the sentence, assigning meanings to the key words in the sentence. For example, in reading the sentence 'He understood that he was coming tonight' you would know to whom each 'he' refers, and you would interpret the word *understood* as meaning 'had been caused to believe' rather than 'comprehended.' Somehow you put all these things together in order to understand the 'plain sense' of what the message says.

Even beyond getting the simple meaning of the material you are reading, you are probably reacting to it in numerous ways. You may be trying to evaluate it for its truth, validity, significance, or importance. You may be checking it against your own experience or knowledge. You may find that it is reminding you of previous thoughts or experiences, or you may be starting to think about its implications for your future actions. You may be making inferences or drawing conclusions from what you read that go far beyond what is explicitly stated in the text. In doing any or all of these things, you are 'reasoning' or 'thinking.' Nobody can tell you exactly what to think; much of your thinking will be dependent upon your particular background and experience. At the same time, some thinking is logical and justified by the facts and ideas one reads, while other kinds of thinking are illogical and not adequately justified by the facts and ideas one reads. One aspect of a mature reader's skill consists in his being able to think about what he reads in a logical and well-informed way. This aspect of reading skill sometimes takes years to attain.

We have described the process of reading in the skilled reader—a process that is obviously very complex. How is this process learned or attained?

As in the case of any skill, reading skill is not learned all at once. It takes a considerable amount of time. Furthermore, the process of learning to read is *not* simply a slow motion imitation of the mature reading process. It has numerous components, and each component has to be learned and practiced.

There are probably a great many ways to attain reading skill, depending upon the order in which the various components are learned and mastered. It may be the case that some ways are always better than others. On the other hand, children differ in their aptitudes, talents, and inclinations so much that it may also be the case that a particular way of learning is better for one child while another way is better for another child. It all depends upon which components of reading skill a given child finds easier to learn at a given stage of his development. In referring to different orders in which component skills would be learned, we do not mean to imply a lock-step procedure in which the child first learns and masters one skill, then goes on to learn and master another skill, and so on.

Actually, a child can be learning a number of skills simultaneously, but will reach mastery of them at different periods in his development. From the standpoint of the teacher, this means that different skills may need to be emphasized at different periods, depending upon the characteristics of the individual child. This is particularly true in the case of the child who is having difficulty in learning to read.

Let us try to specify the components of reading skill. Some of these components come out of our analysis of the mature reading process; others out of a further analysis of *those* components.

1. *The child must know the language that he is going to learn to read.* Normally, this means that the child can speak and understand the language at least to a certain level of skill before he starts to learn to read, because the purpose of reading is to help him get messages from print that are similar to the messages he can already understand if they are spoken. But language learning is a lifelong process, and normally there are many aspects of language that the individual learns solely or mainly through reading. And speaking and understanding the language is not an absolute prerequisite for beginning to learn to read; there are cases on record of children who learn to read before they can speak, and of course many deaf children learn the language only through learning to read. Foreign-born children sometimes learn English mainly through reading. Children who, before they begin to read, do not know the language, or who only understand but do not speak, will very likely require a mode of instruction specially adapted to them.

2. *The child must learn to dissect spoken words into component sounds.* In order to be able to use the alphabetic principle by which English words are spelled, he must be able to recognize the separate sounds composing a word and the temporal order in which they are spoken—the consonants and vowels that compose spoken words. This does not mean that he must acquire a precise knowledge of phonetics, but it does mean that he must recognize those aspects of speech sound that are likely to be represented in spelling. For example, in hearing the word *straight*, the child must be able to decompose the sounds into the sequence /s, t, r, ey, t/.

3. *The child must learn to recognize and discriminate the letters of the alphabet in their various forms* (*capitals, lower case letters, printed, and cursive*). (He should also know the names and alphabetic ordering of the letters.) This skill is required if the child is to make progress in finding correspondences between letters and sounds.

4. *The child must learn the left-to-right principle by which words are spelled and put in order in continuous text.* This is, as we have noted, a very general principle, although there are certain aspects

of letter-sound correspondences that violate the principle—e.g., the reverse order of *wh* in representing the sound cluster /hw/.

5. *The child must learn that there are patterns of highly probable correspondence between letters and sounds, and he must learn those patterns of correspondence that will help him recognize words that he already knows in his spoken language or that will help him determine the pronunciation of unfamiliar words*. There are few if any letters in English orthography that always have the same sound values; nevertheless, spellings tend to give good clues to the pronunciation of words. Often a letter will have highly predictable sound values if it is considered in conjunction with surrounding letters. Partly through direct instruction and partly through a little-understood process of inference, the normal child can fairly readily acquire the ability to respond to these complex patterns of letter-sound correspondences.

6. *The child must learn to recognize printed words from whatever cues he can use—their total configuration, the letters composing them, the sounds represented by those letters, and/or the meanings suggested by the context*. By 'recognition' we mean not only becoming aware that he has seen the word before, but also knowing the pronunciation of the word. This skill is one of the most essential in the reading process, because it yields for the reader the equivalent of a speech signal.

7. *The child must learn that printed words are signals for spoken words and that they have meanings analogous to those of spoken words. While decoding a printed message into its spoken equivalent, the child must be able to apprehend the meaning of the total message in the same way that he would apprehend the meaning of the corresponding spoken message*. As in the case of adult reading, the spoken equivalent may be apprehended solely internally, although it is usual, in early reading efforts, to expect the child to be able to read aloud, at first with much hesitation, but later with fluency and expression.

8. *The child must learn to reason and think about what he reads, within the limits of his talent and experience*.

It will be noticed that each of these eight components of learning to read is somehow involved in the adult reading process—knowing the language, dissecting spoken words into component sounds, and so forth. Adult reading is skilled only because all the eight components are so highly practiced that they merge together, as it were, into one unified performance. The well-coordinated, swift eye movements of the adult reader are a result, not a cause, of good reading; the child does not have to be *taught* eye movements and therefore we have not listed eye-coordination as a component skill. Rather, skilled eye movements represent the highest form of the skill we have listed as 4—the learning of the left-to-right principle. The instantaneous word recognition ability of the mature reader is the highest form of the skill we have listed as 6—recognition of printed words from whatever cues are available, and usually this skill in turn depends upon the mastery of some of the other skills, in particular 5—learning patterns of correspondence between letters and sounds. The ability of the adult reader to apprehend meaning quickly is an advanced form of skill 7, and his ability to think about what he reads is an advanced form of skill 8.

The 'great debate' about how reading should be taught is really a debate about the *order* in which the child should be started on the road toward learning each of the skills. Few will question that mature reading involves all eight skills; the only question is which skills should be introduced and mastered first. Many points of view are possible. On the one hand there are those who believe that the skills should be *introduced* in approximately the order in which they have been listed; this is the view of those who believe that there should be an early emphasis on the decoding of print into sound via letter-sound relations. On the other hand, there are those who believe that the skills should be introduced approximately in the following order:

1. The child should learn the language he is going to read.

6. The child should learn to recognize printed words from whatever cues he can use, but initially only from total configurations.

7. The child should learn that printed words are signals for spoken words, and that meanings can be apprehended from these printed words.

8. The child must learn to reason and think about what he reads.

4. The child should learn the left-to-right principle, but initially only as it applies to complete words in continuous text.

3. The child should learn to recognize and discriminate the letters of the alphabet.

2. The child should learn to dissect spoken words into component sounds.

5. The child should learn patterns of correspondence between letters and sounds, to help him in the advanced phases of skill 6.

This latter view is held by those who argue that there should be an early emphasis on getting the meaning from print, and that the child should advance as quickly as possible toward the word-recognition and meaning-apprehension capacities of the mature reader. Skills 2, 3, and 5 are introduced only after the child has achieved considerable progress towards mastery of skills 4, 6, 7, and 8.

These are the two main views about the process of teaching

reading. If each one is taken quite strictly and seriously, there can be very clear differences in the kinds of instructional materials and procedures that are used. It is beyond our scope to discuss whether the two methods differ in effectiveness. We would emphasize, rather, that methods may differ in effectiveness from child to child. Furthermore, it is possible to construct other reasonable orders in which the various components of reading skill can be introduced to the child. There is currently a tendency to interlace the approaches distinguished above in such a way that the child can attain rapid sight recognition of words at the same time that he is learning letter-sound correspondences that will help him 'attack' words that he does not already know.

For the child who is having difficulty in learning to read, it may be necessary to determine exactly which skills are causing most difficulty. The dyslexic child may be hung up on the acquisition of just one or two skills. For example, he may be having particular trouble with skill 3—the recognition and discrimination of the letters of the alphabet, or with skill 2—the dissection of spoken words into component sounds. On determining what skills pose obstacles for a particular child, it is usually necessary to give special attention to those skills while capitalizing on those skills which are easier for the child to master.

Uncertainties and research problems

The above description of the nature of the reading process is based on the findings of nearly three-quarters of a century of research. A good deal is known about reading behavior, yet there are many questions that have not been answered with precision and certainty. We shall list the most important of these.

Questions about the mature reading process

1. How does the individual's ability to recognize words instantaneously develop? What cues for word recognition are most important? How and when does awareness of spelling clues and inner speech representation recede, if at all? What is the extent of the sight vocabulary of the mature reader? (It should be noted that most studies of word recognition processes have been conducted with adults; there is need for developmental studies in which word recognition processes would be investigated over different chronological age levels.)

2. How do skilled readers process unfamiliar words? To what extent, and how, do they use patterns of letter-sound correspondences?

3. How do skilled readers find the proper readings of homographs and other types of ambiguous words?

4. What are the detailed psychological processes by which skilled readers comprehend the simple meaning of what they read? In what way do lexico-semantic, syntactical, and typographical factors interact to yield this comprehension?

5. How are eye movements controlled by comprehension processes, and how does the individual develop skill in scanning print?

6. How does the mature reader acquire skill in reasoning and inferential processes?

7. What are the major sources of individual differences in rate and accuracy of comprehension in mature readers?

Questions about certain components of reading skill as they affect learning

1. In what way does knowledge of the spoken language interact with learning to read? What kinds and amounts of competence are desirable before the child undertakes any given task in learning to read?

2. What is the nature of the ability to discriminate sounds in the spoken language and to dissect words in terms of these sounds? How does it develop, and what role does it play in the beginning reader's learning of letter-sound correspondences? How can this ability be taught?

3. How do children learn to recognize and discriminate alphabetic letters in their various forms? When children have difficulty with letter recognition, how can these difficulties be overcome?

4. How do children learn the left-to-right principle in orthography, both as applied to individual words and to the order of words in continuous text? Are there children with special difficulties in learning this component of reading skill?

5. Exactly what are the most useful and functional patterns of letter-sound correspondence in English orthography, and in what order should they be learned? How, indeed, *are* they learned? Is it better to give direct instruction in them, or is it better to rely upon the child's capacity to infer these patterns from the experience he acquires as he learns to read? Should the characteristics of particular children be taken into account in deciding this?

6. When a child has acquired the ability to recognize words and read them in order, yet does not appear to comprehend the message as he would if it were spoken to him, what is the nature of the difficulty?

Questions about the ordering of the components of reading skill in the teaching process

1. In what way are the various skills prerequisite for each other? What aspects of each skill are necessary to facilitate progress in another skill?

2. Is there one best order in which to introduce the components of reading skill in the learning process, or are there different orders depending upon characteristics of individual children or groups of children? If so, how can these individual or group characteristics be determined?

3. On the assumption that there is an optimal ordering of skills for any given child, how much mastery of a given skill is desirable before another skill is introduced?

2. 3 Making sense of reading—and of reading instruction

Frank Smith

Children must have two fundamental insights before they can learn to read. These two insights are rarely discussed in the research literature on reading and are generally ignored in reading instruction, which may even suppress the insights in children who have already managed to acquire them. Without these insights reading instruction will remain incomprehensible to children and have the adverse effect of making nonsense of reading.

The two fundamental insights are (1) that print is meaningful and (2) that written language is different from speech. I shall discuss each of the two insights in turn, considering first why the insight is essential for learning to read, then how it is normally acquired, and finally how it may be overlooked or even impeded in reading instruction.

Insight I: print is meaningful

Children are often immersed in spoken language—at home, at play, and even while watching television. But they would make little progress in learning to produce and understand speech unless they could bring meaning to it,[1] and this would be impossible without the fundamental insight that the sounds of speech are not unrelated to other events but in fact make things happen in the world. Children learn language by making sense of the differences that language makes. By 'making sense' I mean that children are able to relate the sounds of the language they hear to understandings they already have. Language makes sense—it is meaningful—when meaning can be brought to it. In fact, I would

Source: *Harvard Educational Review*, 47 (3), 1977, pp. 386–94.

define 'meaning' as the relevance that can be imposed on an utterance.[2]

It is not clear how or when infants acquire the insight that different sequences of language sounds are related to different meanings, that one sequence of sounds cannot be substituted arbitrarily for another sequence. This insight is unlikely to be explicit; I do not see how adults can explain the meaningfulness of language to children, nor how children might formulate the insight in words for themselves. Rather, I regard the insight as an implicit decision that certain events warrant attention because they are related to situations and intentions that the child can make sense of and is interested in. I suspect that the key lies in Halliday's observation that children do not learn language independently of its functions.[3] Language to a child always has a use, and the various uses could provide the child a clue to the purposes underlying differences among utterances. A child soon ignores sounds that do not seem to make a difference. There is, in fact, a powerful mechanism in all children preventing them from wasting time on sounds that they cannot make sense of, that do not appear to have a purpose; that mechanism is boredom. Even if the strangeness of the sounds initially stimulates their interest, children will not continue to pay attention to sounds that do not make meaningful differences. That is why they grow up speaking language and not imitating the noisé of the air conditioner.

A similar insight—that differences on a printed page have a function, that they are meaningful—must also be the basis for learning written language. As long as children see print as purposeless or nonsensical, they will find attention to print aversive and will be bored. Children will not learn by trying to relate letters to sounds, partly because the task does not make sense to them and partly because written language does not work that way. In my view reading is not a matter of decoding letters to sound but of bringing meaning to print.[4] Orthography only indirectly relates print to spoken languages.[5] Phonic generalizations are both cumbersome and unreliable; over two hundred rules with hundreds of exceptions apply to the most common words in our language. Relatively few words can be 'blended' from the sounds of their spelling. To overcome this problem, instruction usually tries to limit alternatives by placing severe restrictions on the words a child will meet. In normal reading, unlikely alternatives are more efficiently eliminated through the sense of the context. Phonics will never enable a child to decode the words *horse, mule*, or *donkey* in isolation. There are at least ten different ways of pronouncing *ho* at the beginning of a word, and /horse/ contains one of the uncommon ones; but if context indicates that a word is either *horse, mule*, or *donkey*, then phonics will indeed work. My view on this controversial issue is that teachers often give phonics too much credit because of the limited objectives to which phonics are usually directed, and children contribute to the myth because the best readers are always good at phonics. It is, however, the sense of the text, if the text has any sense, that enables readers to use spelling-to-sound correspondences effectively.

Prediction through meaningfulness is the basis of language comprehension.[6] By prediction I do not mean reckless guessing but rather the elimination of unlikely alternatives on the basis of prior knowledge. The child predicts that a limited range of relationships is likely to occur between language and its setting or within the language itself. Meaning then is the relationships the child finds. If there is no meaning to be found, there can be no prediction, no comprehension, and no learning. But, to repeat, before meaning can assist a child in learning to read, there must be the insight that print is meaningful.

Acquiring the insight

Research to date has little to offer in the way of relevant data, but it seems a reasonable hypothesis that the majority of children are as much immersed in written language as in speech. I refer to the wealth of print to be found on every product in the bathroom, on every jar and package in the kitchen, in the television guide and television commercials, in comics, catalogs, advertising fliers, street signs, store fronts, billboards, supermarkets, and department stores. All of this print is meaningful; it makes a difference. We do not expect cornflakes in a package labeled *detergent*.

The question is whether children who cannot yet read pay very much attention to all this print.[7] I have reported on a three-and-a-half-year-old boy who obviously could not read the words *luggage* and *footwear* on signs in a department store but who nevertheless asserted that the first sign said 'cases' and the second said 'shoes.'[8] Here was one child who could bring meaning to print long before he could read the actual words—who had acquired the insight that differences in print are meaningful.

I can think of only one way in which such an insight might be achieved, and that is when a child is being read to or observes print being responded to. At this point I am not referring to the reading of books or stories but to the occasions when a child hears 'That sign says "Stop,"' 'That word is "Boy,"' or 'There's the bus for downtown.' Television commercials may do the same for a child. They not only announce the product's name, desirability, and uniqueness in spoken and written language, but they even demonstrate the product at work. The point in all of these cases is that no substitution could be made; the print is directly related to the setting in which it occurs, just as is the spoken language of the home. Once the fundamental insight about the meaningfulness of written language is attained, I see no reason why children should not go on spontaneously elaborating upon it as they do with speech. Children can test hypotheses about the meaning of the printed word *toys* not because anyone reads it to them but because it indicates the location of the toy department.

The relevance of instruction

I must reiterate that to make sense of any aspect of language a child must perceive a purpose for it. In school, I believe, this need implies that children must understand not only the content of the instruction—the materials they are expected to read—but also the purpose of the instruction. However, this often does not occur, and in the next few paragraphs I describe what I consider to be some aspects of reading instruction which are fundamentally incomprehensible.

One such aspect is the decomposition of spoken words to sounds. The spoken word 'cat' makes sense in some contexts, but the sounds /kuh/, /a/, /tuh/ do not. It should not be surprising that children find it difficult to detect these units in speech (until and unless they catch on to the highly conventionalized game that is being taught) because such units do not in fact exist in spoken language, where individual sounds and even words are slurred together. Speech is certainly not understood through an analysis and subsequent synthesis of its parts.[9] Auditory acuity is not essential for reading, although it may be a prerequisite for reading instruction.

Another incomprehensible exercise is the decomposition of written words to letters. The printed word *cat* can make sense in some contexts, since it refers to an object in the real world with which children can meaningfully interact. But the letters *c, a,* and *t* do not have that status. They refer to specialized visual symbols that have nothing to do with anything else in the child's life. Until children have had substantial experience reading, they must find it profoundly unsettling to be confronted with the information that *cat* begins with /see/ or that *bat* and *ball* both start with the same letter. Children who know the alphabet tend to be good readers, but teaching letter names will not turn a poor reader into a good one.[10] Rather, it would seem, fluency with the alphabet comes with being a competent reader.

A third problematic aspect of instruction is the relating of letters to sounds. For a child who has no conception of reading to be told that some peculiar shapes called letters (which have no apparent relevance in the real world) are related in any way to some improbable sounds (that have no existence in the real world) must be the purest Jabberwocky. Of course, with a certain amount of good will and diligence a child might succeed in learning to recite a few of these correspondences. At best, however, such correspondences will not make sense until the child is able to read; at worst, they may persuade the child that reading is a matter of trying to produce meaningless sounds at an impossibly high speed.

The use of metalinguistic terms poses yet other problems. Many of the words that children are expected to understand in order to benefit from reading instruction, in fact, make sense only when one is able to read. The word *letter* is a case in point and so is the word *word*. The status of a word in spoken language is extremely dubious; words cannot be segregated by any mechanical or electronic device from the continuous flow of normal speech,[11] and linguists prefer not to use the term at all. The usual definitions of a word—letters surrounded by white space or a separate item in a dictionary—obviously apply only to written language. It should not be surprising that many novice readers cannot make sense of this and other metalinguistic terms, such as *sentence, paragraph, capital letter*, or even *space*, since only more skilled readers have experienced them meaningfully. Teaching children the definitions of such terms will not make them readers[12] because until they can read, the terms will remain entirely senseless to them.

Finally, many drills and exercises are meaningless. It does not matter how much a teacher might believe or hope that certain exercises have a point; anything that is opaque to a child can contribute nothing positive to reading. Children frequently learn to achieve high scores on boring, repetitive, and nonsensical tasks (especially, once more, those children who happen to be competent readers), but such a specialized skill will not make children into readers. Low scores, on the other hand, can certainly interfere with reading development and not simply because children risk being stigmatized as potential poor readers, but because they may begin to regard rote, meaningless, and difficult activities as a model for what reading is all about.

The content of the material which children are expected to begin reading may also be incomprehensible. As a general rule, isolated words—which are the basis of much initial reading instruction—make no more sense than isolated letters. However, words in a meaningful context—if a child is encouraged to use context—promote prediction, comprehension, and learning. But some elaboration is required. Words that appear by themselves are not necessarily meaningless. In the world outside school, individual words—for example, *gas, exit, burgers*—make a lot of sense. But these single words are not in fact devoid of context; they are given meaning and function by the settings in which they are found. This is not the case when individual words are isolated from any apparent function and are printed alone in lists, on chalkboards, in exercise books, and even under some pictures. Many of the words that are likely to appear in isolation in school have a multiplicity of meanings and grammatical functions. Words like *shoe, house*, and *chalk* can be nouns or verbs, and *open* and *empty* can be adjectives or verbs. To ask children to identify such words is simply to ask them to put a name to them, not a meaning. Conversely, the fact that a word is embedded in a grammatical sentence does not make it meaningful. Sentences can be just as devoid of purpose and meaning as isolated words—*Sam the fat cat sat on the flat mat*—and so can whole paragraphs and 'stories' made up of such sentences.

A consequence of all this potential meaninglessness in reading instruction may be to confound children who are striving to learn through making sense of what they are doing. More seriously, the ultimate danger is that children who have not got the insight that written language should make sense will never achieve it, while children who have got it may be persuaded that they are wrong. Unfortunately, a good deal of reading instruction seems to be based on the premise that sense should be the last, not the first, concern of readers.

Such instruction may not be ineffectual. Many students identified as having reading problems in high school struggle to get every word right, drawing on all their resources of phonics, and in this way they may succeed. But they show no apparent concern for meaning and no evident expectation that sense has any bearing on what they are trying to do. As a cure for their obvious disability, they may often be removed entirely from any possibility of reading meaningful text and returned to a meaningless form of beginning reading. Such meaningless materials and activities are occasionally supposed to exemplify 'getting back to basics.'

Insight II: print is different from speech

Obviously, spoken language and written language are not the same. It is not difficult to detect when a speaker is reading from a prepared text, especially one written for publication, or when a speaker is reading the unedited transcript of a spontaneous talk. Speech and print are not different languages; they share a common vocabulary and the same grammatical forms. But they are likely to contain different distributions of each. It is not surprising that differences exist between spoken and written language, since each is frequently used for quite different purposes and audiences. Spoken language itself varies radically depending on the purpose for which it is used and the relationships among the people using it. Although it is difficult to specify exactly how or why written and spoken language differ, I believe this difference has a simple and distinct basis: spoken language has adapted itself to being heard while written language is more appropriately read.

To understand how such specialized adaptation might have come about, it is necessary to examine the different demands that the two language forms make upon their recipients. For example, consider the obvious fact that spoken language is ephemeral. The word dies the moment it is uttered and can be recaptured only if it is held in one's fallible memory or if one asks the speaker to go to the trouble of recapitulating. In contrast to the facile way in which we can move back and forth through written text, even tape recording does little to mitigate the essential transience of speech. Writing, unlike speech, is largely independent of the constraints of time. Put in another way—and this is still an untested hypothesis—spoken language often makes a considerable short-term demand on memory while written language does not. The reader can not only attend to several words at a time but can also select what those words will be, the order in which they will be dealt with, and the amount of time that will be spent on them.

There is, however, another demand that written language places upon the reader, related not to memory but to the far more fundamental question of how we make sense of language in the first place. The question concerns how language is verified—how we confirm that the information we are receiving is true, that it makes sense, or, indeed, that we understand the message correctly. For everyday spoken language, the matter of verification is simple: look around. An utterance is usually related to the situation in which it occurs. But, if we do not understand or believe what we read, the ultimate recourse can only be back to the text itself. With written language, difficult and possibly unique skills are required in order to verify, disambiguate, and avoid error. Specifically, the skills involve following an argument, looking for internal consistencies, and thinking abstractly.

These requirements of written language have so impressed some theorists that they have argued that writing has introduced a whole new mode to our repertoire of intellectual skills.[13] It might be objected that spoken language is often as abstract, argumentative, and unrelated to the circumstances in which it is comprehended as a scientific paper. But Olson claims that our ability to produce and understand such spoken language is simply a by-product of our being literate.[14] Only because of our experience in reading can we make sense of abstract speech, which in its form is more like writing than everyday spoken language.

The need for the insight

Children who expect to read in the way they make sense of spoken language are likely to have difficulty in comprehending print and thus in learning to read. Their predictions will be all wrong. It does not matter that we cannot define exactly the differences between spoken and written language. We cannot say what the rules of spoken language are; yet children learn to make sense of speech. Nor is there convincing evidence that children need to have the conventions of written language explained to them, provided they can make sense of print. The general requirements of immersion in the problem of making sense, and of getting feedback to test hypotheses would seem to be just as easily met with written language as with speech. In fact, since a number of alternative tests can be conducted on the same material, written language might seem to have advantages as far as hypothesis testing is concerned. By virtue of its internal consistency, the text itself can provide feedback about the correctness of hypotheses, just as the surrounding situation may provide feedback that is relevant to speech. When reading something you comprehend, you can usually tell if you make a mistake that makes a difference—for the very reason that it *makes* a difference—and you can probably go back to find out why. However, none of this will be of any value to children learning to read if the language from which they are expected to learn is not in fact written language or if they do not have the fundamental insight that written language and speech are not the same.

Acquiring the insight

How might children acquire and develop the insight that speech and written language are not the same? There can be only one answer: by hearing written language read aloud. When a child's predictions about written language fail because they are based on prior knowledge of spoken language, then an occasion exists for gaining the insight that spoken and written language are different. As written language is heard and comprehended, hypothesis testing will also help children develop an implicit understanding of the particular characteristics of written language. And children can considerably augment this understanding as they become able to do more and more of their own reading.

I suspect it is the higher probability of hearing written language that accounts for the finding that children tend to become proficient readers if they come from homes where a good deal of reading occurs. (Sartre has related his experience of learning to read in this way.[15]) Children are unlikely to learn to read by osmosis (by the mere fact that books are around them), from direct parental instruction, or because they see the value of reading by watching adults perform what initially must seem a pretty meaningless, silent activity. Rather, I would be inclined to credit the simple possibility that such children are merely more likely than other children to hear written language being read.

Actual stories are the kind of reading that I think most familiarizes children with written language. These can range from the contemporary material found in newspapers and magazines, elaborating perhaps upon something already experienced, to the traditional content of fairy tales and adventure stories, to history and myth. These traditional stories fascinate children—possibly fulfilling some of their deepest needs[16]—without pandering to an alleged inability to handle complex language or ideas. All of these story types are truly written language, produced for a purpose in a conventional medium. There is no evidence that children find it harder to understand such complex texts (when they are read to them) than it is for them to understand complex adult speech. In both cases it usually does not matter if large parts of the language are incomprehensible, provided the general theme and interest carry the reader or listener along. Indeed, it is through exposure to such meaningful complexity that children are able to develop and test their hypotheses about the nature of spoken or written language.

Most of the material which interests children at school—and from which they would be likely to learn—tends to be too difficult for them to read by themselves. This poses a problem for teachers. One solution would be to help children read or listen to such material. But the alternative often selected is to seek or produce less complex material—pseudoforms—in the expectation that children will find them simpler. And if this specially tailored material also confounds beginners, the assumption may be made that the fault lies with the children or with their language development.

Indeed, the language of school texts is probably unfamiliar to most children. But this situation need not have its roots in the particular kind of spoken language with which a child is familiar nor even in the child's possibly limited experience with print. The source is more likely to be the artificial language of school books, whether of the truncated 'cat on the mat' variety or the more florid 'Down the hill hand in hand skipped Susie and her friend.' This language is so different from any other spoken or written form that it is probably most appropriate to put it into an exclusive category, 'school language.'

Of course, such language tends to be quite unpredictable for many children, who may then have enormous difficulty understanding and learning to read from it. Ironically, it is often concluded that written language is intrinsically difficult for children who would be better off learning from 'spoken language written down.' The source for such a hybrid is either someone's intuition of what constitutes spoken language or, worse still, a dialect of that language or even 'children's language,' the description of any of which confounds professional linguists. The result may be something that is quite unlike written language yet has none of the advantages of everyday speech, since it has to be comprehended out of its setting. Children may learn to recite such print, but I have seen no evidence that it makes them readers. And any insight they might have in advance about the nature of written language is likely to be undermined. Worse, children may be persuaded that the print they first experience in school is a model for all the written language that will confront them throughout their lives—a conviction that would be as discouraging as it is misleading.

Conclusions

I have argued that children need two basic insights to begin to learn to read. Also, I have implied that with these insights children can solve all the other problems associated with print by themselves provided that no extraneous confusion or hindrance is put in their way. They must be able to predict and make sense of language in the first place, and they can do this only by bringing meaning to it. This is certainly the way that all children learn spoken language and is probably the reason that many of them succeed in learning to read despite the instructional method used.

As I have argued elsewhere, the implications for instruction are that a child learns to read by reading and that the teacher's role is to make reading easy. I do not mean that reading is made easy by the use of simple material, which can indeed be difficult because of its probable irrelevance and unpredictability. Rather, I suggest helping children to understand any written material that interests them—whether the help is provided by the teacher, an aide, another child, or a tape recording—or simply by permitting children to make errors and omissions without penalty and without the disruption of unwanted correction. Children seek help when they need it and ignore it when they do not.

There are, of course, many factors that can contribute to failure in reading, including lack of motivation, low expectations, fear of failure, and hostility to the school or to the teacher. But failure also implies that a child sees no sense in what is involved in learning to read. A child's commitment to learn reflects an economic decision made on the basis of perceived cost and return. The problem for the teacher is not just to make reading comprehensible (which may be hard enough) but also to make sure that the instruction makes sense and is relevant to all of the child's concerns. Children who can make sense of instruction should learn to read; children confronted by nonsense are bound to fail. The issue is as simple—and as complicated—as that.

Notes

1 John Macnamara, 'Cognitive basis of language learning in infants', *Psychological Review*, 79 (1972), 1–13.
2 Frank Smith, *Comprehension and Learning*, N.Y., Holt, Rinehart & Winston, 1975.
3 Michael A. K. Halliday, *Explorations in the Functions of Language*, Edward Arnold, 1973.
4 Frank Smith, *Understanding Reading*, Holt, Rinehart & Winston, 1971; *Psycholinguistics and Reading*, Holt, Rinehart & Winston, 1973.
5 Noam Chomsky and Morris Halle, *The Sound Pattern of English*, N.Y., Harper & Row, 1968; Carol Chomsky, 'Reading, writing and phonology', *Harvard Educational Review*, 40 (1970), 287–309.
6 Frank Smith, 'The role of prediction in reading', *Elementary English*, 52 (1975), 305–11.
7 The only researchers I know who are working in this area are Yetta Goodman at the University of Arizona, Martha Evans at the University of Maryland, and Ingrid Ylisto at Eastern Michigan University.
8 Frank Smith, 'Learning to read by reading: a brief case study', *Language Arts*, 53 (1976), 297–9, 322.
9 Alvin M. Liberman, 'The grammar of speech and language', *Cognitive Psychology*, 1 (1970), 301–23.
10 S. Jay Samuels, 'The effect of letter-name knowledge on learning to read', *American Educational Research Journal*, 9 (1972), 65–74.
11 Colin Cherry, *On Human Communication: A Review, a Survey and a Criticism*, 2nd ed., MIT Press, 1966.
12 John Downing and Peter Oliver, 'The child's conception of "a word"', *Reading Research Quarterly*, 4 (1974), 568–82.
13 Eric Havelock, *Origins of Western Civilization*, Toronto, Ontario Institute for Studies in Education, 1976; Jack Goody and Ian Watt, 'The consequences of literacy', in *Literacy in Traditional Societies*, ed. Jack Goody, Cambridge University Press, 1968; David R. Olson, 'Utterance to text: the bias of language', *Harvard Educational Review*, 47 (1977), 257–81.

14 Olson, op. cit.
15 Jean-Paul Sartre, *Words*, Penguin, 1969.
16 Bruno Bettelheim, *The Uses of Enchantment: The Meaning and Importance of Fairy Tales*, N.Y., Knopf, 1976.

2. 4 Some curious paradoxes in reading research

John Downing

Sometimes the results of research seem to collide head on with what seems obvious common sense to the practical classroom teacher. Then he or she feels inclined to reject the findings even though they have been obtained by reputable investigators adhering rigorously to the tenets of scientific research, and even when the same surprising or unexpected results have been confirmed independently by several different scholars.

Such paradoxical research findings, however, can be a spur to creative thinking. The resolution of the puzzling problems they create may lead to new perspectives on the ways children learn to read and how teachers can be more effective. This may be particularly helpful if several unrelated paradoxes suggest a common underlying explanation. This seems to be the case with four curious paradoxes in reading research.

(1) *Earlier letter-name knowledge is highly correlated with later reading achievement, yet teaching letter-names does not help children to learn to read.*
Gavel (1958) and many other researchers have found a high correlation between children's letter-name knowledge when they first enter school and their level of achievement in reading at the end of their first year of schooling. It has been found that letter-name knowledge is the best single predictor in reading readiness tests. These findings have led many to propose that, if teachers deliberately taught children the letter-names, it should improve their reading. Yet three independent experimenters (Ohnmacht, 1969; Johnson, 1970; Samuels, 1971) have each tried this out under rigorous scientific control and all reached the same

Source: *Reading*, 8, 1974, pp. 2–10.

conclusion—that letter-name teaching gives the child no help whatsoever in learning to read.

Why this conflict in research findings? Why is it that teaching letter-names is a waste of time and effort but letter-name knowledge is such a good guide to reading readiness?

(2) *Some reading disability cases are superior to normal readers in visual discrimination.*

A second paradoxical research finding is one which seems to fly in the face of obvious common sense. Serafica and Sigel (1970) reported a careful scientific comparison they had made between normal and disabled boy readers. They found that:

> The boys with reading disability in this study do not seem lacking in an analytic ability. If the initial phase of learning to read requires differentiation of graphic symbols from one another, the non-readers were better equipped for that task than were the boys who showed no reading problems.

How can this be? Surely, reading is a visual skill. Why would poor readers be superior to normal readers in visual discrimination?

(3) *Learning to read two languages is easier than learning to read only one.*

Modiano (1968) found in Mexico that teaching Indian children to read their own Indian language first and then later Spanish led to superior achievements in reading Spanish than starting off with just the one language—Spanish. Similarly, Osterberg (1961) in Sweden discovered that children taught to read in a local dialect first and then transferred to standard Swedish afterwards were superior in reading the latter in comparison with children from the same dialect area who were introduced to reading only standard Swedish from the beginning. This is another apparent insult to common sense. How can it be easier to learn to read two languages or two versions of the same language than it is to learn to read only one? Isn't there twice as much to learn?

(4) *It is easier to learn to read in two alphabets than it is in one.*

Many educators who pride themselves on down to earth plain common sense have stated their belief that the i.t.a. approach must be crazy. The pupil learns i.t.a. first, then he must 'unlearn' it and learn all over again the traditional orthography (t.o.) of English. Surely this must be at least double the work of learning to read and write t.o. straight away at the beginning. Warburton and Southgate (1969) in their Schools Council report on i.t.a. examined this 'common sense' belief, but the research evidence from all seventeen British and American investigations led them to conclude:

> There is no evidence whatsoever for the belief that the best way to learn to read in traditional orthography is to learn to read in traditional

orthography. It would appear rather that the best way to learn to read in traditional orthography is to learn to read in the initial teaching alphabet. (pp. 234–5)

The missing link

How can common sense be so often at fault? Because an important psychological element in the process of learning to read has been overlooked. The *adult* 'common sense' formula often fails to take into account the special ways in which children think and talk about reading and language. Adults tend to recognize the (to them) obvious factors in learning to read: visual discrimination because one must use one's eyes to see the printed page; auditory discrimination because one must be able to hear the individual words and phonemes of the spoken language which printed words and letters represent. What they too often overlook is the child's thought processes which must puzzle out the systematic way in which written language is related to speech.

Elkonin (1973), the Russian authority on reading, stated recently:

the perception and discrimination of printed characters is only the external side of the process of reading, behind which lies hidden the more essential and basic behavior, which the reader produces with the sounds of language. The speed of the movement of the eye does not define the speed of reading. Nor does the so-called 'span of apprehension' determine the speed of reading (i.e. the number of graphic symbols perceived simultaneously). Of considerably greater importance than the speed of eye-movements and the span of apprehension is the speed of the underlying more central processes concerned with the behavior creating the sound form of the word and, connected with it, its comprehension.

Thus, reading research may have been overconcerned with the external aspects of reading—perception, eye movements, visual discrimination, letter-name knowledge, etc.—at the expense of neglecting the 'underlying more central processes', those conceptual and reasoning processes of the child, which Elkonin has concluded constitute the heart of the problem of learning to read. If Elkonin's finding is taken into consideration, all four of the paradoxes noted earlier no longer seem so strangely paradoxical.

The disabled readers in the research of Serafica and Sigel were better at visual discrimination than the normal readers because seeing that printed letters are different is less important than knowing when to ignore differences. The reader develops this knowledge through the thought process of categorizing. Then many differences between printed shapes are correctly ignored because they have no significance for the skill of reading. Several years ago Helen Robinson (1953) cited a study by Solomon which also found that some children failed in reading because of undue concern with unimportant details which are quite irrelevant to the reading act. For example, one eleven-year-old boy in a special class for disabled readers visited by the present author could not read *leg* because his teacher wrote the word in italic handwriting. He was confused by the extra curl at the bottom of the *l*. He lacked the bold flexibility of the successful reader who tries to sort unknown symbols into a category which will make sense. Thus the thinking process of categorization can be of much greater importance in reading than the ability to see whether one letter looks different from another.

Another paradox which may be explained if one considers children's thought processes in learning to read is the conflicting evidence about the role of letter-name knowledge in reading. Piaget (1959) has observed that 'verbal forms evolve more slowly than actual understanding'. The natural process is for the child first to develop understanding and to form a concept. Then, when he has formed the new category, he needs a name or label for it. Thus when he begins to grasp the concept of 'letter' he will try to label it, although, as Jessie Reid's (1966) research has shown, the child may at first give it a wrong name. Similarly with individual letters, the first thing that happens is that the child forms a concept of, for example, *G*, then he has something to name and may learn that people call this shape (and some others) 'jee'. The essential point to note is that the concept develops first and the name for it comes later.

Gavel and many others found the high correlation between children's letter-name knowledge on entry to school and their reading achievements at the end of the first year at school because of the connecting link in the child's thought processes. The child who knows many letter-names on first entering school does so because he has developed numerous corresponding concepts about language and the way people write it. He probably has parents who read and write a good deal and talk about what they read and write. This type of environment will also support the school's efforts in teaching reading. In contrast, the child with no knowledge of letter-names does not have the concepts they represent, probably because of a less stimulating environment, and his failure in learning to read will not be surprising. Thus letter-name knowledge is *a symptom* of the state of the child's conceptual growth and in particular of his development of concepts of language. This development of children's concepts and reasoning abilities related to language is a fundamental factor in learning to read.

These considerations show why Samuels and others found it was a waste of time to teach children letter-names. All that the teacher was doing was teaching the symptoms instead of an understanding of the basic concepts. The child could recite the letter-names but he was just as ignorant as ever of the concepts to which they relate. Another Russian psychologist, Vygotsky (1962), in his research on young children's learning of concepts, concluded:

> Direct teaching of concepts is impossible and fruitless. A teacher who tries to do this usually accomplishes nothing but empty verbalism, a parrotlike repetition of words by the child, simulating a knowledge of the concepts but actually covering up a vacuum.

Actually, the rote learning of letter-names may have worse effects than are immediately apparent from Vygotsky's conclusion. Having a vacuum in one's understanding of what the teacher is talking about must cause feelings of puzzlement and a sense of inadequacy. It seems likely therefore that teaching letter-names before the child has understood the related concepts may be an additional cause of what Magdalen Vernon (1957) calls 'cognitive confusion'—confusion in the child's understanding of the concepts and reasoning tasks used in reading. Vernon's comprehensive review of research on causes of reading disability led her to the following conclusion:

> We may conclude that, rather than suffering from some general defect in visual or auditory perception, imagery or memory, the child with reading disability has broken down at some point, and has failed to learn one or more of the essential processes that we have described. He therefore remains fixed at a particular point and is unable to proceed further.

She states also: 'Thus the fundamental and basic characteristic of reading disability appears to be cognitive confusion'.

It follows, therefore, that teachers of reading should avoid any methods which may increase the child's cognitive confusion. Learning the name of something which does not exist in the child's mind surely must be confusing. On the other hand, cognitive clarity is much more likely to be enhanced if the name is learned when the child has developed the thought category that needs a label.

Our third paradox also may be resolved by a consideration of the child's basic need for cognitive clarity. In *Comparative Reading* (Downing (ed.), 1973), the systematic analysis of all the data from fourteen different countries with widely varying environments and very different languages (including Chinese, Japanese, Russian and Hebrew as well as the European languages) seemed to be explained best by making the child's thought processes the focus of concern.

Therefore, the theoretical model as shown in the diagram was developed.

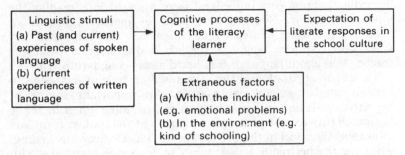

In this model the cognitive processes of the pupil are bombarded with information and other influences from the three directions shown. The ideal situation for the child exists when the 'linguistic stimuli' are in harmony with the 'school expectations', and also if there is a minimum of interference from 'extraneous factors'. In such good conditions sources of cognitive confusion will be at a minimal level and the child should develop steadily increasing cognitive clarity in regard to the concept formation and reasoning processes required in learning to read. This model explains why it was easier to learn to read in two languages than in only one in Modiano's Mexican research. The Indian children who were made to learn to read immediately in Spanish were subjected to an additional source of confusion. Their past experience of their own spoken language had almost no direct link with the written language they were required to interpret. Thus there was a mismatch between their past experience of linguistic stimuli and the expectations of their teacher. In contrast, the Indian children who were allowed to learn to read their own Indian language first were able to develop basic concepts and to understand the logical relationships between speech and writing because there was a direct link between their past experience of linguistic stimuli and their teacher's expectations. Then when they moved on to reading in Spanish they were able to apply the basic concepts and reasoning abilities already learned in their own language to the second language. They could take with them into learning to read Spanish the cognitive clarity gained from having the closer match between spoken and written language in the initial phase of reading in the Indian language.

Osterberg's results showed the same effect. It was easier to learn to read in two dialects of Swedish than one, because beginning in the local dialect presented to the children a clear relationship between the speech they knew and the written form to be acquired.

The resulting cognitive clarity could be taken with them and applied to learning to read standard Swedish. But the children who immediately upon entering school were plunged into reading the unknown standard Swedish were beset by increased sources of cognitive confusion caused by the mismatch between what they knew about spoken language (i.e. their dialect) and what the teacher said about language (i.e. her dialect—standard Swedish).

The apparent paradox of the i.t.a. research conclusions seems to have a similar general explanation. An important source of cognitive confusion in some languages, including English, is the mismatch between the phonemic structure of the spoken form and its graphemic model in the written form. Dialects notwithstanding, when the teacher requires her pupils to associate phonemes with graphemes and to use reasoning processes to decode written English to one of the accepted forms of 'Standard English', this task is much easier in i.t.a. because i.t.a. is a simpler and more regular code for that standard speech. The relationship between the printed symbols and the spoken sounds is clearer. Therefore, the i.t.a. pupil has a better chance of developing cognitive clarity, and, when he transfers to t.o., he can carry this cognitive clarity over to learning the more complex relationship in t.o. This transfer of cognitive development is so important that children who have begun with i.t.a. retain their advantage even in reading t.o., provided that teachers in later classes adapt their teaching to the advanced progress of the i.t.a. pupils they receive.

Conclusion

The practical implication of this discussion is that the way the child thinks and learns should be the starting point for all teaching work. Perhaps teachers could take a leaf out of the industrial psychologist's book. For a good many years now it has been recognized in industry that a dual approach is needed to maximize the worker's efficiency. Training is not enough. Not only must they fit the man for the job, but they must also fit the job to the man. For example, the machinery, information displays, etc., must be designed to suit the men who work with them. A businessman would be regarded as extremely foolish if he insisted that his employees must just learn to use awkward equipment when he could easily increase production by redesigning the equipment.

Similarly in teaching, quite apart from humanistic reasons, child-centred education is more efficient education. Teachers need to be constantly redesigning their teaching equipment to fit the natural ways in which children think and learn. Teachers need to think less about fitting the child to read and more about fitting the reading to the child. In this way their teaching will go with the stream of child thought, instead of, as so often happens, against it.

References

Downing, J. (ed.) (1973) *Comparative Reading*, Collier-Macmillan.

Elkonin, D. B. (1973) 'U.S.S.R.', in Downing, J. (ed.), *Comparative Reading*, pp. 551–79.

Gavel, S. R. (1958) 'June reading achievement of first-grade children', *Journal of Education* (Boston University), 140, 37–43.

Johnson, R. J. (1970) 'The Effect of Training in Letter Names on Success in Beginning Reading for Children of Differing Abilities', paper presented at the American Educational Research Association convention.

Modiano, N. (1968) 'National or mother language in beginning reading: a comparative study', *Research in the Teaching of English*, 2, 32–43.

Ohnmacht, D. D. (1969) 'The Effect of Letter Knowledge on Achievement in Reading in the First Grade', paper presented at the American Educational Research Association convention.

Osterberg, T. (1961) *Bilingualism and the First School Language—An Educational Problem Illustrated by Results from a Swedish Dialect Area*, Umea (Sweden), Vasterbottens Tryckeri AB.

Piaget, J. (1959) *The Language and Thought of the Child* (3rd edition), Routledge & Kegan Paul.

Reid, J. F. (1966) 'Learning to think about reading', *Educational Research*, 9, 56–62.

Robinson, H. M. (ed.) (1953) *Clinical Studies in Reading II* (Supplementary Educational Monographs, no. 77), University of Chicago Press.

Samuels, S. J. (1971) 'Letter-name versus letter-sound knowledge in learning to read', *Reading Teacher*, 24, 604–8.

Serafica, F. C. and Sigel, I. E. (1970) 'Styles of categorization and reading disability', *Journal of Reading Behavior*, 2, 105–15.

Vernon, M. D. (1957) *Backwardness in Reading*, Cambridge University Press.

Vygotsky, L. S. (1962) *Thought and Language*, MIT Press.

Warburton, F. W. and Southgate, V. (1969), *i.t.a: An Independent Evaluation* (Schools Council Report), Chambers.

2. 5 Learning about psycholinguistic processes by analyzing oral reading

Kenneth S. and Yetta M. Goodman

Over the past dozen years we have studied the reading process by analyzing the miscues (or unexpected responses) of subjects reading written texts. We prefer to use the word *miscue* because the term *error* has a negative connotation and history in education. Our analysis of oral reading miscues began with the foundational assumption that reading is a language process. Everything we have observed among readers from beginners to those with great proficiency supports the validity of this assumption. This analysis of miscues has been in turn the base for our development of a theory and model of the reading process.

In this paper we will argue that the analysis of oral reading offers unique opportunities for the study of linguistic and psycholinguistic processes and phenomena. We will support this contention by citing some concepts and principles that have grown out of our research.

We believe that reading is as much a language process as listening is. In a literate society there are four language processes: two are oral (speaking and listening), and two are written (writing and reading). Two are productive and two receptive. In the study and observation of productive language, we may analyze what subjects say or write; however, except for an occasional slip of the tongue, typographical error, or regression to rephrase, speech and writing offer no direct insight into the underlying process of what the speaker or writer intended to say. The study of receptive language—listening and reading—is even more difficult. Either we analyze postlistening or postreading performance, or we contrive controlled-language tasks to elicit reactions for analysis.

Source: *Harvard Educational Review*, 47 (3), 1977, pp. 317–32.

Reading aloud, on the other hand, involves the oral response of the reader, which can be compared to the written text. Oral readers are engaged in comprehending written language while they produce oral responses. Because an oral response is generated while meaning is being constructed, it not only is a form of linguistic performance but also provides a powerful means of examining process and underlying competence.

Consider how Peggy, a nine-year-old from Toronto, reads aloud. Peggy was chosen by her teacher as an example of a pupil reading substantially below grade level. The story she read was considered to be beyond her current instructional level. Peggy read the story hesitantly, although in places she read with appropriate expression. Below are the first fourteen sentences (S1–S14) from 'The man who kept house' (1964, pp. 282–3). In this and other excerpts from the story the printed text is on the left; on the right is the transcript of Peggy's oral reading.

text	*transcript*
(S1a) Once upon a time there was a woodman who thought that no one worked as hard as he did.	(S1b) Once upon a time there was a woodman. He threw . . . who thought that no one worked as hard as he did.
(S2a) One evening when he came home from work, he said to his wife, 'What do you do all day while I am away cutting wood?'	(S2b) One evening when he . . . when he came home from work, he said to his wife, 'I want you do all day . . . what do you do all day when I am always cutting wood?'
(S3a) 'I keep house,' replied the wife, 'and keeping house is hard work.'	(S3b) 'I keep . . . I keep house,' replied the wife, 'and keeping . . . and keeping . . . and keeping house is and work.'
(S4a) 'Hard work!' said the husband.	(S4b) 'Hard work!' said the husband.
(S5a) 'You don't know what hard work is!	(S5b) 'You don't know what hard work is!
(S6a) You should try cutting wood!'	(S6b) You should try cutting wood!'
(S7a) 'I'd be glad to,' said the wife.	(S7b) 'I'll be glad to,' said the wife.
(S8a) 'Why don't you do my work some day?	(S8b) 'Why don't you . . . Why don't you do my work so . . . some day?
(S9a) I'll stay home and keep house,' said the woodman.	(S9b) I'll start house and keeping house,' said the woodman.
(S10a) 'If you stay home to do my work, you'll have to make butter, carry water from the well, wash	(S10b) 'If you start house . . . If you start home to do my work, well you'll have to make bread,

the clothes, clean the house, and look after the baby,' said the wife.

carry . . . carry water from the well, wash the clothes, clean the house, and look after the baby,' said the wife.

(S11a) 'I can do all that,' replied the husband.

(S11b) 'I can do that . . . I can do all that,' replied the husband.

(S12a) 'We'll do it tomorrow!'

(S12b) 'Well you do it tomorrow!'

(S13a) So the next morning the wife went off to the forest.

(S13b) So the next day the wife went off to the forest.

(S14a) The husband stayed home and began to do his wife's work.

(S14b) The husband stayed home and began to do his wife's job.

Peggy's performance allows us to see a language user as a functional psycholinguist. Peggy's example is not unusual; what she does is also done by other readers. She processes graphic information: many of her miscues show a graphic relationship between the expected and observed response. She processes syntactic information: she substitutes noun for noun, verb for verb, noun phrase for noun phrase, verb phrase for verb phrase. She transforms: she omits an intensifier, changes a dependent clause to an independent clause, shifts a 'wh-' question sentence to a declarative sentence. She draws on her conceptual background and struggles toward meaning, repeating, correcting, and reprocessing as necessary. She predicts grammar and meaning and monitors her own success. She builds and uses psycholinguistic strategies as she reads. In short, her miscues are far from random.

From such data one can build and test theories of syntax, semantics, cognition, comprehension, memory, language development, linguistic competence, and linguistic performance. In oral reading all the phenomena of other language processes are present or have their counterparts, but in oral reading they are accessible. The data are not controlled and clean in the experimental sense. Even young readers are not always very considerate. They do complex things for which we may be unprepared; and, not having studied the latest theories, they do not always produce confirming evidence. But they are language users in action.

Miscues and comprehension

If we understand that the brain is the organ of human information processing, that the brain is not a prisoner of the senses but that it controls the sensory organs and selectively uses their input, then we should not be surprised that what the mouth reports in oral reading is not what the eye has seen but what the brain has generated for the mouth to report. The text is what the brain responds to; the oral output reflects the underlying competence and the psycholinguistic processes that have generated it. When expected and observed responses match, we get little insight into this process. When they do not match and a miscue results, the researcher has a window on the reading process.

Just as psycholinguists have been able to learn about the development of oral-language competence by observing the errors of young children, so we can gain insights into the development of reading competence and the control of the underlying psycholinguistic process by studying reading miscues. We assumed that both expected and unexpected oral responses to printed texts are produced through the same process. Thus, just as a three-year-old reveals the use of a rule for generating past tense by producing 'throwed' for 'threw,' so Peggy reveals her control of the reading process through her miscues.

We use two measures of readers' proficiency: *comprehending*, which shows the readers' concern for meaning as expressed through their miscues, and *retelling*, which shows the readers' retention of meaning. Proficient readers can usually retell a great deal of a story, and they produce miscues that do not interfere with gaining meaning. Except for S3, S8, and S9, all of Peggy's miscues produced fully acceptable sentences or were self-corrected. This suggests that Peggy's usual concern was to make sense as she read. In contrast, many nonproficient readers produce miscues that interfere with getting meaning from the story. In a real sense, then, a goal of reading instruction is not to eliminate miscues but to help readers produce the kind of miscues that characterize proficient reading.

Miscues reflect the degree to which a reader is understanding and seeking meaning. Insight can be gained into the reader's development of meaning and the reading process as a whole if miscues are examined and researchers ask: 'Why did the reader make this miscue and to what extent is it like the language of the author?'

Miscue analysis requires several conditions. The written material must be new to the readers and complete with a beginning, middle, and end. The text needs to be long and difficult enough to produce a sufficient number of miscues. In addition, readers must receive no help, probe, or intrusion from the researcher. At most, if readers hesitate for more than thirty seconds, they are urged to guess, and only if hesitation continues are they told to keep reading even if it means skipping a word or phrase. Miscue analysis, in short, requires as natural a reading situation as possible.

Depending on the purpose of the research, subjects often have been provided with more than one reading task. Various fiction and nonfiction reading materials have been used, including stories and articles from basal readers, textbooks, trade books, and magazines. Subjects have been drawn from various levels in elementary, secondary, and adult populations and from a wide range of racial, linguistic, and national backgrounds. Studies have been concluded in languages other than English: Yiddish (Hodes, 1976), Polish (Romatowski, 1972), and American Sign Language (Ewoldt, 1977). Studies in German and Spanish are in progress.

The open-ended retellings used in miscue analysis are an index of comprehension. They also provide an opportunity for the researcher or teacher to gain insight into how concepts and language are actively used and developed in reading. Rather than asking direct questions that would give cues to the reader about what is significant in the story, we ask for unaided retelling. Information on the readers' understanding of the text emerges from the organization they use in retelling the story, from whether they use the author's language or their own, and from the conceptions or misconceptions they reveal. Here is the first segment of Peggy's retelling:

> um . . . it was about this woodman and um . . . when he . . . he thought that he um . . . he had harder work to do than his wife. So he went home and he told his wife, 'What have you been doing all day.' And then his wife told him. And then, um . . . and then, he thought that it was easy work. And so . . . so . . . so his wife, so his wife, so she um . . . so the wife said, 'well so you have to keep,' no . . . the husband says that you have to go to the woods and cut . . . and have to go out in the forest and cut wood and I'll stay home. And the next day they did that.

By comparing the story with Peggy's retelling and her miscues, researchers may interpret how much learning occurs as Peggy and the author interact. For example, although the story frequently uses 'woodman' and 'to cut wood,' the noun used to refer to setting, 'forest,' is used just twice. Not only did Peggy provide evidence in her retelling that she knew that 'woods' and 'forest' are synonymous, but she also indicated that she knew the author's choice was 'forest.' The maze she worked through until she came to the author's term suggests that she was searching for the author's language. Although in much of the work on oral-language analysis mazes are not analyzed, their careful study may provide insight into oral self-correction and the speaker's intention.

There is more evidence of Peggy's awareness of the author's language. In the story the woodman is referred to as 'woodman' and 'husband' eight times each and as 'man' four times; the wife is referred to only as 'wife.' Otherwise pronouns are used to refer to the husband and wife. In the retelling Peggy used 'husband' and 'woodman' six times and 'man' only once; she called the wife only 'wife.' Peggy always used appropriate pronouns in referring to the husband and wife. However, when cow was the antecedent, she substituted 'he' for 'she' twice. (What does Peggy know about the sex of cattle?)

Comparing Peggy's miscues with her retelling gives us more information about her language processes. In reading, Peggy indicated twice that 'said' suggested to her that a declarative statement should follow: One such miscue was presented above (see S2); the other occurred at the end of the story and is recorded below.

text	*transcript*
(S66a) Never again did the wood-man say to his wife, 'What did you do all day?'	(*S66b*) *Never again did the wood-man say to his wife, 'That he . . . what did you do all day?'*

In both instances she corrected the miscues. In the retelling she indicated that after 'said' she could produce a question: 'And then, from then on, the husband did . . . did the cutting and he never said, "What have you been doing all day?"' Even though she had difficulty with the 'wh-' question structure in her reading, she was able to develop the language knowledge necessary to produce such a structure in her retelling.

It has puzzled teachers for a long time how a reader can know something in one context but not know it in another context. Such confusion comes from the belief that reading is word recognition; on the contrary, words in different syntactic and semantic contexts become different entities for readers, and Peggy's response to 'keep house' suggests this. In S3, where the clauses 'I keep house' and later 'and keeping house' occur for the first time, Peggy produced the appropriate responses but repeated each several times. In S9 she produced 'stay home and keep house' as 'start house and keeping house,' and she read the first phrase in S10 as 'If you start home to do my work.' The phrase 'keep house' is a complex one. First, to a nine-year-old, 'keep' is a verb that means being able to hold on to or take care of something small. Although 'keeping pets' is still used to mean taking care of, 'keeping house' is no longer a common idiom in American or Canadian English. When 'stay home' is added to the phrase 'keep house,' additional complexities arise. Used with different verbs and different function words, 'home' and 'house' are sometimes synonyms and sometimes not. The transitive and intransitive nature of the verbs as well as the infinitive structure, which is not in the surface of a sentence, add to the complexity of the verb phrases.

Peggy, in her search for meaning and her interaction with the print, continued to develop strategies to handle these complex problems. In S14 she produced 'stayed home'; however, in S35 she encountered difficulty with 'keeping house' once again and read: 'perhaps keeping house . . . home and . . . is . . . hard work.' She was still not happy with 'keeping house.' She read the phrase as written and then abandoned her correct response. Throughout the story 'home' appears seven times and 'house' appears ten times. Peggy read them correctly in every context except in the patterns 'staying home' and 'keeping house.' Yet she continued to work on these phrases through her interaction with the text until she could finally handle the structure and could either self-correct success-fully or produce a semantically acceptable sentence. Thus Peggy's miscues and retelling reveal the dynamic interaction between a reader and written language.

Oral and written language

The differences between oral and written language result from differences of function rather than from any differences in intrinsic characteristics. While any meaning that can be expressed in speech can also be expressed in writing and vice versa, we tend to use oral language for face-to-face communication and written language to communicate over time and space. Oral language is likely to be strongly supported by the context in which it is used; written language is more likely to be abstracted from the situations with which it deals. Written language must include more referents and create its own context minimally supplemented by illustrations. Written language can be polished and perfected before it is read; therefore, it tends to be more formal, deliberate, and constrained than oral language.

For most people, oral-language competence develops earlier than written-language competence because it is needed sooner. But children growing up in literate societies begin to respond to print as language almost as early as they begin to talk. Traffic signs and commercial logos, the most functional and situationally embedded written language in the environment, are learned easily and early (Goodman and Goodman, in press). Despite their differences and history of acquisition, oral- and written-language processes become parallel for those who become literate; language users can choose the process that better suits their purposes. Readers may go from print to meaning in a manner parallel to the way they go from speech to meaning.

Since the deep structure and rules for generating the surface structure are the same for both language modes, people learning to read may draw on their control of the rules and syntax of oral language to facilitate developing proficiency in written language. This is not a matter of translating or recoding print to sound and then treating it as a listening task. Rather, it is a matter of readers using their knowledge of language and their conceptualizations to get meaning from print, to develop the sampling, predicting, confirming, and correcting strategies parallel to those they use in listening. Gibson and Levin (1975) seem to agree with us that recoding print to sound is not necessary for adults, and Rader (1975) finds that it is not even necessary for children.

We are convinced that oral and written language differ much more in how they are taught than in how they are learned. Although most oral-language development is expected to take place outside of school, the expectation is that literacy development will take place in school programs under teachers' control. Attempts to teach oral language in school are not noted for being as successful as what children achieve outside school. Similarly, literacy instruction is not totally successful. Furthermore, capable readers and writers demonstrate the use and integration of strategies not included in the structured literacy curriculum. Although this paper is primarily concerned with the study of the reading process and not with reading instruction, we are convinced that a major error in many instructional programs has been to ignore or underestimate the linguistic competence and language-learning capabilities of children learning to read.

Reading and listening: active receptive processes

A producer of language can influence the success of communication by making it as complete and unambiguous as possible. The productive process must carry through from thought to underlying structures to graphic or oral production. Written production, particularly, is often revised and edited to correct significant miscues and even to modify the meaning. The receptive process, however, has a very different set of constraints. Listeners and readers must go through the reverse sequence from aural or graphic representation to underlying structure to meaning. Receptive language users are, above all, intent on comprehending—constructing meaning.

Readers and listeners are *effective* when they succeed in constructing meaning and are *efficient* when they use the minimal effort necessary. Thus, through strategies of predicting, sampling, and confirming, receptive language users can leap toward meaning with partial processing of input, partial creation of surface and deep structures, and continuous monitoring of subsequent input and meaning for confirmation and consistency. Many miscues reflect readers' abilities to liberate themselves from detailed attention to print as they leap toward meaning. Consequently, they reverse, substitute, insert, omit, rearrange, paraphrase, and transform. They do this not just with letters and single words, but with two-word sequences, phrases, clauses, and sentences. Their own experiences, values, conceptual structures, expectations, dialects, and life styles are integral to the process. The meanings they construct can never simply reconstruct the author's conceptual structures. That every written text contains a precise meaning, which readers passively receive, is a common misconception detrimental to research on comprehension.

We have argued above that reading is an active, receptive process parallel to listening. Oral-reading miscues also have direct parallels in listening. Although listening miscues are less accessible, since listeners can only report those they are aware of, still these must be quite similar to reading miscues. Anyone who has ever tried to leave an oral message knows that listening miscues are surely not uncommon. In both reading and listening, prediction is at least as important as perception. What we think we have heard or read is only partly the result of sensory data; it is more the result of our expectations.

A major difference between reading and listening is that the reader normally can regress visually and reprocess when a miscue has led to a loss of meaning or structure. The listener, on the other hand, must reprocess mentally, await clarification, or ask a speaker to explain. Furthermore, the speaker may continue speaking, unaware of the listener's problem. Readers are in control of the text they process; listeners are dependent upon the speaker.

The receptive activity during the reading process is especially evident in two different types of miscues—those that are semantically acceptable with regard to the whole text and those that are semantically acceptable only with the prior portion of the text. A miscue may change the author's meaning; but, if it fits the story line, it can be considered semantically acceptable. For example, in S2 of the story Peggy read 'when I am always cutting wood?' for 'while I am away cutting wood?' These two miscues produced a sentence that fitted in with the meaning of the rest of the story. The more proficient a reader is, the greater the proportion of semantically acceptable miscues. The proportion and variety of high-quality miscues suggest that good readers constantly integrate their backgrounds with that of the author as if they are putting the author's ideas into their own language. This ability is often seen in oral language as a mark of understanding. 'Tell me in your own words' is a common request from teachers to discover whether a student has understood something.

Semantically acceptable miscues may be more complex than word-for-word substitutions. Many readers produce reversals in phrase structures such as 'said Mother' for 'Mother said' or other types of restructuring like the one Peggy produced in S12: 'Well, you do it tomorrow' instead of 'We'll do it tomorrow.' Although it seems that Peggy merely substituted 'well' for 'we'll' and inserted 'you,' the miscue is more complex at phrase and clause levels. Peggy inserted an interjection prior to the subject 'you' to substitute for the noun phrase. There was also a substitution of the verb phrase because the verb marker 'will,' indicated by the contraction of 'we'll,' was omitted, and the verb 'do' has been substituted for 'will do.' In addition, Peggy shifted intonation so that the wife rather than the husband says the sentence. Apparently Peggy thought the wife was going to speak, and her shifted intonation reflected changes in the grammatical pattern and meaning, although the sentence retained its acceptability within the story.

A reader's predicting strategies are also evident in those miscues that are acceptable with the prior portion of the text but that do not produce fully acceptable sentences. Such miscues often occur at pivotal points in sentences such as junctures between clauses or phrases. At such points the author may select from a variety of linguistic structures; the reader may have the same options but choose a different structure. Consider these examples from Peggy's reading:

text	*transcript*
(S38a) 'I'll light a fire in the fireplace and the porridge will be ready in a few minutes.'	*(S38b) 'I'll light a fire in the fireplace and I'll . . . and the porridge will be ready in a flash . . . a few minutes.'*
(S48a) Then he was afraid that she would fall off.	*(S48b) Then he was afraid that the . . . that she would fall off.*

Peggy's use of 'I'll' for 'the' in the second clause of the first example is highly predictable. Since 'and' generally connects two parallel items, it is logical that the second clause would begin with the subject of the first clause. The substitution of 'the' for 'she' in the second example occurs frequently in young readers' miscues. Whenever an author uses a pronoun to refer to a previously stated noun phrase, a reader may revert to the original noun phrase. The reverse phenomenon also occurs. When the author chooses a noun phrase for which the referent has been established earlier the reader may use that pronoun. In the second example, Peggy was probably predicting 'the cow' which 'she' refers to. These miscues clearly show that Peggy is an active language user as she reads.

Readers' monitoring of their predictions is observed through their self-correction strategies. Clay's (1967) research and our own (Goodman and Burke, 1973) support the idea that a miscue semantically acceptable to the story line is less likely to be corrected than one that is not acceptable or is acceptable only with the immediately preceding text. For example, of the ten semantically acceptable miscues that Peggy produced in the first excerpt, she only corrected one ('all' in S11). However, of the six miscues that were acceptable only with the prior portion of the text she corrected four. Such correction strategies tend to occur when the readers believe they are most needed: when a prediction has been disconfirmed by subsequent language cues.

Sentences that are fully unacceptable are corrected less than sentences with miscues acceptable with the prior portion of the sentence. Perhaps it is harder for readers to assign underlying structure to sentences in which fully unacceptable miscues occur. Without such a structure, they have difficulty unpacking the grammatical or conceptual complexity of a sentence and so are less able to self-correct. We believe that the two most important factors that make reading difficult are hard-to-predict grammatical structures and high conceptual load (Smith and Lindberg, 1973). What any particular reader finds hard to predict and difficult depends on the reader's background and experience.

The linguistic and conceptual background a reader brings to reading not only shows in miscues but is implicit in the developing concepts or misconceptions revealed through the reader's retelling. Peggy added to her conceptual base and built her control of language as she read this story, but her ability to do both was limited by what she brought to the task. In the story, the husband has to make butter in a churn. Peggy made miscues whenever buttermaking was mentioned. For example, in S10 she substituted 'bread' for 'butter.' The next time 'butter' appears, in S15, she read it as expected. However, in S18, 'Soon the cream will turn into butter,' Peggy read 'buttermilk' for 'butter.' Other references to buttermaking include the words 'churn' or 'cream.' Peggy read 'cream' correctly each time it appears in the text but had trouble reading 'churn.' She paused about ten seconds before the first appearance of 'churn' and finally said it. However, the next two times churn appears, Peggy read 'cream.'

text	*transcript*
(S25a) . . . he saw a big pig inside, with its nose in the churn.	(S25b) . . . *he saw a big pig inside, with its nose in the cream.*

(S28a) It bumped into the churn, knocking it over.
(S29a) The cream splashed all over the room.

(S28b) *It jumped . . . it bumped into the cream, knocking it over.*
(S29b) *The cream shado . . . splashed all over the room.*

In the retelling Peggy provided evidence that her miscues were conceptually based and not mere confusions:

> And the husband was sitting down and he poured some buttermilk and um . . . in a jar. And, and, he was making buttermilk, and then, he um . . . heard the baby crying. So, he looked all around in the room and um, . . . And then he saw a big, a big, um . . . pig. Um . . . He saw a big pig inside the house. So, he told him to get out and he, the pig, started racing around and um . . . he di . . . he um . . . bumped into the buttermilk and then the buttermilk fell down and then the pig, um . . . went out.

Peggy, who is growing up in a metropolis, knows little about how butter is made in churns. Although she knows that there is a relationship between cream and butter, she does not know the details of that relationship. According to her teacher, she has also taken part in a traditional primary-school activity in which sweet cream is poured into a jar, closed up tightly, and shaken until butter and buttermilk are produced. Although Peggy's miscues and retelling suggest that she had little knowledge about buttermaking, the concept is peripheral to comprehending the story. All that she needed to know was that buttermaking is one of the wife's many chores that can cause the woodman trouble.

Reading is not simply knowing sounds, words, sentences, and the abstract parts of language that can be studied by linguists. Reading, like listening, consists of processing language and constructing meanings. The reader brings a great deal of information to this complex and active process. Whenever readers are asked to read something for which they do not have enough relevant experience they have difficulty. That is why even proficient adult readers use such excuses as 'It's too technical' and 'He just writes for those inside the group.' For this reason, proficient readers go to pharmacists or lawyers, for example, to read certain texts for them.

Oral and silent reading

The basic mode of reading is silent. Oral reading is special since it requires production of an oral representation concurrently with comprehending. The functions of oral reading are limited. It has become a kind of performing art used chiefly by teachers and television and radio announcers. We have already explained why we use oral reading in miscue analysis. But a basic question remains: are oral and silent reading similar enough to justify generalizing from studies of oral-reading miscues to theories and models of silent reading?

In our view a single process underlies all reading. The cycles, phases, and strategies of oral and silent reading are essentially the same. The miscues we find in oral reading occur in silent reading as well. Current unpublished studies of non-identical fillers of cloze blanks (responses that do not match the deleted words) show remarkable correspondence to oral-reading miscues and indicate that the processes of oral and silent reading are much the same (Lindberg, 1977; Rousch, 1977).

Still, there are some dissimilarities between oral and silent reading that produce at least superficial differences in process. First, oral reading is limited to the speed at which speech can be produced. It need not, therefore, be as efficient as rapid silent reading. Next, superficial misarticulations such as 'cimmanon' for cinnamon' occur in oral reading but are not part of silent reading. Also, oral readers, conscious of their audience, may read passages differently than if they read them silently. Examples are production of nonword substitutions, persistence with several attempts at problem spots, overt regression to correct miscues already mentally corrected, and deliberate adjustments in ensuing text to cover miscues so that listeners will not notice them. Furthermore, oral readers may take fewer risks than silent readers. This can be seen in the deliberate omission of unfamiliar words, reluctance to attempt correction even though meaning is disrupted, and avoidance of overtly making corrections that have taken place silently to avoid calling attention to miscues. Finally, relatively proficient readers, particularly adults, may become so concerned with superficial fluency that they short-circuit the basic concern for meaning. Professional oral readers, newcasters for example, seem to suffer from this malady.

The reader: an intuitive grammarian

Recently, linguists have equated or blurred the distinction between deep structure and meaning. We, however, find this distinction useful to explain a common phenomenon in our subjects' reading. Moderately proficient readers are able to cope with texts that they do not understand by manipulating language down to a deep structure level. Their miscues demonstrate this. Readers may also correctly answer a question they do not understand by transforming it into a statement and then finding the sentence in the text with the appropriate structure. Thus, when confronted by an article entitled, 'Downhole Heave Compensator' (Kirk, 1974), most readers claim little comprehension. But they can answer the question, 'What were the two things destroying the underreamers?' by finding the statement in the text that reads, 'We were trying to keep drillships and semi-submersibles from wiping out our underreamers' (p. 88). Thus it is dangerous for researchers and teachers to equate comprehension with correct answers obtained by manipulating and transforming grammatical structures. Our research may not prove the psycholinguistic reality of the deep structure construct as distinct from meaning, but it demonstrates its utility. In our research we judge syntactic acceptability of sentences separately from semantic acceptability, since readers often produce sentences that are syntactically, but not semantically, acceptable. In S10 Peggy read 'If you stay home to do my work' as a sentence which she finally resolved as 'If you start home to do my work.' This is syntactically acceptable in the story but unacceptable semantically since it is important to the story line that the woodman 'stay home.'

The first evidence used to separate syntactic from semantic acceptability came from research on the phenomenon of nonwords. Such nonsense words help give us insight into readers' grammatical awareness because sentences with nonwords often retain the grammatical features of English although they lose English meaning. Use of appropriate intonation frequently provides evidence for the grammatical similarity between the nonword and the text word. Nonwords most often retain similarities not only in number of syllables, word length, and spelling but also in bound morphemes—the smallest units that carry meaning or grammatical information within a word but cannot stand alone, for example, the *ed* in carri*ed*. The following responses by second, fourth, and sixth graders represent nonwords that retain the grammatical function of the text (Goodman and Burke, 1973). A different subject produced each response. Notice that 'surprise' and 'circus' are singular nouns and that, in producing the nonwords, the subjects did not produce *s* or *z* sounds at the ends of the words as they would with plural nouns.

expected response	*nonword substitutions*
Second graders:	
The *surprise* is in my box.	*supra, suppa*
Then they will know the *circus* is coming.	*ception, chavit*
'Penny why are you so *excited*?' she asked.	*excedled, encited*
Fourth graders:	
He saw a little *fawn*.	*frawn, foon, faunt*

What queer *experiment* was it?   *espressment,*
                                    explerm, explainment
Sixth graders:
Clearly and *distinctly* Andrew
said 'philosophical.'   *distikily, distintly, definely*
A *distinct* quiver in his voice.   *dristic, distinc, distet*

There is other evidence in miscues of readers' strong awareness of bound morphemic rules. Our data on readers' word-for-word substitutions, whether nonwords or real words, show that, on the average, 80 percent of the observed responses retain the morphemic markings of the text. For example, if the text word is a non-inflected form of a verb, the reader will tend to substitute that form. If the word has a prefix, the reader's substitution will tend to include a prefix. Derivational suffixes will be replaced by derivational suffixes, contractional suffixes by contractional suffixes.

Miscue analysis provides additional data regarding the phenomenon of grammatical-function similarity. Every one of Peggy's substitution miscues in the portion of the text provided earlier had the same grammatical function as the text word. Table 2.5.1 indicates the percentage of miscues made by a sample of fourth and sixth graders that had the same grammatical function. These substitutions were coded prior to any attempt to correct the miscues.

Table 2.5.1 Percent of miscues with grammatical function similarity

Identical grammatical function	4th graders (%)	6th graders (%)
Nouns	76	74
Verbs	76	73
Noun modifiers	61	57
Function words	67	67

Source: K. S. Goodman and C. L. Burke, 1973, p. 136.

Our research suggests that nouns, noun modifiers, and function words are substituted for each other to a much greater degree than they are for verbs. Out of 501 substitution miscues produced by fourth graders, only three times was a noun substituted for a verb modifier, and sixth graders made such a substitution only once out of 424 miscues.

Evidence from miscues occurring at the beginning of sentences also adds insight into readers' awareness of the grammatical constraints of language. Generally, in prose for children, few sentences begin with prepositions, intensifiers, adjectives, or singular common nouns without a preceding determiner. When readers produced miscues on the beginning words of sentences that did not retain the grammatical function of the text, we could not find one miscue that represented any of these unexpected grammatical forms. (One day we will do an article called 'Miscues Readers Don't Make.' Some of the strongest evidence comes from all the things readers could do that they do not.)

Readers' miscues that cross sentence boundaries also provide insight into the readers' grammatical sophistication. It is not uncommon to hear teachers complain that readers often read past periods. Closer examination of this phenomenon suggests that when readers do this they are usually making a logical prediction that is based on a linguistic alternative. Peggy did this with the sentence (S35): 'Perhaps keeping house is harder than I thought.' As previously noted, Peggy had problems with the 'keeping house' structure. She resolved the beginning of this sentence after a number of different attempts by finally reading 'perhaps keeping home is hard work.' Since she has rendered that clause as an independent unit, she has nothing to which she can attach 'than I thought.' She transformed this phrase into an independent clause and read it as 'Then I thought.'

Another example of crossing sentence boundaries occurs frequently in part of a story (Moore, 1965) we have used with fourth graders: 'He still thought it more fun to pretend to be a great scientist, mixing the strange and the unknown' (p. 62). Many readers predict that 'strange' and 'unknown' are adjectives and intone the sentence accordingly. This means that when they come to 'unknown' their voice is left anticipating a noun. More proficient readers tend to regress at this point and correct the stress patterns.

Parts and wholes

We believe that too much research on language and language learning has dealt with isolated sounds, letters, word parts, words, and even sentences. Such fragmentation, although it simplifies research design and the complexity of the phenomena under study, seriously distorts processes, tasks, cue values, interactions, and realities. Fortunately, there is now a strong trend toward use of full, natural linguistic text in psycholinguistic research. Kintsch (1974, p. 2) notes:

> Psycholinguistics is changing its character. . . . The 1950's were still dominated by the nonsense syllables . . . the 1960's were characterized by the use of word lists, while the present decade is witnessing a shift to even more complex learning materials. At present, we have reached the

point where lists of sentences are being substituted for word lists in studies of recall recognition. Hopefully, this will not be the end-point of this development, and we shall soon see psychologists handle effectively the problems posed by the analysis of connected texts.

Through miscue analysis we have learned an important lesson: other things being equal, short language sequences are harder to comprehend than long ones. Sentences are easier than words, paragraphs easier than sentences, pages easier than paragraphs, and stories easier than pages. We see two reasons for this. First, it takes some familiarity with the style and general semantic thrust of a text's language for the reader to make successful predictions. Style is largely a matter of an author's syntactic preferences; the semantic context develops over the entire text. Short texts provide limited cues for readers to build a sense of either style or meaning. Second, the disruptive effect of particular miscues on meaning is much greater in short texts. Longer texts offer redundant opportunities to recover and self-correct. This suggests why findings from studies of words, sentences, and short passages produce different results from those that involve whole texts. It also raises a major issue about research using standardized tests, which utilize words, phrases, sentences, and very short texts to assess reading proficiency.

We believe that reading involves the interrelationship of all the language systems. All readers use graphic information to various degrees. Our research demonstrates that low readers in the sixth, eighth, and tenth grades use graphic information more than high readers. Readers also produce substitution miscues similar to the phonemic patterns of text words. Although such phonemic miscues occur less frequently than graphic miscues, they show a similar pattern. This suggests that readers call on their knowledge of the graphophonic systems (symbol-sound relationships). Yet the use of these systems cannot explain why Peggy would produce a substitution such as 'day' for 'morning' or 'job' for 'work' (S13). She is clearly showing her use of the syntactic system and her ability to retain the grammatical function and morphemic constraints of the expected response. But the graphophonic and syntactic systems alone cannot explain why Peggy could seemingly understand words such as 'house,' 'home,' 'ground,' and 'cream' in certain contexts in her reading but in other settings seemed to have difficulty. To understand these aspects of reading, one must examine the semantic system.

Miscue analysis shows that readers like Peggy use the interrelationships among the grammatical, graphophonic, and semantic systems. All three systems are used in an integrated fashion in order for reading to take place. Miscue analysis provides evidence that readers integrate cue systems from the earlier stages of reading. Readers sample and make judgments about which cues from each system will provide the most useful information in making predictions that will get them to meaning. S2 in Peggy's excerpt provides insight into this phenomenon. Peggy read the sentence as follows: 'One evening when h . . . he came home from work he said to his wife I want you [two second pause] do . . . all day [twelve second pause].' After the second pause, Peggy regressed to the beginning of the direct quote and read, 'What do you do all day when I am always cutting wood?' Peggy's pauses and regression indicate that she was saying to herself: 'This doesn't sound like language' (syntactically unacceptable); 'this doesn't make sense' (semantically unacceptable). She continued slowly and hesitatingly, finally stopping altogether. She was disconfirming her prediction and rejecting it. Since it did not make sense, she decided that she must regress and pick up new cues from which to make new predictions.

In producing the unacceptable language segment 'I want you do all day,' Peggy was using graphic cues from 'what' to predict 'want.' She was picking up the syntactic cues from 'he said,' which suggested that the woodman would use a declarative statement to start his conversation. From the situational context and her awareness of role relationships, she might have believed that, since the husband was returning home from working hard all day, he would be initially demanding to his wife. When this segment did not make sense to Peggy, she corrected herself. She read the last part of the sentence, 'when I am always cutting wood,' confidently and without hesitation. She was probably unaware that 'when' and 'always' are her own encodings of the meaning. She had made use of all three of the cue systems; her words fit well into the developing meaning of the story; therefore, she did not need to correct her miscues. We believe that both children and adults are constantly involved in this process during their silent reading but are unaware that it is taking place.

There are many times when the developing meaning of a story is so strong that it is inefficient to focus on the distinctive graphic cues of each letter or each word. As long as the phrase and clause structure are kept intact and meaning is being constructed, the reader has little reason to be overly concerned with graphic cues. Peggy read 'day' for 'morning' in S13 and 'job' for 'work' in S14. These miscues have a highly synonymous relationship to the text sentence, but they are based on minimal or no graphic cues. In S38 Peggy indicated to an even greater extent her ability to use minimal graphic cues. Her prediction was strong enough; and she was developing such a clear meaning of the situation that 'in a flash' was an acceptable alternative to 'in a few minutes,' although she caught her miscue and corrected it.

Another phenomenon that exemplifies the interrelationships among the cueing systems is the associations readers develop between pairs of words. Any reader, regardless of age or ability, may substitute 'the' for 'a.' Many readers also substitute 'then' for 'when,' 'that' for 'what,' and 'was' for 'saw' in certain contexts. What causes these associations is not simply the words' look-alike quality. Most of these miscues occur with words of similar grammatical function in positions where the resulting sentence is syntactically acceptable. Differences in proficiency are reflected in the ways readers react to these miscues: the more proficient reader corrects when necessary; the less proficient reader, being less concerned with making sense or less able to do so, allows an unacceptable sentence to go uncorrected. This process can only be understood if researchers focus on how readers employ all the cues available to them. For too long the research emphasis on discrete parts of language has kept us from appreciating how readers interrelate all aspects of language as they read.

Sooner or later all attempts to understand language—its development and its function as the medium of human communication—must confront linguistic reality. Theories, models, grammars, and research paradigms must predict and explain what people do when they use language and what makes it possible for them to do so. Researchers have contrived ingenious ways to make a small bit of linguistic or psycholinguistic reality available for examination. But then what they see is often out of focus, distorted by the design. Our approach makes fully available the reality of the miscues readers produce as they orally read whole, natural, and meaningful texts.

Huey (1968, p. 6) once said:

> And so to completely analyze what we do when we read would almost be the acme of a psychologist's achievements, for it would be to describe very many of the most intricate workings of the human mind, as well as to unravel the tangled story of the most remarkable specific performance that civilization has learned in all its history.

To this we add: oral reading miscues are the windows on the reading process at work.

References

Clay, M. M. (1967) 'The reading behaviour of five-year-old children: a research report', *New Zealand Journal of Educational Studies*, 2, 11–31.

Ewoldt, C. (1977) 'Psycholinguistic Research in the Reading of Deaf Children', unpublished doctoral dissertation, Wayne State University.

Gibson, E. and Levin, H. (1975) *The Psychology of Reading*, MIT Press.

Goodman, K. S. and Burke, C. L. (1973) 'Theoretically Based Studies of Patterns of Miscues in Oral Reading Performance, Final Report', Wayne State University (ERIC Document Reproduction Service no. ED 079 708).

Goodman, K. S. and Goodman, Y. (in press) 'Learning to read is natural', in L. B. Resnick and P. Weaver (eds), *Theory of Practice of Early Reading* (vol. 1), Hillsdale, N.J., Erlbaum Associates.

Hodes, P. (1976) 'A Psycholinguistic Study of Reading Miscues of Yiddish-English Bilingual Children', Unpublished doctoral dissertation, Wayne State University.

Huey, E. B. (1968) *The Psychology and Pedagogy of Reading*, MIT Press (originally published 1908).

Kintsch, W. (1974). *The Representation of Meaning in Memory*, Hillsdale, N.J., Erlbaum Associates.

Kirk, S. (1974) 'Downhole heave compensator: a tool designed by hindsight', *Drilling-DCW*, June.

Lindberg, M. A. (1977) 'A Description of the Relationship between Selected Pre-linguistic, Linguistic, and Psycholinguistic Measures of Readability', unpublished doctoral dissertation, Wayne State University.

'The man who kept house' (1964) in J. McInnes, M. Gerrard and J. Ryckman (eds), *Magic and Make Believe*, Don Mills, Ont., Nelson.

Moore, L. (1965) 'Freddie Miller: scientist', in E. A. Betts and C. M. Welch (eds), *Adventures Here and There* (Book V-3), N.Y., American Book Co.

Rader, N. L. (1975) 'From Written Words to Meaning: a Developmental Study', unpublished doctoral dissertation, Cornell University.

Romatowski, J. (1972) 'A Psycholinguistic Description of Miscues Generated by Selected Bilingual Subjects during the Oral Reading of Instructional Reading Material as Presented in Polish Readers and in English Basal Readers', unpublished doctoral dissertation, Wayne State University.

Rousch, P. (1977) 'Miscues of Special Groups of Australian Readers', paper presented at the meeting of the International Reading Association, Miami, May.

Smith, L. A. and Lindberg, M. A. (1973) 'Building instructional materials', in K. S. Goodman (ed.), *Miscue Analysis: Application to Reading Instruction*, Urbana, Ill., ERIC Clearinghouse on Reading and Comprehension Skills and National Council of Teachers of English.

2.6 Language acquisition and the reading process

Robert B. Ruddell

The acquisition of one's native language is indeed a complex process. In fact, little is known about the exact nature of the development of this miraculous phenomenon. Two language acquisition theories which have received greatest acclaim in recent years hold, first, that in a more traditional sense language is acquired through an elaborate association and mediational learning process (51, 54), and, second, that language as the species specific characteristic develops as latent structures are 'triggered' physiologically and influenced by the model language available to the child (9, 27). Convincing arguments have been posited for both points of view; however, it would seem plausible that both theories contribute in some sense to an understanding of language acquisition. Assuming that latent language structures are present and basic to the development of grammatical competency and language performance (21), it is also logical to assume that value stems from consistent social reinforcement and sentence expansion opportunities in refining and extending child grammar (8) as well as lexicon (24). The purpose of this paper, however, is not to review various theories on preschool language acquisition but instead to examine continued language acquisition in the early school years and explore its relationship to the reading process.

As one reads various language research summaries, it is not uncommon to find conclusions which suggest that, upon entrance to the first grade, the child's language development is for the most part mature and that he is sufficiently equipped to handle most

Source: H. Singer and R. B. Ruddell (eds), *Theoretical Models and Processes of Reading*, Newark, Del., International Reading Association, 1970, pp. 1–19.

forms of discourse which embody highly complex structures and vocabulary. Comparatively speaking, the child has made fantastic progress during his six years of life. He can recognize and produce novel sentences; discriminate between grammatical and non-grammatical sentences (e.g., The bike hit the tree. vs. The hit bike the tree.); utilize context and prosodic clues to disambiguate sentences possessing the same surface structure (e.g., They are *visiting* children. vs. They are *visiting children*.); comprehend sentences which possess different surface structures but have identical underlying meaning (e.g., The boy ate the apple. vs. The apple was eaten by the boy.); and also comprehend sentences which possess identical constituent structure but different deep structure (e.g., Miss Rufkin is easy to please. vs. Miss Rufkin is eager to please.).

By the time the child enters the first grade, he has made great strides in language maturation, but it must be recognized that substantial growth in structural and lexical language components must occur in the elementary school years. In this regard it is important that a discussion of language development accounts for language maturity not only in standard but in nonstandard dialects as well. It is also important that the relationship between language experience and the reading process be accounted for. The following discussion will thus be mainly devoted to the acquisition and control of structural and lexical dimensions of the language of standard and nonstandard speakers during the elementary school years, with special concern for the relationship between language production and the reading process.

Control of structural components

Phonological and morphological development

Various status studies have consistently shown that by the time the child enters the first grade he has a high degree of control over his phonological system (31, 56). In fact by the time the child is four to five years of age he has mastered the great majority of English sounds (13). Likewise, his morphological development is well along upon entrance to the primary school (2, 47). Only on occasion will he utilize an inflectional form (e.g., drinked) which deviates from the adult norm (29).

This language progress, however, assumes that the child has been provided with a 'standard English' model and that opportunity has been present for language interaction in a wide variety of language environments. If these assumptions cannot be met then the language maturity criteria for the phonological and morphological systems will need to account for nonstandard forms and performance levels in limited language environments.

Recent work on nonstandard dialects provides evidence of highly regular systems which in past years were considered to be degenerate forms of 'good English.' This regular nature is evident in the l-lessness common to the nonstandard Black dialect and results in consistent production of homonyms so that *toll* becomes *toe*, and *fault* becomes *fought*.* The simplification of consonant clusters in final positions such as /st/ → /s/ and the loss of /t/ and /d/ results in homonyms so that *past* becomes *pass, meant* becomes *men*, and *hold* becomes *hole*. The English-speaking youngster from a Spanish-speaking background may have difficulty with vowel contrasts which distinguish the words b*i*t /i/ and b*ea*t /iy/, b*e*t /e/ and b*ai*t /ey/; and initial consonant contrasts such as *s*ue /s/ and *z*oo /z/. The Navajo child has difficulty with initial consonant distinctions in words like *v*ote /v/ and *b*oat /b/; and *ch*ip /č/ and *g*yp /ǰ/.

These variations in the phonological system may result in meaning confusion between nonstandard and standard English speakers in situations where sentence context is not sufficient to clarify the intended meaning. If we are to understand the relationship between the phonological system and the graphological system, it becomes clear that dialectal variation must be accounted for. Otherwise, the operationalized reading program makes false assumptions about the language performance of the nonstandard speaker and the teacher may attempt to develop sound-letter correspondences which are not possible for the child.

Reading-decoding

Linguists such as Venezky (59), Wardhaugh (61), and Reed (41) have strongly recommended that it is necessary to consider letter patterns beyond the simple sound-letter correspondence level if a more consistent relationship between oral and written language forms is to be realized. This recommendation is based on the linguistic unit known as the morphophoneme, or the intermediate (between phoneme and morpheme) sound-spelling unit. The importance of this unit is obvious at once in the examination of the words supreme and supremity. On the first consideration the second *e* grapheme would appear to possess little regularity in its representation of a given sound. However, when the large spelling

---

* Editor's note: 'l-lessness' is not peculiar to nonstandard Black dialects— readers, including standard-English-speakers, should compare their own pronunciation of 'fault'.

pattern is considered, a highly regular pattern becomes evident. In the alterations—supr*e*me, supr*emity*; extr*e*me, extr*emity*; obsc*e*ne, obsc*enity*—we observe a consistent shift in the sound value (/iy/ to /i/) in adding the suffix *ity*. The same principle is present in the letter pattern using the final *e* marker (e.g., *sit* /i/, *site* /ay/).

Consideration also needs to be given to the possible value of utilizing phonological or sound segmentation rather than morphological or word-affix segmentation in teaching decoding skills. An experiment by Rodgers (42) asked children to repeat words containing two syllables (e.g., toas-ter) and the same words divided between the two morphemes (e.g., toast-er). He found that the children were more successful in redividing words along syllabic or phonological breaks than along the morphological breaks, thus supporting phonological segmentation.

The work by Gibson and her colleagues (18) has indicated that children develop higher-order generalizations in the early stages of reading and that these generalizations follow English spelling patterns. The children in the experiment appeared to perceive regularities in sound and spelling patterns and transfer these to decoding unfamiliar trigrams even though taught by what the researchers refer to as the 'whole word' approach. The above research thus suggests the possible value and need to consider decoding units which extend beyond sound-letter correspondences and account for more complete regularity in the English spelling system.

As the classroom teacher and the theoretician view the relationship between language acquisition and the reading process, both must not only be aware of the previously discussed cultural levels (25, 40), such as standard and nonstandard dialects, but also cognizant of functional varieties of language such as informal, formal, and literary. These varieties may exist within a given cultural level. Additional variation in language performance may be expected to result from the child's limited experience with language forms unique to a particular social environment. As a result one child may be able to function on only an informal functional variety level while a second child from a highly enriched language environment may shift with ease from the informal to the formal level.

By placing oral expression and written language forms on a functional variety continuum ranging from informal through formal to literacy (40), we can examine the 'fit' between these forms of communication for the beginning reader. Table 2.6.1 indicates what we might expect to find. Two problems are immediately obvious. First, the written language material which the child initially encounters in the instructional setting will in most cases be at least one level above his informal and familiar oral language style. Second, the child from a limited language environment, which has provided little opportunity for the development of shift in a functional variety, is at a decided handicap in approaching the printed page which is written for the most part at the formal level. For example, *hafta, gonna, hadda, oughta, hasta,* and *wanna* are quite appropriate in informal conversational settings for oral language, but in written language are realized as *have to, going to, had to, ought to, has to,* and *want to* (29). The contractions *I'll, she'll, he'll,* and *they'll* are most appropriate in informal oral language situations; however, the written equivalents *I will, she will, he will,* and *they will* appear in many children's textbooks at the formal level from the child's earliest encounter with printed matter.

Table 2.6.1 Levels of functional variety in oral and written expression

Functional variety level	Oral language	Written language
Informal	Home and school language	Personal notes, letters to friends, unedited language experience stories
Formal	Classroom lectures, public speeches	School textbooks, edited language experience stories
Literary	Formal papers, speech as an art form	Literature as an art form, aesthetic dimensions of written language.

The problem, then, for the nonstandard speaker is striking when we consider that he must not only account for dialectal deviations but also levels of functional variety in the second dialect. Speakers of standard and nonstandard forms, however, must accommodate the functional variety shift from informal to formal or literary styles. As Goodman (20) has emphasized, certain oral language sequences, which result from morphophonemic rules cutting across morpheme boundaries in the flow of speech, are so common that the young speaker does not differentiate the individual components in the sequence as in *going to* (gonna), *with them* (with'm), *with him* (with'm), *must have* (must'v) and *should have* (should'v). Thus, oral language at the informal level may use one unit, while the early encounter with printed forms at the formal level may require two units. This variation must be taken into account in both the instructional program and abstract explanations of the reading process. More will be said about the problem of stylistic shift in the following discussion which considers syntactical and lexical aspects of language acquisition.

Syntactical development

The control of syntactical patterning by the preschool primary grade child has been demonstrated in various studies including those by Fraser, Bellugi, and Brown (16); Brown and Fraser (6); Strickland (55); Loban (30); Ruddell and Graves (47); and O'Donnell, Griffin, and Norris (38). These studies indicate that, by kindergarten and first grade, the child is able to comprehend sentences and produce expanded and elaborated sentences through the use of movables (words, phrases or clauses with no fixed position in the sentence) and transformed subordinating elements.

The research evidence also suggests that the developmental sequence in syntactical control extends well into and perhaps through the elementary grades. Menyuk's work (33) has identified some sequential components in children's syntax extending from nursery school into the first grade. She noted that even in the first grade some patterns such as 'if' and 'so' clauses, perfects, and nominalizations were still in the process of development. Lenneberg (28) has discussed the difficulty presented by transformations in the passive voice for the mentally retarded child. The work of Strickland (55) shows a definite relationship between sentence complexity and grade level. Loban's research (30) revealed that throughout the elementary grades the average communication unit length increased indicating a developmental sequence of complexity in sentence structure.

The detailed study by Harrell (22) compared selected language variables in the speech and writing of children aged nine, eleven, thirteen, and fifteen using a short movie as the speech and writing stimulus. The investigator found that the length of the compositions and clauses used in oral and written expression increased with age, with a large percentage of subordinate clauses being used by the older children in both written and spoken composition. The children were found to use a larger percentage of subordinate clauses in writing than in speaking. More adverb and adjective clauses were used in written compositions, while a larger number of noun clauses were used in speaking. A larger percentage of adverbial clauses, excepting those of time and cause, were used in the children's speech. The developmental increase of each language variable in relation to age was found to be greater for written compositions than for oral.

The work of O'Donnell, Griffin, and Norris (38) at kindergarten and grades one, two, three, four, and seven also lends support to the general notion of a developmental sequence of syntax acquisition in the elementary grades. These researchers have observed that some transformations (e.g., relative clause, 'The man who was wearing a coat . . .') were used much more frequently in kindergarten than in later grades while other items (e.g., noun modification by a participle, 'The man wearing a coat . . .') were more frequent in later grades. The researchers observed that such a developmental sequence would appear to be a logical one from the standpoint of transformational grammar in that many of the later constructions are derived from more complex deletion rules.

Also of interest in the O'Donnell, Griffin, and Norris research was the finding of distinct variation in the syntax of speech and writing in grades three, five, and seven. At third grade, oral expression was deemed superior to written expression in transformational complexity, while at grades five and seven the reverse was true. These findings are similar to those of the previously mentioned Harrell study and suggest that by the intermediate grades the child has some production control over stylistic variations which require more complex constructions in written expression.

By examining research which contrasts the language development of children possessing hearing deficiency with that of normal children, the relationship between oral language experiences and written language production is brought into sharper focus. Heider and Heider (23) secured written compositions based on a motion picture from a large number of deaf and hearing children ranging in age from eleven to seventeen years and eight to fourteen years, respectively. Although the deaf children were three years older, their compositions were found to resemble the less mature hearing children. The deaf children were found to use fewer numbers of words and clauses than the hearing children, while the hearing children used more compound and complex sentences with a larger number of words in coordinate and subordinate clauses, thus indicating a more advanced development in language production.

The written language of normal and defective hearing children has been examined in Templin's research (57). Children having hearing deficiencies were found to use more words in their explanations of natural phenomena than hearing children of the same age, grade, and intelligence. This finding was interpreted to reflect less adequate control over vocabulary, and perhaps syntax, rather than representing a more complex type of expression. The children with defective hearing apparently needed more words to express a concept due to low efficiency in expressing their ideas through elaborated sentences and more abstract vocabulary.

Both the Heider and Heider and the Templin studies point to a significant relationship between oral and written language development. The opportunity for oral language experience through hearing would appear to directly influence performance in written language.

The language deviations of the nonstandard speaker also result in significant grammatical variations. The previously discussed l-lessness, for example, may affect future forms where *you'll* becomes *you, he'll* becomes *he*, and *they'll* becomes *they*. Thus, when the child reads the sentence 'He will go.' as 'He go.', he is consistently translating the sentence in his dialect. An example used by Shuy (49) states that the written sentence 'John asked if Mary wore a coat.' is frequently read by the ghetto child as 'John asked did Mary wear a coat.' In this instance the substitution of *did* for *if* and *wear* for *wore* does not represent an error in reading in terms of the child's dialect. If, however, the child read 'John asked Mary if did she wear a coat.' or 'John asked Mary if she wear a coat.', the alterations do vary from the consistent nonstandard forms and would represent a reading difficulty. The child's consistent performance may thus be interpreted to indicate that he possesses a high degree of language competence in the same manner as the standard speaker of English.

An understanding of the relationship between the communication process and the standard and nonstandard syntactical forms is of importance to both the classroom practitioner and the theorist. Bernstein's research (3, 4) supports the viewpoint that the 'restricted' code associated with lower socioeconomic status and related language experiences is characterized by limited subordination and is syntactically redundant. In contrast, the 'elaborated' code uses more complex forms of subordination which can account for logical relationships and great causality. The 'elaborated' code makes provision for meaningful explication of specific topics with strangers or new group members. The contribution of syntactical factors to the 'elaborated' code would appear to be in terms of subordination and expression of complex relationships. Although these dimensions can be handled in the 'restricted' code, a definite economy is present in the utilization of the 'elaborated' code with a majority population that does not possess the competency necessary to comprehend the unique features of the 'restricted' code.

The 'elaborated' code would also be expected to make provision for easier transition from oral to written language comprehension and production particularly in terms of greater subordination control required in the stylistic shift from an informal to a formal functional variety level.

Reading comprehension

The close relationship between comprehension ability and language production receives support from a variety of studies. The research of Fraser, Bellugi, and Brown (16) supports the view that children must comprehend grammatical contrasts before they are able to produce these contrasts. The previously cited research of Strickland (55) and Loban (30) report significant relationships between children's reading and listening comprehension achievement and their demonstrated use of movables and subordination in oral language.

From the early study of mistakes in paragraph reading of sixth grade children, Thorndike (58) noted that understanding a paragraph is dependent upon the reader's selection of the right elements and synthesizing them in the right relations. The child's ability to comprehend material whether written or spoken would seem to be a function of his ability to see the relationships between key elements in the sentence. Thus, relating various subordinating elements to the central idea of the sentence is of basic importance for comprehending the discourse.

Using a 'disarranged phrase test,' Gibbons (17) studied the relationship between third grade children's ability to understand the structure of sentences and their reading achievement. She found a high correlation (0.89) between the ability to see relationships between parts of a sentence and the ability to understand the sentence, when intelligence was partialled out. A significant correlation (0.72) was also found between the ability to see relationships between parts of sentences and total reading achievement.

The importance of familiarity with syntactic patterning to reading achievement is evident in MacKinnon's research (32). In a detailed study of beginning readers he observed that children attempted to substitute syntactic patterns which they had previously read and were familiar with in place of unfamiliar patterns in their attempt to decode unfamiliar reading materials.

A study of Ruddell (43), at the fourth grade level, examined the effect on reading comprehension of written patterns of language structure which occur with high and low frequency in children's oral language. By controlling the vocabulary difficulty, sentence length and subject matter content in a series of reading passages, the relationship between reading comprehension and pattern complexity was examined. Reading comprehension scores on passages written with high frequency patterns of language structure were found to be significantly superior to comprehension scores on passages written with low frequency patterns of language structure.

The child's understanding of the sentence structure would be expected to enhance his ability to narrow alternate word meanings and thus contribute to comprehension. For example, the word *that* not only cues a noun which follows but may also clarify or emphasize the semantic nature of the noun (e.g., *That* yellow canary ate the cat. vs. *Some* yellow canary ate the cat.). Miller (35) and Miller *et al.* (36) have demonstrated that words in context following a similar grammatical pattern are perceived more accurately than when in isolation. Additional support for the importance of context in narrowing semantic possibilities is found in the research of Goodman (19). He has shown that although children may be unable to decode words in isolation, they deal successfully with the same words in a running context. These findings support the importance of contextual association which provides sufficient delimiting information to enable the child to determine the semantic role of a word and, further, to recognize and comprehend it in a sentence.

A longitudinal study by Ruddell (45, 46) has demonstrated that the sentence and paragraph meaning comprehension of first and second grade children can be significantly enhanced by emphasizing the meaning relationships between key and structural elements within and between sentences. Additionally, the doctoral dissertation research of Baele (1), which was part of the longitudinal study described above, indicated that by the end of third grade the children who had participated in the treatment stressing the relationship between key structure elements were expressing themselves in written form with longer communication units and with greater clausal depth, thus indicating control over more complex constructions and subordination in the written language performance. This research parallels in some respects the preschool oral language research of Cazden (8). Her work with two- and three-year-old children indicated that the use of full grammatical sentences in response to the children's verbal expression and the expansion of their telegraphic speech to full adult grammatical sentences resulted in an increased level of performance on several measures of grammatical development when contrasted with a control group. The 'richness of verbal stimulation' appeared to be of great import in extending grammatical control. These findings indicate that language comprehension and production can be enhanced in the preschool and early grades by placing emphasis on structural relationships which influence meaning within and between sentences.

Control of lexical components

Concept development

The child's conceptual development makes rapid progress during the preschool years, and he will recognize and possess control over many hundreds of words by his first year of school (52, 53). During this time a variety of concepts are formulated as the youngster associates common properties of an object with the object label. As Vygotsky (60) has pointed out, the preschooler calls a *cow* a *cow* because it has horns, and a *calf* a *calf* because its horns are still small, while a *dog* is called a *dog* because it is small and has no horns. Eventually the child comes to conceptualize the arbitrary nature of language itself as he understands that word labels are assigned to concepts and that a particular label may represent several concepts, depending upon its contextual use.

There is ample evidence to support the view that concepts develop along a continuum from concrete through the semiconcrete or functional to the abstract levels as illustrated in the research of Feifel and Lorge (15). The work of Russell and Saadeh (48) is also illustrative of research supporting such a continuum. These researchers contrasted student conceptual responses at grades three, six, and nine on multiple-choice questions designed to measure various levels of abstraction. They concluded that third grade children favored 'concrete' responses while sixth grade and ninth grade children favored 'functional' and 'abstract' responses. As Ervin-Tripp (14) has emphasized in her extensive research summary of child language, conceptual maturation moves from concrete referents to 'hierarchies of superordinates which may have rather vague features (e.g., mammal, vertebrate) and they [adults] speak of nonvisible referents such as politics and energy.'

Various background variables have been credited with enhancement of language performance. John and Goldstein's verbal mediation research (24) reveals that a child's verbal interaction with a mature speaker is of importance in making provision for testing tentative notions about word meanings. Such opportunity would appear to produce greater verbal control and enable the child to rely on words as mediators facilitating thought. Vygotsky (60) has suggested that the availability of adults for dialogue with the child is of great import to language acquisition. This consideration also receives support from Davis's early research (10), which revealed that in families of only children language facility was found to develop more rapidly than in families of children with siblings; and children with siblings were found to develop language facility faster than twins.

The effect of factors in the home environment on language achievement is evidenced in Milner's investigation (37). Following the selection of high and low achievers in first grade reading, a depth interview was carried out exploring the children's use of language in the home. Milner found that the high achieving children had an enriched verbal environment with more books available and were read to more often by highly esteemed adults than the low achieving children. The high scoring children also engaged in conversation with their parents more often than the low scoring children. She noted further that in many of the home environments of low scoring children a positive family atmosphere was not evident nor did the children have an adult relationship pattern established. There appeared to be little opportunity for these children to interact verbally with adults possessing adequate speech patterns and who were of high personal value to the children.

In classroom instruction the child is frequently required to provide requested information at the formal functional variety level. As Bernstein (3, 4) has emphasized, the child from the low socioeconomic environment using the 'restricted' code is required to use language in situations which he is neither equipped nor oriented to handle. This may be due not only to the past discussion of syntactical factors but also to his limited lexical control and ability to shift from an informal and intimate style developed in situations oriented toward immediate and concrete needs to a formal style characterized by abstractions which carry highly efficient explanatory power. Certainly a limited vocabulary represents a most critical factor in reading comprehension. This problem is highlighted in Metfessel's findings (34) that second grade children from concept deprived backgrounds possessed a comprehension vocabulary only one-third the magnitude of the average of their age-equivalent peers. Again, the classroom teacher and the theoretician must account for the child's lexical control if the wide range of conceptual variation is to be accounted for in practice and theory, respectively.

Comprehension strategies and objectives

The importance of a cognitive strategy to the conceptualization process has been clearly demonstrated in the research literature (7). If the language user is to participate actively in the process of communication, he must evolve a symbol-processing system which will provide for the conceptualization of his experience. This is basic to his success in examining alternate approaches to decoding a new word and in comprehending written material which requires high level inference skill. From his concept formation study with elementary school children, Kress (26) concluded that achieving readers were superior to nonachievers in their versatility and flexibility, their ability to draw inferences from relevant clues, and their ability to shift set when new standards were introduced. There is considerable research to support the relationship between language comprehension and an individual's ability to change, modify, and reorganize previously formed concepts (50).

The child's communicative objectives must also be viewed as critical to the development of his communication skills. These objectives must be of a real and meaningful nature to the child if they are to be operationalized as the individual confronts the reading material. The reading objectives should provide immediate self-direction for the child and will be of value in developing high motivation as revealed in his persistence and drive. This view also obtains support from the previously mentioned study of Kress. He has reported that achieving readers demonstrated more initiative in exhausting solutions and were found to persist in problem solving under changing conditions in contrast to the non-achieving readers. Durkin's extensive work (11, 12) with the preschool child suggests that the early reader is an individual who is serious and persistent, is curious in nature, and possesses the ability to concentrate. The research of Piekarz (39) has identified the high level reader as an individual who provides significantly more responses in interpreting a reading passage, a trait indicating greater involvement and participation. The high level reader was also found to be more objective and impersonal in synthesizing the information sought which may be interpreted to support the importance of establishing reading objectives.

Thus, an individual's cognitive strategy is seen as a method of organizing and assimilating data as well as making provision for hypothesis formulation and testing. Provision for self-directing behavior through formulation of personal and immediate communication objectives would be expected to enhance the child's participation, persistence, and drive leading to more effective language control.

Summary and recommendations

In conclusion, upon the child's entry to formal education he displays language performance which reflects a high degree of competence. Even so, however, four significant factors must be recognized and accounted for in any operational and theoretical formulation of the reading process. First, the child's ability to comprehend language precedes and exceeds his ability to produce language. Second, his language comprehension appears to be a direct function of his control over the grammatical and lexical components of the discourse. Third, his language competence and performance appear to move through a developmental sequence during the elementary school years which in some respects parallels the competency model proposed by the transformational grammarian. And, fourth, his language performance is directly related to his language environment, including the available language model and opportunity for language interaction, his comprehension strategies and objectives, and possibly maturation of his latent language structures.

Many essential informational areas which are required to explain the multitude of interactions which occur during the reading process are blank. The reading-language researcher and theoretician must carefully include the following dimensions in future research exploration:

1. A detailed mapping of the child's developmental performance in gaining control over his grammar during the elementary school years.

2. A parallel longitudinal study which examines the relationship between the child's grammatical performance and his lexical control.

3. A parallel longitudinal study which examines the relationship between his comprehension ability and his grammatical and lexical performance.

4. An intensive investigation designed to explore meaning interference which may be caused by variation in standard and nonstandard and functional varieties in language—including phonological, morphological, morphophonemic, syntactical and lexical items.

5. A study of the unique characteristics of 'language enrichment' approaches and the relationship between these characteristics and the grammatical and lexical development of standard and nonstandard speakers during the preschool and elementary school years.

6. A study of various decoding units (e.g., grapheme–phoneme, morphographeme–morphophoneme) and the relationship between these units and early reading success.

7. A parallel study which will examine the relationship between various decoding units and reading success of children speaking standard and nonstandard dialects.

These problem areas are illustrative of the types of information required in order to formulate a theory of reading which will have explanatory power. Until such information is available, our theoretical formulations of the reading process will remain extremely weak. It is obvious that we have far to go.

References

1 Baele, Ernest R., 'The Effect of Primary Reading Programs Emphasizing Language Structure as Related to Meaning Upon Children's Written Language Achievement at the Third Grade Level', unpublished doctoral dissertation, University of California at Berkeley, 1968.

2 Berko, Jean, 'The child's learning of English morphology', *Word*, 14 (1958), 140–77.

3 Bernstein, Basil, 'Social structure, language, and learning', *Educational Research*, 3 (1961), 163–76.

4 Bernstein, Basil, 'Elaborated and restricted codes: their social origins and some consequences', *American Anthropologist*, 66 (2) (1964), 55–69.

5 Brearley, Molly and Hitchfield, Elizabeth, *A Teacher's Guide to Reading Piaget*, Routledge & Kegan Paul, 1966.

6 Brown, Roger and Fraser, Colin, 'The acquisition of syntax', in U. Bellugi and R. W. Brown (eds), *The Acquisition of Language*, Monographs of the Society for Research in Child Development, 29 (1964), 43–79.

7 Bruner, J., Goodnow, J. and Austin, G., *A Study of Thinking*, N.Y., Wiley, 1956.

8 Cazden, Courtney B., 'Environmental Assistance to the Child's Acquisition of Grammar', unpublished doctoral dissertation, Harvard University, 1965.

9 Chomsky, Noam, 'Review of Skinner's *Verbal Behavior*', *Language*, 35 (1959), 26–58.

10 Davis, Edith A., *The Development of Linguistic Skill in Twins, Singletons with Siblings, and Only Children from Ages Five to Ten Years*, University of Minnesota Press, 1937.

11 Durkin, Dolores, 'Children who learn to read before grade one', *Reading Teacher*, 14 (January 1961), 163–6.

12 Durkin, Dolores, 'The achievement of preschool readers: two longitudinal studies', *Reading Research Quarterly*, 1 (summer 1966), 5–36.

13 Ervin, Susan M. and Miller, W. R., 'Language development', in H. Stevenson (ed.), *Child Psychology*, 62nd Yearbook of the National Society for the Study of Education, University of Chicago Press, 1963, 108–43.

14 Ervin-Tripp, Susan, 'Language development', *Review of Child Development Research*, Russell Sage Foundation, 1967, 55–105.

15 Feifel, H. and Lorge, I. B., 'Qualitative differences in the vocabulary responses of children', *Journal of Educational Psychology*, 43 (1962), 170–4.

16 Fraser, Colin, Bellugi, Ursula and Brown, Roger, 'Control of grammar in imitation, comprehension, and production', *Journal of Verbal Learning and Verbal Behavior*, 2 (August 1963), 121–35.

17 Gibbons, Helen D., 'Reading and sentence elements', *Elementary English Review*, 18 (February 1941), 42–6.

18 Gibson, Eleanor J. *et al.*, 'The role of grapheme–phoneme corres-pondences in the perception of words', *American Journal of Psychology*, 75 (1962), 554–70.
19 Goodman, K. S., 'A linguistic study of cues and miscues in reading', *Elementary English*, 42 (1965), 639–43.
20 Goodman, K. S., 'Words and morphemes in reading', in K. Goodman and J. Fleming (eds), *Psycholinguistics and the Teaching of Reading*, Newark, Del., International Reading Association, 1969, 25–33.
21 Gough, Philip B., 'The limitations of imitations: the problem of language acquisition', in Alexander Frazier (ed.), *New Directions in Elementary English*, Champaign, Ill., National Council of Teachers of English, 1967.
22 Harrell, Lester E. Jr., 'An inter-comparison of the quality and rate of the development of the oral and written language in children', *Monographs of the Society for Research in Child Development*, 22 (1957).
23 Heider, F. K. and Heider, Grace M., 'A comparison of sentence structure of deaf and hearing children', *Psychological Monographs*, 52 (1940), 42–103.
24 John, Vera P. and Goldstein, Leo S., 'The social context of language acquisition', *Merrill-Palmer Quarterly of Behavior and Development*, 10 (1964), 265–74.
25 Kenyon, John S., 'Cultural levels and functional varieties of English', *College English*, 10 (October 1948), 31–6.
26 Kress, R. A., 'An Investigation of the Relationship Between Concept Formation and Achievement in Reading', unpublished doctoral dissertation, Temple University, 1955.
27 Lenneberg, Eric, *Biological Foundations of Language*, N.Y., Wiley, 1967.
28 Lenneberg, Eric, 'Speech as a motor skill with special reference to nonaphasic disorders', *Monographs of the Society for Research in Child Development*, 29 (1964), 115–27.
29 Lindsay, Marie R., 'A Descriptive Exploration of the Growth and Development of Spontaneous Oral Vocabulary of Elementary School Children', unpublished doctoral dissertation, University of California, 1969.
30 Loban, Walter D., *The Language of Elementary School Children*, Champaign, Ill., National Council of Teachers of English, 1963.
31 McCarthy, Dorothea A., 'Language development in children', in L. Carmichael (ed.), *Manual of Child Psychology*, N.Y., Wiley, 1954, 492–630.
32 MacKinnon, A. R., *How Do Children Learn to Read?*, Toronto, Copp Clark, 1959.
33 Menyuk, Paula, 'Syntactic structures in the language of children', *Child Development*, 34 (June 1963), 407–22.
34 Metfessel, Newton S., in J. L. Frost and G. R. Hawkes (eds), *The Disadvantaged Child*, N.Y., Houghton-Mifflin, 1966.
35 Miller, G. A., 'Some psychological studies of grammar', *American Psychologist*, 17 (1962), 748–62.

36 Miller, G. A., Heise, G. A. and Lichten, W., 'The intelligibility of speech as a function of the context of the test material', *Journal of Experimental Psychology*, 41 (1951), 329–35.

37 Milner, Esther, 'A study of the relationship between reading readiness in grade one school children and patterns of parent-child interaction', in H. Stevenson (ed.), *Child Psychology*, 62nd Yearbook of the National Society for Study of Education, University of Chicago Press, 1963, 108–43.

38 O'Donnell, Roy C., Griffin, William J. and Norris, Raymond C., *Syntax of Kindergarten and Elementary School Children: A Transformational Analysis*, Campaign, Ill., National Council of Teachers of English, 1967.

39 Piekarz, Josephine A., 'Getting meaning from reading', *Elementary School Journal*, 56 (1956), 303–9.

40 Pooley, Robert C., *Teaching English Usage*, N.Y., Appleton-Century, 1946.

41 Reed, D. W., 'A theory of language, speech and writing', in Priscilla Tyler (ed.), *Linguistics and Reading* (Highlights of the 1965 Preconvention Institutes), Newark, Del., International Reading Association, 1966, 4–25.

42 Rodgers, T. S., *Linguistic Considerations in the Design of the Stanford Computer-Based Curriculum in Initial Reading*, Institute for Mathematical Studies in the Social Sciences, Technical Report No. 111, USOE Grant number OE5-10-050, 1967.

43 Ruddell, Robert B., 'Effect of the similarity of oral and written patterns of language structure on reading comprehension', *Elementary English*, 42 (April 1965), 403–10.

44 Ruddell, Robert B., 'Psycholinguistic implications for a systems of communication model', in K. Goodman and J. Fleming (eds), *Psycholinguistics and the Teaching of Reading*, Newark, Del., International Reading Association, 1969, 61–78.

45 Ruddell, Robert B., 'Reading instruction in first grade with varying emphasis on the regularity of grapheme–phoneme correspondences and the relation of language structure to meaning', *Reading Teacher*, 19 (May 1966), 653–60.

46 Ruddell, Robert B., *Second and Third Year of a Longitudinal Study of Four Programs of Reading Instruction with Varying Emphasis on the Regularity of Grapheme–Phoneme Correspondences and the Relation of Language Structure to Meaning*, U.S. Department of Health, Education and Welfare, Office of Education Cooperative Research Projects no. 3099 and 78085, 1968.

47 Ruddell, Robert B. and Graves, Barbara W., 'Socioethnic status and the language achievement of first grade children', *Elementary English*, May 1967, 730–9.

48 Russell, David H. and Saadeh, I. Q., 'Qualitative Levels in Children's Vocabularies', *Journal of Educational Psychology*, 43 (1962), 170–4.

49 Shuy, Roger W., 'Some language and cultural differences in a theory of reading', in K. Goodman and J. Fleming (eds), *Psycholinguistics and*

the Teaching of Reading, Newark, Del., International Reading Association, 1969, 34–47.

50 Singer, Harry, 'Conceptualization in learning to read: new frontiers in college-adult reading', in G. B. Shick and M. M. May (eds), *15th Yearbook of the National Reading Conference*, Milwaukee, 1966, 116–32.

51 Skinner, B. F., *Verbal Behavior*, N.Y., Appleton-Century-Crofts, 1957.

52 Smith, Mary K., 'Measurement of the size of general English vocabulary through the elementary grades and high school', *Genetic Psychology Monographs*, 24 (1941), 311–45.

53 Smith, Medorah E., 'An investigation of the development of the sentence and the extent of vocabulary in young children', *Studies in Child Welfare* (State University of Iowa), 5 (1926), 28–71.

54 Staats, Arthur W. and Staats, Carolyn K., *Complex Human Behavior*, N.Y., Holt, Rinehart & Winston, 1964.

55 Strickland, Ruth G., *The Language of Elementary School Children: its Relationship to the Language of Reading Textbooks and the Quality of Reading of Selected Children*, Bulletin of the School of Education, 38 (July 1962), Indiana University.

56 Templin, Mildred, *Certain Language Skills in Children*, University of Minnesota Institute of Child Welfare Monographs, University of Minnesota Press, 1957.,

57 Templin, Mildred C., *The Development of Reasoning in Children with Normal and Defective Hearing*, University of Minnesota Press, 1950.

58 Thorndike, E. L., 'Reading and reasoning: a study of mistakes in paragraph reading', *Journal of Educational Psychology*, 8 (1917), 323–32.

59 Venezky, R. F., 'English orthography: its graphical structure and its relation to sound', *Reading Research Quarterly*, 2 (spring 1967), 75–106.

60 Vygotsky, Lev S., *Thought and Language*, MIT Press, 1962.

61 Wardhaugh, R., 'Linguistics–reading dialogue', *Reading Teacher*, 21 (February 1968), 432–41.

Section 3 From Method to Material

How the reading process is defined is inextricably linked to the teaching method, and the teaching materials are the result of the reading method adopted. If, for instance, one views the reading process in the initial stages as primarily a matter of decoding written into spoken symbols, then the method adopted will be one emphasising sound/letter relationships, and materials will be designed focusing on such relationships. In many cases the materials produced do not explicitly state the model on which they are based, but behind any set of materials used (from the basal reading scheme to teacher-made flash cards) there are assumptions about the way a child learns to read. So, for example, a reading book which includes only twenty words repeated in similar sentences ('Here comes Janet! Here comes John!') assumes that the beginner reader needs to have a tightly controlled reading input, and, incidentally, that structure comes first, with sense a poor second. And if all the words share similar features, e.g. *tough*, *rough*, en*ough*, but not *cough* or thr*ough*, then an assumption has been made that children learn best by learning constant sound/spelling relationships before learning the variability of such relationships.

Different methods have their advocates and their opponents. It is important for the teacher to be familiar with the arguments and the evidence, and to recognise the assumptions on which sets of materials are based. Only with such a background can the teacher critically evaluate the classroom materials and select suitable ones for his/her situation.

The opening article of this section by Elizabeth Goodacre (3.1) describes and evaluates the major trends in reading instruction, showing how these methods have developed from notions about both reading and the learning process. The alphabetic approach is shown to emphasise 'recognition of new words rather than the grasp of meaning' and 'relies heavily on the conditioning aspect of the learning process'. Synthetic methods (phonic, whole word and sentence methods) are all based on the premise that reading can be mastered if the components are treated in isolation. While word and sentence methods do emphasise the importance of reading for meaning, 'they underrate the skill's complexity . . . [and] . . . the importance of being able to use reading in a flexible manner'. In the light of the Section 2 articles (particularly 2.2 and 2.3), such methods can be thought of as concentrating on the decoding skills without full consideration of what the written word means to the child and how reading can be made a meaningful experience. The language-experience approach, as outlined by Goodacre, aims to allow children to 'observe the relationship of speaking to reading and writing' and 'is very dependent upon children attaching importance to writing and reading as valid means of expression'. Formalised spelling instruction and vocabulary development come later. Readers might like to re-read Carroll's article (2.2) and decide to what extent the differences between approaches are really differences in the *order* in which skills are taught.

While much attention has been given to beginning reading and the development of fluency, relatively little concern is voiced about how one needs to read to achieve desired reading outcomes. This imbalance needs to be corrected.

Marion Jenkinson's article (3.2) goes some way towards righting the balance by emphasising the need for a reading programme which continues throughout school life: 'continuous development in reading is now . . . seen as essential for continuing employment in a technological society.' She indicates ways in which pupils can be encouraged to go beyond mere identification of words by drawing upon their experience, the reading context and by developing dictionary skills. The pupil, she emphasises, needs to acknowledge the reciprocal relationship between the reader and the printed page. For example, she notes that 'to derive full comprehension, a reader must first become the co-author, suspending judgement until he has absorbed the concepts presented, and then scrutinizing and assessing the ideas in the light of his own knowledge and experience.' For pupils fully to exploit their reading skills involves adopting flexible strategies suited to both the content and the purpose of their reading. Such an approach to reading cannot be restricted to the reading class but rather must 'be applied to learning in all areas of the curriculum which demand reading of any type of material'.

Methods and materials cannot be looked at in isolation—they are used with pupils and pupils are not *tabulae rasae* on which the three Rs can be inscribed. Downing (2.4) pointed out that methods need to be fitted to the individual child and, from a slightly different perspective, Rebecca Barr (3.3) shows the effect that instructional material has on the child's interpretation of the reading task. The child not only affects what will be learnt but is also affected by what is taught. Barr contends that we can learn how the child reads only by observing him, not by analysing the processes of competent readers (cf. Goodman, 2.5). By looking at the behaviour of readers (e.g. as shown in miscue analysis) one can sometimes 'determine the past instructional influences on a child's reading skill'. A review of research indicates that the initial teaching strategy, such as phonics or word blending, appears to determine how subsequent information about print is used.

The implications of Barr's thesis need careful consideration. If we take as our aim the development of flexible reading strategies in children which allow them to make predictions about word sequences based on the context and their experience, then initial teaching strategies should form the foundation of such reading flexibility. Phonic approaches, for instance, will allow children to produce 'non-words'—that is they will not equip children with the means of identifying the meaning of unfamiliar words. The design and choice of teaching materials must take into account the 'reciprocal relationship between the child's mental structures and instruction', and teachers should ensure that the learning strategies that the child develops are the ones best suited to the process of reading.

John Downing's article (3.4) again draws our attention to the child as an individual in his own right. For the child the written language is an abstract form which he does not necessarily see as useful or meaningful (cf. Smith, 2.3). Children come to the task of reading with a 'lack of any specific expectancies of what reading [is] going to be like, of what the activity consist[s] in, of the purpose and the use of it' (Reid).

Downing's interviews with thirteen children showed that young children have only a vague notion of the nature of the reading task. (Though, as he admits, it is difficult to tell how much they understood but could not express.) It is often taken for granted that the child readily understands the technical terms used during reading instruction. Terms such as 'sound', 'word', and 'sentence' were found by Reid (1966) and Downing (1969) to be incompletely understood by five-year-olds. Even as adults we tend to use such terms rather loosely—you might like to imagine yourself in Reid's experiment and decide what you would call 'sounds' and 'words'. Failure to consider the child's view of the reading task may cause at best confusion in the early stages or, at worst, failure to grasp the meaning and purpose of reading. Read beside Barr's article (3.3),

Downing's paper forces one to re-evaluate the instructional materials and the methods of teaching with which we confront the child. We must concern ourselves with what the child *brings* to the task of reading and what he *takes* from the reading lesson.

3. 1 Methods of teaching reading

Elizabeth J. Goodacre

The main methods of teaching reading are usually understood to be the alphabetic, the phonic, the 'whole-word' or 'look-and-say' and the sentence method. However, the growing emphasis upon the importance of individual differences has led to the discussion in the literature on method of two approaches—the 'language-experience' approach and 'individualized reading'.

The alphabetic method

By this method it is assumed that familiarity with the *form* and *names* of *letters* will help children to recognize and pronounce words. By constant repetition of the letter-names (e.g. 'dee-oe-gee'), this spelling out of words will enable the learner to become familiar not only with the form and name of individual letters but also become accustomed to meeting certain letter-strings or letter-clusters, the component parts of many words. Generally, the main emphasis was laid on the recognition of new words rather than the grasp of meaning. To this extent this method relies heavily on the conditioning aspect of the learning process.

The difficulty with isolating and discussing particular methods is that one never knows exactly how far such methods are successful in their ostensible aims and how far they may inadvertently be teaching other helpful sub-skills. Also, as Diack (1965) has pointed out, it is hard to tell how far specific methods are differentiated one from another. It is not very far from teaching the *names* of the letters to teaching their *sounds*. As Diack notes 'of alphabetic and phonic

Source: *Children and Learning to Read*, Routledge & Kegan Paul, 1971, pp. 25–43.

methods it can indeed be said that "thin partitions do their bounds divide"'. Children make their own deductions and in the case of teaching the letter names, it is quite possible for the bright child to realize that there is a fairly close correspondence between the name of the letter and its sound for *some* of the letters. This can help them to realize that there is a code involved in learning to read and to pronounce initial letters which can be helpful for trying to read unfamiliar words.

Durrell (1968) has suggested that for all the consonants (the letters of the alphabet with the exception of the vowels *a, e, i, o, u*) letter-names, except for the letters *h, q, w* and *y*, contain their phonemes or sounds plus an extraneous vowel, and the names of the vowels are the 'long' sound *ae, ee, ie, oe, ue*. In the names of the 'long-e' letters; e.g. *b, c, d, g, p, t, u, z* (this last in American though not in English), the phoneme comes in front of the vowel in the letter-name—*b-ee, s-ee, etc.*; to say these letters the child uses exactly the same speech mechanisms as in giving the 'sounds'. The names of the 'short-e' letters, e.g. *f, l, m, n, s, x*—have a similar value, with the phoneme following the vowel in the name; e.g. *eh-l, eh-m*. The names *r, k,* and *j* also contain their phonemes or letter-sounds. Durrell considers that the close association between name and sound in 22 of the 26 letters is a great help for word recognition and pronunciation. He cites work which showed that when the letter-name was known, the sound of the letter was easier to learn.

With these considerations in mind, it is interesting to note that in studies of children who learned to read before going to school, interest in and concern with letters was found to be positively associated with early success in reading (Durkin's studies, 1964, etc.). The American government spent an enormous amount of money on a research programme called First Grade Reading Programs which produced as the most important finding the fact that no one method was superior to any other and that the really important factor was the understanding and competence of the teacher. However, another interesting finding was that the best single predictor of success in the beginning stages of learning to read was a test of the letter-names (Bond and Dykstra, 1967). Indeed, work by Hillerich (1967) has suggested that knowledge of the letter-names at the beginning of schooling is a better predictor of later reading achievement than even the scores of a specially designed reading readiness test.

However, such findings should not be interpreted as indicating a causal relationship, or that it is therefore necessary that children must be taught the letter-names in order to read. In trying to discover how children learn to read, Muehl (1962) found that children who were taught letter-names experienced an initial handicap in identifying nonsense syllables because, in trying to identify the printed symbol, the child had to pass through an intermediate step of saying the letter-name before he arrived at the beginning sound of the word. Certainly, many teachers prefer not to teach the letter-names, or to postpone this until after the child has acquired an extensive sight vocabulary.

Porter and Popp (1967) prior to development of a teaching device called an alpha-board made many attempts to teach school beginners the letter-names. They used Lotto-type games, card sorting and spelling games, stories about the letters, and 'alphabet' songs. Their efforts were largely unsuccessful, but their comments are useful. Children could find a letter named by the researcher more easily at this stage than they could name the letters themselves. The researchers came to the conclusion that the popular 'alphabet song' can lead to very serious confusions and that the alphabetical sequence, particularly at the beginning of the alphabet, generated auditory and visual discrimination difficulties; e.g. *b* and *d*. They concluded that letter-names were really 'nonsense syllables' to most of these young children, but a useful concept was to teach the visible difference between *letters* and *words*. Certainly letters whose names are very similar should not be taught at the same time, as this is much too confusing for young children.

It has been suggested that the explanation for the high relationship between knowledge of letter-names and reading success is that a test of letter-names is really a very crude or naïve intelligence test. It measures such things as (1) the child's exposure to print; (2) the amount of attention he has received at home; (3) his ability to retain knowledge gained from these experiences with letters; (4) his ability to pay attention and look closely at letter forms. A recent review of the various readiness measures for predicting reading achievement has suggested that the child's ability to 'attend', to look closely and see differences, and his level of oral development and therefore use of language concepts are factors in reading readiness which need to be more closely investigated. Chall (1967) has also drawn attention to the importance of letter knowledge as a clue to the child's cognitive development.

> The alphabet is a code, an abstraction, perhaps the first that a child learns (and one that is valued because adults value it). Pointing to and naming a letter, or writing a letter, at an early age is quite different from pointing to or drawing a picture of a cat, a truck, or a tree. The child who can identify or reproduce a letter engages in symbolic representation, to borrow a phrase from Jerome Bruner, while the child who is working with a picture of an actual object engages in iconic representation. When the child engages in symbolic representation, he is already practising a *higher form of intellectual behavior*. [my italics].

Work by Wheelock and Silvaroli (1967) suggests that young children can be trained to make instant responses of recognition to the capital letters. What is of interest though is that the training in letter recognition appeared to be of most benefit to the children who came from lower socio-economic homes. Matching letter-shapes, possibly even naming the letters (but not in alphabetic order), are means of helping the young child to pay attention to the letters, and this must be of help in observing differences in the *order* of letters in words and the use of letters as clues to beginning sounds of words. We know from the study of Marchbanks and Levin (1965) that specific letters formed the most salient cues in children's word identification. The 'standing out' quality of first and last letters seemed to be related to the fact that each is isolated on one side by white space, whereas middle letters are 'lost' in the word form. Thus, print and words themselves draw the child's attention to the importance of beginning and end letters, i.e. the positioning of letters as well as their shape.

It has been suggested that the alphabetic method is of limited usefulness for reading words and sentences, and it has been long held that it is a mechanical and difficult method, and that at its heyday it produced uninteresting reading material; e.g. *the cat sat on the mat*. However, we are now at the stage of considering *how* methods can be adapted to children's cognitive development. The teacher's ability to work out means of simplifying the learning task for each child, building on whatever information or knowledge the pupil already possesses, is an important factor.

We know that *some* children will, by the time of beginning school, be interested in letters and how they differ one from another (some boys can easily distinguish letter forms, even names, from experience with car number plates, or engine numbers). In talking about letters, they must be called something and probably at *this* stage their names are the most appropriate term. As Reid (1966) has pointed out, children go through a process of differentiating symbols from pictures, numbers from letters, and letters from words. As she says, later they come to realize that there are different kinds of letters—capital and lower case, and different kinds of words (e.g. the confusing use of the term *name* for children's names, letter-names, etc.). However it seems fairly obvious that very young children need plenty of experience in playing with *letter-forms*, so as to become familiar with their shape and learn their correct orientation; e.g. which way round. Tracing round wooden letters, feeling cut-out letter forms in felt stuck on to paper or card; matching small case letters in in-set trays; matching capital letters—possibly matching capital and lower case letters; making familiar words on felt boards from cellograph letters, or plastigraph letters on plastigraph boards. Some teachers use a system whereby children act out letter-shapes so the memory of the shape is firmly implanted.

The phonic method

In this method, the *sounds* of letters are substituted for the letter-names.

Originally, the sounds of individual letters were taught but mainly in the last decade, linguists have pointed out that letter-sounds are never produced singly but in the context of words, and that usually the positioning of the letter determines its particular sound. If individual letters are sounded there is a tendency for *uh* to be added, so that one gets the distorted pronunciation *huh, ruh*, and *guh*. When the sounds of individual letters are 'blended' or synthesized, one gets the word *bat* sounding more like *barter*, which can be very confusing to some children.

Certain educationists have suggested a more suitable synthesis is achieved by beginning with a consonant–vowel combination (since consonants cannot be accurately sounded except with a vowel), such as *c-at* or *ca-t*. Durrell (1968) favours the former rather than the latter practice. He cites a study of the abilities of school beginners to read unfamiliar words in which it was found that even those children who were taught the *ca-t* approach could get from *cap* to *nap* with greater ease than from *man* to *map*. There are not all that number of three-letter words with medial short vowels in the ordinary child's vocabulary, but *at* is a fairly reliable generalization in comparison with *ca* which can say different things in *came, call, car, care, catch*. Durrell claims that in most of the 225 phonograms from which stem many of the words familiar to young children, the vowel is stable; relatively few change vowel sounds with the *initial* consonant, in the way that the *ant* phonogram changes in the word *want*. Then, of course, the same sound cluster can be spelled in different ways, e.g. the *air* sound more often than not being spelled *car, are, air*. However, this may not be such a difficulty for children when they are *reading* since context can help to indicate the pronunciation if the word is already in the child's oral vocabulary.

Problems and controversies have, and still do, abound in the teaching of phonics. Probably the one that must be dealt with first is the difference in *approach* to the teaching of phonics, since many of the criticisms in the past levelled at phonics as a method, in practice, relate to the approach adopted by the teacher. One type of approach is to introduce children to pictures of an *a*pple, *e*lephant, *I*ndian, *o*strich (not bird!), and *u*mbrella, so that the children are familiar with the short vowel sounds through this use of key pictures. These key pictures carry a phonic clue which provides information about the beginning letter's sound and not its name. This is followed by more pictures of a *squirrel, monkey, fox, rabbit, goat, nest, bear, tiger, pig* and *dog*, to illustrate the more common sounds of the consonants *s, m, f, r, g, n, b, t, f* and *d*. Once the short vowel sounds and the sounds of these ten consonants are learned they are blended together, first into syllables (*su, so, si, se, sa*), then into words (*sun, sob, sit, set, sat*). These initial exercises are followed by reading matter of the following sort (Hay and Wingo, 1948):

> Sam sat in the sun
> The sun is good for Sam.

As can be seen the procedure tends to be a deductive one. That is, beginning with generalizations about the sounds of letters (which may or may not use *picture* clues of objects which may or may not be familiar to the individual child), these are then applied to the pronunciation of specific syllables and words. It tends to be a *synthetic* process in that it initially concentrates on parts of words which are later combined into whole words. As with the confusion between letter-names of similar sound or letters which are similar in form, it may be difficult for some children to differentiate between similar word parts and three-letter words, i.e. words of similar length.

Sometimes in this use of phonics, reading of interesting material is delayed until the pupils have achieved a high degree of mastery of the 'sounds' and are competent at word building. Critics of this way of teaching phonics instance the difficulties of combining letter-sounds into meaningful words by synthesizing, which may lead to awkward articulation and a slower rate of reading. Although the training or conditioning element in the approach can lead to the discovery of phonic generalizations, it is not yet clear how far these expectations can be substantiated in ordinary classroom reading materials, as distinct from the specially designed phonic readers; i.e. what degree of transfer operates.

Also, how valid are these phonic rules?

Clymer (1963) and Bailey (1967) found the two-vowel rule 'the first vowel says its name, the second is usually silent' sometimes stated as 'when two vowels go out walking, the first does all the talking', to be more often wrong than right. They found that others among these so-called 'rules' lack desirable dependability. Programming a computer to spell, some researchers devised 111 vowel rules and 92 consonant rules, but the computer managed to spell correctly only half the 17,000 words demanded of it.

Along with the development of 'sight' methods in the late 1920s in America went a 'new' method of teaching the letter-sounds called *intrinsic*, or *incidental* phonics. By this approach the pupil learned a small sight vocabulary of words (words recognized on sight), usually personally meaningful, and then began to compare these words for similarities and thus to extract from the experience valid phonic generalizations; e.g. when a child knows *my, mother, must* and *me*, or *baby, big* and *baker*, he is ready to make generalizations regarding the sounds of the consonants *m* and *b*. Then as more words become familiar, more generalizations can be made about the sounds associated with other letters or letter groupings. This particular way of progressing in phonics can be termed *inductive* or *analytic*, because specific words are used to discover a generalization regarding the sounds of letters, and whole words are analysed to identify and find recurring letters and their associated sounds. Teachers using this approach play the familiar games 'I Spy' and 'I Went Shopping' (I bought *butter, bananas* and *beef*); they encourage children to collect words beginning with the same sound; list the children's names under the same beginning sound; make displays of objects beginning with the same sound; have children sort and classify toys or small objects beginning with similar but different sounds; e.g. *v* and *f*, or *t* and *f*—difference between voiced and voiceless consonants, between two voiceless consonants. When a child making his own list of words beginning with the consonant *g* comes to the teacher with *ginger* and says it does not begin the same way as the previous word *game*, he has discovered for himself that certain letters have more than one sound, and he may be able to go on after this insight to discover that *c* has two sounds, but *y* has three, and the vowels have many. The last of these generalizations may not be quite the problem adults have considered it, because one researcher has demonstrated that one can get on quite well in reading when dashes are substituted for vowels!

McCullough (1968) writing on balanced programmes has stressed the importance of achieving a balance between teacher guidance and pupils not only discovering but also *using* generalizations about letters and their sounds.

> The child who must do something with what he has learned learns it better because he knows he will have to use it, and he learns it better because he does use it. If the child who has discovered the sound represented by the letter *m* by means of the teacher's models, *milk* and *man*, then has to record his own induction with his own models (such as *mouse* and *match*, which he chooses), he will remember what he has learned better and will have a record from which to retrieve it if he forgets it.

Children can discover a lot of things for themselves about words and their sounds, as they experiment with a word's *head, body* and *tail*, rearranging and twisting them to suit their fancy. This follows on easily from such commercially produced games as 'Jumbled bodies' or 'Misfits'. *Pan* can be turned into *fan, fan* into *fat*, and *bill* into *bell*, or he can try to make new words out of old ones such as making *star* turn into *rats*, or by adding a letter make a *can* into a *cane*, but the effects are limited and usually this word play appeals most to the bright child who studies the structure, changes it and experiments with it in a trial-and-error way.

It should be noted that *phonics* is a method of applying what we know about the study of speech (phonetics) to the reading process and, as such, it involves bringing into play not only the auditory and visual senses, but the ability to combine these two sensory modes of thought. *Phonetics* on the other hand is concerned with classification, description and articulation of the *sounds of speech* and there is a means by which one symbol can represent one sound (International Phonetic Alphabet) but this is not the traditional alphabet. Pitman's i.t.a. or the Augmented Roman Alphabet endeavours to produce a symbol for each sound, and so ensure phoneme/grapheme correspondence; one symbol for each sound. It is useful to make this distinction between phonics and phonetics, as writers, particularly linguists such as Fries, are conscious of the confusion in the literature on reading methods between the two terms.

The word method

The difficulty with categorizing methods and trying to describe them briefly is that one is tempted continually to describe them historically in order to place them in some sort of perspective and to cover the many criticisms or qualifications which can be made by the informed reader. Hunter Diack (1965) does this in a brilliant *tour de force*, and the reader unfamiliar with this historical survey of reading methods is recommended to read it for elaboration of the points being made in this chapter.

As reading research at various times concentrates on different aspects of the reading process, so different methods emphasize different factors in the process, and as a method becomes more acceptable one sees a hardening of its new and valuable 'insight' into the reading process, into rigid dogma which usually justifies teaching techniques as soulless and ill thought out as those the 'new' method was intended to change.

The word method or 'whole-word' or 'look-and-say' way of teaching reading stresses the word and not the letter-name or sound, as has been used as a means of trying to make the reading process more meaningful to children. At least this is the intention and in some ways the popularity or the revival of word methods has provided evidence of the realization by teachers and educationists that the *letter* methods can become boring and meaningless for children if taken to the extreme. In the word methods, it is thought that children's attention can be drawn to an element which is already familiar through the child's speech. Children will see the difference between words on the basis of length and the shape or configuration of the words, and then easily be able to recognize words using such clues. By using words familiar to the child, that is, in the child's own oral vocabulary, it would be possible to get away from the difficult-to-transfer learning situation of phonic word building and blending, and the spelling units of the alphabetic method. Thus children would be more highly motivated to read, and not bored by the 'delayed reading' element which can exist with the use of letter methods, e.g. the synthetic (building up) approach rather than analytic (analysing from known words).

It is useful to distinguish between 'whole-word' and 'look-and-say' methods. Using the former it is possible to associate picture and 'name', that is pictorial representation and the word which stands for it, so that the child is conditioned to accept that the image and the symbol of the word are related. Similarly, objects in the environment can be labelled. This is usually possible only for nouns, and difficulties of interpretation and language experience interfere when it comes to concrete or pictorial representation of verbs, adverbs, adjectives, etc. For this reason 'look-and-say' becomes a means by which the teacher or the adult can tell what the particular word says. As Flesch (1955), a bitter critic of the word method, has insisted, it is in certain circumstances a crude form of conditioning.

> It goes straight back to Pavlov and his famous salivating dogs . . . It was not long before the conditioned reflex psychologists . . . found out that Pavlov's discovery can be used to train a human being . . . Of course you can teach a child to read that way—nothing easier than that. You show him the word *chicken* seventeen times in succession, each time in connection with a picture of a chicken and an explanation by the teacher that this combination of letters means a chicken . . . Don't you see how degrading the whole process is? The child is never told *why* this heap of letters means 'chicken'.

Obviously this method provides little technique for deciphering unfamiliar words. In some classrooms one can see a line of children waiting to be told 'what the word says'. In large classes, the use of this method does produce particular difficulties. Children are encouraged to recognize words by their shape or pattern, but also to think what particular word would fit into the context. I remember reading with a small boy who stuck on a three-letter word beginning with *b*. The reading material was about a washing line of clothes with an appropriate illustration. Foolishly ignoring the picture 'clue' I said, 'Now you think what's on your Mum's line at home that begins with that letter.' A look of anticipated success passed across his face as he cried, 'Mum's bra'. The word in the text was *bib*.

Terms such as 'configuration', 'word-pattern', 'total form' and 'internal characteristics' tend to be used in books on this method rather than the word 'letters' and as Diack (1965) has pointed out 'the mental attitude of thinking about words as not being primarily composed of letters is reinforced'. Not looking closely enough at the letters in words can lead to individual letters being ignored and to guessing; e.g. *bra* for *bib*.

One would have supposed that not being confined by the restrictions of only using regularly phonic words (*mat, hop,* etc.), would lead to the production of more interesting *reading materials* firmly based on children's interests. However, if letter clues are underplayed, it does become difficult for the child to recognize easily the few hundred words necessary for the telling of an interesting story. For children to recognize even 'interest' words it is found necessary to *frequently repeat* them. Also if one has *fewer* words it is still easier. This has led to readers or primers with strict vocabulary control, which in practice tend to be few words frequently repeated. Beginning books in schemes have come to have less than twenty words, and Diack (1965) carrying the idea firmly to its logical conclusion has asked whether even these twenty words are necessary. 'From one point of view, no. The pictures tell what story there is and if reading is *at all stages* a matter of getting meaning from the printed page, then those twenty words are all of them unnecessary. So the wordless method had virtually arrived.'

Although there is insufficient space here to go into it in detail, the Gestalt theory of learning has been used as the theoretical basis for word methods, and basic ideas in this area of thinking are the importance of the *whole*, the innate organization of perception, and the insight or sudden understanding of personal experience. It was thought that young children could recognize the whole word *aeroplane* long before they knew its component letters—that there was a tendency for individuals to perceive 'in wholes'. To a large extent this type of thinking ignores the time element and the effects of previous learning. Indeed skilled readers and adults may part see a word then read it whole. The process or operation of the skill becomes so automatic it is difficult to reflect and realize how the skill has developed. The method has a certain element of imitation in it and to this extent, it can be simply the adult forgetting the difficulties of childhood saying, 'Do as I do, this is the way', and failing to provide the child with the real key to reading, means of visual and auditory analysis. Stressing reading for meaning is much more

programmed reading research project (1)', unpublished duplicated paper, Harvard University.

Reid, J. F. (1966) 'Learning to think about reading', *Educational Research*, 9 (1), 56–62.

Wheelock, W. H. and Silvaroli, N. M. (1967) 'An investigation of visual discrimination training for beginning readers', *Journal of Typographic Research*, 1, 147–56.

3. 2 Ways of teaching
Marion D. Jenkinson

Much has been written about the teaching of reading. No area of the school curriculum has received as much attention or created an equal amount of controversy. Through the centuries there have been many shifts in the methods of teaching reading and there have been special pleas for specific types of training. It is, however, within this century that the need for a reading programme that continues throughout the school life of children has been recognized. Such a programme is necessary so that those who achieve a functional level of literacy do not lapse into semi-literacy. Maintaining literacy has been recognized to be important in terms of achieving higher levels of academic proficiency, but continuous development in reading is now also seen as essential for continuing employment in a technological society.

Though the specifics of teaching reading at the initial level will vary according to the language and the type of alphabet, the establishment of relationship of correspondence between the sound and the symbol usually receives the main emphasis at this point. Yet it is essential that even at the beginning stage the reader realizes that the mere ability to say a word is not sufficient. He must be able to understand the meaning that is presented to him through the symbols. The emphasis in the reading programme will shift once competence in recognizing words has been established. The reading programme will then emphasize skills which ensure the understanding of all types of material at successive levels of difficulty.

Reading, however, must not be separated from other facets of language acquisition. The pervasive influence of general language

Source: R. Staiger (ed.), *The Teaching of Reading*, Paris, Unesco, 1973, pp. 39–58.

development must be recognized at all points in planning the reading programme. Reading performance is undoubtedly improved if those activities designed to foster reading growth are linked with other language activities. There are links between comprehension in listening and comprehension in reading. A variety of writing activities can also reinforce those skills which have been learned in reading.

Moreover, reading is not a subject. Since it has no specific content it cannot be taught separately as are most other subjects on the curriculum. It is part of every other subject and has frequently been regarded as a tool facilitating many other types of learning. But this is not entirely true either, since reading is also an experience; it can enlarge the understanding, develop concepts and extend an individual's experience vicariously. In most schools reading becomes the principal key to learning, and is still the major avenue by which an individual may become a lifelong learner.

This chapter will not be concerned with the initial stages of learning to read. Instead, it will describe the successive development of reading skills and go beyond the attaching of sounds to printed symbols to examine the means by which reading may be used to further learning in all fields. The continuous development of word recognition, knowledge of vocabulary and comprehension at the beginning, intermediate and advanced stages will be discussed. But the focus will be on those aspects which are vital to obtaining meaning from the printed symbols.

Comprehension of material must be taught continuously because two factors influence the processes of reading as the reader progresses. On the one hand, the ideas and concepts which the reader meets tend to become more complex. His understanding of these concepts will need to be checked to ensure that misunderstandings and misconceptions do not occur. Second, these ideas are frequently presented in language which itself is linguistically more complex and usually further removed from the reader's vernacular speech. This dual complexity means that teachers must guide readers in ways of dealing with these twin factors, for it is these which tend to inhibit the reader in obtaining meaning. The interrelationship of the levels of difficulty in language and concepts is further compounded by the greater diversity of material covering many subjects and involving a variety of written styles which the advanced reader has to meet.

Both research and experience have shown that there is no single right way to teach reading. The process will vary according to the school level or according to the type of material presented or to the purposes of the reader. Moreover, different teachers teach in different ways. The teaching style of one successful reading teacher may differ considerably from that of another. It is not possible within a short space to describe in detail the variations in the ways of teaching reading, but an attempt will be made to indicate the fundamentals that are essential to reading programmes at all levels. The general principles which apply to different areas of the programme will be given, and suggestions made for possible ways of adapting these according to the achievement level of the reader, to the type of material presented and to the purposes of the teacher at different stages in the reader's development.

The mainstays of any programme of reading must be the continuing development of word recognition, the extension of knowledge of vocabulary and accurate comprehension. Several other skills must be developed simultaneously, however. Teachers must be aware of the need to balance the emphasis on oral and silent reading in the programme, of the factors involved in reading in the different subject-matter fields and of the necessity of ensuring flexibility in reading habits. All these will be discussed and, in addition, those factors which may interfere with reading development will be noted.

Development of word recognition and extension of vocabulary

Effective word recognition is basic to all progress in reading, but the development of the understanding of word *meaning* is basic to reading comprehension. A variety of word-recognition techniques are given in the initial stages of learning to read. Configuration clues, clues from the context, similarity to known words, structural analysis, and phonic analysis are usually introduced at a very early stage. While economy in breaking the written code, ensuring that the reader makes the appropriate linkages between the sound and symbol, is essential, it has long been acknowledged that such an activity will bear little fruit unless the reader is fully aware of the meaning of the words he utters. Drill in word recognition has little impact upon the development of competent readers. It is necessary to ensure that the skills learnt in word recognition will be transferred to independent reading of connected discourse. This assimilation and transfer of skills must permeate all planned reading activities.

The desire of teachers to increase vocabulary in children is almost universal. Unfortunately, this training in the extension of vocabulary is frequently ineffective because few of the attempts to develop a wide yet functional vocabulary are rarely systematic. Linguistic ability is not merely an ability to memorize words or phrases with a view to being able to reproduce them more or less mechanically in response to a given cue. Though teachers seem to be aware of the necessity of vocabulary development, too frequently this is left to chance, and few opportunities of ensuring widening the understanding of word meanings are presented sequentially.

There are four distinct aspects of vocabulary knowledge and development. Individuals can develop listening, speaking, reading and writing vocabularies. They usually appear in this order. In the case of young children and adults who have not yet learned to read, the listening and speaking vocabularies are obviously much larger than the other two. As progress in reading evolves, however, reading and writing vocabularies may begin to equal—and at later levels may surpass—the spoken and even the listening vocabulary.

Although these vocabularies can be studied separately, there obviously is an overlap between them. It is apparent that most of the words which are used in speech will eventually be legible. Conversely, as the material read becomes more difficult, words will be encountered which will rarely be used in speech. The teaching of vocabulary should work on these four aspects. Constant linking of these four areas of listening, speaking, reading and writing vocabularies is essential if teaching is to result in effective learning.

Another major problem of vocabulary development lies in the ways in which language is used. The shift of function of identical word forms in a given language may cause problems. For example, nouns may become verbs or be transferred to adjectives with no change in word form. A further common problem arises from the development of idioms. In most languages these may be associated with figurative expressions. Though the idioms and aphorisms may be common in the adult vernacular, far too frequently it is wrongly assumed that idiomatic expressions, proverbial sayings and the like, which appear as matters of common sense to those who are linguistically sophisticated, are as readily understood either by children or by those who have limited experience with language.

There are several dimensions of vocabulary which teachers must take into account. First, there is the total size in terms of the number of word meanings known. Second, there is the breadth of understanding of ways in which a number of differing meanings may be associated with certain words; such multiple meanings may relate to single words or to the understanding of the implied meanings of figures of speech. Third, there is a problem of the depth of knowledge of the meaning of a word; this question goes beyond the superficial recognition of synonyms to a fuller understanding of the concepts behind each word. The individual who knows that 'yeast' is a substance which makes bread rise has obviously not the same degree of understanding as one who knows that the action of yeast is caused by certain chemical changes.

From some points of view it might seem that the whole process of education is to develop concepts. Since teaching and learning seem to depend very largely on communicating through language, the accurate use and understanding of words is imperative. Vocabulary development, then, is basic, not only to the teaching of reading comprehension, but is the foundation of understanding which leads to knowledge in any area.

The beginning stage

Pupils at this level gradually acquire a number of words which they can recognize at sight. This recognition is usually based upon the teacher's repetition of the word, clues which are given from pictures, or the context of other words, or by studying the configuration of each word. Many repetitions and presentations of words, in charts, in exercises and through activities designed to make these meaningful, are given.

At this level, most of the words encountered in reading are usually within the listening and speaking vocabularies of the reader; as such they present minor difficulties in terms of understanding meaning. However, a teacher must be on the alert to recognize those occasions when familiar words have another meaning in a particular passage. Thus, frequent checks on understanding of words is essential even at this beginning level.

Even in this early stage, particular attention may need to be paid to decoding structure words—or the 'connectives'. These words do not convey meaning by themselves but are essential in understanding the linguistic patterns. Though 'empty' of meaning individually, these words carry the burden of relating ideas and concepts. All languages contain these markers. In English they are: noun markers—'a', 'the', 'some', 'few', 'all', 'this', 'my' . . .; phrase markers—'up', 'down', 'in', 'out', 'above', 'below', 'between' . . .; clause markers—'if', 'until', 'although', 'because', 'how', 'when' . . .; question markers—'who', 'how', 'when', 'why', 'what', 'where' . . .

The intermediate stage

At this level, the words used in the material frequently go beyond the listening vocabulary of the reader. It is therefore essential that the recognition of words in reading is constantly put to functional use in other language situations. Frequent checks may have to be made, and ways of breaking down words either by syllables or into their structural parts need to be expanded. Emphasis must also be placed upon the way in which the context gives many clues to meaning. The effective use of dictionaries in order to check meanings not obtainable in context also needs to be extended at this level. Increasing awareness, too, of the specificity of meaning as presented within a particular content will need to be developed.

Context clues. Learning meanings in context is the natural way in which human beings learn word meanings in general. It has been found, however, that it is helpful for readers to recognize that a clue to the writer's meaning may be present in the context of the printed page. This fact must be brought to the consciousness of the reader. The following list suggests some ways in which context may reveal meaning:

Direct explanation. A brief explanation of the word may be given in parentheses or a footnote.

Typographical. A word may be set off by bold-faced type, italics or quotation marks to call attention to it. Occasionally, additional explanation may be contained in the following sentence or in a clause set off by commas.

Synonym. A synonym or substitute phrase may be used to indicate meaning. A definition of the word may be given by the content that has just been read or the content that follows the word. Such a definition may have to be obtained by linking the understanding of the concepts as they are presented in the passage.

Comparison or contrast. A word may sometimes be indicated by using an expression which includes a comparison or contrast that would help to illuminate the meaning of the unknown word. The comparison or contrast used are usually those more likely to be familiar to the reader. Sometimes a pictorial illustration may help to clarify a new concept. Such illustrations may be diagrammatic or imaginative in form.

Structural aids. The elements within words and the use of prefixes and suffixes may also be used to aid meaning. Knowledge of the base word plus the transformations which occur with the addition of prefixes and suffixes may begin to be explored at this level. Their precise and effective use, however, may not reach the maximum until the advanced level.

Figures of speech and metaphor. Common idioms and proverbs of a language may not always be understood, particularly by children; frequently additional explanations may need to be given. However, both idiom and metaphor frequently contain imaginative elements which may provide a clue to the unfamiliar word or phrase.

Total context. Sometimes it is only possible to gain the full meaning of a new word by taking into account the total context in which it is presented. This may mean that the reader needs to be aware of not only the literal meaning of words but to infer the less easily apparent aspects of the situation or mood presented by the writer.

Subjective clues. Personal experience in terms of previous

understandings of words in general or words in particular leads, of course, to great differences between readers in the ways in which they can assimilate meaning from context.

Though human beings do learn word meanings from context, the presentation of explicit ways to unlock the meaning of unfamiliar words is extremely helpful.

Dictionary skills. Another way in which readers should be taught to help themselves to acquire a wider range of word meaning is by using glossaries and dictionaries. At the beginning stage picture dictionaries are frequently used, but at the intermediate stage it is necessary to ensure that readers know how to use a dictionary efficiently.

Frequently, learning how to use a dictionary is left to trial and error, with the result that the reader rarely uses a dictionary since he finds it difficult and unsatisfactory, and because it often interrupts the flow of his reading. Although the way in which a dictionary is compiled is somewhat complex, it has been discovered that it is possible to facilitate dictionary use by stressing the development of certain skills. These skills may be identified as location skills, pronunciation skills, and meaning skills:

Location skills. Learning the sequence of the alphabet. Facility in recognizing and arranging words in alphabetical order by initial letter, by second letter and by third or fourth letters. Familiarity with a dictionary so that it may be opened quickly to the section in which the word is located. Ability to use the guide words at the top of a page. Facility in recognizing the abbreviations used in the dictionary to indicate pronunciation of special terms, for example, medical or slang expressions, foreign words and phrases, etc.

Pronunciation skills. Ability to use the pronunciation key of the particular dictionary. Interpretation and use of the accent mark. Understanding and use of diacritical marks. Location and use of the guide to pronunciation. Ability to recognize the differences between spellings and pronunciations where there is a lack of exact relationship between phoneme and grapheme.

Meaning skills. Ability to understand meanings of new words by reading simple but typical dictionary definitions. Ability to select from several meanings listed in the dictionary and to determine which one fits the present context. Awareness that one word may have different meanings according to the syntax and its particular word function. Ability to use the sentences given for illustration in the dictionary. The understanding of special meanings, idioms, slang expressions, proverbs, figures of speech. Recognition of root words and the ability to relate derived forms of a word to the basic word. Ability to interpret multiple meanings of a word and to recognize the nuances which distinguish these meanings. Ability to understand synonyms. Ability to recognize the fine distinctions between synonyms. Ability to know when meaning has been satisfied through dictionary usage.

However, it must be recognized that the dictionary definitions do not circumscribe all the meanings of a word. They are only points of departure. The interaction between the reader's experience, the present reading context and the dictionary entry must all take place before meaning can be derived.

Too frequently, however, using a dictionary becomes a chore which many readers dislike undertaking because it interferes with the thread of thought. Only if readers become really facile in their use of the dictionary will they recognize the fascination and assistance dictionaries can provide in the over-all goal of enlarging an awareness of meaning. Undoubtedly, motivation is a problem in maintaining interest in vocabulary study.

Fortunately, many students become interested in words, but teachers must continue to captivate this interest in as many ways as possible.

Advanced stage

At this level it is not sufficient to assume that all the word recognition skills taught earlier will be used constantly to maximum effect in the student's independent reading. Work must continue on attention to context and use of the dictionary.

At this later level a study of such things as verbal relationships and simple etymology often assists in the continuing expansion of vocabulary. The historical study of the origin and development of words frequently interests many students. Root words with a variety of prefixes and suffixes may also aid in understanding. Moreover, the shift or changes in word meaning have an intrinsic interest as do the words borrowed from foreign languages but now part of the vernacular. Speakers of a native language are often unaware of the background from which words have evolved. Such a study might well include derivations of idioms and proverbs and continue with an examination of the ways in which meaning is conveyed through simile, metaphor and hyperbole.

Additional study of verbal functioning might also include more extended work with synonyms and antonyms, the relationships between these and the fine shades of nuances of meaning which may occur. The intimate interrelationships of language and thought, of semantics and syntax, may also be explored with more advanced students.

Conclusion

In summary, to encourage readers to pay conscious attention to new words as they are encountered but to offer direct, overt ways in which meaning may be derived, are essential practices towards ensuring an ever-increasing reading vocabulary.

Comprehension

Reading has been defined as the act of responding to printed symbols so that meaning is created. It has long since been recognized, however, that *getting* meaning from the printed page is too limited a definition of reading. *Bringing* meaning to the printed page indicates more accurately the reciprocal process between the printed symbols and the mind of the reader. Constructing meaning is a vital prerequisite of all reading. But reading is also a form of thinking, problem-solving or reasoning, which involves analysing and discriminating, judging, evaluating and synthesizing. All these mental processes are founded on past experience, so that the present context of the reading matter must be scrutinized in the light of the reader's own experiences. Any definition of the reading process, therefore, must include interpretation and evaluation of meaning as well as construction of meaning.

Exercises and activities designed to check comprehension rarely probe beyond the understanding of the literal level of a passage. It is important to recognize the relevant details, and to be able to abstract the main idea, but this may only take place at the literal level. The accomplished reader must also read between the lines, and frequently extend and assimilate the author's thought. To do this he must interpret and evaluate what is read. To derive full comprehension, a reader must first become the co-author, suspending judgement until he has absorbed the concepts presented, and then scrutinizing and assessing the ideas in the light of his own knowledge and experience.

Interpretation and evaluation have often been linked under the label of critical reading. While it is true that the extent of comprehension activities may depend both upon the reader's purpose and the content of the material read, the effective reader seems to examine automatically the ideas received.

The following lists may be used by teachers as a check to ensure that all aspects are covered. As reading is so complex, the analysis has been divided into the three sections suggested above, construction, interpretation and evaluation of meaning. Obviously, all these activities cannot be taught at all levels and to all pupils. Teachers should choose from this list the ones which they think should be taught to their pupils at their particular level of development, but the list should be checked frequently to ascertain that no main aspect is overlooked. It is not possible to teach 7-year-old children to draw conclusions in the same way as in the case of a 14-year-old pupil. However, even at an early age children can be taught to anticipate outcomes by suggesting the ending of a story or an alternate conclusion for example. To produce functional readers in a technological society, growth in reading must parallel and reinforce children's developmental cognitive growth.

Construction of meaning

This area is basic to all other aspects of comprehension. The following abilities must be developed to construct complete meaning:

To recognize and understand words or groups of words that are meaningful as units; to recognize ever increasing groups or units of words; this includes word meaning, paragraph meaning, meaning of continuous written discourse (prose and poetry).

To realize the appropriate vocabulary of meanings and to understand nuances of meanings between words.

To detect figurative language and well-turned phrases and interpret the effect upon meaning.

To recognize the function of grammar and syntax in controlling meaning.

To interpret typographical devices as clues to meaning.

To grasp the literal meaning, or to understand direct statements made by the author.

To identify parallel statements.

To recognize paraphrases.

To identify things mentioned most frequently.

To recognize topic sentences and where divisions might come in a single paragraph.

To state the main topics of separate paragraphs.

To understand the main idea in a passage.

To follow the sequence of ideas and to anticipate this sequence.

To understand the basis on which a passage is organized.

Interpretation of meaning

In addition to understanding the direct meaning of a passage, comprehension must also include the ability to recognize implied and inferred meanings. This part of the reading process necessitates further mental activity and involves abilities to infer, deduce and construe the import, purport and significance of a passage. This composite meaning will only be accomplished if the reader has been trained to interpret the passage in the light of the context and of his own previous knowledge and experience.

Interpretation will include the following abilities:

To understand the meanings of words and to realize the effect of the context upon meaning.

To understand why the author included or excluded certain things.

To assess the relevance of the materials.

To summarize the passage.

To select a suitable title.

To identify the type of passage, e.g. fiction, history, factual, description, exposition, etc.

To be able to recognize and state the author's purpose in writing.

To establish a purpose for reading.

To keep the question or problem in mind while reading for the answer.

To see the motives of the author.

To draw and support conclusions.

To make inferences or predictions.

To identify the tone of the passage.

To determine the author's attitude towards the reader.

Evaluation of meaning

The evaluation of a passage will result from the synthesis and integration of the two previous sections, constructing and interpreting meaning. Evaluation involves critical reaction to the material read, which may include many intellectual processes such as discriminating, imagining, analysing, judging and problem-solving. It must be emphasized, however, that the function of criticism is not to be derogatory, but rather to establish principles for judging well.

The following abilities should be developed to obtain evaluation of meaning:

To appraise the passage for its ideas, purpose and presentation.

To maintain an objective attitude which demands proof and checking of sources.

To recognize objective evidence and to distinguish between fact and opinion.

To be aware of basic assumptions the author expects the reader to take for granted.

To make critical judgements; such as: (a) to evaluate statements that conflict with or contradict one another; or (b) to judge if an argument is supported.

To identify a valid objection not answered by the author.

To detect special pleading such as emotional appeal or propaganda.

To judge the effectiveness of devices used by the author, e.g. metaphor, simile, rhetorical questions, etc.

To understand that materials will differ greatly in validity and reliability because of the time written, pressure of circumstances, bias of writers and many other factors.

As a child progresses through school there must be increasing emphasis on developing more than the literal meaning of what is read and on undertaking the two latter aspects of comprehension. The fact that many of these activities can only be developed as the child becomes cognitively more mature has led to the extension of the teaching of reading beyond the initial learning-to-read stage. It has been shown that the earlier definite training in comprehension is given, the firmer the foundation will be, thus ensuring full maturity in reading at later levels.

It is in this area of comprehension that gifted children often need considerable help as well as those of average ability. They can profit greatly from this type of training. Too frequently the gifted pupil fails to extend the breadth and depth of his reading comprehension. He can usually grasp the literal meaning with little effort, so that unless he is made aware of these wider aspects of comprehension he rarely develops his full potential.

Teaching comprehension

The description so far makes it clear that reading is a form of thinking triggered by printed symbols, and that these symbols usually represent words. The reader must use his experience and knowledge to construct the concepts presented by the writer; but this mental process is a dynamic one and remains in a constant state of flux as long as the reading goes on. As he apprehends each word or phrase, the reader has to take into account the total context, the problems, the perplexities and the novelties of the ideas presented. Thus, training in reading must focus on the systematic examination of the ideas propounded and somehow facilitate the reciprocal exchange between the reader and the writer.

The major art of teaching comprehension lies in the ability of the teacher simultaneously to check the accuracy of what is read, to probe the pupil's ability to assimilate and interpret more than superficial meaning and to ensure that by participating in concepts and ideas presented by the author the reader not only receives information, but, through his cognitive interaction, also has a novel experience.

Unfortunately, comprehension activities far too frequently imply vivisection. Enjoyment and profits from reading are often dissipated by a lack of variety in the activities stimulating understanding. Repetitive activities usually result in rote reactions which tend to hinder continuous growth in comprehension. The following suggestions are merely points of departure, from which teachers might diverge. Though the routes may be many, the destination is common: the comprehensive understanding of the printed word.

During this century the ways in which children can be taught to recognize words have been systematized and a variety of well-established procedures have been evolved. The teaching of comprehension has tended to be haphazard. Too frequently it has been assumed that the asking of questions will serve not only to assess the understanding of content, but also to develop strategies enabling the readers to follow intricacies of thought.

To develop mastery in reading comprehension, teaching must be specific and systematic and include a wide variety of diverse activities. But systematic teaching for comprehension should not attempt to teach all aspects at one time. One facet of comprehension should be mastered before proceeding to another related aspect. It may be necessary to concentrate on one skill for several lessons until the pupils have developed facility in utilizing this skill in connexion with all types of material. For example, literal meaning should be firmly grasped before any attempt is made to teach the student how to make inferences or draw conclusions, as the ability to assess relevant from irrelevant detail appears to precede that of deriving a main idea.

The art of questioning. The posing of provocative questions by the teacher about reading content is one of the most effective ways of stimulating children to think as they read about what they read. Though questioning has proved a most effective teaching method since the time of Socrates, it is only comparatively recently that attempts have been made to analyse the effectiveness of certain types of questions. Several studies have shown that the majority of questions test repetition of irrelevant facts rather than stimulate productive thought.

As the activity lists suggest, questions which go beyond simple recognition and recall, demanding higher levels of cognitive activity, are those which demand interpretation and evaluation. Though these types of questions may be partially linked to the cognitive growth of the child, and may be related to the evolution of a hierarchy of levels of abstract thinking, appropriate training should begin in the very earliest stages. Within the limits of understanding and experience, a child at the initial stage of learning to read can give judgements about the truth of reasonableness of what he has read; can realize the author's tone and mood; and can make intelligent comments about the content through questions which elicit comparisons with his own experience. At the early levels it is important that teachers frame these questions in concrete rather than abstract terms. The early reader may not be able to determine the main idea, but can usually say what is 'the most important thing' he has learned.

Teachers should ensure a repertoire of questions which over a period of time will cover all aspects of the reading programme. Questions should be framed appropriately; teachers must also be aware of the effects of their responses on the pupil. Questions which frame purposes of reading or demand information to be verified from the text are most common and, at the beginning stages, are essential. Leading questions which give an incidental guide or clue to the desired answer often form the bridge from the recall to the inference type question. Frequently, however, in order to probe more deeply into reader reaction, teachers pose questions requiring judgement or demanding that the answer be justified either from personal experience or general knowledge.

The response patterns of the teacher are also important in promoting reading growth. Research has shown that most responses fall into four major categories. First is the response that has the effect of cutting off the pupil's thinking, often termed a 'closure' response. Many teachers however give a verbal reward, and in some way or other signify to the child that his answer has merit, and that he is contributing to the lesson. Responses which sustain and reinforce the pupil's thinking not only reward but usually serve as a useful type of motivation. Finally, the questions that seek to extend and raise the level of complexity of the reader's reaction are those which, in the long term, ensure that understanding of printed material will develop and mature.

At later levels, exercises designed to check comprehension are presented in the form of short passages usually followed by a variety of questions designed to assess literal as well as derived meanings. Though all the questions may be answered by the learners, the teacher may need to select for teaching purposes those questions which give practice in a certain skill. Errors in comprehension are more likely to be eradicated if one specific skill—for example, gleaning relevant from irrelevant facts—is selected and worked upon, rather than attempting to cover the gamut of reader reactions as surveyed in the exercise questions. Such directed concentration has been shown to yield better results than incidental learning from continued exposure to comprehension exercises. Unfortunately, too often these activities serve to reinforce errors rather than improve understanding.

The reading curriculum, however, is a spiral one, and it must be reiterated that success in obtaining the main idea at an intermediate level may not secure an individual from making errors at a more advanced level. The increasing complexity of vocabulary, concept and linguistic forms at later stages usually necessitates checks by the teacher to ensure that the earlier skill is now being put to functional use.

Two major cautions about questioning should be noted. When a question is asked, care must be taken to prevent a focus which determines the reader's level of comprehension. Far too frequently, questions circumscribe the mental operations involved, the points which are explored and the modes of thought undertaken by the individual. At the same time, both teachers and student (and test constructors) usually assume that there is a single right answer. Though this is usually true of recall and recognition questions, any activity which involves interpretation has some subjective element, and should result in alternative judgements. Through discussion the reader becomes aware of the discrepancies between his interpretation and those of others. If opportunities are presented for the reader to substantiate his positions based on the text and his own pertinent experiences, he is forced to weigh the evidence in favour of alternatives. Even at the level of recall and recognition a discussion of the mistakes made by children either individually or as a group is usually productive.

Though a reader may learn to react appropriately to all the methods of questioning suggested here, these are but the means to an end. Reading is a solitary activity, and in most normal reading occasions there is no external goad to prod the reader's thought and focus his thinking. The main aim of all this activity is to stimulate the reader to develop the art of the self-posed question. However provocative the questions about reading are, they rarely cover the special needs or difficulties peculiar to each individual. From the earliest stages children should be encouraged to ask questions as they read, first orally, later silently. Such training is also an essential step in teaching them how to study.

Reading is one of the prime modes of receptive learning, but it will only become a functional learning tool if readers are both critical and discriminating.

Reading and other language activities. Reading is only one aspect of language growth and development. Thus, whenever possible, reading comprehension should be linked with other language activities.

It has been reiterated often that full reading comprehension cannot be obtained until the reader can formulate the author's ideas in his own words. This is the basis for the French emphasis on '*la lecture expliquée*', in which pupils are encouraged not to parrot the author's words but to present an oral interpretation of his concepts and style. Mention has already been made of the usefulness of discussion in examining differing answers to questions. Fruitful debate may also centre upon nuances of meaning, upon underlying assumptions, upon the author's purpose and upon his use of language. Such discussion should never seek to impose ideas, but should rather encourage reflective thought which may lead individuals to recognize that some interpretations may be more appropriate than others and that each idea must be judged in its own right in the light of the total context.

The intimate relationship between reading and writing is also frequently ignored. Activities which teachers designate as writing often cannot be accomplished without adequate achievement in reading. Learning to write a paragraph becomes more meaningful if the paragraphs of other writers are examined. Such an activity may be linked with an examination of how the main idea is presented, and the ways in which details are included. Similarly, a scrutiny of the ways in which different authors organize their ideas may be linked with essay writing. Outlining, note-taking, summarizing and précis writing, if based on material read, reflect reading and writing abilities equally, while at a much lower level efficient word recognition may be mirrored in spelling accuracy.

The *cloze* procedure of measuring reading has recently received much attention. A *cloze* test is constructed by omitting every '*n*th' word through a passage and substituting in their places blanks of a standard length. The reader then attempts to anticipate meaning from the context and to supply accurately the words deleted from the message. The term *cloze* is derived from the psychological notion of closure, the tendency to fill in a gap to make a well-structured whole. Though only one word is permitted, in some instances synonyms may also be scored. This technique is not mere guessing; on the contrary, the reader is being asked to use his cognitive powers to the fullest. He is forced to use context clues of every type as well as his knowledge of vocabulary, of language patterns and of previous experience. He is being asked to comprehend so thoroughly that he can make logical connective deductions between the ideas presented.

Though the *cloze* procedure is usually used to measure reading comprehension, the discussion of alternate completions has also been found to be a rather useful technique for fostering reading comprehension.

It is a major paradox that at the later levels of teaching reading, both teachers and researchers have been more concerned with measuring information gained from a passage than determining appropriate strategies for obtaining meaning. Though there is a paucity of both research and empirical evidence in this area, all the measuring devices have been successfully adapted to teaching procedures.

Factors which may interfere with comprehension

Many studies suggest that not only intelligence, but appropriate levels of cognitive development, including vocabulary and concept formation, are prerequisites to comprehension.

Another major factor which apparently results in many comprehension errors committed by readers may be their failure to identify or empathize with the thought of the writer. Several research studies have shown how comprehension is subject to the biases and attitudes of the reader and have suggested that such prejudices may be a product of the total environment, within and without the schools. It has also been shown that the interests and the purposes of the reader will alike affect his level of comprehension. A further problem occurs in that there may be cognitive limitations of the reader in terms either of his developmental maturity or of his unfamiliarity with the topic of this material.

The genre or type of presentation the author chooses to use, in addition to the constraints that may result from the cognitive discipline under which he is operating, may also present many problems to readers who are unaware of the nature and impact of these controlling factors. Moreover, research has shown that not only substantive content but also level and concentration of concept presentation may also form a barrier. In addition, the tone of the writer, his attitude towards his topic and towards the reader, all apparently influence the level of comprehension.

It has also been established that though there is a minimal 'general' factor in reading comprehension, major differences arise with respect to reading in various subject-matter fields. As far as cognitive processes are concerned, it is self-evident that each substantive field of knowledge utilizes different modes of thinking; these will inevitably be reflected in the written form. It is therefore necessary to ensure that students learn to adapt their reading strategy according to the content of the material.

Reading in curriculum areas

If reading skills are to become functional they must be applied to learning in all areas of the curriculum which demand reading of any type of material. In spite of many new visual aids, learning through the medium of reading still plays a major part.

There is considerable evidence that good general reading ability does not guarantee that a student will automatically read well in all subject areas. Reading skills need to be refined, broadened and adapted if they are to facilitate learning in other areas of the curriculum. Vocabulary and the concepts behind the words are fundamental to understanding in any content area. In addition, however, the reader must be made aware that each subject field tends to have its distinctive mode of thinking which in turn is often reflected in the style of writing. Many attempts have been made to delineate the demands made by varying content upon the reader. Space only permits a brief synopsis of some of the reading problems faced in literature, in mathematics, in science and in the social sciences.

Literature

Though the prime aim of the reading of literature is to develop appreciation, one of the major problems arising is the variety of genres with which the student is faced. Literature demands that the reader exercise his imagination to the fullest; but even here, as the stimuli differ so do the methods by which mental images are evoked. Drama, for example, calls upon the reader's imagination to a far greater extent than does the novel. In the case of a play, the reader has to create the setting from very meagre suggestions, and the characters have to be evaluated by their speech and actions, without benefit of additional description or analysis by the author. But the novel too makes its own specific demands upon the reader. It calls for sustained awareness and often suspended judgement of characters and events, until the author reaches his dénouement. Understanding of character and analysis of plot are usually emphasized; but frequently, the significance of the theme, the writer's purposes and the elements which foster true appreciation are neglected.

The reading of poetry demands a high degree of reader skill. Here the reader has to recognize meaning which has been distilled through the highest arts and techniques of the language. Experiences and emotions are presented through condensed and vivid metaphors, which in turn should evoke both auditory and visual imagery. Similarly, the distinctive forms of short stories, essays and other types of literature elicit diverse imaginative responses.

Most of the comprehension activities suggested previously are appropriate for literature, but here a dual problem arises. Though literature demands imagination, its substance must be rooted in the author's presentation; the reader should not descend into subjective convoluted fantasies. Equally dangerous is the tendency to murder literary appreciation by dissection. Skilled reading of literature calls for skilled teaching.

202 Marion D. Jenkinson

Mathematics

Teachers of mathematics frequently complain that students who have been able to master the fundamentals of addition, subtraction, multiplication and division are unable to do problems concerned with these fundamental processes. It is rarely recognized that the problem is primarily one of inability to read effectively in this subject. Some of the new approaches in mathematics emphasize the language of mathematics not only in terms of its special symbolization but also because it has a distinctive syntax.

The vocabulary of mathematics is more compact and exacting than in any other subject area. There is a precision of meaning, a succinctness of sentence structure and sequence of thought which must be understood. Reading rate is necessarily slow and before full comprehension can be obtained there may have to be several re-readings. For example, the question to be answered in a problem usually is in the final sentence, and this often necessitates a re-reading, in order to determine the relevance of the facts stated.

The variety of mathematical symbols must be understood, and, as in the reading of word symbols, the reader must possess a knowledge of mathematical concepts. The complexity of understanding needed for the solution of comparatively simple problems is frequently overlooked. A problem such as: 'Find the rate of discount on a nine dollar pair of shoes that sold for five dollars', may be simple to read in the sense of saying the words aloud, but one must consider the previous learnings that are necessary to solve the problem. The pupil must know the difference between the marked price, the selling price, discount and rate of discount. His knowledge of these terms must cover the relationship between each of these concepts, as well as implied meanings; for example, that rate of discount is usually given as a percentage. Unless his knowledge of these concepts is complete he will not be able to read to solve the problem.

Moreover, in mathematics as in other areas, ideas may be expressed in a variety of ways. Students need to be aware of multiple meanings as well as the fact that a single concept may be conveyed differently. For example, the area of a rectangle 6 feet wide and 4 feet long is 6×4 square feet, or 4×6 square feet, or $6 \times 4 \times 1$ square feet, or 'the product of its dimensions'.

Terms which are unique to mathematics are usually carefully introduced, yet it cannot always be assumed that this vocabulary will be accurately understood in new situations. In mathematics, the reader is required to merge mathematical language with the vernacular.

Science

As in other areas, one of the major problems in scientific reading is the understanding of the complex, technical vocabulary involved. Two unusual features of the scientific lexicon must be noted. In the modern world many technical terms are in common usage—for example, 'vitamin', 'atomic fission', 'atomic fusion', 'antibiotics' —and are frequently used in a non-scientific way. Conversely, it is frequently necessary to teach the specialized meanings of words which are familiar to students in their everyday usage but have specific meanings in science; for example, 'element', 'force', 'effort', 'resistance'.

Scientific writing is usually turgid with facts that follow each other in quick succession. The reader is thus confronted with a mass of information that must be related, for science content usually demands both inductive and deductive mental activity. The reader must not only recognize relevant information, but must classify and order it so as to understand how a particular principle is evolved.

One of the grave dangers in science reading is that the apprehension of fact will remain at a literal and superficial level. The relationships between facts, their cumulative evidence, whether positive or negative, that gradually link up so that a principle may be obtained, demand the highest reading skill. The accurate reading of diagrams and charts should help, not hinder, this understanding.

Social sciences

The reading skills learned in the general programme are applied and refined in reading the social sciences. The ability to find reference material with the minimum of effort, to be able to consult indexes, outlines, typographical aids, to use maps, charts, graphs and diagrams, as well as to skim for particular information, are all required in social sciences. Too frequently, however, teachers assume that once pupils have learned these skills, they will automatically apply them efficiently in any future situation.

As in other areas, a broad general vocabulary is a prerequisite for success. A unique feature, however, of the language used in social sciences is frequently overlooked: the metaphorical nature of many terms. For example, unless the student realizes the analogy and depth of meaning involved in terms such as 'the cold war', 'the iron curtain', 'tariff barrier', he will fail to obtain the full import of the writing. Furthermore, it is essential that students have accurate concepts of time and space. Frequently, spatial and temporal terms are imperfectly understood by many students, which leads to considerable confusion in thinking.

Material in the social sciences is also loaded with factual information. Here again the reader must go far beyond the literal interpretation. He has to use his imagination to transcend the limits of time and space, and to conjure up figures of the past or people of far-off places. This imagination, however, must be grounded in reality and spring from knowledge rather than from fantasy. Though his background of experience may be limited, his reading should enable him to extend and enhance his awareness and knowledge.

The material of the social sciences is usually very pertinent to training in the interpretative and evaluative skills of reading. Opportunities to compare accounts of the same event from diverse sources lead to skills in detecting biases, assessing sources and qualities of argument. The techniques of propaganda and advertising rhetoric can also be examined. It is very frequently in this area of the curriculum that the techniques of modern journalism, whether newspapers, journals or comics, are scrutinized.

As in literature, the major source of information in the social sciences is still the printed word. It is therefore imperative that teachers in these areas recognize that efforts to understand the field will be fruitless unless the student is capable of gaining comprehensive meaning from what he reads.

Rate of comprehension

The explosive expansion of knowledge during the last two decades has been paralleled by a deluge of printed materials. This has led to many demands for ways of accelerating the reading process in order to cover more of the material. Though this area is still subject to great controversy, certain statements appear to be valid.

The term 'rate of comprehension' is perhaps more accurate than the one which has received the greatest usage, 'rate of reading'. There is little value in skimming quickly over words and pages if little or no understanding ensues. Furthermore, there is obviously a connexion between an individual's rate of thinking and the speed with which he can comprehend; this appears to vary considerably between individuals. Several studies have shown, however, that adults who are mature readers tend to read too slowly.

Authorities are agreed that an efficient, accomplished reader will reveal flexibility and versatility in his reading performance. He has the ability to adjust his rate of reading according to his purposes, to the nature and type of material, and in accord with his own background of experience. Some materials may be scanned, or skimmed; yet, for material demanding reflective thought, the proficient reader will shift his reading gears.

In the early stages of learning to read, rate will of necessity be very slow—as the process of mastering the recognition of individual words is of necessity slow—and much of the reading may be done orally. When silent reading becomes prevalent at later stages, speed of reading increases with little external assistance. However, even at the advanced level, efficiency and versatility are rarely achieved by every reader unless some special training is given.

There are several reasons why some readers fail to reach their maximum flexibility. Many readers do not completely eliminate vocalization; that is, they still move their lips, saying the words either sub-vocally or mentally. Many slow readers are guilty of mind wandering. This is particularly true when the individual's rate of reading is slower than the rate of thinking: the process of assimilating ideas from print is so slow that the attention wanders. In addition, slow readers frequently focus their attention upon word elements rather than on the ideas behind the words. Such readers are still at the elementary level in which the mechanical aspects of word recognition prevent comprehension of difficult material. This phenomenon may also be caused by immature perceptual habits in responding to words; that is, they have a narrow span or a slow speed of recognition. Unfamiliar or difficult vocabulary may also curtail speed of reading.

Some students have good comprehension but find reading laborious. Such slowness often impedes their enjoyment and progress; for these students attempts should be made to diversify reading tactics and accelerate comprehension.

Mechanical devices are available which either control the rate at which the reader can read or which attempt to increase his perceptual span. These devices often have an excellent motivating effect on deficient readers, but many gains can be made without them. Every possible means should be employed to develop a student's familiarity with words and their meanings and to speed his thought processes. Improvement in rate has resulted merely by increasing motivation for reading. Reading passages of different types of carefully timed material has resulted in gains due to self-competition. Both scanning and skimming techniques should be available to an individual when these are appropriate to the material he is reading. Above all, however, the reader should be mentally comfortable as he reads; he should never be complacent. An excited reader is usually versatile.

Oral reading

Though it is possible to learn to read without articulating words orally, pronunciation of words enables the teacher to check on the accuracy of word recognition during the early stages, and may also serve to reinforce the learning of the beginning reader. Once the essentials of word recognition have been mastered it is essential that pupils make the transition to silent reading, for this allows the individual to read independently at his own rate.

At one time oral reading predominated and became much abused. Pupils were asked to read in turn, all from the same book at the same page. Each student mumbled or stumbled through two or three sentences and then thankfully sat down, and usually ignored the text for the remainder of the lesson. Such reading activities led to boredom on the part of both the teacher and the pupils Moreover, the eye–voice span in oral reading tends to be very small, and if word-by-word reading persists it is likely to impede progress in silent reading. Gradually, teachers have recognized the futility of reading by turns and have substituted other ways for assessing and assisting reading progress at the intermediate and advanced levels, and even at the beginning stage.

Although it is true that most adult reading is silent, there are many occasions when oral reading is necessary, as in the minutes of a meeting. Since the main purpose of oral reading after the beginning stage is concerned with communication through the spoken word, some attention to oral interpretation needs to be given. Since the focus is upon communication, the reader must first comprehend what he is reading. When reading for an audience, therefore, it is important to let the student read silently and, if necessary, give him time to prepare his reading for an intelligible presentation. Not only are there innumerable occasions in adult life when the ability to read aloud is important; there is also the fact that a great deal of literature, for example, poetry and drama, can only be appreciated if it is heard.

Oral interpretation should develop the following abilities: to recognize and pronounce words accurately; to use the voice meaningfully and pleasingly; to read in thought units; to transmit the meaning directly; to be accurate in reading, e.g. not to omit or substitute or transpose or repeat words; to interpret thoughts and feelings; to match voice and manner to the thoughts and feelings of others; to sense audience reaction; to control breathing, bodily movements and mannerisms; to adjust expression to changes in the mood of characters or the mood of materials; to assume the character for oral reading of dramatic materials or stories; to make gestures where they are purposeful, natural and meaningful; and to make necessary vocal adjustments to bring out the rhythm and feeling in prose and poetry.

Although it is usual for silent reading to precede oral, there are occasions when oral reading at sight is desirable. Sight reading can be an invaluable tool for diagnosing reading difficulties, particularly in word recognition. Omissions, substitutions, lack of knowledge of sound-symbol relations, insertion of words, faulty enunciation, can all be noted, as well as the lack of comprehension which may be revealed by awkward phrasing, wrong emphasis and quality of expression.

Thus, though oral reading no longer holds the prime position which it held in the nineteenth century, functional oral reading still has a place in the curriculum.

Teaching adults

Since the early days of the industrial revolution it has been recognized that the industrial machine cannot run smoothly unless its cogs are literate.

The enlarging of the definition of literacy from the ability to read and write one's own name to that of functional literacy is well known. Functional literacy implies a minimum of four years of education with a sufficient command of reading and writing to ensure that the skills will not be forgotten and can be used with minimum efficiency in everyday life. While this level may have been adequate as recently as twenty years ago, the demands of an automated society will make those who reach this level economic outcasts. These people will be semi-literates or the subliterates with insufficient educational qualifications to compete in today's labour market. Such marginal literates constitute one of the greatest social and economic problems in modern highly industrialized nations.

Therefore, it may be necessary to redefine literacy. Technological literacy must involve more than the ability to decipher words, follow simple directions and read advertisements. In countries with an advanced level of technological development, it now appears essential to have a minimum of about seven years of schooling before the citizen can adapt to the pervasive changes of such a society. Since the rote tasks of industry have been taken over by automation, this upgrading of literacy is imperative. Such a level demands not only considerable skill in word recognition, but a wider reading vocabulary as well as an increasing ability to cope with the expanding complexities of ideas and their expression. The ability to assimilate information, assess its relevance and use it efficiently and critically, will be basic requirements for any reading programme.

However, reading programmes often tended to disappear once the functional level of literacy was reached. One of the surprising and paradoxical features of societies which have reached a high technological level has been the public demand in adult education for courses designed to promote reading efficiency.

While the skills to be taught will be similar to those outlined in this chapter, teachers of adult reading courses will need to adapt methods and choose materials suitable for their adult clients.

Since attendance of adults is usually voluntary, motivation is rarely a problem and results usually occur more quickly. Their maturity in life experience, their will-power, perseverance and practical judgements should all facilitate reading growth. The relative command of language and the more mature faculties for logic and reasoning which adults normally possess may, however, be offset by rigidity of thoughts and habits, and a complete lack of awareness of the linguistic differences between the spoken vernacular and the more formal syntax of the printed word.

Material used with adults therefore should arouse immediate interest and be pertinent to the purposes which seem relevant to the adult. Moreover, adults usually learn most effectively if tasks are presented within a clearly defined system. As they frequently have a greater capacity for sustained effort than children, adults should have activities which demand such expenditure, but which are also overtly related to their expressed needs. Since most adults know what they want they quickly become critical of methods and materials which fail to satisfy their needs. Newspapers, magazines, trade journals, any general reading matter which caters to their vocational, domestic or artistic needs should be used as source materials. Failure for adults, however, has even more immediate consequences than it does for children, while their sense of achievement can also be reflected in phenomenally rapid progress.

It is no longer sufficient to master the techniques of word recognition and literal comprehension. Both self-respect and self-development develop in an individual once he can use reading as his key to learning. In today's world the unread are the unready and the unemployed. Though literacy programmes are making headway, we must take care lest the uneducated become the undereducated.

Conclusion

This chapter has attempted to suggest the many ways in which the reading processes that result in productive thinking can be developed, whatever the content of the thought and whatever the language in which the ideas are expressed. Language and nationality are closely linked, but ideas contained in print know no boundaries of time or space.

While general guidelines have been given, no attempt has been made to outline specific lesson plans. These will change with the teacher's purposes, the level of development of the learner, the type of material, and the setting. The creativity, ingenuity and understanding of teachers make them the life-core of education. They will need to use all their acumen and wisdom to inspire, conspire and frequently perspire to ensure that every student reaches his reading potential.

3. 3 Influence of instruction on early reading

Rebecca Barr

A learning theory concisely formulates the relationships among learning outcomes, situations, and learner characteristics; it should define the parameters and specify the interactions among apparently diverse learning phenomena. Theorists typically differ in how much they emphasize situational or learner characteristics as influences upon learning.[1] For example, most traditional learning theorists have assumed that learner characteristics are either inconsequential or that they should be held constant; hence, for example, the use of pure genetic strains of rats. These theorists accepted some situational constraints without scrutiny (the maze, the Skinner box, the associational task) and focused on others (reinforcement or practice) that appeared to influence learning or performance. The consequence was the development of learning theory able to account for simple learning in constrained situations but clearly inadequate to account for the situational characteristics that influence the complex learning of humans, who have a history of prior learning, and who learn in complex social settings like classrooms.

Other theorists, concerned with human development, focus mainly on the characteristics of learners, and how their behavior changes over time; they typically ignore environmental variations that may precipitate or support change, and attribute development to experience in general.

It seems strange, when schooling and other forms of education are clearly a preoccupation of our society, that we have failed to develop a theory of learning to account for complex human learning; perhaps we have not tried, beyond using simple analogies drawn from experimental studies, to address the more complex pheno-

Source: *Interchange*, 5, 1974, pp. 13–21.

mena. Nevertheless, I propose that the foundations can be laid for such a theory by studying cases of complex learning in order to (1) identify situational characteristics that form and maintain a learned manner of responding, and (2) specify the procedures for organizing new information and the operations for transforming information that learners normally bring to new learning situations.

In this paper I focus on early reading as a case of complex human learning. Most formulations about how children learn to read are derived logically from theories of competent reading processes (e.g., Goodman, 1964; Gough, 1972; Venezky and Calfee, 1970); are based on a behavioral analysis of the reading task (e.g., Coleman, 1970; Gagné, 1970; Samuels, 1973); or are extensions from formulations of language acquisition based on linguistic theory (e.g., Brown, 1970; Ryan and Semmel, 1969). Generally, these formulations are of little help in thinking about instructional issues. Williams (1973) noted in a review of theories and models of learning to read: 'We are quickly proceeding to the point where our theoretical formulations—and empirical findings—may become too refined and sophisticated to be of great use in helping to determine instructional procedures' (p. 123). I agree that current formulations may be of little use in instructional design, *not* mainly because of their refinement and sophistication, but rather because of their narrowness. Specifically, with the exception of the behaviorally based formulations, task dimensions are almost totally neglected in current formulations. Little attention is directed toward how modification of the reading task might influence the reading processes or the strategies used by beginning readers. Not only do most formulations fail to conceptualize differences among print environments, but some assume instruction to have a neutral or even negative influence: the learner is viewed as actively organizing his experiences with print with little support, and sometimes interference, from instruction. Rarely is the influence of the social setting on children's learning to read considered in current formulations.

Conceptions of the processes of competent readers are an important consideration in early reading instruction because they establish instructional goals; nevertheless, processes used by competent readers are not necessarily those used by novices, and not always does the whole equal the sum of the parts. In order to understand the processes used by beginning readers, we cannot use analogy from or logical analysis of the processes used by competent readers, but rather must obtain independent evidence on what beginning readers do by observing them as they learn to read. By examining the correlation between changes in learner responses and instructional variation, inferences can be made about the nature of learning, its underlying processes, and the conditions that affect and support change. Although subsequent experimental evidence is required to confirm formulations developed in this manner, these conceptualizations have the advantage of constituting valid representations of the learning phenomena and the conditions that typically influence early reading.

Though massive numbers of investigations have been directed toward understanding the influence of instruction on early reading, most have limited their focus to the effect of instructional conditions on general reading achievement (Bond and Dykstra, 1967; Chall, 1967). However, in order to understand instructional effects, qualitative as well as quantitative differences in children's learning in response to aspects of instruction must be documented.

Few studies have attempted to answer the question now posed: how does the nature of instruction (method or materials, or both) influence the manner in which children structure the problem of learning to read? In an attempt to do so, I review selected studies conducted in natural settings. First, the nature of reading instruction is examined as well as the use of children's oral reading responses to infer the underlying processes; then evidence from studies of reading instruction and learning in natural settings is summarized and interpreted; and finally, instructional and learner influences on early reading are identified.

Nature of reading instruction[2]

Though instructional methods and materials are often treated as a unit, they are conceptually and operationally distinct. Method is usually conceptualized as a scheme that guides the activity of a teacher: a unit of print is focused upon, appropriate responses to particular units of print (e.g., the letter, word, or sentence) are taught, and certain behavior is encouraged when children read a story, especially that pertaining to comprehension and the identification of words not recognized by children. Reading materials, by contrast, are described along certain stimulus dimensions: individual words in terms of graphophonemic regularity, length, and aural referent; the word sample in terms of the number of words and their repetition; and sentences in terms of syntax and meaning. In subsequent discussion I refer to the former as 'teaching method' and the latter as 'printed material' or 'print environment'; both are components of the reading instruction provided for most children.

The probable reason that most discussions of reading instruction treat teaching method and printed materials as a unit is that certain combinations typically occur. One way in which printed materials are commonly designed is through the systematic introduction and repetition of a limited number of words varied in length and pattern within contextual material. Typically, only a few new words are introduced within each new story and each word introduced is systematically repeated in subsequent stories. In most reading series, word control continues during the first several years of instruction and in some series through the sixth grade. Because the 'word' is the unit of print around which these materials are designed, I refer to these materials as 'sight-word materials.' Chall (1967) noted that teachers using materials of a particular design rarely supplement them with materials from outside the particular basal series they use. Certain teaching methods are commonly used with sight-word materials: the introduction of new words contained in a story; the discussion of story characters, sequence, and outcome; and the development of phonics and structural skills for identifying unknown words.

A second type of printed material is easily identified: contextual material composed of words similar in pattern and length. The 'letter' unit of print is considered in the design of these materials. Whereas first grade materials of this type initially contain words composed of only a limited number of letters, by the end of first grade they contain multisyllabic words varied in pattern. I refer to these materials as 'phonics materials.' The predominant teaching method used with these materials involves teaching letter-sound associations and the skills of blending phonemes and matching the blended sequence with a word from natural language. Little attention is usually directed toward story comprehension.

The design of materials around certain units of print may solve certain problems, but it creates others for the learner. While letters are probably the simplest units of print in terms of the number to be discriminated and of their visual complexity, letters also create certain problems for the learner—they usually correspond to meaningless units of speech. For children to identify words, they must learn new skills for blending and matching the phonemes corresponding to letters with words from natural language. By contrast, words as units of print do correspond to meaningful speech units, and thereby may permit children to use processes that they have previously used in the perception and memory of faces, objects, and pictures. Nevertheless, the visual complexity of words and the number of words to be discriminated may create problems for children.

Whether children are instructed with sight-word or phonics materials, they must learn to relate printed words, in the first case, and blended phonemes, in the second case, to lexical units in natural language.[3] But once the words of the text are matched to the words of natural language, normal children at the age of most beginning readers may still have difficulty synthesizing meaning from word symbols.[4] Synthesis of words for meaning appears to be a process distinguishable from the processes involved in translating print to speech. Sight-word instruction, because of its emphasis on comprehension, may teach this synthesis for meaning whereas phonics instruction, because of little emphasis on comprehension, may not.

Oral reading response characteristics

Many recent studies of reading development examine the reading response characteristics of children in order to infer what children have learned and what cues they use to translate print into speech. Error characteristics, in particular, are analyzed to infer underlying reading processes. Among the error types commonly studied are a child's substituting a different word for the printed one, and omitting or making no response to a printed word. Substituted words frequently do not appear to be random guesses but rather calculated responses cued by print and/or prior sentence context or by other more general cues (pictures, story theme, previous reading in the same book). Several assumptions underlie the use of response analysis to infer underlying process; first, that correct responses to printed words are produced in a systematic fashion, and second, that reading errors reflect, in a manner similar to correct responses, the workings of an underlying process.

Just as a linguist is able to identify the geographical region of a person's language acquisition through dialect characteristics, a reading specialist can sometimes determine the past instructional influences on a child's reading skill through an examination of error characteristics. Disabled readers, even years after their initial exposure to reading instruction, and beginning readers sometimes display identifiable reading response patterns. For instance, the following examples show how two disabled readers read the sentence, 'Now he does not try to take his dog.'[5] Kay, 8 years of age, responded, 'Now *his dose* not *tray* to take his dog.' Bill, 10 years of age, read, '. . . he *did* not *take* to take his dog.' Reading responses of these children to printed words presented in isolation can be compared with those made when they read text. For example, Kay substituted *erv* for the printed word *every, doan* for *done, road* for *round*, and *those* for *these*. Bill's responses to the same words were *very* for *every, did* for *done, about* for *round*, and *what* for *these*.

The response deviations from the text can be examined to determine whether the errors are appropriate to prior sentence context (for sentence reading) and to letter cues (for sentence and word reading). For example, Kay's contextual substitutions were appropriate to the prior sentence context in one of three cases (*his* but not *dose* and *tray*), whereas Bill's were appropriate in two of two cases (*did* and *take*). Kay produced some non-word substitutions, whereas Bill produced none. Whereas Kay's substitutions (contextual and isolated word) tended to correspond with several letter cues from the printed words, Bill's substitutions tended to match either at the beginning or end or not at all. Further description and interpretation of response patterns are made later in the paper.

Influence of contextual experience on early reading

Biemiller (1970) was among the first to speculate about the reading processes of children on the basis of changes in their oral reading responses. Using oral reading errors made by children during first grade instruction, Biemiller identified three main phases of development that reflect differences in the manner in which learners use contextual and graphic information. In the initial phase, the responses of beginning readers showed a predominance of contextually constrained errors, i.e., substituted words appropriate to the preceding sentence context. The second stage was defined by an increase (50% or more of all errors) in non-response errors. During this phase children made significantly more graphically constrained errors than in the first, i.e., they substituted more words that shared a common initial letter with the printed word. In the third phase, characterized by a drop in non-responses below 50% of all errors, children used both graphic and contextual information.

Biemiller maintained that this pattern of development in children's use of graphic and contextual information occurred for most American children learning to read with contextual materials. He said little about the instructional program in which the children he studied learned to read and, to that extent, leaves the impression that his hypothesized stages occur regardless of the specific characteristics of teacher methods as long as the reading material is contextual.

The failure to examine instructional factors that may influence learning is reminiscent of the failure of many cognitive theorists to examine conditions (e.g., play environment, authority relations, schooling) that may lead to cognitive restructuring. The assumption that experience is not distinctive in its effect on learning encourages little or no examination of environmental conditions and also precludes a test of the initial assumption that experience is uniform in its influence on learning.

Influence of teacher method on early reading

Barr (1972) proposed that Biemiller's phases might actually reflect changes in teaching method, rather than development, occurring through experience with contextual materials.[6] She noted that the responses occurring during Biemiller's second phase—a higher proportion of non-response errors and an increase in graphically constrained substitution responses—are characteristic of children instructed by a phonics method, whereas fewer non-responses and substitutions showing little use of graphic information but considerable dependence on contextual information are typical among children taught by a sight-word method. For example, Gates (1927) made this observation: 'In this work the nonphonetic pupils usually showed a greater disposition to depend on the context and to attack the larger word units or features of configuration; the phonic groups resorted more to detailed analysis of the new words encountered' (p. 225).

Barr (1972) suggested that Biemiller's subjects may have used a sight-word strategy during the first phase, but by the second phase may have begun to identify words through phonics synthesis; she further suggested that this assumed strategy shift reflected a shift in teaching method or emphasis.

In order to test whether teaching methods affect changes in the characteristic manner in which children respond to printed words and whether changes in response patterns are similar to the patterns observed during Biemiller's first and second phases, Barr examined the short-term word-learning of 41 prereading first grade children taught by two instructional methods. When the 41 children were taught by the sight-word method, their non-response errors were low and most substitution responses showed little use of graphic information. In addition, Barr observed that most words erroneously substituted for the printed ones by children instructed by the sight-word method were other words taught at the same time. Rarely were the substitute words those taught at some previous time, untaught words, or non-words. In effect, the set of words learned, or those to which the children were exposed, constrained the substitution responses.

By contrast, when the same 41 children were instructed by a phonics method, they produced significantly more non-response errors and their substitution responses showed the influence of graphic information. In addition, responses among children receiving phonics instruction, by contrast, consisted of a high proportion of words *other than those taught*, and a substantial number were non-words or words from the child's total aural vocabulary.

The similarity between the responses of Barr's children instructed by the sight-word method and those of Biemiller's subjects during the first phase, and the similarity between responses of the same pupils instructed by a phonics method and those of Biemiller's subjects during the second phase, led Barr to conclude that changes in the methods emphasized by teachers might account for Biemiller's observations. Yet, the Barr study was limited in two respects: the instruction was of short duration, and responses were obtained from test words presented in isolation rather than in context. As Barr noted, the importance of further examination of the influence of teaching method and printed materials on reading development lies in the fact that if instruction can be shown to affect reading skills differentially, a child's reading response patterns can be used diagnostically to specify appropriate instruction. By contrast, if reading strategies are related to unspecified experience with contextual materials in which the influence of instruction is not ascertained, there is no way to account for shifts in behavior and no way to aid a child caught in one phase of reading except to provide more of the same experience or to provide alternative experiences haphazardly.

Instructional influence on later reading

Other investigations of the relationship between instructional conditions (methods and materials) and reading response patterns suggest that neither experience with contextual materials nor teacher method alone account for observed changes in early reading.

DeLawter (1970) studied the reading responses of New York City children taught either by a decoding (phonics) or a meaning (sight-word) method after two years of instruction. Most substitutions by children taught by the decoding method were non-words closely resembling test words in most graphophonemic elements. By contrast, most substitutions by children taught by the sight-word meaning method were real words showing a relatively low graphophonemic correspondence to test words. In both groups almost all real word substitutions were syntactically acceptable while about half were semantically acceptable.

Elder (1971) compared the responses of children taught by a sight-word method and by a phonics method after two-and-a-half years of instruction. He found that the responses of Scottish children taught with a strong phonics emphasis showed fewer word-recognition errors, including fewer word substitutions, but more non-word substitutions on the Gray Standardized Paragraphs than the responses of an American group receiving the same amount of instruction with a sight-word meaning emphasis. In addition, a significantly greater proportion of the word substitutions tended to change the meaning of the sentence and remain uncorrected among the Scottish than among the American children.

The DeLawter and Elder evidence suggests that children form one main strategy for identifying words and that this strategy is determined by instructional conditions. The distinctiveness of the response patterns of children after two to two-and-a-half years of instruction suggests that initial strategies remain dominant for at least some period of time.

The evidence supporting this conclusion consisted of mean response patterns for groups of learners; deviations of individual learners from the group means could easily be masked. Therefore, case study research (Barr, 1974–5) was undertaken to determine whether response characteristics of groups were displayed by individual children in the groups, and whether the characteristics were similar among children experiencing the same instruction and different among those experiencing different instruction. The December and May word substitution responses of 32 first graders, half instructed by phonics materials and method and half by sight-word materials and eclectic methods, were classified in terms of two criteria: (1) the number of non-words produced and (2) the percentage of words substituted that had been introduced previously in the reading text (i.e., reading-text words). Children tended to display one of the two following response patterns: (1) some non-words were produced *and* a small percentage of reading-text words were substituted or (2) no non-words were produced *and* a high percentage of reading-text words were substituted (75% or more). In December 10 pupils taught by the phonics materials and method showed the first pattern and six the second. In May 14 children showed the first pattern and 2 the second. Of the children instructed by the sight-word materials and eclectic methods, in December 15 showed the second pattern and 1 the first. In May 2 children, among the most able taught by the sight-word materials, were no longer constrained by the reading-text set of words, and 1 of the 2 produced non-words; all the remaining pupils substituted real words, mainly from the reading set. The findings show that the response patterns of most children reflect instructional conditions and are consistent from December to May of first grade. Nevertheless, some shifts in response pattern did occur, mainly among the pupils instructed by the phonics materials and method, indicating a strategy shift in accord with instructional materials and method.

If indeed eclectic teaching methods resulted in the development of several reading strategies, we should anticipate the development of two strategies for children reading from sight-word materials. One strategy, corresponding to the sight-word instruction, would be used for discrimination among previously learned sight words and the other, corresponding to instruction in phonics and structural analysis, would enable the identification of unknown words. That children should develop skill in both these areas is an explicit goal of eclectic teaching methods. Contrary to this expectation, the evidence from the Elder, DeLawter, and Barr studies suggests that beginning readers taught by eclectic methods do not commonly use phonics synthesis to identify unfamiliar words. The substitutions tended to be real words rather than non-words, with relatively little reliance on graphophonemic cues in comparison with the substitutions of children instructed with phonics materials and methods.

Two conclusions seem inescapable: (1) teaching methods that are eclectic in emphasis do not result in the parallel development of alternative word-identification strategies; instead, children operate generally from a single initial strategy; (2) whether this strategy is phonics synthesis or sight-word recognition depends greatly on initial instruction conditions.

Reading strategies

Children's reading strategies consist of information and expectations, developed and organized by them from past experiences in order to deal with similar new experiences with text. Strategies for translating print into meaning or speech can be inferred from the response characteristics just described. Children instructed by phonics materials and methods characteristically respond with some non-words or partially pronounced words and words not exclusively found in the set of reading words, but rather in their speaking vocabularies. Most of their substitutions show a high correspondence between letters and phonemes. The strategy of children receiving phonics instruction appears to involve the synthetic blending of phonemes corresponding to letters and the matching of the synthesized sequence of phonemes with the words of natural language; when a child fails to find a match, he either produces a non-word or makes no response.

Learners apparently discriminate and remember letters or letter combinations and phonemes associated with them. The relationships between print and speech are explicitly provided in instruction; the child does not have to infer them. In addition, children must learn the operations of blending phonemes and matching the blended sequence with words from natural language. That this strategy is more difficult for children than a sight-word strategy is suggested by the percentage of children (37.5) instructed with phonics materials who initially used a sight-word strategy (Barr,

1974–5). Nevertheless, by the end of the first year of instruction, the strategy of most phonics-instructed children (87.5%) did conform to the instructional emphasis. Their expectations appear to be derived from their experience with print; they seem to make relatively little use of expectancies developed from their oral language experiences.

The strategies of children taught by sight-word materials and eclectic methods are more difficult to predict from an analysis of instruction. A meaningful unit of print is selected and repeated, but the child must identify the relationships among printed words. As reported by Barr (1972, 1974–5), DeLawter (1970), and Elder (1971), the responses of children taught by a sight-word emphasis were characterized by a relatively low degree of correspondence between letters and sounds, and few or no non-word responses.

In addition, several investigators noted that almost all substitution responses came from the set of reading words. For example, Biemiller (1970) noted that a large proportion of the substitution and insertion responses during contextual reading came from the set of reading words, 99% in the first phase of reading acquisition, 94% in the second, and 91% in the third. This tendency to produce only reading-word responses is the same as that observed for children studied by Barr (1972, 1974–5) and others (Gates and Boeker, 1923; Wiley, 1928) for children tested on isolated words or word lists.

On the basis of this evidence, sight-word learning appears to involve a strategy of distinguishing words previously taught as reading words. That is, when children make substitution errors they select wrong words from words appearing in their instructional materials but not from the larger array of words comprising their spoken vocabularies. Biemiller's investigation appears to describe the children's search for cues, contextual as well as graphic, that facilitate discrimination among reading words. Substitution responses were initially appropriate to sentence context but not to the graphic form of the word. However, the use of graphic cues increased significantly during the second phase; children relied either on contextual or graphic information, but usually not on both kinds. By the third phase children apparently relied on both sources of information in combination since most of their substitution responses were contextually as well as graphically appropriate. But within each phase, children generally used the contextual and/or graphic information to distinguish words within their reading word sets.

Wiley's (1928) subjects were instructed by sight-word methods and read from sight-word contextual materials but word learning was tested by having the children read words presented in isolation during their first two months of first grade reading instruction. In order to determine the word characteristics or features used by children to distinguish one word from the next, Barr (1975) reanalyzèd the responses made by Wiley's children. The responses substituted for a given printed word during the first months of first grade reading instruction differed little in length from the stimulus word and typically shared letters in the initial and/or final position of that word. Given the total set of words learned by the pupils, substitution responses could be predicted very accurately.

These findings suggest that when children are tested with words presented in isolation, and therefore use graphic information for discrimination, they rely, at least during the first several months of instruction, on two characteristics of print: the length of the printed words and the form of letters appearing at the beginning and/or end of a word.

Several conditions may account for the discrepancy observed in the reported use of graphic cues between Biemiller's subjects during the first phase of reading and Wiley's children during their first two months of reading instruction. First, the test conditions may account for the differences: Wiley's children were tested on words presented in isolation and therefore could use only graphic cues; Biemiller's children, tested during contextual reading, had the opportunity to use contextual cues as well as graphic cues. Second, the criteria for determining the use of graphic cues differed: in the reanalysis of the Wiley data (Barr, 1975), match at the beginning and/or end of words was used to index graphic similarity whereas in the Biemiller study only initial letter match was used. Because children were limited in their responses to the set of reading words and because few words in the sample similar in length may have begun with the same initial letter in the beginning stages of reading, the opportunity for children to demonstrate the use of graphic cues defined in terms of initial letter match may have been limited.[7]

In sum, children taught by a sight-word emphasis appear to learn the set of reading words introduced in their instructional materials. They discriminate words by identifying features of printed words that distinguish them from other printed words in the same instructional set. Sight-word learners may learn to focus on and remember only those features useful for discrimination, and to associate those characteristics of the printed word with its aural counterpart. Their expectations seem to be derived not only from their experiences with print, but also from their oral language experiences generally. A successful strategy appears to integrate information from both these sources.

This formulation of discrimination learning on the basis of distinctive features is not new; it has been used to account for learning in several areas (Gibson, 1969; Jakobson and Halle, 1956). Typically in reading and in most discrimination tasks (pictures, objects, faces), learners must infer the characteristics that in various combinations serve to distinguish one particular unit, or word in this case, from another. Only rarely does reading instruction specify characteristics that differ among words and then usually only in the beginning stages of instruction. Further, features useful in distinguishing a set of reading words at a given time may become insufficient once additional words containing the same characteristics are introduced. At this point, as existing cues become insufficient for discrimination, children refine, expand, and coordinate their use of graphic and contextual information to distinguish the expanding set of words they encounter in reading.[8] Some children may even form the alternate strategy of phonics-synthesis. The changes in response characteristics noted by Biemiller (1970) and Barr (1974–5) seem to support this inference.

Refinement of reading strategies

During early reading it is not surprising that children must evolve some systematic strategy for translating print to speech. A printed symbol system that relates in systematic ways to speech defines the essential nature of reading. However, comparing the response patterns of early readers with those of competent readers suggests that considerable refinement of these early strategies must occur.

Pupils using a phonics strategy are not constrained by a set of reading words; they draw on words from natural language. They also, however, come up with nonsense words, and as Elder (1971) showed, their word substitutions do more violence to sentence meaning than do those of pupils using a sight-word strategy. So I conclude that even though children using a phonics strategy draw from natural language, they are not really treating reading as a natural language experience.

However, children using a sight-word strategy draw from natural language in the sense that they are typically more observant of contextual constraints and that they do not make nonsense word responses; nevertheless, they cannot treat reading as a general natural language experience because they are constrained by the set of previously learned reading words.

The intriguing question is this: how do children modify and expand their initially dominant strategy into mature strategies that treat print as a representation of natural language? Because little reading research using the concept of strategy as an organizing principle has been undertaken, the following discussion is speculative in nature.

The idea developed by Farnham-Diggory (1972) that reading development involves attention to increasingly larger print units[9] appears to be a plausible hypothesis for the refinement of a phonics strategy. Printed materials composed of words that increase in length and complexity would support such development. Probably, phonics strategies become adapted in two ways. First, as printed words become extremely familiar to children, their features become associated with morphemic units in natural language. This association may occur only after children attend to root word and affix units in print. Second, children must learn to synthesize words into meaning. The exclusive focus on phonics-synthesis during the first months of instruction may be necessary in order to discourage the use of a sight-word strategy. Nevertheless, once a phonics strategy is established, comprehension instruction might facilitate the development of a strategy for synthesizing words into meaning, and support the evolution of mature reading strategies.

Evidence from the Biemiller (1970) study and the Barr (1974–5) case study suggests that most children who form a sight-word strategy use information provided by their teacher to distinguish better among previously learned reading words rather than to develop new strategies. Generally, the initial strategy appears to determine how subsequent information about print is used.

That sight-word strategies appear to be refined through the incorporation of information into a separate print system rather than into the general language system is not surprising when one considers the nature of the sight-word materials. In sight-word materials, words that vary in length and pattern are introduced in limited number and systematically repeated in contextual materials. Teachers normally introduce the new sight words that children will encounter in a particular story. Given this very controlled printed environment, why should children develop a strategy for identifying unfamiliar words? The expectation that all words encountered are previously learned ones is viable under this circumstance. Further, the variety of word patterns included in the material might interfere with a child's use of word parts from known words for the identification of unfamiliar words. For example, Söderbergh (1971) made a detailed longitudinal study of a child in the initial stages of learning to read Swedish, a highly affixed language. The child initially learned by a sight-word method but subsequently used affixes and root words from previously learned words to identify other words. By contrast, the sample of English contained in reading texts designed so that words vary in pattern and length may interfere with the abstraction of word parts. The reading task itself may make it difficult, as well as unnecessary for children to refine their strategy for word discrimination into one suitable for identifying unfamiliar words.

The fact that a few of the better readers studied by Barr (1974–5) who initially used a sight-word strategy were no longer constrained by the reading word sample by the end of first grade suggests that refinement of the strategy occurs in this direction. Printed words that are unfamiliar to children may be identified through the coordinated use of contextual expectancies and graphic cues occurring at the beginnings and/or ends of words. Some children may even develop the alternate strategy of phonics-synthesis, as did one child in the Barr case study.

Influence of learner characteristics

The evidence from the studies reviewed suggests that children reading from particular materials do adopt a strategy for translating print to speech or meaning that is generally functional. Most children reading sight-word materials organized their strategy around the word unit of print, while most reading phonics materials focused on the letter unit. One learner characteristic that appears to influence subsequent learning is the initial strategy. Nevertheless, children using the same general strategy differed markedly in the manner in which this dominant strategy was used and refined. For example, within the sight-word strategy group, the expectation that all words are those previously learned as reading words appears to be held by all children, but the use of contextual and graphic information to discriminate among words in the set varies. Average and good readers show increasing attention to graphic cues and are able to coordinate the use of graphic and contextual cues during their first year of instruction, whereas children of low reading ability show little increase in attention to graphic cues or coordination of this information with contextual information (Biemiller, 1970).

Whereas most readers evolve a strategy or set of strategies that is useful in coping with most reading tasks, disabled readers are often marked by poorly refined strategies. Further study within general strategy groups of children is needed to identify various solutions to problems posed by reading materials that lead either to continued refinement of reading strategies or a fixation that is maladaptive within a strategy. An analysis such as that undertaken by MacKinnon (1959), where children's responses to printed sentences were monitored over time in order to identify unresolved problems, may represent one useful approach toward increased understanding of reading difficulty *if* attention is directed toward individual differences among learners.

Nature of instructional influences

Two conclusions can be drawn from this analysis of how instruction influences early reading. First, the reading skills developed by all children reading contextual materials are *not* identical. Rather, the design of the printed material and teaching methods directed toward the unit of print around which the materials are organized determines the dominant strategy that children use for translating print to speech.

Second, eclectic teacher methods do *not* result in the parallel development of several distinctive reading strategies. Rather, the beginning reader's dominant strategy, once established, appears to determine how subsequent information provided by the teacher is used. Longitudinal research during the second and third years of instruction needs to be undertaken in order to determine the stability of this effect.

The analysis of reading response patterns suggests the hypothesis that the occurrence and manner of strategy refinement are directly related to modifications in the learner's printed materials. Just as children's organization of information about their natural environment(s) is stable because of the constancy of their experiences, so, on a much smaller scale, their organized experiences with distinctive print environments will remain stable so long as continuing experiences demand no adjustment. For example, I suspect that children initially using a sight-word strategy could be encouraged to focus on print-speech relationships within words if their printed materials contained unfamiliar words, similar in pattern to previously learned words. Printed materials presently used for sight-word instruction may delay or interfere with the children's discovery that their reading responses need not be limited to previously learned reading words.

This formulation about early reading suggests a reciprocal relationship between the child's mental structures and instruction. The identification of a unit of print and its reinforcement in reading materials influences the characteristics of the structure organizing a child's experience with printed words. This mental structure, once formed, serves to determine what subsequent information about printed words can be incorporated and how it will be organized. Nevertheless, it too will be modified gradually over time in accord with changes in the print environment.

The value of research conducted in natural settings is that it provides a many faceted view of the phenomenon, the dimensions of which can be productively formulated. Because of the manner in which the formulation is derived, no artificial problems of how to relate isolated skills are created, as is frequently the case when associational learning models are used to describe early reading. Similarly, the unique problems that a new printed symbol system poses for children can be adequately documented through naturalistic study; these problems are not identified when formulations are imposed on early reading from existing theories of learning and development.

This study of early reading suggests that complex human learning cannot be understood through simple analogies; rather, each kind of learning demands both investigation in its own right and comparative investigation in order to identify its unique and general characteristics. Further, the general context in which learning normally occurs must be examined to specify characteristics that form and maintain a learned manner of responding. That a child brings to learning certain procedures for organizing new information and certain operations for transforming information is an idea that must be taken seriously. Finally, theories of skill learning must eventually be able to account for learning phenomena in their most complex manifestations, and, accordingly, must specify variations in learners, in situations, in forms of instruction, and in outcomes.

Notes

1 White (1970) suggested that these differences in theoretical orientation arise from alternative conceptions of the nature of man: 'In this writer's judgment, the conflict between the learning theory tradition and the tradition of genetic psychology was and is another chapter of the ancient and honorable conflict between empiricist and rationalist views of man' (p. 664).

2 For a comprehensive description of reading instruction, see Chall (1967).

3 It is not a purpose of this paper to discuss the nature of children's language. Natural language, as used in this discussion, refers to the language-conceptual skills that children have developed auditorily that became manifest through speaking and listening. Reading, at least during the first years of development, is considered to be a secondary system that relates printed symbols initially through speech to meaning and only at a later time directly to meaning. Considerable evidence exists that children's language concepts differ in important respects from those of adults: whereas children organize language concepts in terms of their subject response to events, adults classify lexical items hierarchically in terms of classes. Reading instruction apparently aids children in abstracting word units from natural language that corresponds to printed words, something they do not do if left to their own devices. For example, Karpova (1955) found that Russian children between three and a half and seven years of age generally could not segment an aurally presented sentence into lexical units. Huttenlocher (1964) demonstrated that pre-school children could not reverse word pairs or indicate lexical boundaries. Holden and MacGinitie (1972) found that many of their kindergarten subjects were not familiar with

conventional word boundaries in print in relation to units from speech, and they were also not able to understand these concepts even after they had brief instruction.

4 Several researchers have documented this tendency (Farnham-Diggory, 1970; Hall *et al.*, 1970). For example, Farnham-Diggory (1967) found that whereas children learning pictographs and logographs respond correctly with words appropriate to symbols, they have difficulty reading and acting out simple sentences composed of two or three logographs, such as 'jump over block' and 'clap hands.' Farnham-Diggory concluded from the responses of 50 normal children that 'it is not until the age range of 6–8 to 7–3 that normal children begin to demonstrate reliable proficiency in the ability to synthesize sentences from word symbols' (p. 228). This age range coincides with the time that most normal children receive formal reading instruction.

5 This sentence is excerpted from passage 2A of Spache's (1963) *Diagnostic Reading Scales*.

6 Because the printed materials were organized around the word unit of print and remained consistent in design during first grade, material characteristics would probably not account for the changes observed by Biemiller.

7 Indeed, during Biemiller's second phase, the increasing number of words in the reading word sample beginning with the same initial letter may have increased the opportunity for graphically constrained errors; at the same time, several words possessing the same distinguishing characteristics may have created confusion and led to an increase in non-response.

8 The set of Roman letter characters is small in number, in contrast to the set of English words commonly introduced to children. Thus, some problems created by an accumulating number of words to be distinguished may be avoided with the small set of letters.

9 For example, she described four aspects of print speech relationships: '(A) letter-sound association systems, (B) spelling pattern sight-and-sound systems, (C) word-sound systems, and (D) phrase-sound systems. Each of these can be built from the preceding system. The more complex systems require more skill and become fluent at a later age' (p. 434).

References

Barr, R. (1972) 'The influence of instructional conditions on word recognition errors', *Reading Research Quarterly*, 7, 509–29.

Barr, R. (1974–5) 'Case study of the effect of instruction on pupils' reading strategies', *Reading Research Quarterly*, 10 (4), 555–82.

Barr, R. (1975) 'Processes underlying the learning of printed words', *Elementary School Journal*, 75, 258–68.

Biemiller, A. (1970) 'The development of the use of graphic and contextual information as children learn to read', *Reading Research Quarterly*, 6, 75–96.

Bond, G. S. and Dykstra, R. (1967) 'The cooperative research program in first-grade reading instruction', *Reading Research Quarterly*, 2.

Brown, E. (1970) 'The bases of reading acquisition', *Reading Research Quarterly*, 6, 49–74.

Chall, J. (1967) *Learning to Read: the Great Debate*, N.Y., McGraw-Hill.

Coleman, E. B. (1970) 'Collecting a data base for a reading technology', *Journal of Educational Psychology Monograph*, 61, 1–23.

DeLawter, J. (1970) 'Oral Reading Errors of Second Grade Children Exposed to Two Different Reading Approaches', unpublished doctoral dissertation, Teachers College, Columbia University.

Elder, R. D. (1971) 'Oral reading achievement of Scottish and American children', *Elementary School Journal*, 71, 216–30.

Farnham-Diggory, S. (1967) 'Symbol and synthesis in experimental "reading"', *Child Development*, 38, 221–31.

Farnham-Diggory, S. (1970) 'Cognitive synthesis in Negro and white children', *Monographs of the Society for Research in Child Development*, no. 135.

Farnham-Diggory, S. (1972) *Cognitive Processes in Education: A Psychological Preparation for Teaching and Curriculum Development*, N.Y., Harper & Row.

Gagné, R. M. (1970) *The Conditions of Learning*, 2nd ed., N.Y., Holt, Rinehart & Winston.

Gates, A. I. (1927) 'Studies of phonetic training in beginning reading', *Journal of Educational Psychology*, 18, 217–26.

Gates, A. I. and Boeker, E. (1923) 'A study of initial stages in reading by pre-school children', *Teachers College Record*, 24, 469–88.

Gibson, E. J. (1969) *Principles of Perceptual Learning and Development*, N.Y., Appleton-Century-Crofts.

Goodman, K. S. (1964) 'Reading: a psycholinguistic guessing game', *Journal of the Reading Specialist*, 4, 126–35.

Gough, P. B. (1972) 'One second of reading', *Visible Language*, 6, 291–320.

Hall, V. C. *et al.* (1970) 'Cognitive synthesis, conservation, and task analysis', *Developmental Psychology*, 2, 523–38.

Holden, M. H. and MacGinitie, W. H. (1972) 'Children's conceptions of word boundaries in speech and print', *Journal of Educational Psychology*, 63, 551–7.

Huttenlocher, J. (1964) 'Children's language: word-phrase relationship', *Science*, 143, 264–5.

Jakobson, R. and Halle, M. (1956) *Fundamentals of Language*, The Hague, Mouton.

Karpova, S. N. (1955) 'Osonznanie slovesnogo sostava rechi rebenkom doshkol'nogo vozrasta', *Voprosy psikhologii*, 4, 43–55. (For an abstract in English, see D. I. Slobin, 'Abstract of Soviet studies of child language', in F. Smith and G. A. Miller (eds), *The Genesis of Language*, MIT Press, 1966.)

MacKinnon, A. R. (1959) *How Do Children Learn to Read?*, Toronto, Copp Clark.

Ryan, E. B. and Semmel, M. I. (1969) 'Reading as a constructive language process', *Reading Research Quarterly*, 5, 59–83.

Samuels, S. J. (1973) 'Success and failure in learning to read: a critique of the research', *Reading Research Quarterly*, 8, 200–39.

Söderbergh, R. (1971) *A Linguistic Study of a Swedish Preschool Child's Gradual Acquisition of Reading Ability*, Stockholm, Almquist & Wiksell.

Spache, G. D. (1963) *Diagnostic Reading Scales*, Monterey, Calif., CTB/McGraw-Hill.

Venezky, R. L. and Calfee, R. C. (1970) 'The reading competency model', in H. Singer and R. Ruddell (eds), *Theoretical Models and Processes of Reading*, Newark, Del., IRA.

White, S. (1970) 'The learning theory approach', in P. H. Mussen (ed.), *Carmichael's Manual of Child Psychology*, 3rd ed., N.Y., Wiley.

Wiley, W. E. (1928) 'Difficulty words and the beginner', *Journal of Educational Research*, 17, 278–89.

Williams, J. P. (1973) 'Learning to read: a review of theories and models', *Reading Research Quarterly*, 8, 121–46.

3. 4 How children think about reading

John Downing

Research on young children's thinking indicates five important conclusions about teaching reading:

1 Children's thoughts about reading, their notions or conceptions of its purpose and nature, present the most fundamental and significant problems for the teacher of reading.

2 The young beginner's *general* ways of thinking are extremely different from those of adults.

3 The very different logic of young children causes two serious difficulties in teaching them to read and write.

(a) they have difficulty in understanding the *purpose* of the written form of their language.

(b) they cannot readily handle the *abstract* technical terms used by teachers in talking about written or spoken language.

4 Teaching formal rules (e.g. of phonics or grammar) for their thinking is (a) unnecessary and (b) may cause long term reading difficulties.

5 It is vitally important to provide rich and individually relevant language experiences and activities which (a) *orientate* children correctly to *the real purposes* of reading and writing, and (b) enable children's natural thinking processes to *generate understanding of the technical concepts of language.*

Why children's thinking processes are of central importance for the reading teacher

Although this first point may seem commonsense to many classroom teachers, the curious fact is that most college textbooks about

Source: *Reading Teacher*, 23 (3), 1969, pp. 217–30.

reading have no chapter on children's thinking. This topic is also notably under-researched, and comparatively few articles about it have been published in the journals. In contrast, there is a wealth of published material, for example, on visual perception in reading. Perhaps, this is due to the obvious need for a study of visual perception because printed symbols have to be looked at visually in reading. Perhaps thinking is neglected because it is an invisible process.

Yet, the most comprehensive and thorough review of research on children's failure in reading ever to be undertaken arrived at the conclusion that it was a breakdown in *the thinking processes in learning to read* which consistently appeared as the real problem in study after study. Vernon (1957), in her classic review, *Backwardness in Reading*, concluded: 'Thus the fundamental and basic characteristic of reading disability appears to be cognitive confusion and lack of system.' If *cognitive* confusion is the 'fundamental and basic characteristic of reading disability', then clearly the *cognitive* processes of beginning readers must be the central concern of reading teachers seeking to prevent disability through any such confusion. Thus research says research resources and teachers' efforts should be directed more towards a concern for the child's own ways of thinking in learning to read.

The child's mode of thought

It is impossible to understand the revolution which has occurred in British primary schools over the past two decades if one does not recognize the contribution to British educational theory made by the studies of Jean Piaget. His influence is most noticeable in math and science teaching, probably because part of his work was directly concerned with the development of mathematical and scientific concepts in children. However, Piaget's (1959) theory of the development of logic in children is a general one and must be applied to the child's learning of the written form of language too. His book, *The Language and Thought of the Child*, provides the starting point.

Piaget's concept and description of *ego-centric* language and thought in children below the age of about seven or eight years is fundamental to an understanding of the child's mode of thinking at the typical beginning reading age. It becomes clear that the logic of such young children is qualitatively different from that of adults. Marshall (1965) expresses simply and clearly what this means for the practical teacher. She is referring particularly to the revolution which started first in a change of teachers' attitudes towards art education. 'The new conception of child art simply takes into account that children are not solely adults in the making, but creatures in their own right, as tadpoles differ from mature frogs, or caterpillars from butterflies.' This statement is generally true of the thought of children before the age of eight years, and it is especially true of their thinking about reading.

Difficulties in children's thinking about reading

Vygotsky (1962) replicated and expanded the research started by Jean Piaget on the relationship between children's thought and language, and Vygotsky did turn his attention directly to the problem of teaching Russian children the written form of their spoken language. He describes his investigations designed to 'account for the tremendous lag between the school-child's oral and written language'. (Incidentally it is interesting to compare this great Russian educational psychologist's recognition of a 'tremendous' reading problem in his country with the naive assertion that Ivan knows so much more than Johnny does!)

This fundamental Russian research led Vygotsky to draw just two main conclusions:

1 'Our studies show that it is the *abstract* quality of written language that is the main stumbling block.'
2 The child 'has little motivation to learn writing when we begin to teach it. He feels no need for it and has *only a vague idea of its usefulness.*'

Both these conclusions could be predicted from Piaget's general theory of the development of thinking. At the conventional age for beginning reading, abstract ideas are least appropriate and the child's ego-centric view of his environment is not conducive to a natural understanding of the purpose of the written form of languages—an artificial two-dimensional product of civilization.

At the University of Edinburgh, Reid (1966) has conducted an investigation which provides independent evidence to support Vygotsky's conclusions. Reid's original research will undoubtedly be recognized as one of the outstanding reading research contributions of this decade. Her method was to conduct intensive interviews with twelve five-year-old children in their first year in the infants' class at an Edinburgh city school. She interviewed them first when they had been two months in school, and then twice more, after five months and nine months of school.

Reid's protocols provide fascinating insight into children's thoughts about reading, and her article should be priority reading in every course for teachers of first grade reading. The first conclusion she reports is that, for these young beginners, reading 'is a mysterious activity, to which they come with only the vaguest of expectancies'. They displayed a 'general lack of any specific expectancies of what reading was going to be like, of what the activity consisted in, of the purpose and the use of it'.

The other finding of Reid's was that these children had great difficulty in understanding the abstract technical terms which adults use to talk about language, e.g. 'word', 'letter', 'sound', etc.

New research

Jessie Reid's original study stimulated the author of this present article to follow up her line of investigation. Her three focused interviews are being replicated with thirteen five-year-olds in an infants' class at Hemel Hempstead. In addition, some experimental methods are being used to test predictions based on Reid's conclusions. Already, the first of the three interviews and experimental sessions has been completed with all the children. The results generally confirm Reid's findings and expand our knowledge of how children think about reading. The following paragraphs provide an interim report of the new Hemel Hempstead research.

None of Reid's Edinburgh children could actually read, and all but one knew it. Some of the Hemel Hempstead children were beginning to read their basal (i.t.a.) readers, and this seems to account for the fact that seven children said they could read, two were uncertain, and four said 'no'. The children were fairly realistic about the extent of their reading. For example, Jane (5 years 0 months) answered the question, '*Can you read yet?*' by replying, 'Not quite, I can read a little bit', and Felix (5 years 3 months) said 'No. . . . I can read *something*. . . . I can read my Sam book' (A pre-primer).

What is in books?

The question, '*What is in books?*', produced responses at Hemel Hempstead which were quite similar to those of the Edinburgh children. Only two children said 'writing' and no child mentioned words. Four said 'pictures'. The usual response was to quote the names of characters in the basal reader (e.g. 'Sam and Topsy') or in a story book at home (e.g. 'Humpty Dumpty'). Three children quoted a specific phrase or sentence from the basal reader.

No child said anything to suggest that books conveyed information, and only one (William, 5 years 1 month), the most mature child in the class, said 'stories' spontaneously. As Reid also had found that children did not think of books containing stories, the Hemel Hempstead children were asked specifically '*Do books have stories in them?*' Then, seven children agreed that they did, but it was usually books which had been read to them, more often at home, that they thought of as containing stories. Felix actually differentiated between the school books and the books he had at home, the former having no stories, while the latter did have them. One boy, Mark (5 years 0 months), denied that books have stories. He declared that one gets stories 'on the floor—near the piano'. (This is a reference to the teacher's arrangement for reading stories to the class.)

How do grown-ups read?

Two of Reid's children did not know if their parents could read. Similarly, three of these Hemel Hempstead children were uncertain about their parents' ability to read.

Only one of the Edinburgh children mentioned symbols in trying to tell what their parents did when they were reading. At Hemel Hempstead the response was similar. Kay (4 years 11 months) said 'They just look at the writing', and Sandra (4 years 11 months) said 'They look at the numbers'. The other children referred to the more obvious behaviour of adults when they read. For example, William simply said, 'by looking', and both Tina (5 years 2 months) and Vanessa (5 years 2 months) said, 'They sit down.'

Questioning more closely, '*What part do they look at?*', did not improve this vague picture of what their parents did when reading. Three then said, 'the pictures'. But only William gave the most sophisticated reply 'the words'.

Because such young children have difficulty in verbalizing about a new experience, at this point in the Hemel Hempstead interviews a book without pictures was placed open before the child, with the comment, '*Show me what they look at.*' Then six of the children used their fingers to indicate that it was the print, and more technical linguistic terms were used by the children. Four said it was 'writing', one said 'words', and two said 'letters'.

Reid asked the Edinburgh children, '*How does mummy know what bus to take?*' All but one said it was 'by the number', and none mentioned the destination. The same question at Hemel Hempstead produced rather poorer results, only about half the children mentioning 'the number'.

A comment by Reid on this point is that, 'In some cases it was unclear whether they really knew the number was visible, or whether they just thought of it as something the bus was called by ("the twenty-four").' To investigate this problem, after the Hemel Hempstead interviews, the children were shown three model buses each with different number and destination boards at front, back and on the side, and asked, '*How do you know which one to get on?'* When they were provided with this more concrete situation, all the children except one pointed correctly to the number and destination boards on the model buses. Felix cried, 'There it is! That's the seven-oh-eight!' and 'There's the one-oh-three!'

Another concrete aid added to the Hemel Hempstead interviews was a page with two pictures of cars. One car had an 'L' ('learner') plate clearly visible. Eight of the thirteen correctly chose the 'learner' car and pointed correctly to the 'L' plate to show how they knew. William said the 'L' was 'the red number', but Jane and Kay called it 'a letter'.

The results with the model buses and the pictures of the cars are particularly interesting because, in comparison with Reid's interview situation which depends solely on an exchange of spoken words, these young children could achieve so much more with actual concrete objects than they could in the more abstract verbal situation. This provides an example of the normal course of development in children's thinking. Actual understanding comes first, while ability to verbalize about it naturally comes later.

What is writing?

The Hemel Hempstead children gave identical responses to the request *'Can you write something for me?'* to those made by Edinburgh five-year-olds. All but one in both samples produced some kind of symbols. In both samples, just one child interpreted 'write' as draw. At Hemel Hempstead, Michael (5 years 0 months) said, 'I can write people with a round face', and drew a human figure which he said was 'my Mum'.

The larger majority of the Hemel Hempstead five-year-olds wrote recognizable numbers, letters, or words. Only two produced what appeared to be a row of unrecognizable hieroglyphs. Vanessa said they were 'letters', but Gary (5 years 1 month) revealed that he was confused about the distinction between writing words and drawing pictures. He said, about his row of symbols, 'that's about my Mum', and, when asked *'What are these* (the symbols) *for?'* added (pointing to one) 'that's for the leg'. Sandra, too, may have been demonstrating a similar confusion, because although she produced a quite well written 'H', which she said was 'for house', she pointed at a part of the letter and said it was 'the door'.

Asked, *'Tell me about what you have written'*, three children correctly named the numbers or letters which they had written, and one sounded the phoneme it represented. Tina mixed letter names and phonemes. She said 'HOK' was 'aitch, oh, kuh'. Three children said correctly the word they had written. Two called the symbols correctly 'letters' and one said they were 'names'.

Writing their own first name was spontaneously chosen as something they would write by three of the children. All the others were asked to do this as a second writing task. Of these, three were doubtful of their ability to do so, and one indicated that she could do it only with a fair copy, 'I need some writing what it's like.' All the children did try to write their names, but three of them produced only unrecognizable marks. Five children spelled their names correctly; but five others got only the initial letter correct, plus, in two cases, some other letters of their name. Such children usually said they had been taught to write their names by their mothers.

Mark made a spontaneous comment which provides supporting evidence for another of Reid's findings. Asked to write his name, he said, 'You don't write muh.' Asked, '*why not?*' he added, 'Not the muh on the card.' What he wrote was not recognizable, but he was probably referring to the lower case letter 'm' as being on 'the card', whereas he knew that his name began with a capital 'M'. He added an explanatory comment: 'You write an older one.' It is quite clear that young beginners perceive upper case and lower case letters as looking different, and they believe that this must have some special significance. Thus 'm' is 'muh' but 'M' is not 'muh'.

This replication of Jessie Reid's first interview of five-year-olds clearly confirms her conclusion that such young children have only a vague notion of the purpose of the written language and of what activities are actually involved in reading. The Hemel Hempstead children, like the Edinburgh children, displayed a great deal of confusion over the use of abstract technical terms, such as word, number, letter, name, writing, and drawing. However, the concrete aids—the model buses, the pictures of cars, and the presentation of an actual book—stimulated motor and verbal responses which indicate that the Hemel Hempstead five-year-olds were groping towards an understanding of the technical concepts of language, although they were very much less able to use them accurately in verbal responses.

A concept attainment experiment

Reid admits in a footnote that 'the fact that a child does not, when given opportunities to do so, use a certain term is not proof that it is unknown to him . . . He may, for instance, understand it when someone else uses it.'

The abstract technical terms 'word' and 'sound' often are used by teachers in talking to young beginners with the assumption that children understand just as well as adults do what 'words' and 'sounds' actually are. Reid's interviews suggest that this assumption may be quite unfounded, but her method leaves the problem unanswered. In an attempt to investigate this question further the following experiment was conducted with the thirteen Hemel Hempstead five-year-olds after their interviews.

The experiment began by training the children to give the type of response needed in the experimental test. This training was introduced as 'the yes/no game'. Each child was told that he would be shown some cards. On some of them he would see a picture of a bird. The others would not have a bird on them. The experimenter said, 'Say "yes" if you see a bird, and "no" if you see something that is not a bird.' All the children learned to make this discrimination response very quickly. To check that they could generalize the response to other discrimination tasks, they were tested on their ability to say 'yes' when they saw a pencil and 'no' when they were presented with other objects which were not pencils. All the children could do this at once after the training on the bird/not bird picture cards.

The hypotheses to be tested were:
1 These five-year-old beginners are not able to discriminate between auditory stimuli on the basis of the concept of a 'word'.
2 They are not able to discriminate between auditory stimuli on the basis of the concept of a 'sound'.

The test material for checking both these hypotheses consisted in a tape recording of twenty-five auditory stimuli of five types:
(a) a non-human noise (e.g. bell ringing)
(b) a phoneme (all vowel sounds)
(c) a word (e.g. 'milk')
(d) a phrase (e.g. 'fish and chips')
(e) a sentence (e.g. 'Dad's digging in the garden').

The human utterances (b, c, d, e) were spoken by a seven-year-old in the same school. Each stimulus was introduced by the experimenter's voice saying, seven seconds earlier, 'get ready'. Each type had five different examples, and the order of presentation of the types was randomized.

To test the first hypothesis, the child was asked to 'listen for a word. Say "yes" if you hear a word, and "no" if you hear something which is not a word.'

The tape began with a series of five stimuli for practice before the real test began. This made it possible to be certain that the child understood the instructions as far as he was able.

The second hypothesis was tested with the same tape, except that now the child was asked to respond 'yes' for a 'sound' and 'no' for 'not a sound'.

Experimental results

The results of these two tests were as follows.

The word concept

1 Five children made no *discrimination* between the auditory stimuli (one thought that none were 'words', four that they were all 'words').

2 Three children thought that all the stimuli were 'words' *except the non-human noises*, i.e. what they thought was 'a word', in actual fact, was anything from a single phoneme to a whole sentence.

3 Five children (one not certain—possibly belongs to category 2 above) thought that the *phonemes as well as the non-human noises were 'not words'*. These pupils were the most advanced in the attainment of the concept of 'a word'. The category 'word' in their thinking included phrases and sentences as well as single words, but not phonemes.

The sound concept

1 Six children made *no discrimination* (four thought that all the stimuli were 'sounds', two that none were 'sounds').

2 Three children thought that all were 'sounds' *except the non-human noises*.

3 Two children *excluded both phonemes and non-human noises*.

4 One child's category of 'sound' *included only the non-human noises*.

5 One child *included both phonemes and non-human noises* in his category 'sound'.

Both hypotheses are strongly supported by these test results. 'A word' for five of these thirteen children was a meaningless and useless category. Three had begun to connect it with human utterance, and five more had progressed a little further to connect it with a meaningful human utterance. *But none thought of it as the segment of human speech defined by adults as 'a word'*.

The term 'sound' was even less well understood. About half the children could make no use of it as a category. Three more children associated it with any human utterance. Only two children had a narrow category for 'sound'. One seems to have used it to classify noises which were not human. The other added phonemes to this category.

No child thought of 'a sound' as being exclusively the phoneme. But perhaps it is not surprising that 'a sound' is not understood as meaning a phoneme. When we observe these children's confusion, it is clear that the term 'sound' is in fact a confusing one, because, in everyday life outside the reading lesson, the word 'sound' is used by people for a variety of noises. Perhaps reading teachers should learn from the experience of New Math, and provide concrete experiences associated with accurate, clear, and rigorous terminology of a more sophisticated kind. There seems no reason why 'phoneme' should not be used directly to the children *when* a technical term is needed for this unit of speech.

Experimental conclusions

The replicated interviews together with this new experimental evidence provides emphatic endorsement of the earlier research of Vygotsky (1962) and Reid (1966):

(a) Young beginners have serious difficulty in understanding the *purpose* of written language.

(b) They have only a vague idea of how people read, and they have a particular difficulty in understanding *abstract* linguistic terminology.

The futility of verbal rules

These fundamental difficulties *in the essential nature* of children's thinking on the one hand, and the written form of language on the other, pose the practical question for reading teachers—*How can we overcome these two problems?*

First they must beware of falling into the trap of believing naïvely that they need just *tell* their pupils how to think about reading. There is abundant evidence that teaching formal rules for thinking is both unnecessary and may even delay or prevent the development of the full understanding of the concepts essential in making children readers.

Unnecessary

Piaget's research led him to conclude, 'A child is actually not conscious of concepts and definitions which he can nevertheless handle when thinking for himself.' 'Verbal forms evolve more slowly than actual understanding.'

One has only to consider how very young children perform wonders in manipulating the grammar and phonemic structures of language, without anyone's telling them the rules or their being able to describe them, to see that it is quite unnecessary for rule following behaviour to be based on verbal formulation of the rules.

Dangerous

Teaching verbal rules is worse than unnecessary. It is likely to fool the teacher and delay or prevent the child from developing appropriate behaviour and attitudes for reading.

Vygotsky's research led him to conclude:

> Direct teaching of concepts is impossible and fruitless. A teacher who tries to do this usually accomplishes nothing but empty verbalism, a parrotlike repetition of words by the child, simulating a knowledge of the corresponding concepts but actually covering up a vacuum.

Such a vacuum is being covered up when a child can recite 'When two vowels go walking the first one does the talking', but can't read 'meat', 'pie', 'road', or 'faint'. Such ritualistic teaching methods go against all that research has revealed about the development of young children's thinking.

It is a serious error to assume that children always learn only what the teacher thinks she is teaching. This is why teaching methods are extremely important. They are important not for the usual reasons which people give, but *because of the concealed lessons which are unintentionally taught* by different methods.

Teaching verbal rules, before children have made generalizations from their own concrete experiences and arrived at an understanding of the nature of the tasks and problems they are required to undertake, reverses the natural order of development. The order in nature is from concrete experience, via understanding, to the ability to verbalize about such experience and understanding. Reversing this order confuses children about the purpose and nature of the skills of reading and writing.

When children are taught verbal rules about reading, they learn that reading is a kind of ritual which they have to perform to please adults. They also learn that reading and writing are dull and boring tasks which have little or nothing to do with the interesting things in their lives outside school. Thus, many children take a very long time to learn the essential truth about reading which is that it is to convey interesting information from the author to his reader. Quite a large proportion of pupils never learn this vital truth and so never become readers.

Foss (1967) has expressed this in more general psychological terms: 'It is while learning to read that a child first meets symbolic representations, and one would expect the method of teaching and the age of learning to have important consequences for his later symbolic and non-symbolic behaviour.'

Strang (1968) makes the point more specifically as regards the effects of such unintentional learning from beginning methods of teaching reading on later reading behaviour. In her lucid criticism of Chall's (1967) *Learning to Read: the Great Debate*, Strang comments: 'To begin with the synthetic or code-emphasis method may (1) decrease the child's initial curiosity about printed words as he encounters and uses them, (2) deprive him of the experiences of discovering sound-symbol relationships in words for himself, (3) give him the wrong initial concepts of reading, and (4) if pursued too extensively and too long, interfere later with speed of reading and maximum comprehension.'

All these are unintentional learnings caused by beginning reading with synthetic phonics, but Strang's criticism number three, that this method may give the child 'the wrong initial concepts of reading', seems the most serious ill effects of such methods. What makes this still more serious is that this ill effect may do long term damage to the child's development in reading.

Adapting teaching to the child's thinking

Bruner's (1960) dynamic view of readiness is an application of the basic psychological research on children's cognitive development to the problems of teaching young children. His well known statement, 'The foundations of any subject may be taught to anybody at any age in some form', has often been misunderstood because of insufficient consideration of its last three words, 'in some form'. This is filled out when Bruner adds in another place, 'It is only when such basic ideas are put in formalized terms as equations or *elaborated verbal concepts* that they are out of reach of the young child, if he has not *first understood them intuitively* and had a chance *to try them out* on his own.'

An object lesson in this is provided by two recent experiments on reading readiness. Tanyzer *et al.* (1966) reported that 'introducing a consistent medium such as i.t.a. to kindergarten children in a formal reading program does not result in significantly better reading and spelling achievement than that attained by children who begin formal reading instruction in first grade in i.t.a. when both groups are measured (in T.O.) at the end of first grade.' But this is hardly surprising because the materials used were the i.t.a. Early-to-Read series *designed for six-year-olds*! In contrast, Shapiro and Willford (1969) used i.t.a. materials which were designed for *five-year-olds* (the i.t.a. Downing Readers and other special materials) and obtained significantly superior results from the children who began i.t.a. a year earlier. Similar errors with i.t.a. have been made in school systems. The i.t.a. Early-to-Read series designed for American six-year-olds was used with Canadian five-year-olds at Halifax, Nova Scotia, with such poor results that i.t.a. was abandoned altogether. This was a pity because i.t.a. can be of great benefit *if taught in a way adapted to the thinking of younger children*.

The essential need of beginning readers, whether in i.t.a. or in T.O. at any age below seven or eight, is rich and personally relevant language experiences and activities which

(a) *orientate* children correctly to the true purposes of reading and writing, and

(b) enable children's natural thinking processes *to generate understanding* of the technical concepts of language.

Almy (1967) states: 'An environment that provides the children with many opportunities for varied sensory and motor experiences is essential. So, too, is the presence of people who talk *with* (not merely to or at) the child, people who read and write and who share these activities with children.'

When the non-reader shares a reading experience with a reader, he is having the most fundamental learning experience of his life, because he is learning the vital truth that reading is gaining information from the printed page. Similarly through creative writing experiences such as those proposed in Allen's (1961) *language experience approach*, children learn by induction what it means to be an author, and thus that writing and reading are essentially a purposeful and relevant means of communication. The Plowden Commission report (DES, 1967) states: 'Books made by teachers and children about the doings of the class or of individuals in it figure prominently among the books which children enjoy. They help children to see *meaning* in reading and to appreciate *the purpose* of written records.'

In Britain, i.t.a.'s chief value has been in making this policy more effective, because children's independent authorship and the individualized approach to learning have come easier and earlier with i.t.a. Gayford (1969), headmistress of a British infants' school, reports this in her new book on i.t.a., and the same theme is expressed by Warburton and Southgate (1969) in their report on i.t.a. for the Schools Council which has followed up the scientific experiments on i.t.a. conducted by the present author (Downing, 1967).

The new Schools Council report says:

> The majority of teachers commented that the greater regularity and simplicity of i.t.a. enabled children to help themselves, far more than was possible with T.O. Children did not find it necessary to ask the teacher to tell them every new word they met. They soon discovered that they could 'puzzle it out for themselves'. The resultant change in procedure represented a swing away from instruction towards individual, independent learning.

It seems very sad that this aspect of i.t.a. has been missed by the majority of American schools adopting i.t.a. The American Early-to-Read i.t.a. series, for example, uses a formal synthetic phonics approach very different from the way in which i.t.a. has been introduced in British schools. Featherstone's (1967) articles provide a fine description of the revolution in methods in British schools which has been achieved in recent years. In a private letter to the author of this present article, Featherstone comments:

> Your justifiable concern that i.t.a. is being misused in America underlines the real danger: before we talk of i.t.a. or any innovation in teaching reading, however good, we must talk about making the whole approach to reading as flexible and individual as possible. When this is done, a useful innovation like i.t.a. will be very welcome, and there will be some chance that it will be used properly—that, for example, the children won't be set to memorizing the (forty-four) letters of i.t.a.'s improved alphabet, a spectacle that you and I would rightly agree in condemning.

Sadly, this is the common practice in many American i.t.a. classes, but fortunately not in all. The language experience i.t.a. program in Oakland County Schools, Michigan, is the most notable exception, and a similar program has been developed in some of the i.t.a. classes in Stockton, California, for example. But in Britain, i.t.a. fortunately has been more generally recognized as an aid to individualized learning and the development of creative self-expression through teaching approaches which have been described so expressively by such intuitively great teachers as Marshall (1963) and Ashton-Warner (1963).

Such authors have the rare gift of being able to portray the special insight into and sympathy with children's special ways of thinking which good teachers use in adapting the demands of the adult world to the natural development of their pupils. Psychological researchers like Piaget, Vygotsky, and Bruner provide the scientific evidence which confirms the judgment and great artistry of these intuitive teachers.

References

Allen, R. V. (1961) 'More ways than one', *Childhood Education*, 38, 108–11.

Almy, Millie C. (1967) 'Young children's thinking and the teaching of reading', in J. L. Frost (ed.), *Issues and Innovations in the Teaching of Reading*, Chicago, Scott Foresman.

Ashton-Warner, Sylvia (1963) *Teacher,* Secker & Warburg.

Bruner, J. S. (1960) *The Process of Education*, N.Y., Vintage Books.

Chall, Jeanne (1967) *Learning to Read: the Great Debate*, N.Y., McGraw-Hill.

Department of Education and Science (1967) *Children and their Primary Schools* (Plowden Report), 3 vols, HMSO.

Downing, J. (1967) *Evaluating the initial teaching alphabet*, Cassell.

Featherstone, J. (1967) *The Primary School Revolution in Britain*, pamphlet reprinting of three articles in the *New Republic*.

Foss, B. (1967) 'A psychological analysis of some reading processes', in J. Downing and Amy L. Brown (eds), *The Second International Reading Symposium*, Cassell.

Gayford, Olive (1969) *i.t.a in Primary Education*, Initial Teaching Publishing.

Marshall, Sybil (1963) *An Experiment in Education*, Cambridge University Press.

Piaget, J. (1959, revised edition) *The Language and Thought of the Child*, Routledge & Kegan Paul.

Reid, J. F. (1966) 'Learning to think about reading', *Educational Research*, 9, 56–62.

Shapiro, B. J. and Willford, R. E. (1969) 'i.t.a.—kindergarten or first grade?', *Reading Teacher*, 22, 307–11.

Strang, Ruth (1968) 'Is it debate or is it confusion?', *Reading Teacher*, 21, 575–7.

Tanyzer, H., Alpert, H. and Sandert, L. (1966) *Beginning Reading: the Effectiveness of i.t.a. and t.o.* (Report to the Commission of Education), Washington, D.C., U.S. Office of Education.

Vernon, M. D. (1957) *Backwardness in Reading*, Cambridge University Press.

Vygotsky, L. S. (1962) *Thought and Language*, MIT Press.

Warburton, F. W. and Southgate, Vera (1969) *An Independent Evaluation of i.t.a.* (Schools Council Report), Chambers.

Section 4 Looking at Texts

The papers in Section 3 showed the ways in which teaching materials affect and are affected by the pupil. Materials were shown to be related to methods of reading instruction which in turn depend on one's view of the nature of the reading process.

This Section includes papers which look at ways of assessing texts in terms of their level of difficulty, their readability, and in terms of their inherent biases. The choice has been highly selective and is not intended as representative of all factors which a teacher takes into account when matching reading material to pupils.

George Klare's article (4.1) looks at the assessment of text difficulty with the use of readability indices. The article covers the major readability formulae developed and, as such, can be viewed as a resource article for those wishing to explore the techniques in more detail. While some of the formulae look rather forbidding, readers are recommended to try and apply a couple of the indices to classroom materials. Only if one realises the 'diverse purposes' for which the formulae are used, and matches these to one's needs, can readability indices be developed with the 'maximum predictive validity'.

It is worth noting the reservations made about readability indices. Finding that, for example, word length and sentence length are relatively good predictors of readability does not necessarily imply that 'they *cause* ease or difficulty . . . they are merely good *indices* of difficulty.' Furthermore such indices are objective measure of the text itself which do not take into account the reactions of readers. Factors such as motivation may mean that the reader finds some material easier to read than other, even though 'objectively' they may be of the same measured level of difficulty.

In addition to readability indices we can assess text difficulty with the use of cloze procedure: 'an empirical measure which uses the performance of children upon the text being measured to obtain the readability level.' Donald Moyle (4.2) outlines the working of cloze procedures showing how it involves on the part of the child 'accuracy . . . fluency, and a knowledge of grammatical structure. Further, it necessitates understanding the text and therefore comprehension.' Clearly these are laudable aims, though as the description of the procedure shows, cloze tests need very careful treatment. Its application is not restricted to grading texts in terms of their difficulty. It can also be used as a diagnostic tool, as a teaching aid and as a test of attainment. Thus it provides a powerful tool for the classroom teacher, but like all powerful tools needs to be used sensitively.

Both cloze procedure and readability formulae provide a means to assess objectively the suitability of texts for pupils at different reading levels. Deciding on the 'suitability' of texts in terms of the values presented in them is necessarily subjective. The articles by Glenys Lobban (4.3) and Bob Dixon (4.4) look at the content of reading materials in terms of its influence on children's attitudes to the world and to themselves.

> Current knowledge suggests that children's books and particularly their first readers do influence children's attitudes. They do this by presenting models like themselves for the children to identify with and emulate. In addition they present an official view of the real world and 'proper' attitudes. (Lobban, 1974)

Lobban (4.3) takes issue with the sex-role content of children's reading primers. She found that females were predominantly featured as passive figures engaged in domestic activities, while males were adventurous and innovative. She notes: 'The world they depicted was not only sexist, it was more sexist than present reality'.

Dixon (4.4) looks at the racist bias of children's books, noting that 'a particularly strong aspect of the indoctrination carried on in children's literature is that of racism'. The examples he draws from children's books show how racial stereotypes permeate literature. Anecdotes of children, reflecting their race-consciousness, demonstrate the prevalence of racialist attitudes.

Acknowledgment of bias in text (it can never be eliminated) is at least a step towards correcting the balance.

As Lobban puts it: 'If we as educationalists care about the full development of each individual child, it is time we became fully aware of how materials such as reading schemes denigrate females. . .' And in a similar vein, Dixon states:

I've felt it necessary to quote the findings of these experiments in some detail because many people—and amongst them, depressingly, a great number of teachers—are reluctant to admit that small children are affected by racism and more reluctant still to admit that racist attitudes can be transmitted via literature.

4. 1 Assessing readability

George R. Klare

One of the problems in public education and mass communication is how to tell whether a particular piece of writing is likely to be readable to a particular group of readers. Several possible solutions are available.

A first is to guess. Writers and teachers have long been making estimates of readability with skill probably developed largely from experience and feedback from readers.[1] A second solution—particularly suitable when a precise index of readability is needed—is a test. In this case, a comprehension test covering the material must usually be built and refined before readability can be determined. With the large amount of reading material being published and available today, still another approach is often needed. Readability formulas have come to provide a third possible solution to the problem.

A readability formula uses counts of language variables in a piece of writing in order to provide an index of probable difficulty for readers. It is a predictive device in the sense that no actual participation is needed. Comprehension tests, on the other hand, are not predictive devices in this sense. Some kind of measurement of or by readers is needed in order to determine the difficulty of certain material for a larger population of readers.

A readability formula, which has been devised statistically to predict comprehension test scores, is more likely to be actually used. Some notion of the acceptance of readability formulas for this purpose can be seen from the development and popular use of

Source: *Reading Research Quarterly*, 10 (1), 1974–5, pp. 62–102 (abridged).

over thirty such formulas, plus at least ten variations, up to 1960 (Klare, 1963).

Use, of course, is not by itself evidence of predictive validity, as has been pointed out many times. Formulas are not perfect predictors (Klare, 1963, pp. 24–5, 111–56); evidence of how good they are must come from development and evaluation studies. Most of the formulas developed to date have used the McCall–Crabbs *Standard Test Lessons in Reading* (McCall and Crabbs, 1925, 1950, 1961) as a criterion. These lessons have been convenient statistically because there are a large number of reading passages, covering a wide range of difficulty, resting upon extensive testing, and providing detailed grade scores.

Recently the cloze procedure, developed by Taylor (1953), has begun to compete with and replace the usual multiple choice test in the measurement of readability. In its most common form, preparing a cloze test involves removing every fifth word in a passage and replacing it with a standard-sized blank. The reader is asked to fill in each blank, with only the deleted words (except for minor misspellings) accepted as correct answers. In research applications, it has become common to employ all five possible versions in which every fifth word is deleted (that is, one version with words 1, 6, 11 . . ., another with 2, 7, 12 . . . etc.). In this way, all words in a passage are subject to test. Other experimental arrangements have been used, such as varied deletion ratios and deletion of selected categories of words,[2] but these are uncommon.

Where cloze scores on a large number of passages covering a wide range of difficulty are available (Coleman, 1965; Bormuth, 1969), they can be used as criteria in formula development. This has recently become a popular method, to a great extent because of its objectivity and convenience for computer analysis. Furthermore, as Miller (1972, 1974) pointed out, formulas consistently yield higher predictive validity coefficients using cloze scores as a criterion than when using multiple choice test scores of the sort provided by the McCall–Crabbs *Standard Test Lessons in Reading*. Only infrequently are formulas developed using judgments of readability as a criterion, and sometimes these also have very high predictive validity coefficients.

This paper is concerned primarily with formulas and related devices for predicting readability that are available to a potential user. No attempt has been made to cover all devices. Summaries of work up to 1960 and between 1960 and 1974 are available elsewhere (Klare, 1963, 1974–5). Formulas have been included here only when they are still widely used, have been modified recently for continual use, or when necessary to clarify matters. Where possible, brief mention will be made of the criterion used in formula development and of the ability of the formula to predict that criterion or other criteria. Cross validation data will also be included.

The formulas and other devices presented will be grouped under three categories:

1 Recalculations and revisions of existing formulas.
2 New formulas, for general-purpose or special-purpose use.
3 Application aids, for both manual and machine use.

Certain publications will fit under several of the above headings. They will be listed where they seem most appropriate, but cross-reference will be made where desirable for clarity or completeness.

Recalculations and revisions

In the past formula developers have seemed quite willing to recalculate or revise their own formulas when they noted an error or came up with a new or better idea. More recent writers have also done so. The recalculations and revisions reported below will be grouped around the original version of the formula rather than presented chronologically.

The Lorge formula

Irving Lorge published the first version of his formula for children's material in 1939. The formula, designed to cover grades 3–12, was perhaps the first of the modern, easy-to-use formulas. It further set the stage for many to follow by using the *Standard Test Lessons in Reading* (McCall and Crabbs, 1925) as the criterion of difficulty. Lorge's first formula (below) correlated 0.77 with this criterion.

$$x_1 \text{ (grade placement)} = 0.07\, x_2 + 0.1301\, x_3 + 0.1073\, x_4 + 1.6126$$

Where: x_2 = average sentence length in words;
x_3 = number of prepositional phrases per 100 words;
x_4 = number of different hard words not on the Dale list of 769 words.

Lorge recalculated his formula in 1948, in order to correct an error that had been discovered (Lorge, 1948). It then took the following form (which the symbols defined as above):

$$X_1 \text{ (grade placement)} = 0.06\, x_2 + 0.10\, x_3 + 0.10\, x_4 + 1.99$$

The grade placement score in the first formula signified the reading ability necessary to answer correctly three-fourths of the test questions on a McCall–Crabbs passage. In the second formula, the grade placement score indicates that one-half the questions can be answered; if the three-fourths standard is desired, 1.866 should be added to the formula score.

Barker and Stokes (1968) proposed that the Lorge formula be simplified by using a count of the letter-length of words to approximate the count of words not on the Dale list. Tretiak (1969) also proposed that the Lorge formula be simplified, but in this case by dropping the count of prepositional phrases, since he found the count unreliable and of little added value for prediction in his recalculation of the Lorge formula using the 1961 edition of the McCall–Crabbs *Standard Test Lessons in Reading*.

The Flesch formulas

In 1943, Rudolf Flesch published his first formula, using the original McCall–Crabbs *Lessons* as a criterion. He designed it for general adult reading matter; in contrast to existing formulas, it gave, he felt, proper attention to abstract words as well as sentence length (Flesch, 1943).

$$\text{Grade placement} = 0.1338\, x_s + 0.0645\, x_m - 0.0659\, x_h - 0.7502$$

In this formula, grade placement refers to a 50 per cent comprehension level; adding the constant 4.2498 to that of 0.7502 gives the 75 per cent level of comprehension if desired. The formula was based partly on calculations of Lorge which were found to contain an error. Lorge, therefore, presented the following recalculation of Flesch's formula (Lorge, 1948):

$$\text{Grade placement} = 0.07\, x_m + 0.07\, x_s - 0.05\, x_h + 3.27$$

Where: x_m = number of affixes;
x_s = average sentence length in words;
x_h = number of personal references.

Flesch subsequently found (1948) that his count of affixes was time-consuming, that the count of personal references was misleading, and that the scoring system was unsatisfactory. He provided, therefore, two new formulas, again based upon the original McCall–Crabbs *Standard Test Lessons in Reading*.

RE (Reading Ease) = $206.835 - 0.846\, wl - 1.015\, sl$
HI (Human Interest) = $3.635\, pw + 0.314\, ps$

Where: wl = number of syllables per 100 words;
sl = average number of words per sentence;
pw = average of personal words per 100 words;
ps = number of personal sentences per 100 sentences.

The Reading Ease formula correlated 0.70 with the McCall–Crabbs criterion; the Human Interest formula correlated 0.43. Flesch contended that both the old affix count and the new syllable count measured abstractness, although he proposed a direct count of definite words as a way of getting at abstraction in a later formula (Flesch, 1950). Neither this 'Level of Abstraction' formula nor the several other formulas Flesch developed later were ever as popular with users as his earlier formulas. His Reading Ease formula, on the other hand, became one of the most widely used in the history of readability measurement.

As noted, Flesch's formulas, as well as those of Lorge and many others, used the original (1925) edition of the McCall–Crabbs *Standard Test Lessons in Reading* as a criterion. A 1950 revision of this set of passages provided an excellent opportunity for revalidation of existing formulas. Powers, Sumner, and Kearl (1958) seized this opportunity to recalculate several widely used formulas; Tretiak (1969) also followed this procedure later, as has been noted. Powers, Sumner, and Kearl provided the following version of the Reading Ease formula:

$$RE = -2.2029 + 0.0778 \, sl + 0.0455 \, wl$$

They also noted that the correlation of the revised Flesch formula scores with the 1950 McCall–Crabbs scores was 0.64, whereas it had been 0.70 with the 1925 McCall–Crabbs scores.

The Dale–Chall formula

Dale and Chall presented their formula for adult materials in 1948; it quickly became, along with Flesch's Reading Ease formula, one of the two most widely used. It was designed—as Flesch's revision had been—to correct certain shortcomings in the original Flesch formula. Similar to Flesch's, it used the 1925 McCall–Crabbs *Standard Test Lessons in Reading* as a criterion. It had a 3,000-word list, which was deemed preferable to the 769-word Dale list used by Lorge, especially for the more difficult levels of readability. Flesch's count of personal references was avoided as unnecessary, and in order to keep it easy to use, only 2 factors were used. The Dale–Chall formula correlated 0.70 with McCall–Crabbs criterion scores.

$$X_{c50} = 0.1570 \, x_1 + 0.496 \, x_2 + 3.6365$$

Where: X_{c50} = reading grade score of a pupil who could answer one-half the test questions on a passage correctly;

x_1 = Dale score, or percentage of words outside the Dale list of 3,000;

x_2 = average sentence length in words.

As they had of Flesch's Reading Ease formula, Powers, Sumner, and Kearl (1958) provided a recalculated version of it, based upon the 1950 edition of the McCall–Crabbs *Lessons*. They found a correlation using their recalculated formula with 1950 McCall–Crabbs scores of 0.71, which is virtually the same as the 0.70 found with the 1925 McCall–Crabbs scores by Dale and Chall (1948). This, plus other consistent evidence, suggested that the Dale–Chall was the most accurate general-purpose formula available up to 1960 (Klare, 1963). The recalculated formula presented by Powers, Sumner, and Kearl follows.

$$X_{c50} = 3.2672 + 0.0596\, x_2 + 0.1155\, x_1$$

Nyman, Kearl, and Powers (1961) attempted to shorten the list of 3,000 familiar words used with the Dale–Chall formula in order to make it easier to use. They found they could reduce the list to 920 words by including only those of the 3,000 found also in the AA (most frequent) group of words in the Thorndike–Lorge count (Thorndike and Lorge, 1944). Their revised version of the Dale–Chall formula using this list was found to correlate with the McCall–Crabbs *Lessons* (1950 edition) to the extent of 0.58 ($R^2 = 0.34$). This version yielded the same R^2 values as the Gunning formula (Gunning, 1952) and the Farr–Jenkins–Paterson formula (Farr, Jenkins, and Paterson, 1951). The original version of the Dale–Chall formula using the 3,000-word list yielded an R^2 value of 0.51, however; so the authors concluded that the regular list should be used. They also suggested, however, that other schemes for shortening the regular list should be tried.

Brown (1965) developed his revision of the Dale–Chall formula for another purpose. He felt that science books were being rated more difficult than they should be because the Dale list lacked commonly known science words. He found that by using the regular Dale–Chall formula except for adding 7 such words from a list he had developed to the 3,000-word Dale list, two science books were given scores two grades lower than before.

Holmquist (1968) went several steps further in his analysis than Brown. First, a new version of the McCall–Crabbs *Standard Test Lessons in Reading* appeared in 1961. Following the example of Powers, Sumner, and Kearl (1958), Holmquist recalculated the Dale–Chall formula, with the following results (symbols as defined by Dale and Chall)

$$X_{c50} = 0.0512\, x_2 + 0.1142\, x_1 + 3.442.$$

Then, following the lead of Brown, and in fact using his list of science terms, Holmquist found 102 words known to 80 per cent of fourth graders (and therefore of the same level of difficulty as

Dale's 3,000 words). He recalculated the Dale–Chall formula on the basis of analyses made with the expanded list of 3,102 words, with the following formula resulting.

$$X_{c50} = 0.0510 \ x_2 + 0.1195 \ x_1' + 3.4457$$

Where: x_1' = words not on the expanded Dale list of 3,102 (all other symbols as defined by Dale and Chall).

Holmquist found that his recalculated formulas, with and without the added science terms, provided multiple correlations of 0.69 and 0.68 respectively. These are very similar to that of 0.70 found by Dale and Chall for their original formula and that of 0.71 found by Powers, Sumner, and Kearl for their recalculated Dale–Chall formula. Holmquist did find, however, that his two formulas and that of Powers, Sumner, and Kearl had a somewhat lower standard error of estimate than the original Dale–Chall formula: 0.80, 0.79, and 0.77 respectively. On this basis, he raised the question of whether changes that have occurred in the vocabularies and reading abilities of pupils since Dale and Chall's work might not have lowered the validity of the Dale–Chall formula for today's use. He felt that such newly recalculated and revised versions as his own might therefore be preferable.

The Farr–Jenkins–Paterson formula

In 1951, J. N. Farr, J. J. Jenkins, and D. G. Paterson proposed a formula that was similar to Flesch's Reading Ease formula but simpler to apply. The authors felt that substituting a count of one-syllable words for Flesch's syllable count could reduce analysis time and remove the need for the analyst to know syllabication rules, yet the result would be equally predictive. Their formula did in fact produce scores on two sets of passages which correlated 0.93 and 0.95 with Flesch scores on the same passages.

New Reading Ease Index = $1.599 \ \text{nosw} - 1.015 \ \text{sl} - 31.517$

Where: nosw = number of one-syllable words per 100 words;
 sl   = average sentence length in words

Just as Powers, Sumner, and Kearl (1958) had recalculated the Flesch Reading Ease and Dale–Chall formulas, they also recalculated the Farr–Jenkins–Paterson formula on the basis of the 1950 revision of the McCall–Crabbs *Standard Test Lessons in Reading*. They provided the following version, which was found to produce scores which correlated 0.58 with McCall–Crabbs criterion scores.

$$X_{c50} = 8.4335 + 0.0923 \ \text{sl} + 0.0648 \ \text{nosw}$$

The Fog Index

Another formula which, like the Farr–Jenkins–Paterson, was related to Flesch's Reading Ease formula, was Robert Gunning's Fog Index (1952). Rather than counting number of syllables as Flesch did or counting one-syllable words as Farr, Jenkins, and Paterson did, Gunning proposed counting words of three or more syllables. These he termed 'hard words,' which were entered in the following formula.

Reading grade level = 0.4 (average sentence length + percentage of words of three or more syllables).

Once again, Powers, Sumner, and Kearl (1958) provided a recalculated version using the 1950 McCall–Crabbs *Standard Test Lessons in Reading* as a criterion. They found that scores for the McCall–Crabbs passages based upon their newly recalculated formula correlated 0.59 with the reading grade scores on the passages.

$X_{c_{50}}$ = 3.0680 + 0.0877 (average sentence length) + 0.0984 (percentage of monosyllables).

The Spache formula

George Spache developed his original formula for children's material of grades 1 to 3 in 1953.

Grade level = 0.141 x_1 + 0.086 x_2 + 0.839

Where: x_1 = average sentence length in words;
x_2 = number of words outside the Dale list of 769 words.

Spache validated his formula against level of classroom use for 152 books in grades 1 to 3, finding a multiple correlation coefficient of 0.818.

Stone (1956) felt that the accuracy of Spache's formula could be increased by replacing 173 words in the Dale list of 769 with an equal number from Krantz's 'The Author's Word List' and his own *A Graded Vocabulary for Primary Reading*. He found that using the revised list in Spache's formula yielded a lower rating than the original Dale list used in the formula. Spache, in his own subsequent publications, followed this procedure in using Stone's Revised Word List (Spache, 1966). Very recently, Spache (1974) revised his formula on the basis of use of the Harris–Jacobson *Basic Elementary Reading Vocabularies*. He has reported a correlation of 0.95 between formula scores and grade level of primary books.

New formulas

A number of new formulas were developed after 1960, some for general application and some for use with special kinds of materials. Both types will be presented together in chronological order, with an added note where special application is intended.

The Devereaux formula

Edgar A. Smith published the first version of his general formula in 1961 (Smith, 1960–1). He called it the Devereaux formula, after the foundation where he then worked. It differed from previous formulas primarily by using a count of character-spaces (that is, letters, numbers, punctuation marks) to estimate word difficulty. At that time Smith felt that this count was faster or easier than other counts, particularly for users who were not versatile with English or grammar. In addition, the ·count made for easy automation.[3] The original version of Smith's formula, designed to cover grades 4–12, was as follows:

$$\text{Grade placement} = 1.56\,W_L + 0.19\,S_L - 6.49$$

Where: W_L = word length in character spaces;
S_L = sentence length in words.

Smith also presented the following simplified version, which did not result in grade levels, but from which tabled values of grade levels could be read.

$$\text{Index} = 8\,W_L + S_L$$

The Botel formula

The Botel method of predicting readability is not, as are most others, a regression equation. Since it has been used as a general formula, however, it is included with others here. Botel's method (1962) is to predict reading level from the median difficulty of samples of words whose grade levels are determined through the presence in or absence from a 'Graded Vocabulary List.' This gives the *Botel Readability Score*, which may vary from pre-primer level to grade 12 in difficulty.

The Danielson–Bryan formula

The general formula developed by Danielson and Bryan (1963) used the same variables as had been used by Smith (1961): characters per space and characters per sentence. Smith had felt his formula was easier to use manually as well as, later, to automate. Danielson and Bryan, on the other hand, developed their formula specifically for automated use—the first one developed specifically for this purpose. Actually, they presented two versions of their formula—the first a pure regression equation and the second scaled to provide most scores in the 0–100 range used in the Flesch Reading Ease and Farr–Jenkins–Paterson formulas. And, as Flesch had done, they used the McCall–Crabbs *Standard Test Lessons in Rèading* as a criterion, achieving a correlation of 0.575 between formula scores and passage scores. Their formulas were the following:

DB no. 1 = 1.0364 CPSp + 0.0194 CPSt − 0.6059
DB no. 2 = 131.059 − 10.364 CPSp − 0.194 CPSt

Where: CPSp = characters per space;
CPSt = characters per sentence

The Readability Graph

Fry proposed a 'Readability Graph' in 1965 for predicting readability, recommending it as a way of saving the user's time and effort. It first appeared in his book *Teaching Faster Reading: a Manual*, published in England (Fry, 1965), and later in American publications (Fry, 1968a, 1968b, 1969; Gaver, 1969). Fry used the common formula variables of syllables per 100 words and words per sentence and actually referred to his method as a formula (probably for reader convenience) in the title of one of his papers (Fry, 1968a), but no formula as such was presented. The user simply enters the counts of the above variables in a graph and reads the readability grade score directly from it.[4] Fry's graph has been validated on both primary and secondary materials, and the scores derived from it correlate highly with those from several well-known formulas. Maginnis (1969) has recently extended the Fry graph downward through the preprimer level.

The Coleman formulas

In 1965, Coleman completed a research project sponsored by the National Science Foundation in which he presented four readability formulas for general use.[5] Coleman's formulas are notable for first use of the cloze procedure as a criterion rather than the commonly used McCall–Crabbs *Lessons* or rankings by judges. Coleman's four formulas took the following forms:

C% = 1.29w − 38.45

$$C\% = 1.16w + 1.48s - 37.95$$
$$C\% = 1.07w + 1.18s + 0.76p - 34.02$$
$$C\% = 1.04w + 1.06s + 0.56p - 0.36prep - 26.01$$

Where: C% = percentage of correct cloze completions;
     w = number of one-syllable words per 100 words;
     s = number of sentences per 100 words;
     p = number of pronouns per 100 words;
 prep = number of prepositions per 100 words.

Coleman found multiple correlations of 0.86, 0.89, 0.90, and 0.91, respectively, for his formulas with cloze criterion scores. In a cross-validation, Szalay (1965) found correlations of 0.83, 0.88, 0.87, and 0.89, respectively, for the four formulas with cloze scores on a new set of passages. The use of cloze scores as a criterion, as was noted, consistently provides higher validation coefficients than does use of McCall–Crabbs scores; and this is at least a partial reason for the high correlations presented above.

The Easy Listening formula

Fang, in presenting his 'Easy Listening Formula' (1966–7), argued that 'listenability' is not necessarily 'readability.' Consequently, he used newscasts in studying the validity of his measure, called ELF. Since, in addition, he argues that a formula for listenability should be simply stated if it is to be used, he arrived at the following version, where an average sentence score below 12 is considered desirable for mass listenability.

ELF = number of syllables above one per word in a sentence

Fang found a correlation of 0.96 between scores from his formula and from Flesch's Reading Ease formula on thirty-six television scripts and thirty-six newspaper samples.

The Elley formula

The method of assessing readability devised by Elley (1969) is not a regression equation, as are most formulas. But since, as in the case of Botel's method, it is used as a formula, it is included here. Elley found, through various approaches, that the best single predictor of readability was some measure of vocabulary load. He settled upon nouns and found that noun frequency in five series of passages correlated more highly than did other measures with judges' criteria of difficulty for the passages. The 0.90 median correlational value he found was not reached even by any combination of two measures. His method consists of selecting passages long enough to contain at least twenty different nouns, then determining their mean frequency according to the NZCER (New Zealand Council for Educational Research) *Alphabetical Spelling List*. Reading age levels can then be determined by means of a table.

SMOG grading

In 1969, McLaughlin published his SMOG grading formula, a technique which he believes to be quicker, simpler, and more valid than previous methods of assessing readability. He believes that both word length and sentence length measures are needed but that they should be multiplied rather than added. By counting the number of words of three or more syllables (polysyllable count) in the proper number of sentences (30), he has been able to remove the usual multiplication procedures, and provide the following simple formula for use with the sentences:

SMOG grading = 3 + square root of polysyllable count.

McLaughlin validated his formula against the McCall–Crabbs passages, but used the 100 per cent comprehension criterion rather than the 50 or 75 per cent criteria used by most previous writers. For this reason, his formula gives scores two grades higher (less readable), generally, than the Dale–Chall formula. The validity of his formula may be best judged, he feels, by the standard error of estimate of its predictions, which is 1.5 grades. Though this is somewhat higher than that for other formulas, he believes that the grade-level corrections made by others make his formula's predictions comparable to theirs.

The Bormuth formulas

In 1969, Bormuth published the most extensive readability analyses yet made. He used 330 passages of about 100 words each, ranging in difficulty from first grade to college and covering a wide range of subject matter. He used the cloze procedure as his criterion of difficulty, deleting every fifth word but using all five parallel versions of this deletion ratio. His subjects were 2,600 fourth to twelfth grade pupils, who took a total of 650 different passages. This gave him a total of approximately 276 responses per deleted word, or something over 2 million responses to analyze. It is perhaps not so surprising, then, that he would have checked the potential value of as many as 169 variables against these data, and from them have developed twenty-four readability formulas. He also provided certain kinds of new measures not given by previous writers: independent readability formulas to predict word length, minimal punctuation unit length, and sentence length, as well as the usual passage length. Finally, he provided formulas to predict 35, 45, and 55 per cent cloze criterion scores as well as mean cloze criterion scores. No attempt will be made to present all of Bormuth's formulas here, especially since his 'unrestricted' formulas contained from fourteen to twenty variables each. Instead, only a sample of the formulas of greatest interest, notably those for manual computation, will be listed. The interested reader can check Bormuth's paper (1969, pp. 57–71) for the other formulas.

1 $C(M) = 1.051674 - 0.099691 (LET/W) - 0.004236 (LET/MPU) + 0.000015 (LET/MPU)^2$

2 $GP(35) = 0.861207 + 1.279050 (LET/W) + 0.050548 (LET/MPU) - 0.000172 (LET/MPU)^2$

3 $GP(45) = 1.849494 + 1.307968 (LET/W) + 0.053930 (LET/MPU) - 0.000191 (LET/MPU)^2$

4 $GP(55) = 1.231834 + 2.764035 (LET/W) - 0.023845 (LET/W)^3 + 0.051591 (LET/MPU) - 0.000186 (LET/MPU)^2$

5 $C(M) = 0.578543 - 0.014349 (LET) + 0.000054 (LET)^2 - 0.0000004 (LET)^3 - 0.047842 (W) - 0.000748 (W)^2 + 0.000005 (W)^3$

6 $C(M) = 0.900063 - 0.092991 (LET) + 0.000382 (LET)^3 - 0.063139 (NR) - 0.006637 (ML) + 0.009844 (NR)^2 - 0.044190 (L-S) - 0.035738 (SYL)$

7 $C(M) = 0.812807 - 0.100400 (LET) + 0.000410 (LET)^3 - 0.037406 (SYL)$

Where:
C (M)	=	cloze mean;
GP (35)	=	grade placement cloze score of 35;
GP (45)	=	grade placement cloze score of 45;
GP (55)	=	grade placement cloze score of 55;
LET/W	=	letters per word;
LET/MPU	=	letters per minimal punctuation unit;
NR	=	right depth of sentence, based on Nida's analysis;
ML	=	left depth of sentence, based on modern analysis;
L-S	=	lexical words minus structural words;
SYL	=	syllables.

Formulas 1 to 4 are passage-level formulas; 5 is a sentence-level formula; and 6 and 7 are word-level formulas (the first with words in context and the second with words in isolation). Bormuth, as a careful researcher, presented multiple correlation coefficients with his criteria both for validation and cross-validation (in the case of passage-level formulas). They are, for the seven formulas taken serially, with the validation figure first and the cross-validation figure second, where appropriate: 0.81 and 0.83, 0.79 and 0.83, 0.80 and 0.84, 0.79 and 0.82, 0.62, 0.53, 0.52. In the case of the unrestricted formulas having up to twenty variables, the cross-validation coefficients dropped considerably below the validation coefficients. As Bormuth points out, the formulas were simply too complex for their predictiveness to be maintained in cross-validation.

The Mugford Readability Chart

Mugford (1970) has developed a predictive method for readability which, like Fry's, provides a graphic solution instead of a formular solution. Though the Mugford Readability Chart was initially intended for 5½ to 15 year reading ages, the Chart has been extended to cover material for adults. It uses the common variables of word-length in syllables and sentence-length in words, but also takes repetition into account; deriving a score involves only the addition of four whole numbers. Mugford has compared the scores from his Chart against authors', teachers', and publishers' ratings; but he urges further research with it.

The Syntactic Complexity formula

Botel and Granowsky (1972a, b) have suggested that a difficulty measure for primary grade materials based upon syntactic complexity should parallel the usual readability formulas, which emphasize vocabulary. They have rated the complexity of various sentence structures on a 0–3 basis and have suggested that, for measurement purposes, an arithmetic average be taken of the complexity count of sentences in the material to be graded. Botel and Granowsky have suggested a number of uses for the formula, but they indicate that their work is, at this time, 'a directional instrument' and 'a directional effort.' Note, in this connection, that other beginning attempts have been made to use syntactic complexity—by Brewer (1972) and Endicott (1973). Brewer used an automated syntactic analysis technique based on linguistic and psycholinguistic theories. He found a number of significant correlations between syntactic measures and McCall–Crabbs scores, but the major contributors were simply sentence and passage length. He achieved a multiple regression of 0.48 but an unacceptable level of error with his syntactic complexity measure and the words per passage. Endicott proposed a scale for syntactic complexity based upon the 'co-meme' unit. These units are of four types—base, syntactic, compression, and morphemic—and can be used to provide sentence counts. As Endicott notes, however, the scale has not as yet been weighted for readability, which he feels would be a desirable next step.

The FORCAST readability formula

Caylor, Sticht, Fox, and Ford (1973) have carried out an extensive study of the reading requirements of military occupational specialties. In the course of their work, they found existing readability formulas to have certain limitations when used with US army materials, and consequently decided to develop a formula specifically for such an application. They developed cloze versions of military materials, and used a 35 per cent comprehension criterion (equivalent to approximately 70 per cent on a multiple choice test) with army recruits as subjects. After checking the correlation of fifteen variables with that criterion, they developed the following formula, based on a 150-word (as opposed to the more common 100-word) sample.

$$RGL = 20.43 - (0.11) \text{ (number of 1-syllable words)}$$

Where: RGL = reading grade level.

In order to simplify this formula, they made some minor adjustments, as shown below, and called it the FORCAST readability formula.

$$\text{FORCAST RGL} = 20 - \frac{\text{number of 1-syllable words}}{10}$$

The RIDE scale

Carver (1974) has recently proposed the RIDE scale, which is simply the average number of letters per word (using certain decision rules). He established the validity of the scale by comparing it to the values from five traditional readability formulas—the Flesch Reading Ease, the Dale–Chall, the Automated Readability Index, the SMOG index, and the Fry Graph—on the cloze scores for the thirty-six passages developed by Coleman (1971). Carver proposed five levels of difficulty of reading materials based on RIDE scores: Level 1, or approximately beginning reading; Level 2, or approximately elementary school materials; Level 3, or approximately, secondary school materials; Level 4, or approximately college level materials; and Level 5, or approximately graduate school materials. Carver has found his scale to be somewhat less valid than the Flesch Reading Ease (1948) and Dale–Chall (1948) formulas, a fate it shares (in his research) with that of Smith (1960–1), McLaughlin (1969), and Fry (1965).

The Harris–Jacobson Primary Readability formulas

Two new formulas were described recently by Harris and Jacobson (1973). One was developed for grades 1–3 and the other for grades 1–6 (but chiefly for grades 4–6). Both were found to correlate 0.90 with reader grade level; the former was found to have a standard error of estimate of 0.38 years, the latter of 0.71 years. Complete description and directions for application will appear in Harris and Sipay (1975). It is interesting to note that Jacobson, in unpublished work, also found that he could use spelling patterns as the basis for readability prediction. He found that by using one group of twelve spelling patterns for primary and another group for middle-grade material he was able to achieve a multiple-correlation of 0.965 with grade level of material. A computer and a complex program are needed for application. Jacobson (1974) also found that by using thirty-seven spelling patterns combined in a multiple regression equation he could achieve a correlation of 0.92 with primary reading difficulty.

Application aids

Readability formulas have, in most cases, been intended for wide usage, but time and effort, if not fear of numbers, have long restricted this. Consequently, there have been a number of efforts to make formulas easier and/or quicker to apply. The first such efforts were intended to help those applying formulas by hand, but beginning in the early 1960s, writers began to provide automated versions of formulas; almost all such automated versions were, of course, computer programs. The application aids mentioned in this section will be grouped by formula, and then separated into manual and machine aids.

The Lorge formula

Machine aids. Fraser (undated) provided one of the earliest attempts to automate available readability formulas to come to the author's attention. He developed FORTRAN IV programs for both the Lorge formula and the Flesch Reading Ease formula. This is the only attempt to automate the Lorge formula known to the author. Many other programs for the Flesch formula have since become available (see below), and more recent work does not require the pre-editing of text, as Fraser's approach did.

The Flesch Reading Ease formula

Manual aids. One of the first application aids to be provided for any formula was the set of tables provided by Farr and Jenkins (1949) for Flesch's 'Reading Ease' and 'Human Interest' formulas (1948). Flesch himself provided a chart for quick determination of scores with these formulas in his *How to Test Readability* (1951), and General Motors provided a plastic hand calculator for this same purpose soon after. Powers and Ross (1959) provided a calculating diagram for use with the Flesch Reading Ease formula as recalculated by Powers, Sumner, and Kearl (1958). Though these aids are still useful, more recently interest has shifted almost exclusively to the automation of the original version of the Flesch Reading Ease formula.

An exception to the preceding statement is the ingenious method developed by Kincaid and McDaniel (1974) for using an electronic metronome to pace manual counts. They report (McDaniel, 1974) faster and more reliable counts for this method than the usual manual method, with the values approaching the counts for the Automated Readability Index (Smith and Senter, 1967).

Machine aids. The first attempts to automate the Flesch Reading Ease formula were those of Fraser (undated) and Fang (1968), who provided the first syllable counters. Klare *et al.* (1969) borrowed from the work of Fang, Berkeley (1967), and Coke and Rothkopf (1970) in preparing a syllable counter and an automated version of Flesch's formula. Coke and Rothkopf's automated version of the Flesch formula, however, was not based upon a direct syllable count, but rather upon the simpler but somewhat less accurate method of estimation of number of syllables using vowels/word, consonants/word, and letters/word algorithms. Felsenthal and Felsenthal (1972) also used a letter count to estimate the number of syllables in their automated program (TEXAN) for the Flesch Reading Ease formula. They have, in addition, provided an automated version of the rarely used Human Interest formula. General Motors (undated) has provided a commercial computer program for the Flesch Reading Ease formula called STAR (Simple Test Approach for Readability). This program has a syllable counter. It also provides a derived 'Dale Index' (Dale–Chall score) based on the computed 'Flesch Index' (Flesch Reading Ease score). Finally, the University of Texas Instructional Materials Service (undated) uses computer programs for the Flesch Reading Ease formula (and also three other formulas, noted below).

The Farr–Jenkins–Paterson formula

Manual aids. Farr, Jenkins, and Paterson (1951) provided an application aid along with the publication of their formula. Powers and Ross (1959) subsequently published a calculating diagram for the Powers, Sumner, and Kearl (1958) revision of the formula.

Machine aids. Danielson and Bryan (1963), as noted, published the first computer program for readability measurement in developing their own formula. However, it was in developing a computer version of the Farr–Jenkins–Paterson formula that they came to do so; both may therefore be considered the 'first computer formula.' Klare *et al.* (1969) and University of Texas (undated) also provided a computer version of the formula.

The Fog Index

Manual aids. Gunning's original Fog Index (1952) was set up in such a manner that manual application aids of the typical sort are not necessary, although he himself admits (1968) that it has some unnecessary complications. Powers, Sumner, and Kearl's revision (1958) is not as easily applied as Gunning's original, however; and Powers and Ross (1959) consequently presented a calculating diagram for it.

Machine aids. Klare *et al.* (1969) and Felsenthal and Felsenthal (1972) have provided computer programs for applying Gunning's Fog Index.

The Dale–Chall formula

Manual aids. Klare (1952) developed the first manual aid, a table, for rapid determination of Dale–Chall readability scores (Dale and Chall, 1948). Subsequent modifications were suggested by Goltz (1964) to save additional time. Koenke (1971) then provided a graphic method for quick computation of scores. Powers and Ross (1959) provided a calculating diagram for the revised Dale–Chall formula developed by Powers, Sumner, and Kearl (1958), and Williams (1972) provided a table for rapid determination of revised Dale–Chall scores.

Machine aids. Because of the special rules for use, it has been more difficult to develop a computer program for word-list formulas, such as the Dale–Chall (or Spache, 1953, 1966), than for syllable-count formulas, such as the Flesch, Farr–Jenkins–Paterson, or Gunning. However, Krueger and Stolurow (1965) were able to use the computer to develop an extended word list (base words plus endings) for the Dale–Chall formula. MacRae and Miller (1971a) were able to make use of the list in developing an assembler program for the Dale–Chall formula. They achieved the desired accuracy in their program by providing a number of pre-editing functions for the card puncher to follow. Soon afterward, several other automated versions of the Dale–Chall program appeared. Rakes (1972) prepared such a program as part of his study involving the application of the Dale–Chall formula, as well as the Gunning (1952) and Fry (1968) methods to adult basic education materials. Branch (1972) developed a highly detailed version of the Dale–Chall formula that appears to be able to handle the 30-odd special rules for its application (which few such programs can do). It was written in PL-1 language for the IBM S360/40 computer. R. J. Butz (1973) has also developed a sophisticated program, called READABL, for applying the Dale–Chall formula. This appears to be the same program used at the University of Texas, Instructional Materials Service (undated). It provides such related data for scores as 95 per cent confidence intervals, standard deviations, standard errors of means, and skewness indices. Finally, as noted, General Motors' STAR computer program (undated) provides Dale–Chall scores derived from Flesch Reading Ease scores.

The Spache formula

Manual aids. Safier (1959) provided a short method for using the 1953 version of the Spache formula (Spache, 1953), designed to save application time. The only change from the usual application procedure was to count exactly 100 words (rather than to count to the end of a complete sentence) and use a conversion table for sentence length.

Machine aids. Felsenthal and Felsenthal (1972) have provided a computer program (TEXAN) for applying the revised Spache formula (Stone, 1956; Spache, 1966).

The Bormuth formulas

Machine aids. Bormuth (1969) provided six readability formulas designed specifically for computer application. They involved variables which a computer could calculate directly from a literal keypunching of a passage or from scanning of a text. Four of the formulas were designed for passage-level material, one for sentence-level material, and one for word-level material. MacRae and Miller (1971b) provided a computer program to apply the Bormuth passage-level machine formula.

The Automated Readability Index (*Devereaux*)

Machine aids. As indicated earlier, Smith developed a formula for manual use that he called the Devereaux formula (Smith, 1960–1). Since it used the variables of character-spaces per word and sentence, it was readily convertible to machine analysis. Such a program was developed (Smith and Kincaid, 1970, p. 464), but not before a unique typewriter-based, automated count called the Automated Readability Index (ARI) was developed (Smith and Senter, 1967). The ARI is calculated automatically as data are collected during typing of material on a modified electric typewriter.

Summary

The potential user of a readability formula has many formulas to choose from—almost too many. It is tempting to recommend one over another in order to help. Formulas are, however, so varied and are used for such diverse purposes that the recommendations are likely to be either too simple to be accurate or too complex to be convenient. The course chosen here, therefore, is to provide a set of guideposts for choosing among the formulas reviewed.

Which formula to use must, of course, depend first upon the user's needs; if he has a special purpose, he may be able to find just what he wants. Under such circumstances, formulas are likely to have their maximum predictive validity.

The user of a general-purpose formula, one intended to cover a wide range of difficulty in general materials, can first decide whether he wishes to apply a formula manually or by machine. If he has a relatively small amount of material to analyze, manual application is the more practical, especially if available manual application aids are used. If he has a great deal of material to analyze, computer programs can be very helpful.

A review of the general formulas available provides further suggestions. Unless a user is interested in doing research, there is little to be gained from choosing a highly complex formula. A simple two-variable formula should be sufficient, especially if one of the variables is a word or semantic variable and the other is a sentence or syntactic variable. Beyond these two variables, further additions add relatively little predictive validity compared to the added application time involved, and a formula with very many variables is likely to be unreliably applied by hand. As a matter of fact, a formula with as many as twenty variables may well be an unreliable predictor even if applied by machine.

The word or semantic variable is consistently more highly predictive than the sentence or syntactic variable when each is considered singly. This appears to be the case for other languages as well as English. When a word variable is to be counted, there are two common choices: count word length, or count number of words not on a particular list of familiar words. If the count is to be made by hand, counting syllables in some fashion (all syllables, one-syllable words, or multi-syllable words) is somewhat faster than using most word lists. If the count is to be made by machine and the user wishes to write his own program, counting letters will give fairly good results and a computer can be instructed much more easily how to make a reliable count.

Using a list of familiar words appears to give a slightly more predictive index than counting word length, probably because length is a (secondary) reflection of familiarity. Zipf's principle, as well as other evidence (see Klare, 1968), indicates that as words are used more frequently they become shorter. Using word lists does create practical problems, however. The most important is that one cannot hope to include all words in a piece of writing on a list. The longer a list gets, in the attempt to approach this, the more likely it is to discourage the user (eventually, even, the computer user).

Fortunately, the list need not be extremely long, since humans tend to repeat familiar words so much more frequently than unfamiliar. Ten words may make up as much as 25 per cent of college freshman writing; 100 words may make up as much as 95 per cent of adult telephone conversations. Furthermore, one can get a relatively accurate picture of readability by noting the familiarity of the content words alone, that is, the nouns, verbs, adjectives, and adverbs. Of these, the nouns appear to be most critical. Several writers, using this kind of logic, have suggested that special terms be added to increase a list's predictive validity for special purposes (for example, scientific materials or religious materials). Such additions appear to be of limited value, however, and they restrict the circumstances when the formula can be used.

The sentence variable, though not as predictive of difficulty as the word variable, does have an important contribution to make to formulas. Though sentences can be evaluated in several ways, a simple count of length is generally sufficient either by hand or machine. Sentence complexity is probably the real causal factor in difficulty, but length correlates very highly with complexity and is much easier to count.

It may seem surprising that counts of the two simple variables of word length and sentence length are sufficient to make relatively good predictions of readability. No argument that they *cause* ease or difficulty is intended; they are merely good *indices* of difficulty. Consequently, altering word or sentence length, of themselves, can provide no assurance of improving readability. How to achieve more readable writing is another and much more complex endeavor. But as long as predictions are all that is needed, the evidence that simple word and sentence counts can provide satisfactory predictions for most purposes is now quite conclusive.

Notes

1 For a review of attempts by judges to estimate reading ability, and their accuracy in doing so, see Klare (1976).
2 See Klare, Simaiko, and Stolurow (1972) for a review of related literature.
3 This is discussed further under *Application aids* on p. 263 of this article.
4 In this sense, Fry's graph is close to what is discussed under *Application aids* (p. 263) but since it is actually also a new predictive device, it is covered here.
5 Since the Final Report of the project in which they appeared (Coleman, 1965) is not easily obtained, note that they may also be found in Szalay's cross-validation of their predictiveness (Szalay, 1965) and in Coleman's chapter in a book edited by Rothkopf and Johnson (1971).

References

Barker, D. G. and Stokes, W. W. (1968) 'A simplification of the revised Lorge readability formula', *Journal of Educational Research*, 61, May–June, 398–400.

Berkeley, Edmund C. (1967) *Computer-assisted Explanation*, Cambridge, Mass., Information International.

Bormuth, John R. (1969) Development of Readability Analyses, Final Report, Project no. 7–0052, Contract no. OEC–3–7–070052–0326, USOE, Bureau of Research, US Department of Health, Education, and Welfare, March.

Botel, Morton (1962) *Botel Predicting Readability Levels*, Chicago, Follett.

Botel, Morton and Granowsky, Alvin (1972a) 'A formula for measuring syntactic complexity: a directional effort', *Elementary English*, 49, April, 513–16.

Botel, Morton and Granowsky, Alvin (1972b) 'A New Formula for Measuring Syntactic Complexity', paper presented at International Reading Association Convention, Detroit, Michigan, April.

Branch, Lee Edward (1972) 'The Dale–Chall Readability Formula as Programmed for the Computer', unpublished doctoral dissertation, Claremont Graduate School, *Dissertation Abstracts*, 30, 2316A–2317A.

Brewer, Richard Kemp (1972) 'The Effect of Syntactic Complexity on Readability', unpublished doctoral dissertation, University of Wisconsin, *Dissertation Abstracts*, 23, 2404A–2405A.

Brouwer, R. H. (1963) 'Onderzock naar de Leesmoeilijkheid van Nederlands Proza', *Paedagogische Studien*, 40, 454–64.

Brown, Walter R. (1965) 'Science textbook selection and the Dale–Chall formula', *School Science and Mathematics*, 65, February, 164–7.

Butz, Roy J. (1973) Personal correspondence, Oaklands Schools, Pontiac, Michigan, 14 February.

Carver, Ronald P. (1974) Improving Reading Comprehension: Measuring Readability, Final Report, Contract no. N00014–72–C0240, Office of Naval Research, Silver Spring, Maryland: American Institutes for Research, 14 May.

Caylor, John S. *et al.* (1973) Methodologies for Determining Reading Requirements of Military Occupational Specialities, Technical Report no. 73–5, HUMRO Western Division, Presidio of Monterey, Cal., Human Resources Research Organization, March.

Coke, Esther U. and Rothkopf, Ernst Z. (1970) 'Note on a simple algorithm for a computer-produced Reading Ease score', *Journal of Applied Psychology*, 54, June, 208–10.

Coleman, Edmund B. (1965) On Understanding Prose: Some Determiners of its Complexity, NSF Final Report GB–2604, Washington, D.C., National Science Foundation.

Coleman, Edmund B. (1971) 'Developing a technology of written instruction: some determiners of the complexity of prose', in E. Z. Rothkopf and P. E. Johnson (eds), *Verbal Learning Research and the Technology of Written Instruction*, N.Y., Teachers College Press, Columbia University.

Dale, Edgar and Chall, Jeanne S. (1948) 'A formula for predicting readability', *Educational Research Bulletin*, 27, 21 January and 17 February, 11–20, 37–54.

Danielson, Wayne A. and Bryan, Sam Dunn (1963) 'Computer automation of two readability formulas', *Journalism Quarterly*, 39, spring, 201–6.

Elley, Warwick B. (1969) 'The assessment of readability by noun frequency counts', *Reading Research Quarterly*, 4, summer, 411–27.

Endicott, Anthony L. (1973) 'A proposed scale for syntactic complexity', *Research in the Teaching of English*, 7, spring, 5–12.

Fang, Irving E. (1966–7) 'The "easy listening formula"', *Journal of Broadcasting*, 11, winter, 63–8.

Fang, Irving E. (1968) 'By computer: Flesch's Reading Ease score and a syllable counter', *Behavioral Science*, 13, May, 249–51.

Farr, James N. and Jenkins, James J. (1949) 'Tables for use with the Flesch readability formulas', *Journal of Applied Psychology*, 33, June, 275–8.

Farr, James N., Jenkins, James J. and Paterson, Donald G. (1951) 'Simplification of Flesch Reading Ease formula', *Journal of Applied Psychology*, 35, October, 333–7.

Felsenthal, Norman A. and Felsenthal, Helen (1972) 'Utilizing the Computer to Assess the Readability of Language Samples', paper presented at annual meeting of the American Educational Research Association, Chicago.

Flesch, Rudolf F. (1943) *Marks of Readable Style: a Study in Adult Education*, N.Y., Bureau of Publications, Teachers College, Columbia University.

Flesch, Rudolf F. (1948) 'A new readability yardstick', *Journal of Applied Psychology*, 32, June, 221–33.

Flesch, Rudolf F. (1950) 'Measuring the level of abstraction', *Journal of Applied Psychology*, 34, December, 384–90.

Flesch, Rudolf F. (1951) *How to Test Readability*, N.Y., Harper.

Fraser, Ian E. (n.d.) 'Determining Readability with a Computer', report from a dissertation presented in partial fulfilment of the requirements of the Degree of Master of Education at the University of Western Australia, mimeographed.

Fry, Edward B. (1965) *Teaching Faster Reading: a Manual*, Cambridge University Press.

Fry, Edward B. (1968a) 'A readability formula that saves time', *Journal of Reading*, 11, April, 513–16, 575–8.

Fry, Edward B. (1968b) A Readability Graph Validated at Primary Levels, Technical Report no. 2, Contract no. OEG–0–8–085762–2502(056), Harvard Computer-Aided Instruction Laboratory.

Fry, Edward B. (1969) 'A readability graph for librarians, part I', *School Libraries*, 19, Fall, 13–16.

Gaver, Mary V. (1969) 'A readability graph for librarians, part II', *School Libraries*, 19, Fall, 23–5.

General Motors (Marketing Staff, Service Research Group) (n.d.) STAR: General Motors computerized simple test approach for readability, a tool for improved communications.

Goltz, Charles R. (1964) 'A table for quick computation of readability scores using the Dale–Chall formula', *Journal of Developmental Reading*, 7, spring, 175–87.

Gunning, Robert (1952–1968) *The Technique of Clear Writing*, N.Y., McGraw-Hill.

Gunning, Robert (1968) 'The Fog Index after twenty years', *Journal of Business Communications*, 6, winter, 3–13.

Harris, Albert J. and Jacobson, Milton D. (1973) 'The Harris-Jacobson Primary Readability Formulas', paper presented at the annual convention of the International Reading Association, Denver, Colo., May.

Harris, Albert J. and Sipay, Edward R. (1975) *How to Increase Reading Ability* (6th ed.), N.Y., McKay, Appendix D.

Holmquist, John B. (1968) 'A Determination of whether the Dale–Chall Readability Formula may be Revised to Evaluate more Validly the Readability of High School Science Materials', unpublished doctoral dissertation, Colorado State University; see also *Dissertation Abstracts*, 29, 407A.

Jacobson, Milton D. (1974) 'Predicting reading difficulty from spelling', *Spelling Progress Bulletin*, 14, spring, 8–10.

Kincaid, J. Peter and McDaniel, William Charles (1974) An Inexpensive Automated Way of Calculating Flesch Reading Ease Scores, Patent Disclosure Document no. 031350, US Patent Office, Washington, D.C.

Klare, George R. (1952) 'A table for rapid determination of Dale–Chall readability scores', *Educational Research Bulletin*, 13, February, 43–7.

Klare, George R. (1963) *The Measurement of Readability*, Iowa State University Press.

Klare, George R. (1968) 'The role of word frequency in readability', *Elementary English*, 45, January, 12–22.

Klare, George R. (1974–5) 'Assessing readability', *Reading Research Quarterly*, 10 (1), 62–102.

Klare, George R. (1976) 'Judging readability', *Instructional Science*, 5, 55–61.

Klare, George R. *et al.* (1969) 'Automation of the Flesch "Reading Ease" readability formula, with various options', *Reading Research Quarterly*, 4, summer, 550–9.

Klare, George R., Simiako, H. W. and Stolurow, L. M. (1972) 'The cloze procedure: a convenient readability test for training materials and translations', *International Review of Applied Psychology*, 21 (2), 77–106.

Koenke, Karl (1971) 'Another practical note on readability formulas', *Journal of Reading*, 15, December, 203–8.

Krueger, Scott and Stolurow, Lawrence M. (1965) Extended Dale–Chall Word List Alphabetized within Word Length, Technical Memorandum no. 15, Training Research Laboratory, University of Illinois, July.

Lorge, Irving I. (1939) 'Predicting reading difficulty of selections for children', *Elementary English Review*, 16, October, 229–33.

Lorge, Irving (1948) 'The Lorge and Flesch readability formulae: a correction', *School and Society*, 21, February, 141–2.

McCall, William A. and Crabbs, Lelah M. (1925, 1950, 1961) *Standard Test Lessons in Reading*, N.Y., Bureau of Publications, Teachers College, Columbia University.

McDaniel, William Charles (1974) 'Inter-analyst Reliability and Time Measures for the Automated and Manual Flesch Counts'; unpublished master's thesis, Georgia Southern College.

McLaughlin, G. Harry (1969) 'SMOG grading—a new readability formula', *Journal of Reading*, 12, May, 639–46.

MacRae, R. and Miller, Lawrence R. (1971a) Assembler Program to Compute the Dale–Chall Readability Formula with 7,000 Word List, Computer program, Ohio University.

MacRae, R. and Miller, Lawrence R. (1971b) Assembler Program to Compute the Dale–Chall, Bormuth Machine Computation, and Coleman no. 4 Readability Formulas, Computer program, Ohio University.

Maginnis, George H. (1969) 'The readability graph and informal reading inventories', *Reading Teacher*, 22, March, 516–18, 519.

Miller, Lawrence R. (1972) 'A Comparative Analysis of the Predictive Validities of Four Readability Formulas', unpublished doctoral dissertation, Ohio University.

Miller, Lawrence R. (1974) 'Predictive powers of the Dale–Chall and Bormuth readability formulas', *Journal of Business Communication*, 11, winter, 21–30.

Mugford, Len (1970) 'A new way of predicting readability', *Reading*, 4, 31–5.

Nyman, Patricia, Kearl, Bryant E. and Powers, Richard D. (1961) 'An attempt to shorten the word list with the Dale–Chall readability formula', *Educational Research Bulletin*, 40, 13 September, 150–2.

Powers, Richard D. and Ross, J. E. (1959) 'New diagrams for calculating readability scores rapidly', *Journalism Quarterly*, 36, spring, 177–82.

Powers, R. D., Sumner, W. A. and Kearl, B. E. (1958) 'A recalculation of four readability formulas', *Journal of Educational Psychology*, 49, April, 99–105.

Rakes, Thomas Arthur (1972) 'A Readability Analysis of Reading Materials Used in Adult Basic Education Classes in Tennessee', unpublished doctoral dissertation, University of Tennessee; see also *Dissertation Abstracts*, 1973, 4072A.

Safier, Daniel (1959) 'Notes on readability', *Elementary School Journal*, 59, May, 429–30.

Smith, Edgar A. (1960–1) 'Devereaux readability index', *Journal of Educational Research*, 54, April, 289–303.

Smith, Edgar A. and Kincaid, J. Peter (1970) 'Derivation and validation of the automated readability index for use with technical materials', *Human Factors*, 12, October, 457–64.

Smith, E. A. and Senter, R. J. (1967) Automated Readability Index, AMRL-TR-66-22. Wright-Patterson AFB, Ohio, Aerospace Medical Division.

Spache, George (1953) 'A new readability formula for primary grade reading materials', *Elementary School Journal*, 53, March, 410–13.

Spache, George D. (1966) *Good Reading for Poor Readers*, Champaign, Ill., Garrard.

Spache, George D. (1974) *Good Reading for Poor Readers* (9th ed.), Garrard.

Stone, Clarence R. (1956) 'Measuring difficulty of primary reading material: a constructive criticism of Spache's measure', *Elementary School Journal*, 57, October, 36–41.

Szalay, T. G. (1965) 'Validation of the Coleman readability formulas', *Psychological Reports*, 17, December, 965–6.

Taylor, Wilson L. (1953) 'Cloze procedure: a new tool for measuring readability', *Journalism Quarterly*, 30, Fall, 415–33.

Thorndike, Edward L. and Lorge, Irving (1944) *The Teacher's Word Book of 30,000 Words*, N.Y., Bureau of Publications, Teachers College, Columbia University.

Tretiak, Richard (1969) 'Readability and Two Theories of English Grammar', unpublished doctoral dissertation, Columbia University; see also *Dissertation Abstracts*, 30, 1441A, 1442A.

University of Texas, Instructional Materials Service (n.d.) Readability Formulas Today: a Brief Summary.

Williams, Robert T. (1972) 'Table for rapid determination of revised Dale–Chall readability scores', *Reading Teacher*, 26, November, 158–65.

4. 2 Readability: the use of cloze procedure

Donald Moyle

Cloze procedure, as a new approach to the assessment of readability, was first used by Taylor (1953). It is an empirical measure which uses the performance of children upon the text being measured to obtain the readability level. Though it would seem obvious that an examination of the performance of children on the actual text has more face validity than the use of formulae, it has as yet been employed infrequently. In the USA, where both reading materials and subject texts are often assessed for readability before publication, formulae are normally employed no doubt due to the greater expense and trouble which would be occasioned if an empirical measure were used. In Britain there has to date been little interest in measures of readability other than the grading of books by committees of experienced teachers using subjective judgments, e.g. Pascoe (1962) and Lawson (1968). Cloze procedure has to date been employed only experimentally and even here usually at high levels of reading attainment.

Cloze procedure: what is it?

Gestalt psychologists applied the term 'closure' to the tendency to complete a pattern which has a part missing. Thus we tend to see a circle even when a small gap is left in the drawing. The fluent reader will often substitute a word of similar spelling and meaning to the one in the text or read correctly a word from which a letter has been omitted. A current advertising stunt to promote pre-packed bacon is based upon this principle. Spelling errors are to be located, one

Source: J. Merritt (ed.), *Reading and the Curriculum*, Ward Lock Educational, 1970, pp. 159–68 (amended by author).

being the omission of the 'h' from the word 'when'. Though this appears in large print in a four word sentence a group of intelligent adults took on average 3½ minutes to locate the error.

Cloze procedure, applied to reading, requires the subject to fill in a gap, usually a whole word, which has been left in the text. In order to do this the subject must complete the language pattern of the writer by filling the gap, e.g. by supplying 'ran' in 'The dog—after my cat'. In order to complete such blanks in an extract from a book, the child must be able to react according to a number of criteria:

1 select a word according to grammatical rules
2 select a word with the correct meaning
3 choose a word which fits in best with the language patterns and vocabulary employed by the author.

For example, in the sentence given above the word omitted could equally well have been 'runs'. However if the sentence had been preceded by 'Yesterday my cat scratched a dog' the word 'runs' would no longer be acceptable for the omission must be a verb in the past tense. The synonym 'chased' could possibly be employed but is perhaps less likely to occur than 'ran' in the given text.

Cloze procedure involves accuracy, in that the child cannot hope to fill in the blanks if he cannot recognize the majority of words given. It also involves fluency and a knowledge of grammatical structure. Further, it necessitates understanding the text and therefore comprehension. As such it would seem to measure total readability much more nearly than any of the formulae or other measures so far developed.

Cloze procedure: how does it work?

There are a number of alternative approaches to the application of cloze techniques. It is usual to sample the text by taking a short passage from the early pages, another midway through the book and a third from near the end. This gives some idea of the internal consistency of the book with regard to reading level. Sampling of course has the danger that the extracts used may not be fully representative of the level of the book as a whole. It is necessary therefore to examine the complete text subjectively to assess whether the extracts used are representative.

Passages can be presented either with deletions, i.e. the use of the original text with chosen words obliterated, or with omissions, i.e. with the passage retyped, each word omitted being represented by a blank of equal size. Both methods have their advantages and disadvantages. In the former the presence of illustrations and the clue given to the size of the word omitted may influence results. In the latter the use of a different type face may alter the difficulty of the task, especially among very young children.

Omissions or deletions from the text can be selected on a structural or lexical basis. Rankin (1959) found structural deletions correlated at a significantly higher level with vocabulary and reading comprehension scores than did lexical deletions.

In structural deletion a certain percentage of words are removed from the text no matter what words these prove to be. In lexical deletion certain parts of speech are omitted, e.g. nouns or verbs.

Structural deletions can be determined by a table of random numbers or the omission of say every tenth word. Taylor (1953) found that though both methods achieved a similar grading of the passages he employed, the deletion of every fifth word gave the best discrimination between passages. It must be added, however, that Taylor was working with adult subjects and it may be that there will be differences from one age to another in the deletion rate which gives the best discrimination. Indeed Smith and Dechant (1961) suggest that among young children a passage cannot be understood if more than one word in ten cannot be read. If this is so then to omit more words than one in ten would prevent the child using his ability to understand the text in order to fill in the blanks.

The two passages below have been treated in an identical manner, every tenth word being deleted. Actual deletions are shown in italics. Quite by chance the parts of speech selected are heavily different and it could be that the difficulty of the passages presented as cloze tests could be significantly affected by the nature of the words selected. The two passages are graded by their respective authors as having a reading level of nine years. No information is available on how this grading was achieved.

Passage 1 From *The Village That Was Drowned* by P. Flowerdew (Oliver & Boyd, 1965)

'You haven't seen Foxy. Isn't he a pretty little *thing*?'
Carol gave the animal scarcely a glance. She was *bursting* with news of her own.
'Have you heard?' she *asked*.
'Heard what?'
She paused to give full effect to *her* coming announcement.
'This village,' she said in a dramatic *voice*, 'this village is going to be drowned. All the *houses* will be covered by water. The church will be *covered*. The school will be covered. The whole valley will *become* one great lake.'
'What do you mean?'
'What are *you* talking about?'
'It's true. People in the town of *Westhill* haven't enough water, so it's going to be stored here for them.'

Passage 2 From SRA International Reading Laboratory IIA

About forty men live on this island, each man *an* expert in one of the many jobs there are *to* do.
'Any luck yet?' Bill asks, as he and *his* team get ready to take over from another drilling *team*.
'No,' one man tells him, shaking his head. 'And *you* won't find gas on your shift. Rock's hard now *and* there's still half a mile to go.'
The experts *had* said that there might be gas at this point, *but* it would be two miles under the sea. Bill *and* his team take over.
To reach the place under *the* sea-bed where the gas is trapped, great drills are used.

Cloze procedure: possible uses

1 The method would seem to commend itself to authors and publishers as a realistic means of assessing the reading level of books of all types prior to publication.
2 The teacher could employ the technique for grading the books within his/her own classroom.
3 Teachers might well find that a brief cloze test taken from the text of a given book and administered to the child before he reads the book itself would prevent a child experiencing failure through reading a book that is too difficult for him.
4 Cloze supplies a quick and easy way of checking important aspects of comprehension.
5 A battery of standardized cloze tests could simplify attainment testing in reading.

Preliminary report on a pilot study using cloze procedure in assessing the readability of a reading scheme

The purpose of this pilot study was simply to obtain evidence on the possibility of using cloze procedure in the grading of books for children in the early stages of reading. The Griffin and Dragon Books written by S. K. McCullagh and published by E. J. Arnold were selected. These books were chosen as they have proved popular with children and are well graded. The only criticisms heard have been that the Griffins are heavily weighted towards the interests of boys and that the scheme is rather steeply graded at certain points.

Estimates of the difficulty of the books by teachers' committees have varied somewhat. For example, Griffin Book 1 has been given reading levels varying from five to more than six years.

The Griffin Books present a single story in twelve parts which tell the adventures of three pirates. The Dragon Books were added as supplementary readers at a later date. Again there are twelve books but each presents a complete story. Here the characters are more numerous and the content would seem equally attractive to girls and boys.

Two passages of 100 words were selected from each of the twenty-four books, one beginning with the first complete sentence on the second page of the text and the other ending at the last complete sentence on the next to last page of the text. Structural deletion was employed and every tenth word was covered with masking tape. Children read the passages orally from the actual text and the actual responses were recorded though in fact only the author's original words were counted as correct responses for the purposes of the analysis which follows. All the children were given a practice passage before they used the Griffins and Dragons and all read the page before the one containing the cloze test. The books were presented in the order suggested by the publishers and therefore practice in using the cloze technique may have reduced the discrimination of the tests between the early and later books.

Children from two schools varying in age from 6.0 years to 9 years 10 months were used as subjects. The schools were chosen to represent a wide range of ability and socio-economic status. Ninety children were tested on the Schonell Graded Word Recognition Test and the Schonell Silent Reading Test R4B. Thirty-eight children were eventually selected for the evaluation of cloze results on the basis that the mean chronological age of each of the four age groups was equal to the mean reading age.

A further eighteen children were matched with the eight-year-old group and these children read the same passage without deletions. Their total reading errors were recorded.

A third measure was obtained by submitting the passages used for the cloze tests to analysis using the Fry (1968) Readability Graph. This computes a reading level from a combination of the number of syllables and the number of sentences per 100 words.

Results

Table 4.2.1   Reading age levels of Griffin Books 1 to 6 according to the Fry Readability Graph

Griffin Book	Reading age
1	6 yrs 11 mths
2	8 yrs 10 mths
3	8 yrs 1 mth
4	9 yrs 8 mths
5	7 yrs 6 mths
6	7 yrs 5 mths

Table 4.2.2 Results of cloze tests

Book	Average age n	Percentage correct: closures 9.6 5	8.6 17	7.6 11	6.6 5	Total closures (possible 760)	Mean (possible 20)
Griffin	1	76	74	55	53	503	13.24
	2	72	71	49	35	457	12.03
	3	70	68	39	25	412	10.84
	4	70	67	39	17	403	10.61
	5	64	51	23	9	337	8.86
	6	67	66	31	12	372	9.79
	7	64	54	26	9	313	8.24
	8	54	41	15	5	231	6.08
	9	50	39	14	8	223	5.87
	10	44	35	13	2	193	5.08
	11	39	30	8	0	160	4.21
	12	36	25	6	0	134	3.53
Dragon	A1	79	71	49	62	490	12.89
	A2	81	75	51	52	501	13.18
	A3	73	69	48	35	447	11.76
	B1	72	63	44	29	411	10.82
	B2	70	69	39	21	412	10.84
	B3	65	46	26	13	291	7.66
	C1	68	49	26	11	305	8.03
	C2	60	39	21	6	244	6.42
	C3	61	37	16	4	227	5.97
	D1	50	33	15	2	198	5.21
	D2	44	25	12	0	157	4.13
	D3	39	28	9	0	152	4.00

Until applying this formula to the Griffin Books, I had found it to be reasonably reliable considering its simplicity. The weaknesses of assessing readability by sentence and syllable length are fully shown up here. One of the very strong points of McCullagh's writing is her ability to produce vivid description within the limits of a restricted vocabulary. However, descriptive writing usually employs long sentences and this explains in part the high reading levels given throughout. A second feature of course is the fact that American children start school, and usually therefore reading, later than British children.

The sudden jump of two years from Book 1 to Book 2 is interesting, for the passage selected in Book 2 consisted of the pirate's song. This has rhythmic repetition and children usually read it easily. However, it has very long sentences and the name 'Acrooacre' occurs frequently. Thus the Fry score is raised considerably on both items which it measures. It will be noted that the cloze test did not suffer any distortion because of this passage.

Table 4.2.3 Results of estimating difficulty by counting the number of errors made in oral reading of the passages employed in the cloze tests of Griffin Books 1–6[a]

Griffin Book	Average number of errors
1	3.7
2	4.9
3	5.1
4	6.2
5	9.9
6	9.6

[a]This table is based on the performance of 18 children—average chronological and reading age 8 years 6 months.

Table 4.2.4 Griffin and Dragon Books in publisher's suggested order

Main scheme (Griffin)	Supplementary (Dragon)
Book 1	
Book 2	
Book 3	
	Book A1
	Book A2
	Book A3
Book 4	
Book 5	
Book 6	
	Book B1
	Book B2
	Book B3
Book 7	
Book 8	
Book 9	
	Book C1
	Book C2
	Book C3
Book 10	
Book 11	
Book 12	
	Book D1
	Book D2
	Book D3

The results of the counting of errors method suggested by McLeod (1962) is shown for the first six books of the Griffin series. It will be seen that the grading of the books is identical in order to that given by the cloze procedure results. All three measurements used in fact suggest that Book 5 is more difficult than Book 6. Certainly teachers have often commented that Book 5 causes difficulty for children and it has been suggested that the high literary quality of the language used to describe the storm involves sentence constructions and figures of speech which are rather difficult at this reading level.

The counting of errors procedure would seem to have two weaknesses as a measure of readability. Firstly, it emphasizes reading accuracy rather more than comprehension, and secondly it demands individual application whereas the cloze procedure test can be given as a group test.

The cloze tests seem to suggest that with the exception of Book 5 the Griffin scheme is extremely well graded.

Contrary to expectations the cloze tests did not show any difference in readability levels between boys and girls. However one cannot rule out the possibility of a cumulative effect where, on reading the whole series, boys may eventually gain from the exercise because they find the subject matter of the books more attractive.

The Griffin Books were written specifically for the retarded reader in the junior school. It seems significant therefore that the only break in the smooth gradient from book to book at all age levels and between the age groups is shown in the difference between children in the 7 years 6 months and 8 years 6 months groups. The big jump in scores on the cloze tests between two age groups is so marked that it could hardly have occurred by chance. It could be that the concepts and language used are more related to those of the older child. If this is so then there is a further argument for not using remedial readers in the infant school, no matter how attractive they may seem to the teacher.

As the Dragon Books are a series of supplementary readers and are individual stories grouped in sets of three, their precise positioning from a readability point of view is perhaps not quite so important within each set of three books.

The cloze tests suggest only minor modifications in the order planned by the publishers. On only one occasion, namely the case of B3 and C1, is there a suggestion that the presentation in groups of three is incorrect.

It should be noted that the reordering based on the results of the cloze tests is not a plan for action by teachers. To suggest for example that Griffin Book 5 should be read before Book 6 would make nonsense of the story content of the readers. Rather, the teacher should ensure that children have adequate help to overcome any difficulty they might experience with Book 5. In the case of the Dragon Books certain reordering in the placement could be made without any real damage to the scheme as a whole. However it must be remembered that the scheme has been constructed around a system of vocabulary control. Thus any change in order suggested by total readability must be weighed against a break in the sequence of vocabulary growth provided by the scheme.

Table 4.2.5 Reordering of the scheme based on results on cloze procedure

Griffin	Dragon
Book 1	
	Book A2
	Book A1
Book 2	
	Book A3
Book 3	
	Book B2
	Book B1
Book 4	
Book 5	
Book 6	
Book 7	
	Book C1
	Book B3
	Book C2
Book 8	
	Book C3
Book 9	
	Book D1
Book 10	
Book 11	
	Book D2
	Book D3
Book 12	

Cloze procedure commends itself as an empirical measure of readability which would provide information complementary to the teacher's own subjective assessments of printed materials. There are however a number of aspects upon which we need further information:

1 What is the appropriate number of deletions for each age group?
2 Will deletion or omission have an effect upon results gained and

might this vary as to whether the test is given orally or in group form?

3 What variables affect performance e.g. vocabulary, sentence completion or comprehension attainment, intelligence and socio-economic status?

4 What effect on cloze scores is observed when there are heavy deletions of particular parts of speech?

5 Can a percentage score be suggested which can be equated with an individual's frustration or independent reading level?

In recent years the wider use of cloze procedure in the assessment of readability and comprehension and its use as a teaching and diagnostic aid have resulted in certain question-marks about its validity as a measure of readability. For example, it has been noticed that there is a variability of performance in relation to different types of material and the extent to which deletion is weighted towards particular parts of speech. A further complication which raises questions—as yet unanswered—comes from a study by Campbell-Wignall (1977). Here, even within the same passage, matched groups of children performed unequally when the words deleted were different words, even though a check had been made for balance according to the percentage of each part of speech deleted. In fact, the mean difference in reading age at which 45 per cent of the words were replaced by the author's original word was as high as three years. The suggestion must be, therefore, that there is a further dimension as yet not delineated which could arise from the complexity of the grammatical structure, the conceptual difficulty or meaning density of the word deleted, or the language which provides the context clue to its discovery.

References

Campbell-Wignall, B. (1977) 'The Standardization of a Cloze Procedure Test', unpublished MA thesis, Edgehill College of Higher Education.

Fry, E. A. (1968) 'A readability formula that saves time', *Journal of Reading*, 11 (7), 513–16.

Lawson, K. S. (ed.) (1968) *Children's Reading*, University of Leeds Institute of Education.

McLeod, J. (1962) 'The estimation of readability of books of low difficulty', *British Journal of Educational Psychology*, 32, 112–18.

Pascoe, T. W. (ed.) (1962) *A Second Survey of Books for Backward Readers*, University of London Press.

Rankin, E. F. (1959) 'The cloze procedure—its validity and utility', in *Eighth Yearbook of the National Reading Conference*, 131–44.

Smith, H. P. and Dechant, E. (1961) *Psychology in Teaching Reading*, Englewood Cliffs, N.J., Prentice-Hall.

Taylor, W. L. (1953) 'Cloze procedure: A new tool for measuring readability', *Journalism Quarterly*, 30, 415–38.

4. 3 Sex-roles in reading schemes

Glenys Lobban

The major premise underlying the current debate about class and race bias in reading schemes is that the content of the schemes influences children's attitudes to the world and to themselves. Reading schemes are presumed to be particularly influential because they are usually the child's first introduction to the written word and they are presented within a context of authority, the classroom, and most children read them. They are hence presumed to convey official approval of attitudes the child will have already learned in the pre-school years from parents, the media and other persons in the society. Current knowledge suggests that children's and particularly their first readers do influence children's attitudes. They do this by presenting models like themselves for the children to identify with and emulate. In addition they present an official view of the real world and 'proper' attitudes.

It is now generally agreed that reading schemes such as the 'Ladybird' scheme, which show a white middle-class world peopled with daddies in suits, and mummies in frilly aprons, who take tea on the lawns in front of their detached houses, are likely to be irrelevant and harmful for urban working-class and black children. They do not provide them with models like themselves, they implicitly, if not explicitly, denigrate these children's culture and imply that what is real and proper is also white and middle class. If this argument is accepted for race and class bias in reading schemes then it must equally apply to another type of inequality within our society, namely sexual inequality.

Ours is a patriarchal society where females are economically and legally discriminated against, where males control all the major

Source: *Forum*, 16 (2), 1974, pp. 57–60.

social institutions, and where two distinct sex-roles, the 'feminine'-passive and the 'masculine'-active, exist. As nobody has proved any genetic difference between females and males other than those related to reproduction, we must conclude that the sex differences in temperament, interests, abilities and goals, are the results of socialisation. If we assume that despite class and race discrimination in our society, reading schemes should not mirror this and denigrate these groups, then we should also demand that such schemes do not mirror male-dominated sex-roles and denigrate females.

To my knowledge few people have extended the argument in this way, and indeed no broad-ranging study of the way sex-roles are presented in British reading schemes even exists. This article will describe a preliminary study on sex-role content in readers which I undertook to begin to remedy this lack of information.

The sex-role content of six popular British reading schemes was coded. I chose two schemes published before 1960 ('Janet and John' and 'Happy Venture'), two published in the 1960s ('Ready to Read' and 'Ladybird'), and two recent schemes ('Nipper' and 'Breakthrough to Literacy') which are designed specifically for urban children. I coded the content of 225 stories in all. 179 of these had people as their central characters and I listed the toys and pets, activities and adult roles these showed for each sex and both the sexes. Table 4.3.1 gives a summary of these results. It lists the toys and pets, activities and adult roles for each and both of the sexes that figured in three or more of the six reading schemes. In all cases single sex activities are those which figured as single sex in five of the schemes and in some of the readers in the remaining scheme.

A glance at Table 4.3.1 shows that the schemes rigidly divided the sphere of people's activity into two compartments, 'masculine' and 'feminine' with very few common characteristics. The number of 'masculine' options exceeded the number of 'feminine' ones in every category and they tended to be more active and instrumental and to relate more to the outside world and the outdoors than the 'feminine' options which revolved almost entirely around domestic roles. Only 35 of the 179 stories I coded had heroines, while 71 had heroes. The heroines were seldom being successful in non-'feminine' spheres, while the heroes were frequently brave and adventurous. In the 'Nipper' scheme, for example, a heroine who ran away got lost, caught the wrong tube and found herself back home and gave up, whereas boys who went off on their own frequently found adventure. In the remaining 73 stories there were female and male central characters but it was almost always a boy who took the lead in all non-domestic activities and let the girl help or watch. In the 'Janet and John' scheme, for example, while both

Table 4.3.1 The sex-roles that occurred in three or more of the six schemes coded

The sex for which the role was prescribed	The content of the children's roles				The adult roles presented
	Toys and pets	Activities	Taking the lead in both sex activities	Learning a new skill	
Girls only	1 Doll 2 Skipping rope 3 Doll's pram	1 Preparing the tea 2 Playing with dolls 3 Taking care of young siblings	1 Hopping 2 Shopping with parents 3 Skipping	1 Taking care of younger siblings	1 Mother 2 Aunt 3 Grandmother
Boys only	1 Car 2 Train 3 Aeroplane 4 Boat 5 Football	1 Playing with cars 2 Playing with trains 3 Playing football 4 Lifting or pulling heavy objects 5 Playing cricket 6 Watching adult males in occupational roles 7 Heavy gardening	1 Going exploring alone 2 Climbing trees 3 Building things 4 Taking care of pets 5 Sailing boats 6 Flying kites 7 Washing and polishing Dad's car	1 Taking care of pets 2 Making/Building 3 Saving/Rescuing people or pets 4 Playing sports	1 Father 2 Uncle 3 Grandfather 4 Postman 5 Farmer 6 Fisherman 7 Shop or business owner 8 Policeman 9 Builder 10 Bus driver 11 Bus conductor 12 Train driver 13 Railway porter
Both sexes	1 Book 2 Ball 3 Paints 4 Bucket and spade 5 Dog 6 Cat 7 Shop	1 Playing with pets 2 Writing 3 Reading 4 Going to the seaside 5 Going on a family outing	—	—	1 Teacher 2 Shop assistant

children had dogs, Janet's was a puppy while John had a big dog. Boys were more frequently responsible for the care of the pets, and owned larger versions of a common toy such as a boat, and usually did better at common activities; e.g., the boy reached the top of the tree while sister sat on a lower branch. In the classroom situation both sexes were equally good at reading and writing, but they were frequently shown with toys or apparatus conventionally appropriate to their sex. Frequently in situations where the children participated equally, their parents played out conventional roles. When both sexes made or built anything the boy usually did so more or excelled and Dad was the instructor unless they were learning to make cakes. Mum was never shown teaching them to build anything or to play sport.

It is illuminating to contrast the female and male worlds the schemes showed. The female world was almost entirely oriented around domestic activity and childcare. The message that the schemes conveyed was that a woman's place is in the home and that little girls should spend their time learning 'feminine' skills such as cooking and childcare. It is significant that the only new skill learned by girls in three or more of the schemes was taking care of a younger sibling. The adult models available were all situated in the home and shown doing domestic activity. The 'Nipper' scheme was the only one which showed working mothers and this was for a minority of the mothers shown. The fact is that the majority of women in Britain are in paid employment outside the home and many of them are neither shop assistants nor teachers (the only both-sex jobs in the schemes). This makes the schemes' relegation of women to the home even more invidious. The only two girls' activities that allowed physical activity were skipping and hopping. Neither of these develop group co-operation nor the varied motor skills that the range of boys' activities and games offered.

The male world the schemes described did not include toys or activities that allowed expressive or nurturant behaviour. Boys' toys and activities were such as to allow the learning of independence and a variety of instrumental and motor skills. The boys' world was oriented outside the home and their toys and their adult models suggested a variety of future occupational goals. Boys, unlike girls, spent time watching adult males, who weren't relatives, performing their occupational roles. The idea that it was the boys who would have jobs was often explicitly stated. While girls were told they'd be like Mum or voiced such ideas, the boys expressed the desire to be train-drivers and the like. In only one of the 'Nipper' readers was a jobless father shown, and this dad was just temporarily out of work, while virtually all mums were jobless permanently. Thus, while the scope of adult male roles was somewhat limited, the schemes clearly conveyed the idea that it was males who had jobs, and who were responsible for the maintenance of all aspects of the 'real' world except for childcare and cooking.

The schemes also showed the interaction within the family in rigidly traditional terms. 'Nipper' was the only scheme which showed female single parent families and none of the schemes showed male single parent units. None of the schemes showed Dad doing housework or cooking anything other than a cup of tea. (The one exception was in 'Ready to Read' when Mum was in hospital having a baby.) Dad was always the one who drove 'his' car (only one reader in one scheme showed a woman driver), his authority was ultimate and he usually initiated and directed all family activities. All the schemes abounded in pictures of Dad reading the paper or watching television, while Mum bustled about preparing and serving food, and washing up, often with the help of daughter. Once again, as in the case of female employment, the schemes' version of the family was even more rigidly traditional than current practice. Many British women drive cars and do handiwork, and in many homes cooking and cleaning are tasks which are shared by the family, but none of this was reflected in the schemes.

In summary the reading schemes showed a 'real' world peopled by women and girls who were almost solely involved with domestic activity and whom the adventurous and innovative males might occasionally allow into their world (the rest of human activity and achievement) in a helpmate capacity. The world they depicted was not only sexist, it was more sexist than present reality, and in many ways totally foreign to the majority of children, who do have working Mums, and at least some experience of cross sex activities.

The question that now arises concerns the impact of these readers on the attitudes of girls and boys to themselves and the world. If, as research suggests, characters like themselves suggest new modes of behaviour for children and define what they should do and want, then the models of their own sex available to the readers could only serve to reinforce the patriarchal sex-roles the children have already learned. The present policy in primary schools (see the Plowden Report (Central Advisory Council, 1967)) is for all the pupils to do traditionally one sex activities like cooking and metalwork. The content of the reading schemes is opposite to this policy, and might well neutralise these non-sextyped experiences, or convince the children that experiences in school are unrelated to the 'real' world outside. The schemes, like the rest of children's and adults' literature (see Millett, 1971), concentrate on the exploits of males. The girls who read them have already been schooled to believe, as our society does, that males are superior to females and better at everything other than domestic work, and the stories in the schemes cannot but reinforce the damage that our society does to girls' self-esteem. The total lack of female characters who are successful in non-'feminine' activities and jobs and who are independent, ensures that girls with these aspirations will receive no encouragement. In the same way, boys who feel the need to express gentleness and nurturance will find no male models to emulate. In short, these schemes in no way question the correctness of a society which deprives both sexes of full expression of their capabilities, and, in fact, they endorse a set of sex-roles that are even more rigid than our present role division.

One of the arguments that might be given to justify male bias in reading schemes is that boys have more reading problems. Certainly girls learn to read in spite of the male bias in readers but at what price to their self attitudes? If the primers children were given paid them the compliment of being intelligent beings able to comprehend complexity and depicted a world real to the majority of children (with girls who were tough, children of varied colour and nationalities, boys who cried, motherless or fatherless families, working parents, family fights, violence, television and other phenomena familiar to them) they would involve all the children. If we as educationalists care about the full development of each individual child it is time we became fully aware of how materials such as reading schemes denigrate females as well as other groups. It is time we acknowledged and attempted to change this sexist aspect of their content, and of our society, along with the class and race inequalities.

Reading schemes used

'Breakthrough to Literacy' (D. Mackay, B. Thompson and P. Schuaub, Longmans, for the Schools Council, 1970).
'Happy Venture Reader' (F. J. Schonell and I. Sarjeant, Oliver & Boyd, 1958).
'Janet and John' (M. O'Donnell and R. Munro, James Nisbet, 1950).
'Ladybird Key Words Reading Scheme' (W. Murray, Loughborough, Wills & Hepworth, 1964).
'Nipper' (Macmillan, 1968).
'Ready to Read' (M. Simpson, Methuen, 1964).

References

Central Advisory Council (England) (1967) *Children and their Primary Schools*, 2 vols, HMSO.
Millett, K. (1971) *Sexual Politics*, Hart-Davis.

4. 4 All things white and beautiful

Bob Dixon

A particularly strong aspect of the indoctrination carried on in children's literature is that of racism. It'll be useful, first of all, to consider the English language itself.

It still has to be brought to the conscious attention of most native speakers of the language that the word '*black*', when not used in a purely literal sense, has overwhelmingly pejorative associations. Meanings are, for the most part, connected with: evil, as in 'the black arts' and 'black magic'; death, as in 'the black death' and 'the black flag'; disgrace, as in 'black books', 'black mark', 'black list', 'black sheep', 'to blackball' and 'to blacken'; and have criminal connotations, as in 'blackmail' and 'Black Maria'. Other associations, such as 'black-leg', 'blackguard' and 'a black look' merely add to the negative picture which is filled out by such phrases as 'the nigger in the wood-pile'. Words associated with blackness, such as 'dark', 'pitch', 'shadow' and 'night', and phrases and sayings based on them, have similar connotations. With the word '*white*', it's just the opposite. Although there are exceptions, the linguistic associations are overwhelmingly with goodness, beauty and purity. Most Indo-European languages seem to follow a similar pattern. In Czech and Russian, the words for 'black' and 'devil' are similar, while further afield, certain aspects of this pattern of associations can be found, even in Chinese. The idea that such a situation arose through the association of fear with the darkness of night before racial contacts had taken place on a large scale doesn't, of course, contradict the idea that real psychological damage is caused by this type of semi-conscious racism built into everyday language.

Source: *Catching Them Young*, vol. 1, *Sex, Race and Class in Children's Fiction*, Pluto Press, 1977, pp. 94–127.

Adult literature, as might be expected, is full of such figurative and symbolic usages—where it isn't openly racist. Shylock and Fagin, Othello and Caliban all deserve a second look, for there's no need for anyone to accept racism in literature, not even if expressed in deathless blank verse.

Children's literature, especially that intended for very small children, gives rise to particularly difficult problems as it more often works on a symbolic and unconscious level. It's difficult to combat racism instilled in this way by argument, as small children aren't able to cope with the necessary ideas. It's only possible to combat such racism effectively through literature for children which embodies civilised attitudes carried at the same emotional and symbolic level. Here, however, it's necessary first to give some account of racism in children's literature as it affects black people.

There are, clearly, different degrees of racism to be found, some more vicious and destructive than others. I've chosen examples to show as great a variety as possible. They range from fairly realistic stories to outright fantasies and from unconscious to open racism. I don't think it follows, though, that the more real and overt kinds are the more harmful. It's at least arguable that the less apparent racism is—that is, the more it's carried in symbolic terms—the more psychologically damaging it can be. The fact that the more symbolic forms are usually intended for younger children may be an important part of the argument since such children are all the more impressionable. And when we speak of psychological destruction, it should be understood that racism, in children's fiction as elsewhere, is harmful to all people, black or white, or whatever colour they may be, though, of course, non-white people obviously suffer from its effects far more.

The world of fiction for very small children often includes recognisable elements from a child's everyday life. Naturally, it's important for a young reader, as for any other, to be able to identify with what's being read. Thus, we can account for the popularity of toys as characters in fiction for small children. Though bears figure largely in folk and fairy tales, it's the teddy bear as a traditional and very popular toy that must have given rise to the numerous fictional bears. The golliwog also started as a toy and now, it seems, no fictional 'nursery' is complete without one. Essentially, a golliwog is a doll with crudely stylised racial characteristics which are African in type. He belongs to the patronising and condescending category of racism which includes 'coons' and 'nigger' minstrels. If we feel affection for him at all it's such as we might feel for a pet animal.

Enid Blyton, however, in the 'Noddy' stories, gives the reader or the listener little opportunity to develop any such affection. Here, the golliwogs are usually 'naughty' and constitute a threat to Noddy, with whom the child is obviously meant to identify. The association of the golliwogs with fear and darkness is clearly seen in the following passages from *Here Comes Noddy Again*:[1]

> At twelve o'clock that night Noddy got out his little car. He jumped when a voice came out of the darkness. 'Are you ready? I'm here?' [*sic*]
>
> It was the golliwog. He was so black that Noddy couldn't see him, and bumped into him when he walked out to find him.
>
> 'Oh, sorry,' he said. 'Yes, I'm ready. Here is the car. Jump in.'
>
> The golliwog climbed in. Noddy switched on the lights of the little car. They weren't very good, only just enough to see by as he went down the streets of Toy-Town. The golliwog began to sing a peculiar song.
>
> 'It isn't very good
> In the Dark Dark Wood,
> In the middle of the night
> When there isn't any light;
> It isn't very good
> In the Dark Dark Wood.'
>
> 'Don't sing that,' said Noddy. 'You make me nervous. I shall drive into a tree or something. Be quiet, Golliwog.'
>
> So the golliwog was quiet, but he kept making little chuckling noises which Noddy didn't like at all.
>
> 'I wish I hadn't come,' he thought. 'I do wish I hadn't come!'

Once in 'the Dark Dark Wood', Noddy becomes even more nervous:

> 'Where's this party of yours?' asked Noddy. 'I don't want to drive any deeper into the wood.'
>
> 'Well, stop just here, then,' said the golliwog, and Noddy stopped. Where was the party? And the band? Where were the lights, and happy voices?
>
> 'It's so quiet,' he said to the golliwog. 'Where *is* this party?'
>
> 'There isn't a party,' said the golliwog in a very nasty sort of voice. 'This is a trap, Noddy. We want your car for ourselves. Get out at once!'
>
> Noddy couldn't move an inch. He was so full of alarm that he couldn't say a word. A trap! Whose trap? And why did they want his car?
>
> Then things happened very quickly. Three black faces suddenly appeared in the light of the car's lamps, and three golliwogs came running to the car. In a trice they had hold of poor Noddy and pulled him right out of his little car.
>
> The golliwog who had come with him took the wheel, laughing loudly. 'What did I tell you?' he said. 'It isn't very good in the Dark Dark Wood! Hey, you others, there's room for one beside me and two sitting on the back of the car.'

'Wait a minute,' said one of the other golliwogs. 'This little driver has got some rather nice clothes on. We might as well have those, too!'

'Oooh yes,' said another golliwog. 'I'll have his lovely hat—it's got a jingle-bell at the top.'

'And I'll have his shirt and tie,' said a third golliwog. He pulled them off poor little Noddy. Then the driver leaned out and told the others to get him Noddy's dear little trousers and shoes.

[We should note that the black people are taking Noddy's property from him.]

Soon Noddy had no clothes on at all. He wriggled and shouted and wailed. 'No, no, no! I want my hat, I want my shirt. You bad, wicked golliwogs! How dare you steal my things?'

But it wasn't a bit of good. What could the little nodding man do against four big strong golliwogs? Nothing at all.

The golliwogs piled into the little red and yellow car. Two were in front, two sat in the back of the car. One of them had Noddy's hat on. The moon shone down on it suddenly through the trees and Noddy wailed loudly.

'My dear little hat! Oh, do, do leave me that!'

'Ha, ha, ho, ho!' laughed the bad golliwogs and drove off at top speed. 'R-r-r-r-r!' went the little car, and the sound grew fainter and fainter, till at last it couldn't be heard any more.

Noddy was all alone in the Dark Wood. He remembered the song of the golliwog. 'It isn't very good in the Dark Dark Wood,' and he stood up, trembling.

'Help!' he called. 'Oh, help, help, HELP! I'm little Noddy and I'm all alone and LOST!'

The child reader or listener can be left in little doubt as to where his or her sympathies should lie. The emotionally loaded epithets applied to Noddy—'poor' and 'poor little'—are even carried over to his possessions, his 'dear little trousers and shoes', his 'dear little hat' and his 'little red and yellow car'. This manipulation of the emotions is strongly backed up by the coloured illustrations. There is, for instance, a full-page picture of two villainous-looking golliwogs ripping the clothes off Noddy while the other two look on with broad smiles on their faces. The illustration following the extract just quoted shows a pathetic and frightened Noddy, naked in the dark wood. (A young acquaintance of mine found this book in my house when he was about four-and-a-half years old. He couldn't read, but brought the book to his mother, pointing to the picture just mentioned. 'Oh, look, Mammy!' he said, in some distress. Then he hammered his fist on the picture on the facing page, which showed the golliwogs driving off and Noddy on the ground. So the message got across, through pictures alone.) Retribution follows, of course, and the golliwogs are tracked down, tied up in a big sack and carried off to prison by the policeman.[2]

It has to be emphasised, perhaps, that there's nothing necessarily wrong in a black doll, as such. We need to centre our concern upon two things. Firstly, as already touched upon, the golliwog is a racial caricature, of an African type. Since its first literary appearance, in the USA in *The Adventures of Two Dutch Dolls* (1895) by Bertha Upton, with illustrations by her sister Florence, it's been remarkably standardised, both as a toy and in illustrations. It's interesting that Florence Upton was apparently inspired by a grotesque doll belonging to her grandmother. Secondly, we have to consider the role played by golliwogs in literature. As in the *Noddy* extract, they're normally cast in 'naughty', evil and menacing roles—that is, where they're not merely merry coons. Blyton, in her simple way, found their blackness a sufficient cause for dislike, as at the beginning of the first story in *The Three Golliwogs*: 'There were once three golliwogs who were most unhappy in the nursery cupboard. None of the other toys liked them, and nobody ever played with them, because their little mistress, Angela, didn't like their black faces.' The three golliwogs here are called Golly, Woggie and Nigger,[3] and nine of the eleven stories in the book are based upon mistaken identity as the three all look alike, of course. That's another irritating thing about black people.

Before passing on, two small details should be added here, to complete the picture as far as Blyton's concerned. The association of the golliwogs with fear has been mentioned in reference to the 'Noddy' extract. Two references from two of her books intended for much older children confirm the connection and associate the fear with black *faces*, in particular. In *Five Fall into Adventure*, a book which will be analysed in greater detail later, Anne, one of the 'Five', wakes up at night:[4]

> She felt for her torch, and switched it on.
> The light fell on the window first, and Anne saw something that gave her a terrible shock. She screamed loudly, and dropped her torch in fright. George woke up at once. Timmy came bounding up the stairs.
> 'Julian!' wailed Anne. 'Come quickly. I saw a face at the window, a horrible, dreadful face looking in at me!' . . . Anne was trembling, and Julian put his arm round her comfortingly.
> 'What was this dreadful face like?' he asked her. Anne shivered in his arm.
> 'I didn't see very much . . . It had nasty gleaming eyes, and it looked very dark—perhaps it was a black man's face! Oh, I *was* frightened!'

The reference to a black face is entirely gratuitous. There isn't a black person in the book, even. Another example of gratuitous racism from Blyton occurs in *The Mystery of the Spiteful Letters*: Frederick Algernon Trotteville, leader of the five 'Find-Outers' and otherwise known as Fatty, has been disguising himself to play a joke on Constable Goon. Afterwards, referring back to the incident, he tells the others, 'One day I'm going to make myself up as a black boy and give you all a fright.'

Little Black Sambo isn't a doll, but the illustrations of him in the many books in which he's featured show him as a racial caricature of a black boy. Here again, we have the fuzzy hair, the large, round eyes and the wide (and simple) grin which give the game away, as much in respect of Sambo's race as of his relatives—the Kentucky Minstrels, the coons and the black servants of early Hollywood films. Here we have the condescending, the patronising end of racism, where the principals are merry, simple, childlike people—at best, amusing and at worst, stupid. In a racial context, they are the counterparts of working-class characters in a class context as portrayed in, for instance, *The Family From One End Street*. The two stereotypes are acceptable in this form: one to white racist sentiments and the other to middle-class attitudes. Children—white children, that is—can laugh at Sambo's antics and feel superior.

The Story of Little Black Sambo, the first of the series, was published in London in 1899 and the following year in the USA. Its success was such that Helen Bannerman, the author, was encouraged to produce a number of similar books with titles such as *The Story of Little Black Mingo* and *The Story of Little Black Quasha*.[5] All were illustrated by the author. They've been widely translated, and since 1911 *The Story of Little Black Sambo*, along with the others, has been published in Britain by Chatto and Windus. Over a period of eight years recently, its sales averaged 28,500 copies per year, amounting altogether to more than a quarter of a million, which is good business, if nothing else. The fact that the characters are more like African stereotypes while the setting is, vaguely, India is, perhaps, one of the lesser problems presented by the series.

In *The Story of Little Black Sambo*, the hero goes for a walk in the jungle, wearing 'a beautiful little Red Coat' and 'a pair of beautiful little Blue Trousers' made for him by his mother, Black Mumbo. He's also wearing 'a lovely little Pair of Purple Shoes with Crimson Soles and Crimson Linings' and carries 'a beautiful Green Umbrella'. These were bought for him in the bazaar by his father, Black Jumbo. Meeting various tigers, one after another, who wish to eat him up, Little Black Sambo fobs them off, in turn, with all these possessions, giving the jacket to one tiger, the umbrella to another, and so on, until he's stripped to his underpants. Each tiger thinks it will be the grandest tiger in the jungle with whatever Little Black Sambo has surrendered to it but when they all meet together there is, of course, a dispute amongst them and, clutching one another's tails, they all rush faster and faster round a tree until there's nothing left but a big pool of melted butter, or 'ghi'. Black Jumbo finds the ghi and takes it home where Black Mumbo makes a huge heap of pancakes with it and Little Black Sambo eats a hundred and sixty-nine.

The book has been much criticised in recent years, but I think that not enough attention has been paid to the illustrations. After all, the story is almost identical with the Swedish folk tale, *Little Lisa*[6]—so close that coincidence must be ruled out—and Bannerman must have got it from this source. Apart from changing the setting, she only added the pictures and the mumbo-jumbo.

All the stories in the series are about food and eating, and follow a basic pattern: firstly, animals threaten to eat up the children; then the animals are outwitted or fobbed off by some means; thirdly, there's the food, or a feast, which the children or friendly animals have and, lastly the hostile animals melt away, tear one another to shreds, are blown into fragments or dismembered or eat one another up and so cancel themselves out. (The order of the third and fourth elements may be reversed.) This pattern holds good, even for *Pat and the Spider: The Biter Bit*, which is about a little white boy, not a caricature, dressed in a sailor suit.

Bannerman, whose husband was an army doctor, lived in India for most of her adult life. A radio programme of a few years ago, which was concerned largely with the letters she sent to her children who were being educated in Britain, gave an interesting insight into her attitudes. At one point, she related how an Indian cook, who had been dismissed from the Bannermans' service, stayed on to impersonate (as she alleged) the new one, who hadn't arrived. 'They're all just alike,' said Dr Bannerman. 'So they are,' agreed his wife.

Before leaving Little Black Sambo, it's interesting to relate a story from a primary school in North London. The school, with a partially black population, had had the usual trouble with the white children bandying about the names 'blackie' and 'wog'. Then one day, the school put up posters showing Little Black Sambo, and 'Sambo' was added to the list. If the school had been using the 'Adventures in Reading' series published by the Oxford University Press, the pupils might possibly have read two stories by Gertrude Keir, *The Old Mill* and *The Circus*, where a monkey called Sambo appears, on one occasion dressed in a bright red jacket with silver buttons. It's not difficult to imagine what fun this linking of events could have given rise to amongst the children. 'Ifs and ans', you might think, but isn't it by the constant and maybe sometimes chance assembling of hosts of such details that racist attitudes are built up? Sambo is a name normally applied to people of African race: here, it's applied to a monkey. What kind of psychological associations do we expect children to form? If, later, the same children had seen some of the programmes in the television series *Love Thy Neighbour* they would have seen the same kind of name-calling presented as entertainment. And on the table at breakfast or tea-time, these same children might well notice a jar of Robertson's jam or marmalade with the usual golliwog grinning at them. Some people like to think that such things have no significance but it's an increasingly hard line to defend.

The Epaminondas stories, by Constance Egan, are favourites of long standing, with an interesting history. Their first appearance in written literature was in 1911 in 'Stories to Tell to Children' by Sara Cone Bryant. This included *Epaminondas and his Auntie* described as 'A Negro nonsense tale from the Southern States of America'. Epaminondas is a type of the foolish or silly hero very common in folk literature but what's most important here is that the stories were taken over, expanded and developed by white people for the entertainment, largely, of white children. Furthermore, unlike many simple 'heroes', Epaminondas doesn't triumph, and the story may well represent, even in the original folk form, a 'housing' (to use Paulo Freire's term) of the ideology of the oppressor in the oppressed. The stories show a greater degree of realism, both in text and illustrations, than the 'Little Black Sambo' stories but the hero is still of the simple type. In *Epaminondas Helps in the Garden*, Epaminondas's Mammy plants some peas, saying she hopes they'll come up quick and then goes off to take her eggs to the market leaving the little boy to look after things. She tells him not to let the hens get into the vegetable garden because, if they do, 'they'll have the peas up in no time.' Later, Epaminondas, growing rather confused, chases the hens into the garden in order to make the peas come up: '"Oh! Mammy," he says when she returns, "I thought the hens would help the peas to grow. I minded wot you said, Mammy, an' I was to take special care of them hens. An' I did, I drove them specially into the garden to help the peas come up quick."' His Mammy calls him 'just one foolish, foolish piccaninny' but she relents at his tears and they kiss and make up.

Here, we can recognize another type of racism presented through the literary stereotypes of the coal-black mammy and the little piccaninny. A. E. Kennedy's illustrations bear this out very strongly. The Mammy, who's very fat, wears a long blue and white dress with a large, white apron. On her head she wears a large scarf, dotted with red and tied at the front. Some kind of flat, red footwear completes the picture. Epaminondas is rather spindly, has short, red trousers, a red-striped shirt and no shoes. Both are coal-black with big, rather round eyes and enormously thick, red lips. (The hens are realistically drawn.) An illustration towards the end of the story shows, in profile, the mother and son kissing. Their lips are so thick, however, that the rest of their faces are still about four to six inches apart. Actually, a good deal of human warmth comes over in the story at the time of Epaminondas's distress at his mistake and his reconciliation with his mother. It's a pity that it's presented in a form derived from the concept of the 'plantation nigger'.

Interestingly, a group of infant teachers, conducting research into the influence of certain stories on their pupils, reported of the children's reaction to *Epaminondas and the Eggs*: 'They were ready to gloat as Epaminondas broke the eggs.'[7] Perhaps these children, a few years later on in life, will become acquainted with the mischievous and ill-founded theories of Jensen, Eysenck and others, which are supposed to show that people of African race have 'intelligence' inferior to whites. Of course, such psychologists assume that they know what 'intelligence' is, and, further, that what they take to be 'intelligence' should be accepted by others. It's rather a pity that Epaminondas, along with so many other fictional characters, lends support to such theories.

Moving on to a more overt and yet more offensive aspect of racism, we move also to an older age range. Hugh Lofting's Dr Dolittle has been on the go for more than fifty years now. The twelve books featuring him have been hailed as children's classics and several million copies have been sold in English alone. The first title published, *The Story of Doctor Dolittle*, came out in 1922 and has been translated into twelve languages: I examined a copy of the 26th English impression, issued by the publishers, Jonathan Cape, in 1959. Here, it isn't necessary to survey in detail the racism and white supremacist attitudes which permeate the series. It'll only be necessary to look at the character of Prince Bumpo, a major figure who turns up in three of the stories, and in particular, at a certain event in his life which happens in *The Story of Doctor Dolittle*. Prince Bumpo is the son of the King of the Jolliginki. The names, as elsewhere in Lofting's work, set the tone. It would, perhaps, be rather difficult to have serious characters with names like that, or like King Koko, King Kakaboochi or Chief Nyam-Nyam. However, they never appear in serious roles but always as comic, childlike, simple-minded figures of fun. Prince Bumpo, funny fellow that he is, wishes to be white and with blue eyes, too, as we learn in *The Story of Doctor Dolittle*. His father has imprisoned Dolittle and most of his animal friends as they were on their way home after curing the sick monkeys of Africa. Polynesia, the parrot, who has escaped imprisonment, sees from a tree, Prince Bumpo come into the garden. The Prince lies down on a seat to

read fairy stories. After a while, he lays down the book and
Polynesia hears him musing: 'If I were only a *white* prince!'
Polynesia puts on a small high voice pretending to be 'Tripsitinka,
the Queen of the Fairies'. She tells Bumpo that the 'famous wizard,
John Dolittle' can change Bumpo into 'the whitest prince that ever
won fair lady!' Then, Polynesia goes back to Dolittle and says to
him, 'You *must* turn this coon white' and tells him to do it in
exchange for their release. Dolittle is doubtful about whether he
can perform this task, but thinks, 'perhaps zinc ointment, as a
temporary measure, spread thick . . .' Bumpo comes to the prison
and explains that, years before, he'd travelled to find the Sleeping
Beauty whom he'd read about in a book. He found her and kissed
her as the book said he should, 'But,' he says, 'when she saw my
face, she cried out, "Oh, he's black!" And she ran away and
wouldn't marry me.' (Jip, the dog, is of the opinion, as we learn
later, that Bumpo probably mistook some 'farmer's fat wife' for
the Sleeping Beauty.) Bumpo settles for having his face, only,
changed to white, and his eyes to blue, while he, for his part, is to
help the prisoners to escape. He has to dip his face into a bowl
where a lot of medicines have been mixed up. Then, we read, 'the
Prince's face had turned as white as snow, and his eyes, which had
been mud-coloured, were a manly grey! . . . When John Dolittle
lent him a little looking-glass to see himself in, he sang for joy and
began dancing around the prison.' Dolittle is doubtful about
whether the medicine will last and says, 'Most likely he will be as
black as ever when he wakes up in the morning . . . But then again
he *might* stay white . . . Poor Bumpo!'

Dolittle, we learn at the end, is going to put everything to rights
by sending Bumpo some candy. The message is clear: the black
man, quite naturally, wishes to be white but he can never become
white, with all that whiteness signifies, no matter how hard he tries
and how great his longing. Of course, it *is* silly for Bumpo to wish
to be white but for reasons other than those Lofting sets forth in
the crude symbolism of this story.

Here, we come upon a pattern familiar in the world of literature
as a whole—the transmogrification, shape-shifting, or magic
change—though it's more common in folk and children's
literature, where the change is brought about by the magic potion
or the kiss. The frog, the beast, the black man are all prisoners,
waiting for release. Within the larger pattern of physical change,
there's an area where the symbolism carries racial associations. Of
course, the change obvious to the eye merely signals some more
profound change, some entry to a new life or a better world once
the spell, however figurative it might be, is broken. But poor
Bumpo! When he began, the wicked fairy got among the genes and

touched them with melanin. How can he ever hope to change? 'And the Sleeping Beauty!' the Doctor asks Polynesia in *The Voyages of Doctor Dolittle*, 'did he ever find her? / 'Well, he brought back something which he *said* was The Sleeping Beauty. Myself, I think it was an albino niggeress.' Poor Bumpo! It should be noted that in his own illustrations to the stories, Lofting always portrayed black people as grotesque.

Finally, before leaving Lofting in this context, it's both curious and sad to relate that the man who wrote the episode of Bumpo's 'change' wrote also the words:

> If we make children see that all races, given equal physical and mental chances for development, have about the same batting averages of good and bad, we shall have laid another very substantial foundation stone in the edifice of peace and internationalism.

We can now follow this particular pattern, of the racially significant change, through two further examples which, although the settings are very different from that of Lofting's story, show a remarkable similarity on a symbolical level.

The Little Black Doll by Enid Blyton was first published in 1937 and was re-issued in 1965 by World Distributors, Manchester, with new illustrations. The copy I used was bought in 1972 and the book may still be on sale. The story begins:[8]

> Sambo had a black face with very white teeth, black hair, a red coat, and blue trousers. He belonged to Matty—but she didn't like him.
> 'I think you are ugly, Sambo,' she said. 'I don't like your black face. I don't mind Golly's face being black, because gollies always are—but I don't like *your* face.'
> Sambo was very sad. He couldn't help being black and all the other toys said the same as Matty. They didn't like him either.
> They wouldn't let him join their games, ride in the train or even sit in the little toy deck-chair that they all loved. The humming top wouldn't hum for him, and the clockwork mouse ran away, because it was afraid of his black face.
> Sambo felt angry and unhappy. How could he help being a black doll? It wasn't fair to punish people for what they couldn't help.

He decides to run away and slips out of the house at night. After tramping along for a while, he begins to feel cold, 'for his red coat was not very thick'. He shivers and sneezes and decides he's caught a cold. Unfortunately, he's come out without a handkerchief but help is at hand when he meets a pixie:

> She had silver wings that shone in the moonlight and the prettiest pointed face, with big pointed ears that stuck up through her shining hair. 'I have a little toadstool house in the hedge here. Come in a minute and I'll find you a handkerchief,' said the pixie.

Sambo was delighted. It was lovely to hear some one talking to him so kindly. He followed the pixie and stared in surprise at the neat little house in the hedge. It was an enormous toadstool, with a door neatly cut in the stalk, and two small windows in the top part.

'I'm afraid,' said the pixie, 'you will think my house is most untidy. But the little brown mouse, who is my servant, has had to go and look after her mother, who is ill. So I've had no one to see to things.'

The device of the cold and the handkerchief leads to Sambo's opportunity to prove his worth, though as a servant:

She opened a drawer and gave him a clean white hanky with tiny silver stars in the corners.

'I say!' said Sambo, 'this is too good for me! And I don't know how I'll be able to wash it.'

'Well, keep it,' said the pixie. 'I've plenty!'

'You are kind!' said the black doll. 'Can't I do anything for *you*? Let me tidy up. I am good at sweeping.'

'I think *you* are kind, now!' said the pixie. 'You've got such a kind face.'

'But it's black,' said Sambo mournfully.

'I don't see that it matters what colour your face is if your heart is kind. I do wish you would stay with me till my mouse comes back. I've a party on tomorrow, and I'll never get done in time!'

Sambo blew his nose with joy. To stay in this dear little house and help the pretty little pixie!

Soon he had told her all his troubles, and had arranged to stay and do the housework till the mouse came back. He had a dreadful cold, but he didn't care! Here was some one who liked him at last!

Sambo devotes himself to looking after the pixie's house but she catches his cold and becomes very ill. Eventually, he decides he must fetch the doctor (a near-by gnome) and, braving thunder, lightning and pouring rain—such is his love for the pixie—he runs across the field and brings the doctor back with him.

[The gnome] gave the pixie some medicine that made her feel better at once—and she turned to thank Sambo.

But she didn't say a word! Instead, she stared and stared! For the rain had soaked all the black off his face and body, and he was as pink as the pixie! Yes, really!

'Oh!' squealed the pixie, in delight. 'You aren't black any more, Sambo. You've got the dearest, pinkest, kindest face that ever I saw!'

Sambo could hardly believe his ears. He was a nice-looking doll now, as good as any other. He *was* pleased.

The little mouse came back the next day, so Sambo had to say good-bye.

'I shall often come and see you,' he said. 'I have had a lovely time here. I am going back to the nursery now, and perhaps the toys will like me, now that I am no longer different.'

This proves to be the case:

> 'You are a brave doll!' they told him. 'We wouldn't have gone out in that thunderstorm! Please be friends with us, we're sorry we made you run away. We couldn't see your kind heart under your black skin!'
>
> 'Well, that was foolish of you,' said Sambo. 'But I forgive you, perhaps you can no more help being foolish than I could help being black! I do wonder what Matty will say when she sees me!'
>
> Well, Matty didn't know Sambo at all! When she found him in the toy cupboard the next day, all pink and shining, she couldn't think *who* he was! But she liked him very much, and now she plays with him as much as with the other toys. No wonder he's happy—little pink Sambo!

Some details are familiar from the books by Blyton referred to earlier—the black face which is disliked or feared and the idea of the social outcast. More important, however, is the symbolic message (which here, however, is fairly explicit and overt)—that blackness is a stigma which has to be removed before Sambo can be accepted. He has to suffer, act as a servant and undergo the ritual purification by water. Then he becomes 'a nice-looking doll . . . as good as any other' and thinks that perhaps the toys will like him now that he's 'no longer different'. The primitive fear of something or someone different is part of the powerful conservative complex which pervades the whole of Blyton's work and racism has its place in this. The fact that the other toys failed to detect Sambo's kind heart under his black skin does little to alter the overall effect of the story. At the end, Sambo is 'pink' and the others are prepared to show affection towards him. He has had to change: that's what is significant. Two other points seem to me to be worth noting in this story: one is that, as in the incident concerning Prince Bumpo already referred to, the ancient instrument of change, the magic potion, also occurs here though in the form of medicine and more indirectly; the second point concerns Matty's remarks at the very beginning about Golly's black face being (just) acceptable because that's part of the natural order of things, while, in the case of Sambo, it's implied that, somehow, it's his fault that he's black—in spite of the statement in the next paragraph that he 'couldn't help being black'. At first sight, this seems curiously muddled, but if we see it in the context of an idea outlined earlier, in which we found that black people at the level of the golliwog, the merry coon and the 'nigger' minstrel were assimilable to white racist sentiments, the position becomes clearer.[9] Blyton's Sambo has some pretensions to being a recognisable human being. He's not a golliwog but 'a black doll' and the illustrations bear this out strongly just as, elsewhere, they bring out the spirit of the text. The pixie, for instance, is of a distinct blond, Nordic type. Although there's a wide choice, it would be difficult to find a story more psychologically destructive, to white as well as to black children.

In 1976, Collins brought out, in their Armada books, a new edition of *Story Party at Green Hedges*, a collection of Blyton's stories including *Little Black Doll*. In this edition, a very confused attempt has been made to give this story a face-lift. The episode of the pixie has been completely left out and Sambo, washed white by the rain, is brought back to the nursery by the toys, who have undergone a change of heart towards him. They now wish he was black, as before, and restore him to his former self by rubbing his face with black ink. This black-washing attempt doesn't seem much of an improvement to me and although the racism of the original has been toned down, Sambo is still subject to the whims of the other toys. Probably, in a few years' time, there'll be a new version in which he'll be painted in black and white stripes, but cosmetics—of any kind—are no treatment for cancer.

The Black Penny by Alan Drake (University of London Press, 1971) is the least explicit and overt, in racial terms, of all the examples we've been looking at, although, in symbolic terms, it provides very close confirmation of the pattern which has emerged from the last two books. (It couldn't be considered, I think, as one of the more harmful stories.) As far as explicitness goes, this story is only one stage on from the basic racism built into the English language which was noted at the outset of this chapter.

The story, for children of about eight years of age, tells of how David gets a new money-box. He says that all the coins he puts into it must be new and shiny, too, but one day he's given a very old penny which is almost black. Although he likes the penny and puts it into his box, it isn't liked by the other coins:

> 'I ask you!' said the fivepenny coin and pulled a face. 'Black! Pooh!' . . .
> The fifty pence piece frowned very hard.
> 'I am not sure that he should be here at all,' he said. 'All of us are shiny and bright. He is dirty and black.'

When David and his parents go for a drive into the country, however, it's the black penny which saves them when the car breaks down. A waterplug has blown out and the old penny is just the size to fit into the plughole. This enables the family to reach a garage. David says, of the black penny, 'I am going to keep it for ever. I will polish it. It will look new and shiny.' His father, however, has the idea of gilding the old penny and, when this is done, the old penny has a very different reception from the other coins:

They bowed. They all made room for the gold coin . . .
'What a beautiful gold coat you have!' said the five-penny piece. 'You
must be a very high person indeed.'
The old penny tells them,
'I am still that old, black, out-of-date penny underneath . . . I am
sorry about that,' he said. But he did not look it. You and I know why.

Yes, we know why he didn't look sorry about his change from
black to gold. The pattern—the move from rejection, through a
powerful visual change, to acceptance—is a familiar one. It's worth
noting that the idea of a test, a proving of worth, is common to the
two examples just quoted: Sambo has to prove his devotion to the
pixie by braving the rain and the black penny's worth is shown
when the car breaks down. Each, in an emergency, was tried and
found to be not wanting. After this initiation rite, they could move
on to better lives. Here, the fact that the colour change is mixed up
with other elements, such as the old-new component and the idea of
status and hierarchy amongst the coins, is merely incidental. It's
worth remarking, too, that, in the original version of the story,
there was no differentiation between the black penny and the other
coins in terms of the old, and decimal, currencies to obscure the
issue. Racism, in any case, is a part, though a very large one, of the
notion of hierarchy which often seems, still, to form the basic
framework of human thinking, though it relates more to the
less-than-human ancestry of humanity than to anything that might
be called civilised. It is remarkable how, twenty-three centuries
later, *The Black Penny* should recall Plato's *Republic* and his men
of gold, silver and bronze.

Two novels for older children—those in their lower teens,
perhaps—can give us a very good idea of what discussion has
centred on in recent times. *Sounder* by William H. Armstrong and
Theodore Taylor's *The Cay* were both published in 1969 in the
United States; both were hailed as outstanding, the first winning
the Newbery Medal and the second five lesser awards; both have
been published in Britain, in hardback and paperback editions;
Sounder was made into a film, already seen in Britain, and there's a
television version of *The Cay*.

Sounder tells of a black sharecropping family in the United
States, ground down by poverty and white oppression. In spite of
all their trials, the story has a curious, unemotional, distanced
atmosphere. The only one to show much emotion in the story is
Sounder, the dog, who intervenes when the father is arrested by the
white law officers for stealing to feed his family. (The fact that, in
such situations, many wrongs were often internalised and emotions
curbed, for self-protection, scarcely explains the rather numb

characters. They're more likely explained by the fact that it's a religious family.) A lot of questions need to be asked about this book. Why's it called *Sounder*? Why is the dog the only one to be given a name?—the people are merely referred to in such terms as 'the woman', 'the man' and 'the boy'. Albert V. Schwartz, in an article about the book, puts this in a wider context and one we've already touched on in the case of Bannerman:[10]

> Within the white world, deep-seated prejudice has long denied human individualisation to the Black person. At the time of the story's historical setting, white people avoided calling Black people by their names; usually they substituted such terms as uncle, auntie, boy, Sambo; or they called every Black person by the same name. The absence of name helped to avoid the use of the polite salutation.

Why does the boy seem more concerned about the loss of the dog than about the loss of his father? When, after years of imprisonment, the man limps home, crippled as a result of a dynamite blast in a prison quarry, why does the family, unlike the dog, show so little reaction? It scarcely seems to fit the occasion. Why is there even less reaction to the father's death? Other things add to the anonymous, impersonal atmosphere of this story. We're told, for instance, that 'The boy did not remember his age.' The fact that the family scarcely have any contacts with other black people emphasises this atmosphere still further. It all seems to take place in a kind of aquarium.

It's strange that such a story should have been so acclaimed in a country where, in general, the debate on racism in books is so much more advanced than in Britain. Here, in fact, it's hardly begun.

Most of the story of *The Cay* takes places on a small, Caribbean island (a cay) over thirty years ago. Here, the author sets up his thesis which is supposed to show the gradual enlightenment of the white, eleven-year-old, racist Phillip. (Islands are very popular for fictional experiments because writers can isolate the factors they wish to deal with.) On this one, Phillip and Timothy, an elderly West Indian, are stranded. We can look at each in turn, to see what happens. Phillip Enright is established as a racist at the beginning. He's repelled by the smell, the appearance and the touch of Timothy. However, he's very dependent upon the experienced seaman for survival and becomes even more so when he goes blind. This is symbolic because the most important aspect of his blindness is that he's colour blind. The reader is clearly meant to date his conversion from this point. As for Timothy, we first meet him as an 'ugly' 'Negro', who's afterwards referred to as a 'black man'. Later we learn from him his first name, which, he says, is the only name he has. A master—servant relationship is immediately set up when the two meet, Timothy calling Phillip 'young bahss'. Later, Phillip asks Timothy to call him by his first name. Eventually, according to the old literary cliché, found in race, class and sex contexts in about the order of frequency, the 'inferior' gives her/his life for the 'superior': Timothy, in a storm, sacrifices his life protecting Phillip. The author doesn't make very much of his death and this, together with the fact that, unlike Phillip, he doesn't seem to have relatives or friends anywhere, or if he does they don't matter, again gives a sort of isolated, fish-tank effect. At the end we're expected to believe that Phillip is a changed character but it obviously doesn't go very deep.

Now, especially in the light of the earlier examples we've studied, it may be easier to comprehend the account an infant headmistress gave of a small West Indian girl who covered herself with white chalk and then announced proudly, 'I'm a little white girl now.' Also, Bernard Coard's account—in *How the West Indian Child is made Educationally Sub-normal in the British School System* (New Beacon Books, 1971)—of how black children portrayed themselves, and him, as white in their paintings and drawings, begins to be understandable. The attitudes and values expressed in the kind of literature we've been considering naturally lead to this kind of self-rejection. When such warped concepts are presented through the powerful medium of literature, and reinforced by the child's environment and through other media, not forgetting geography and history textbooks in school, it isn't difficult to understand how such incidents happen. At the very least, a black child can find little to identify with in literature and little that's recognisable as her or his own culture. Looking into literature, for such children, is like looking into a mirror and either not seeing your face reflected back or, worse, seeing a distorted mask.

Some people find difficulty in believing that very small children are race-conscious and since we've been considering dolls, some reference to sociological research making use of them may be instructive here. In the United States, where there's a long tradition of valuable research into the sociological and psychological aspects of racism, the results of the first experiments involving children and dolls were published as long ago as 1947. Kenneth B. Clark and Mamie P. Clark in their article, 'Racial Identification and Preference in Negro children', report as follows:[11]

> Dolls Test: The subjects were presented with four dolls identical in every respect save skin color. Two of these dolls were brown with black hair and two were white with yellow hair. In the experimental situation these dolls were unclothed except for white diapers. The position of the head, hands, and legs on all the dolls was the same. For half of the subjects the dolls were presented in the order: white, colored, white,

colored. For the other half the order of presentation was reversed. In the experimental situation the subjects were asked to respond to the following requests by choosing *one* of the dolls and giving it to the experimenter:
1. Give me the doll that you like to play with—
   (a) like best.
2. Give me the doll that is a nice doll.
3. Give me the doll that looks bad.
4. Give me the doll that is a nice color.
5. Give me the doll that looks like a white child.
6. Give me the doll that looks like a colored child.
7. Give me the doll that looks like a Negro child.
8. Give me the doll that looks like you.

253 black children were involved in this experiment. In age, they ranged from three to seven years. They were, roughly, equally distributed between the northern and southern states and according to sex and, as regards skin colour, by far the majority were classified as 'medium', the next highest total being 'dark'.

Ignoring the variations according to age, their own skin colour and the area where the children lived, all of which variations were, however, recorded, the experimenters found that the majority of the children preferred the white doll and rejected the colored doll. Furthermore, '59 per cent of these children indicated that the colored doll "looks bad" while only 17 per cent stated that the white doll "looks bad" . . . Only 38 per cent of the children thought that the brown doll was a "nice color".' Some of the remarks the children made during the experiment are at once pitiful, funny and horrifying:[12]

> On the whole, the rejection of the brown doll and the preference for the white doll, when explained at all, were explained in rather simple, concrete terms: for white doll preference—''cause he's pretty' or ''cause he's white'; for rejection of the brown doll—''cause he's ugly' or ''cause it don't look pretty' or ''cause him black' or 'got black on him' . . . A northern five-year-old dark child felt compelled to explain his identification with the brown doll by making the following unsolicited statement: 'I burned my face and made it spoil.' A seven-year-old northern light child went to great pains to explain that he is actually white but: 'I look brown because I got a sun-tan in the summer.'

The children's words oddly strike through the detached, scientific prose of the study but their actions speak louder still: 'some of the children who were free and relaxed in the beginning of the experiment broke down and cried or became somewhat negativistic during the latter part when they were required to make self-identifications. Indeed, two children ran out of the testing room, unconsolable, convulsed in tears.' In case anyone should wonder what this has to do with the situation in present-day Britain, I can report that David Milner recently carried out similar experiments with dolls in Britain, and his results confirmed, in considerable detail, the findings of the Clarks' study. Milner worked with three groups of children: Asian, English and West Indian, and reported that, when the children were asked to say which doll they would 'rather be', 100 per cent of the English children, 82 per cent of the West Indians and 65 per cent of the Asians chose the white figure instead of, in the case of the black children, the relevant figure in terms of race.[13] In fact, a great deal of research has been done on the foundations of racial attitudes in both black and white children in, for instance, South Africa, New Zealand, Mexico and Hong Kong. All the evidence seems to show that the patterns of racism: the deprivation of cultural identity; the creation of self-rejection; the relegation to sub-human status—are everywhere and always the same.

I've felt it necessary to quote the findings of these experiments in some detail because many people—and amongst them, depressingly, a great number of teachers—are reluctant to admit that small children are affected by racism and more reluctant still to admit that racist attitudes can be transmitted via literature. Faced with the kind of evidence we have drawn from children's literature, it's rather hard to contend that racism is not actually present, though many people insist on being blind to it. Again, even when it's conceded that children's literature is often racist, the point of view is often advanced that, nevertheless, this does no harm as it is, for the most part, at a subconscious or symbolic level. There can be little doubt that people can be influenced subconsciously—the evidence from subliminal advertising and research into learning during sleep would seem to confirm this. However, it seems reasonable to believe, quite simply, that we are influenced by whatever happens to us and that the more subconscious an influence is the more dangerous it can be.

We've been considering the child readers who are on the receiving end of the attitudes and values present in what authors write. It need not be supposed that the writers themselves are conscious of the values they hold. They would all, no doubt, be highly indignant at the charge of racism. After all, very few people will admit to being racist—it's usually at a subconscious level. An incident from my own personal experience brought this home to me very forcefully. I'd been advising a student on teaching practice and had been observing her work with a class of children of about eight-years-old. One particular English lesson involved the writing of accurate descriptions. The student had found six large pictures of faces and had set these up on the blackboard at the front of the class. Then, she'd asked the children to imagine that these were pictures of people wanted by the police. The children were to choose one and write a description so that the person could be identified. Although I wasn't particularly happy about this enlisting of the children in vigilante roles, I let that pass. What I was more concerned about was the fact that all the pictures were of black men. (The fact that they were all pictures of *men* is something I only realised later.) At the time, I concentrated on the fact that they were all pictures of *black* men. When I pointed this out to the student, she was amazed. Clearly, it had never occurred to her, and she told me that she had merely leafed through copies of magazines and selected what she thought to be suitable pictures. Things being what they are, it's scarcely possible to believe that there could have been an overwhelming number of pictures of black people in the magazines in question—rather the reverse. I pointed out that the children were being asked to associate criminality with blackness. (The fact that black people are usually disproportionately represented in prisons in mixed-race countries is a vital, but perhaps different, question.) It's only fair to add that the student was very concerned when she realised the significance of what she'd done and she did her best, in subsequent lessons, to bring about a better sense of values in the children's minds. This was not a student who wished ill to any child, white or black. She had simply, and unconsciously, absorbed the values of the society in which she'd grown up and was in the process of transmitting them. The end of the story is also instructive. The student confided to me that she'd discussed the matter, later, with other members of the staff. All, except one, thought that I'd been making a fuss about nothing.

The charge of making a fuss about nothing is a familiar one to those concerned with values in children's literature. As far as racism is concerned, the charge often appears in the more serious form of 'stirring it up'. These elements came out very strongly in the *Little Black Sambo* controversy of 1972 which began when Bridget Harris of the Teachers Against Racism group gave a statement on *Little Black Sambo* to *The Times* which was to print an article on the new, boxed set of the complete works of Helen Bannerman. The statement aroused a storm of fury from outraged readers who had loved *Little Black Sambo* when they were children and who thought that Teachers Against Racism were seeing harm where none existed. *The Times* published at least twenty letters attacking the position outlined by Harris and only three in favour. It's interesting to compare this ratio with the conclusion arrived at by E. J. B. Rose in *Colour and Citizenship* (Oxford University Press, 1969)—that only 17 per cent of the population are not racially prejudiced—though the letters might be seen, rather, as revealing the views of *The Times'* readership. More important, however, is the fact that the three letters were all from black people. One of them was Dorothy Kuya, senior Community Relations Officer in Liverpool, who has done a great deal of valuable work in bringing about a conscious awareness of racism in children's books. She wrote:[14]

> The days have gone when the British could talk of Sambos, greasers, wogs, niggers and Chinks, and not find one of them behind him, refusing to accept his description and demanding to be treated with dignity.
>
> We now have to take note that we live in a multi-racial society, and need to consider not whether the white children find LBS lovable, or the white teachers think it 'a good repetitive tale', but whether the black child and teacher feel the same way.
>
> As a Black Briton, born and educated in this country, I detested LBS as much as I did the other textbooks which presented non-white people as living entirely in primitive conditions and having no culture. I did not relate to him, but the white children in my class identified me with him.

What strikes me is that so many writers of the other letters apparently found it enough to assert that they, personally, had found the stories, or Little Black Sambo, charming, lovable, amusing, interesting or enjoyable. This kind of view often goes with an it-never-did-any-harm-to-me attitude. But what are such arguments—if they can be called that—supposed to prove? Both these attitudes are quite beside the point. It's what *all* racist books have done to *all* children over a long period of time that matters. Whether a particular child was affected by a particular book or not is irrelevant. People exposed to infectious diseases don't always catch them. Also, of course, we don't have to take their word for it when people say a book never did them any harm.

Although there's little enough to choose from, fortunately it's possible to report that some positive attempts have been made within the field of children's literature to bring about a better state of affairs than the one we've been examining. It seems to me that they vary in the degree of success achieved and that, within the positive, as within the negative field, there are variations in ideological viewpoint. It's important to remember that the battle, especially as far as small children are concerned, must be conducted on a symbolic level. After all, it would be difficult to discuss the racism of *The Little Black Doll* with a six-year-old, who wouldn't be capable of the necessary reasoning.

Judy and Jasmin by Jenefer R. Joseph (Constable Young Books, 1967), which is a story intended for children of about six years of age, is an attempt, although, I think, one based on a mistaken attitude, to bring about a positive sense of values with regard to race. It provides, perhaps, the most obvious, if the lowest, starting-point for an examination of the more positive side. The story is of two small girls who are friends. Judy is, apparently, British, and Jasmin is Indian. The only indication of race comes at the very beginning where we are told that Judy had 'curly, fair hair' and that Jasmin had her hair in a 'long, straight, black plait', though the attractive illustrations show the two girls as of clearly different colours. We see a picture of the house where, semi-detached, they live side by side, we see them skipping together and we see them going to school with their mothers differentiated only, apart from their skin colour, by the colour of their raincoats and boots, though Jasmin's mother wears a sari and Judy's mother wears 'western' dress. At school, they go into a tent and change dresses so that, 'When they crawled out again, Judy was wearing Jasmin's yellow dress, and Jasmin was wearing Judy's red dress.' Further, when they lie down to rest 'after lunch', each takes the other's bed. Throughout the rest of the day, the other children get the two girls muddled and we are told that 'even their teacher wasn't sure which was Judy and which was Jasmin.' At the end, however, their mothers correctly claim their respective daughters and they all go home again. On one level, it's strange that the illustrations flatly contradict the story. No one, looking at the pictures, could have any doubt as to the identity of the two children. On another level, it can be seen that this, in literary terms, is the equivalent of the integrationist attitude towards those groups who have emigrated to Britain since the second world war. Jasmin's racial identity is completely ignored, in the face of all obvious evidence. It may be better to be ignored than despised, as Sambo, the Little Black Doll, was but it's still not a solution.

Nor do the picture books of Ezra Jack Keats, for children of about the same age, offer a solution, in racial terms, though they are well-intentioned and beautifully illustrated by the author. In such stories as *Snowy Day, Whistle for Willie* and *Goggles* (Penguin Books), there's certainly no attempt to pretend that the black children are white. They are black enough, but it's only skin deep. Nothing would be affected in Keats's stories if the characters were white. The whole social, political and cultural significance of being black is left out. In fact, it has been remarked that '"Snowy Day" said that Black kids were human by presenting them as colored white kids.' The symbolic significance of the snow becomes apparent. The message seems to be that it's a white world but that black people can enter into it, integrate with it, with success and enjoyment. However, notwithstanding these reservations, it has to be remembered that Keats's stories represent a positive achievement, as is overwhelmingly obvious when they are compared with *Little Black Sambo*, the 'Epaminondas' series and *The Little Black Doll*. Here is no simple little 'coon', no doll despised in his very blackness and nor is there any caricature either in words or pictures.

It is *Stevie* by John Steptoe, however, which seems to me to succeed in every way. The story is meant for children of about nine years old but it operates at such a depth of human understanding that anybody might wonder whether the term, *children's literature*, is really valid. Certainly, although the children in the story are black, and it's set in the United States, I'd expect almost any child to be able to identify with Bobby (who tells the story in his own language) on a simple, human level. It's a story of Bobby's encounter with jealousy and of how he learns something from it. We see it start at the beginning of the story:[15]

> One day my momma told me, 'You know you're gonna have a little friend come stay with you.'
> And I said, 'Who is it?'
> And she said, 'You know my friend Mrs Mack? Well, she has to work all week and I'm gonna keep her little boy.'
> I asked, 'For how long?'
> She said, 'He'll stay all week and his mother will come pick him up on Saturdays.'

We see jealousy and resentment growing in Bobby:

> I could never go anywhere without my mother sayin' 'Take Stevie with you now.'
> 'But why I gotta take him everywhere I go?' I'd say.
> 'Now if you were stayin' with someone you wouldn't want them to treat you mean,' my mother told me.
> 'Why don't you and Stevie try to play nice?'
> Yeah, but I always been nice to him with his old spoiled self. He's always gotta have his way anyway. I had to take him out to play with me and my friends . . .
> 'Ha, ha. Bobby the baby-sitter,' my friends said.

We see, after Stevie has gone and things have returned to normal, Bobby reflecting on what happened:

> We used to have some good times together.
> I think he liked my momma better than his own, 'cause he used to call his mother 'Mother' and he called my momma 'Mommy'.
> Aw, no! I let my cornflakes get soggy thinkin' about him.

In the end he concludes:

He was a nice little guy.
He was kinda like a little brother.
Little Stevie.

The black experience is there and, at the same time, is unimportant, unobtrusive. The story contains a common humanity, all too uncommon in the world of children's literature.

To move to an older age range again and to very recent works, we have two novels of a rare excellence, *The Slave Dancer* by Paula Fox and *Nobody's Family is Going to Change* by Louise Fitzhugh. Both originated in the United States and have now been published in Britain, the first in 1974 and the second in 1976. From the point of view of attitudes to race, it's very interesting to compare them with *The Cay* and *Sounder*—and fair to add that *The Slave Dancer*, like *Sounder*, was awarded the Newbery Medal.

Nobody's Family is Going to Change is about children's rights, though it moves on to women's rights fairly late in the book. It happens to be about a black, middle-class family, as well. However, this is not to say much about it. What's chiefly remarkable in this story is the psychological insight of the author shown in her creation of characters, especially that of Emma, the eleven-year-old compulsive eater with the overwhelming ambition to become a lawyer. Especially compelling are the few pages at the climax of the story when Emma realises that her father doesn't want her to be a lawyer and, in fact, doesn't love her. She'll always be a loser, she realises, as long as she wishes to gain his love and until she stops 'being a mess to please him'. She sees she has to come to terms with this and change herself to cope with it because her family, both her father and her mother, is not going to change. If the book gives rise to any doubt at all, it is that such great insight might not be possible for an eleven-year-old. Perhaps, though, we should have the humility to think, and hope, that it might.

The Slave Dancer is a novel of great horror and as great humanity. It seems to me that it approaches perfection as a work of art. The story is of Jessie, a white boy thirteen-years-old, who's kidnapped in his home town of New Orleans and taken on a voyage in an illegal slaver in 1840. His job is to play his fife and 'dance the slaves' to exercise them during the long return journey across the Atlantic. At the end of the voyage, he's one of two survivors but his life is changed for ever. He tells us, 'At first, I made a promise to myself: I would do nothing that was connected ever so faintly with the importing and sale and use of slaves. But I soon discovered that everything I considered bore, somewhere along the way, the imprint of black hands.'

Notes

1 Sampson Low, Marston and Co. and Richards Press, undated, pp. 36–43.

2 Noddy returned to television in the spring of 1975 in a new series of programmes about twenty years after his first—but without the golliwogs. They were removed by Ruth Boswell, the adaptor, who also admitted the nastiness of the original Noddy and was trying to give him a better image. •

3 In the edition published by Pan Books in 1973 their names were changed to Wiggie, Waggie and Wollie. An expurgated hardback edition is also available.

4 Leicester, Brockhampton Press, 1968, pp. 28–30.

5 This name comes from the Ashanti or Fanti (West African) name Kwasi which was taken to the West Indies and used as a general term for Africans. Here, as with the name 'Sambo', and as in the illustrations, Bannerman shows she's thinking in stereotypes, even to the extent of not distinguishing between African and Asian peoples.

6 I'm indebted to Leila Berg for pointing this out.

7 Various authors, 'The influence of certain stories on groups of East Suffolk children aged 4–8 years', *School Librarian*, 11 (2), July 1962, p. 123.

8 Manchester, World Distributors, 1965 (pages unnumbered).

9 The contradiction can't be resolved, however. Compare Angela's attitude to her three golliwogs, p. 81.

10 Children's Rights Workshop (eds), *Racist and Sexist Images in Children's Books*, London, Writers and Readers Publishing Co-operative, 1975, p. 27.

11 T. M. Newcomb and E. L. Hartley (eds), *Readings in Social Psychology*, N.Y., Holt, 1947, p. 169.

12 Ibid., p. 178.

13 David Milner, *Children and Race*, Penguin, 1975, pp. 117–26.

14 1 May 1972, p. 15.

15 Longman Young Books, 1970 (pages unnumbered).

Section 5 Evaluating Reading Progress

While we can assess materials in terms of their approach to the reading process, their complexity or their biases, to find out which materials are of greatest value, we also need to look at the effect they have on the pupils' progress.

Testing techniques in the reading field are reviewed by Peter Pumfrey (5.1). Teachers have the task of both teaching and assessing the effect of teaching. They need to be aware of the kinds of tests available, how to use them and what to use them for. Rejection of test techniques may, as Pumfrey points out, be a reflection of the way people use a test rather than of the test procedure itself. The article stresses the importance of understanding what is involved in formal reading tests, and also shows that testing not only involves finding out what happened but also involves deciding what to do next: 'Reading tests enable and encourage one to make precise observations, replicable and communicable descriptions leading to an enhanced understanding of the phenomenon under consideration.'

Pumfrey distinguishes between standardised tests and criterion-referenced tests. The distinction is an important one. Standardised test results, whether at a national, local or school level, are intended to help the administrator decide whether general standards are satisfactory and whether additional resources need to be deployed in particular areas. Diagnostic observations, on the other hand, are of value only if they provide information which can lead to more precise help being given to an individual child. Both types, as Pumfrey explicates, have their own limitations. Limited tests lead to limited teaching, and diagnostic instruments are effective only in the hands of a skilled and sensitive teacher. The paper, however, is optimistic about the future development and use

317

of tests, noting that 'without reading tests, the skills, under-standings and insights of the most effective teacher cannot be made public and used to advance our professional expertise.'

Burke and Lewis (5.2) review six studies of the reading standards of British schoolchildren. They set out the questions which reading surveys have attempted to answer, and critically evaluate the ways in which their results have been interpreted. Results from such surveys usually receive wide coverage by the national press and results are often relayed without mention of research limitations. Burke and Lewis take note of the ways in which reading can be assessed (comprehension, speed, accuracy, etc.), the types of samples that are used and the ways in which results are interpreted. They point out that 'it is important . . . not only that the implications of such research be understood but that its limitations be appreciated.' It is interesting to note that they conclude from their appraisal that there is no justification for a belief that reading standards are declining. The forthcoming surveys being set up by the Assessment of Performance Unit (see Pumfrey, 6.4) should allow us to study more accurately the rise or fall of reading attainment levels.

The final article of this section by John Pikulski (5.3) looks at another type of evaluative tool—the informal reading inventory. In reviewing the nature and uses of IRIs, he quotes William Powell: 'the strength of the IRI is not as a test instrument, but as a strategy for studying the behavior of the learner in a reading situation and as a basis for instant diagnosis in the teaching environment.' Informal assessments such as IRIs are closely related to what is taught and therefore akin to criterion-referenced tests described by Pumfrey (5.1). In fact in some American reading clinics Pikulski found that IRIs were viewed as such standardised diagnostic instruments. The IRI is compared with reading miscue inventories (see Goodman and Goodman, 2.5) and shares with other informal procedures the risks of 'imprecision and uncertainty'. Consideration is also taken of the effects of classroom practice. As Pikulski points out, 'the method used for teaching reading will influence the configuration of scores' (cf. Barr, 3.3). The final comment on this paper applies, perhaps, to all evaluation of pupil performance. To paraphrase: the usefulness of IRIs in providing a close match between testing and teaching can be adequately explored only if methodological questions are closely scrutinised and understood.

5. 1 Reading measurement and evaluation: some current concerns and promising developments

Peter D. Pumfrey

It has been suggested that the appreciation of the theoretical and practical value of any new scientific technique passes through five stages. In the first no one, other than its inventors, is particularly interested. Indeed, workers in allied fields may be hostile. During the second stage the technique begins to gain support on the basis of its promise. Stage three is characterised by extensive and even indiscriminate use by those working in the field, often irrespective of whether or not they are competent to assess its value. The reaction that occurs in the fourth stage leads to a disillusionment with the technique without the critical examination logically demanded in such circumstances. The fifth stage occurs when both the strengths and weaknesses of the technique are acknowledged and it is applied appropriately.

History

The use of reading tests based on conventional test theory is an example of such a technique (Magnusson, 1967). Currently the value of standardised reading tests is being called into question. Other approaches are being suggested as alternatives. There is a danger that the reaction is fuelled by emotion based on unwarranted expectations.

Basic psychological research concerned with the nature of human abilities led, during the last century, to the development of techniques by which mental abilities could be assessed. Certain

Source: paper presented at UKRA Conference, Durham, 1976 (abridged). A version of this paper appears in John Gilliland (ed.), *Reading: Research and Classroom Practice*, Ward Lock Educational, 1977, pp. 205–27.

assumptions concerning the nature and distribution of mental abilities underpinned the testing movement. The first was that inter-individual differences in cognitive abilities existed and the second that in many instances the distribution of these differences approximated the 'normal law of error'.

Research workers in various European countries contributed concepts and techniques essential to the development of a technology of mental measurement that enabled abilities to be identified and inter-individual differences assessed. The initiative in relation to the assessment of reading attainments and the associated theory and practice of test construction moved to the USA. It is largely due to the extensive work of American researchers over the last seventy-five years that most major advances have been made in this area (Linden and Linden, 1968). Although resources were not as readily available in Great Britain, some notable contributions have been and are being made. Pioneers included the first officially appointed educational psychologist, the late Sir Cyril Burt, and Professors Ballard and Thomson. Their contributions have led to many initiatives.

Current British contributions

The Scottish Office of Education, the Godfrey Thomson Unit for Academic Assessment and the Moray House College of Education have recently produced an excellent series of reading tests known as the Edinburgh Reading Tests. The Scottish Council for Research in Education has published a new standardisation of the Burt Graded Word Reading Test. The National Foundation for Educational Research in England and Wales is active in the development of test theory and construction and in the dissemination of reading test information. Early in 1976 it was commissioned by the Department of Education and Science to provide reading tests as an interim step in response to the call in the Bullock Report to make a national survey of the reading standards of primary school children. Both the Schools Council and the Social Science Research Council have supported projects involving the development of reading tests. The DES is currently supporting the construction of the British Intelligence Scale under the direction of Dr C. D. Elliott at the University of Manchester. This is probably the most sophisticated psychometric instrument yet devised (Elliott, 1975). Its twenty-four scales include tests of word reading, word definitions, naming vocabulary, verbal comprehension and verbal fluency.

The publication of the Bullock Report is likely to have considerable long-term effects. Within the broader context of the learning and teaching of English in our schools, the Report makes many recommendations that, if implemented, will improve the uses made of reading tests within our schools.

Recent trends

The importance of measurement and testing in the teaching of reading is being increasingly recognised in this country. There is, however, a different tide which cannot be ignored. The Zeitgeist, the fashions of thought and feeling current in our society, affect us all. Discrimination between individuals is not as acceptable a notion as it once was. Men and women are equal in the sight of God and of the ballot-box, and must be treated equally under recent legislation. Discrimination on the basis of sex or race is deemed undesirable. Labelling individuals is seen to have certain adverse consequences that are to be avoided. Teachers' expectations amplify differential performances by their pupils, and the professional validity of such expectations is also questioned. In schools, streaming or setting is often seen as suspect. There is a backwash from this spirit of the times which can be detected in a rejection of the use of tests that discriminate between individuals. It is interesting, however, that the book by Jencks and his colleagues, *Inequality*, could not have been written without the evidence of both inter- and intra-individual and group differences operationally defined by scores on a wide variety of tests (Jencks *et al.*, 1975).

Is diagnosis possible?

Not infrequently both lecturers and, in their turn, reporters overstate a case for effect. The headline, 'Tests no guide to reading', appeared in a professional periodical over a summary of a conference held in Birmingham on 'New approaches to reading'. An infant school headmistress who has written a book on the teaching of reading was reported as saying, 'There is no such thing as diagnostic testing in the teaching of reading.' Her argument was that since we do not understand how children learn to read, we cannot diagnose weaknesses or learn how to remedy them. She pointed to the fact that some good readers scored no more or no less than poor readers on certain tests. It was surprising to find this followed by her statement that the greatest handicap to reading was poor concentration which, it was reported, did not show up in the tests. In other words, after claiming diagnosis was not possible, one was made. This was followed by a prescription for alleviating children's lack of concentration. We were given an intuitive diagnosis of the cause of children's difficulties in learning to read, and a prescription based on that diagnosis. To find both of these following immediately after a rejection of the possibility of diagnosis and prescription, using reading tests, gives reason for doubting the validity of the headmistress's initial assertion and the logic of her own analysis.

At the level of teacher politics one finds an executive member of the National Union of Teachers warning of the danger of turning schools into 'nightmare test factories'. In the same address the speaker is reported as saying: 'We do not want to divert even more public money into the blind alley of producing even finer and more sophisticated tests of ability.' Yet he also recognised the need to reassure parents on the objectives and aims of our schools including the prime duty of our schools to demonstrate their ability to help children to change and to learn. The need to monitor certain standards, as the Bullock Report recommends, was also conceded. However, this was followed by the statement that this did not make a case for developing 'so-called [note the pejorative implication!] highly sophisticated tests to be applied indiscriminately'.

If any educationist is using tests indiscriminately, the criticism might more appositely be placed on the individual who decides to use a particular test rather than on the test itself. Using a stop-watch to hammer in a nail hardly justifies criticism of the watch's ineffectiveness as a hammer.

One welcomes informed criticism of any educational practice. Argument is essential to advance. It is, however, disconcerting to see stage four in the evaluation of the testing movement receiving from its opponents such impoverished criticism.

The value of reading tests

There are many misconceptions current among the teaching profession concerning the nature of psychological tests in general and reading tests in particular. For many, testing is an annoying and unnecessary erosion of valuable teaching time. Others see testing as essential to effective teaching. The majority of teachers find tests of some value, but have reservations. These reservations often arise from erroneous and limited ideas of what a reading test is, from justifiable anxieties concerning the particular instruments and from a lack of training in the uses and limitations of reading tests (Pumfrey, 1974).

A reading test is a means of obtaining information that will help teachers, inspectors, psychologists, administrators, Education Committee members, parents and pupils to answer questions and make decisions more adequately than would be possible without the test results. The five key characteristics of the formal reading test are:

(a) it provides public data;
(b) the test is so devised that information for a particular purpose is obtained efficiently;
(c) the results obtained are valid, in other words the test measures what it is intended to measure;
(d) the results are reliable and provide a consistent means of assessing whatever aspect of reading behaviour is being tested; and
(e) the information obtained leads to more efficient teaching.

We are aware of the complexity of the reading process. No single reading test yet devised is able to provide information on all the aspects of reading in which the teacher is likely to be interested. Some tests measure more than one aspect; for example the Edinburgh Reading Tests Stage 2 provides measures of six reading skills. Many tests, however, measure only one aspect. The most popular reading tests in use in Britain today are of this type. The Schonell Graded Word Reading Test R1 and the Burt (rearranged) Word Reading Test were used respectively in 72.5 and 34.3 per cent of the sample of 936 primary and middle schools that provided evidence for the Bullock Committee. Frequently these tests are expected to provide more information than their authors designed them to elicit. As well as providing normative information on the child's reading age and the amount of progress since the last administration of the test, some teachers expect to obtain diagnostic information that will identify the types of difficulties a pupil has with particular types of words. In practice the absence of a sufficient number of words of a given type makes it impossible to carry out a reliable diagnosis.

There is a wide variety of reading tests suitable for various purposes at all ages from the pre-reading to university level. Although the appreciation of the range available is not as great or as extensive as might be, the UKRA has attempted to improve this situation in two of its recent publications (Turner and Moyle, 1972; Pumfrey, 1976).

The Bullock Report recommends that standardised reading tests 'should ideally have been developed and evaluated within the last ten years' (DES, 1975, p. 249). Two points merit comment. First, if a ban was placed on all reading tests more than ten years old, much of the testing of reading currently done would have to stop. Second, many schools are using sets of norms established in different years. Are these schools wasting the time they spend on using these tests?

The Bullock Committee's point derives from the ever-changing nature of both spoken and written language. Words become obsolete, neologisms proliferate and only the fittest survive. Phrases can become archaic, divorced from the language experience of the child on which his reading skills will be developed. To be valid, the content of reading tests must reflect these changes. The recent rearrangement of word difficulty of the two most popular tests used in England shows the need for such revisions (Shearer and Apps, 1975; SCRE, 1976).

Further, reading standards change over time. The extensively documented and discussed increase in the reading attainments of successive groups of·eleven-year-old pupils tested on the same sentence completion test of reading comprehension between 1948 and 1971 is one example at the national level. If the same test had not been used, it would have been difficult to have assessed the extent of the changes. The subsequent finding in 1971 that standards of reading had apparently not continued to improve would also not be open to discussion, and the Bullock Committee might never have been set up (Start and Wells, 1972; Burke and Lewis, 1975).

It can be perfectly valid to use tests that are more than ten years old as long as that the data they provide are helpful to the school. A school may have the records of pupils over many years. This helps the staff to become aware of fluctuations in the reading standards in their own school. Additionally one must accept that because of the slowness of biological evolutionary processes, the nature of the cognitive abilities underpinning reading is unlikely to change rapidly. Examination of a variety of word frequency lists shows that the twelve most commonly used words have not changed for a very long period. The pupils' ability to recognise these words on sight is a legitimate index of one aspect of a school's reading programme. The number of pupils able to do this at given age level in successive years does give an indication of whether a school is or is not maintaining standards in this aspect of reading. The influx of a large number of non-English-speaking children is likely to reduce this and other indices of reading attainments in the short term at the very least.

Types of reading tests

Reading tests enable and encourage one to make more precise observations, replicable and communicable descriptions leading to an enhanced understanding of the phenomenon under consideration.

There are two major types of reading tests. That most widely known is the normative objective reading test. The items making up such an instrument are deliberately selected so that they optimise individual differences in test scores on the particular aspect of reading being measured. It follows that items passed by all or by no pupils are of no value in normative test construction since they tell one nothing about inter-individual differences within the group. Items which discriminate between children on the ability being tested are selected on both psychological and psychometric grounds. The result is an instrument that enables the user to make valid inter-individual comparisons with a known degree of reliability. Provided that the test has been standardised on a suitable sample of children, it is then possible to compare with the original sample the attainment of an individual or group to whom the test is subsequently administered. If standardisation is carried out on a nationally representative group, the attainments of an individual, a class, a school or an LEA can be compared with the national norms.

It would be possible to coach or allow practice on the test. This would increase the pupils' raw scores and reading ages, giving the impression of a higher standard of reading than was in fact the case. To coach or allow pupils to practise normative test items is to fail in one's professional duty.

Normative tests have come under considerable criticism because they do not provide direct guidance as to what should be taught to a child. For a number of years increasing attention has been paid to testing that is objectives-based. A more common name is content criterion-referenced testing. Unlike the standardised test where a pupil's score is compared to those of other pupils as the basis of interpretation, criterion-referenced test results are interpretable in terms of explicitly stated objectives that are operationally defined. The notion behind this approach is no more than a sophisticated extension of the grade system to allow for individual differences in a flexible manner. The tests are sometimes referred to as mastery tests. An example taken from a practice common in schools illustrates the idea. If a teacher is using a graded reading scheme, a child who has read one book and wishes to continue to the next is typically asked two questions. The first is, 'What was the story about?'; the second, 'Will you read these words, please?' This refers to the out-of-context list frequently found at the back of the book. If the child shows an understanding of the text and is able to read correctly all, or nearly all, of the out-of-context words that comprise the book's content, the child proceeds to the next graded reader with the teacher's blessing. If the child does not meet the criteria of understanding and word recognition, he will not proceed to more difficult work but will be directed to something at a level in keeping with his instructional needs.

This aspect of testing reading leads logically to the use of checklists of skills that the child should master (Dean and Nichols, 1974). The great strength of this approach is that there are a clearly defined number of quite specific objectives that the child is expected to reach. The teacher can set to work to teach the skills to the children. In contrast to the normative test, failure to encourage the children to master the content-criterion-referenced tests is a dereliction of one's professional responsibilities. The content-criterion-referenced test tells one what must be taught and learned.

In such tests the teacher is not concerned with individual differences between pupils in their mastery of a given reading skill. From one point of view, all children should score full marks on the criterion test. A whole new industry is being built up to produce content-criterion-referenced reading tests. The following extract from one firm's catalogue indicates the line taken (Instructional Objectives Exchange, 1976):

> educators are becoming increasingly disenchanted with standardised tests as a measure of educational performance. Standardised testing is giving way to criterion-referenced (objectives-based) testing. Unlike the typical standardised test in which a student's score must be compared to the scores of other students in order to be interpretable, criterion referenced tests results are interpretable in terms of explicitly stated objectives.

One of the most advanced of these systems is the Prescriptive Reading Inventory. This is designed to allow the diagnostic teaching of reading based on ninety clearly defined objectives. The analysis of the results is linked to the prescription of suitable reading activities likely to help the pupil to develop the skills he has not yet mastered. At present the system is keyed to more than thirty-two reading schemes (Pumfrey, 1976). Its scope and promise are extensive. One awaits with interest research reports on the reading progress of children with whom it has been used.

Test profiles

Increasing use is being made of diagnostic reading tests that provide information on different aspects of the reading attainments of an individual. Frequently the results obtained are presented in the form of a profile of intra-individual differences. The initial and intuitive approach to interpreting a profile is by a visual identification of areas of apparent strength and weakness. The purpose is usually to decide in which sub-skills of the reading process the child needs help, and how to use relative strengths to minimise or rectify weaknesses.

In the case of a normative diagnostic test, such an intuitive interpretation ignores several important points. Looking at the profile one may consider the pupil's score on one sub-test to be higher than that on another. Before starting a pupil on a course of remedial teaching, one would wish to be reasonably certain that a further administration of the test would result in a similar profile. Other considerations than the visual pattern therefore matter. The following questions must be asked. First, how reliable is each of the sub-tests? Second, to what extent are the sub-tests intercorrelated? This information is vital because the lower the reliabilities of the sub-tests, the higher is the standard error of measurement of the differences between sub-test scores. Unreliable sub-tests can give only unreliable profiles and unreliable differences between them. Additionally, the correlations between sub-tests affect the interpretation of the differences between the sub-tests. The more highly correlated the sub-tests, the less likely are any differences between sub-test scores to recur (Pumfrey, 1977). The position is well summarised by the following extract from an article on the interpretation of multiple measurements (Cooley, 1971, p. 603):

> One very serious shortcoming of such within-profile contrasts, especially within the achievement area, is the unreliability of difference scores. This unreliability is partly the result of the high correlations among the traits measured by the battery. Some publishers attempt to 'solve' this problem by not reporting these correlations! [Later in the article Cooley says] To provide a battery that measures a set of highly related traits and then to encourage educators to make interpretations regarding trait differences for students without even reporting the typical correlations among these traits is certainly an irresponsible practice.

The simplicity of the visual presentation of a normative profile of reading skills is deceptive. Expertise in the interpretation of a reading profile requires considerable study, practice and application. It demands an awareness of mental measurement concepts, of test theory. Devising a remedial programme requires further qualities. Experience of various methods and materials, an appreciation of their respective efficacies in helping children to acquire or develop skills, and a theory of development which includes reading are essential corollaries to the efficient use of a normative diagnostic reading test. Fortunately, a number of teachers are aware of the complexities of profile interpretation. There is evidence that the approach using normative intra-individual tests is a promising, albeit complex, one (Naylor, 1973).

The content-criterion-referenced approach differs from the normative, largely because items are not selected to maximise individual differences. Having drawn up an analysis of the reading process, the skills to be learned by the child are taught. The major dangers that can occur from working to such a scheme of operationally defined objectives arise from the fact that there is, even in a criterion-referenced test, a measure of individual differences. Often the number of items in a content-criterion-referenced test is small, and hence not very reliable, though this cannot be assessed as with a normative test. The validity is usually face-validity only, and the aspects of reading measured are highly intercorrelated. The psychometrics and theory of mastery tests is still in a rudimentary stage. Their major contribution to improving the teaching of reading is because their use involves analysing the reading process, defining observable and measurable objectives for the children and teaching the mastery of these objectives. The hierarchy of skills on which certain content-criterion-referenced reading tests are based is often suspect.

Of the two approaches, the content-criterion-referenced measurement approach will have more immediate appeal to teachers because it tells them what to teach. The normative is probably of more interest to the research worker.

Perhaps the most interesting developments in diagnostic reading tests attempt to combine both normative and criterion-referenced approaches. It has been said that today's norm, that is the average reading attainment of a group, becomes tomorrow's criterion to be achieved by all. Such an aspiration should be treated with caution, as was noted earlier. Landing on the moon without the technology of NASA would be easier than achieving the initial aspirations of the 'Right to Read' Programme.

In terms of its theoretical development, content-criterion-referenced profile analysis is at a rudimentary level, but has some promise.

Early identification of potential reading failure

This area is one of great conceptual and practical complexity (Wedell and Raybould, 1976). Research findings have helped greatly in establishing which factors within the child and his environment are predictive of potential failure. Thus, on the basis of the National Child Development Study (NCDS), Davie is able to say: 'the need for special educational help will be six times higher for children in Social Class 5 than in Social Class 1'. Yet the power of social class as a predictor cannot be used in explanation of the differences which emerge, because 'It is a crude reflection or measure of a large number of factors, some of them genetic and some environmental'. Despite the validity of social class as a predictor of later need of help, the predictions are based on groups of children and not on individuals.

In terms of individual children, the chances are about 3 to 1 against any individual child aged seven years in Social Class 5 needing such help (Davie, 1976). (Of course some critics argue that the NCDS is like Hamlet without the Prince, as no measure of intelligence other than the 'Drawing a Man' test (Goodenough, 1926) was included in the initial test battery.) Despite this, the point is made that the use of such an approach to identify children likely to need help will result in the identification of a large number of children who will prove to have been mistakenly identified. Such pupils are referred to as 'false positives'. This will be paralleled by the failure to pick out a considerable number of children who will later meet difficulties.

These problems arise in part as a consequence of the unreliability of difference scores between correlated variables referred to in the comment on the need for caution in profile interpretation. The major point is the tentative nature of an identification procedure for an individual that is based on a survey of a group. If any survey is carried out and we identify a number of cases requiring help in reading, we can expect a considerable number of those cases to disappear when re-tested. This is because we have capitalised on unusual combinations of errors of measurement. There have been cases with plus errors on one test and negative errors on the other. Such individual cases will not hold up if looked at more closely. One of the consequences of such a screening or identification procedure is that a number of apparently miraculous improvements will occur. These are likely to be attributed to whatever approach has been used and may thus lead to entirely unjustified claims concerning the efficacy of the identification procedure and the treatment. One way of minimising such undesirable consequences is to develop increasingly valid tests.

Some LEAs use identification procedures that do not involve the use of normative tests. Thus at the end of the child's infant school education, teachers may be asked to nominate those pupils who have not progressed beyond a given level in the graded reading scheme used in the school. As it is well established that early progress in reading is positively related to later progress, the idea of identifying poor readers and providing such help as they require is an appealing one. The simplicity of the scheme also appeals to teachers who are able to say with some confidence which pupils are failing to reach an objective criteria. One authority organised a screening procedure that resulted in a profile of information on criterion measures plus the teachers' recommendations concerning which individual children needed help in reading. Because promotion to the junior school occurred in September, the system resulted in a dramatic over-referral of summer-term-born slow-learning pupils. The absence of a normative test with monthly age allowances led to autumn-term-born children and summer-term-born children being compared on their reading attainments in an absolute sense in July. For children of a given ability, those born in the autumn term both were older than the summer-term-born pupils and had experienced a longer period of infant education. Their reading attainments were understandably superior to those of the younger pupils in an absolute sense, but who would argue that this justified giving special help mainly to the summer-born children? Had the date of transfer been amended to January, then the autumn-term-born pupils would have been over-recommended (Pumfrey, 1975). It seems plausible that the need for special help with reading is evenly distributed in that approximately half of the yearly groups requiring this help should come from each of the three school terms in which their date of birth fell. Only a standardised test with monthly age allowances could identify children whose difficulties were relatively equivalent.

This cautionary point is made so that those looking at identification procedures will realise that for such purposes content-criterion-referenced tests have at least one major weakness. A further danger is that in identifying children 'at risk', one has established a self-fulfilling prophecy. The pupils may respond to the teachers' expectations and exhibit the anticipated difficulties in learning to read.

Normative tests have an important role in the early identification of children likely to find difficulty in learning to read. Research findings give valid indications concerning the host of variables that are predictive of later success or failure in reading. The teachers' responsibility is to be aware of these predictors and to endeavour to find ways of defeating them. If they are successful, then our understanding of and control over the reading process will have been enhanced. But without reading tests, the skills, under- standings and insights of the most effective teacher cannot be made public and used to advance our professional expertise (Askov *et al.*, 1972; Bilka, 1972).

Conclusion

Testing, measurement and quantification do not necessarily lead to precision, to unambiguous communication, to objectivity and understanding. Figures often function as a smokescreen. The Ulsterman who said he was 100 per cent behind the anti-terrorist campaign and then, as if suddenly aware of the ravages of inflation, amended his statement by adding, 'To tell the truth, I'm 200 per cent behind it', is an example. The young apprentice engineer described how he had to work accurately to a ten-thousandth of an inch. When asked how many of these units there were in an inch, after a period of struggle he replied 'millions'.

There are occasions when the use of basic concepts in mental measurement that are essential to the effective use of reading tests is either unfamiliar to or misunderstood by teachers. What are the relationships between raw scores, ranks, percentiles and standard scores of various types? What exactly do we mean by the various types of validity and reliability, and how are they related? What is the standard error of a reading test score? Do such esoteric ideas merely confuse simple issues? Or does such knowledge help one to deal with other questions such as the following? How can we interpret reading test profiles? What is the best way to identify both groups and individual children likely to experience difficulties in reading?

The profession is becoming increasingly conscious of the important role that testing plays in the efficient teaching of reading and is keen to improve its ability to use reading tests effectively (Pumfrey, 1977). In this respect the literacy of our pupils is to some degree dependent on the numeracy of their teachers. Let us as a profession move as quickly as possible to that fifth stage in the development of reading test technology when both the strengths and weaknesses are acknowledged and it is applied to the benefit of all.

References

Askov, W., Otto, W. and Smith, R. (1972) 'Assessment of the De Hirsch predictive index tests of reading failure', in R. C. Aukerman (ed.), *Some Persistent Questions on Beginning Reading*, Newark, Del., International Reading Association.

Bilka, L. P. (1972) 'An evaluation of the predictive value of certain readiness measures', in R. C. Aukerman (ed.), *Some Persistent Questions on Beginning Reading*.

Burke, E. and Lewis, D. G. (1975) 'Standards of reading: a critical review of some recent studies', *Educational Research*, 17 (3), 163–74.

Cooley, W. W. (1971) 'Techniques for considering multiple measurements', in R. L. Thorndike (ed.), *Educational Measurement*, Washington, D.C., American Council on Education, 2nd ed.

Davie, R. (1976) 'Children at increased educational risk: some results and some reservations', in K. Wedell and E. C. Raybould (eds), *The Early Identification of Educationally 'At Risk' Children*.

Dean, J. and Nichols, R. (1974) *Framework for Reading*, Evans.

DES (1975) *A Language for Life* (Report of the Committee of Inquiry appointed by the Secretary of State for Education and Science under the Chairmanship of Sir Alan Bullock), HMSO.

Elliott, C. D. (1975) 'British Intelligence Scale takes shape', *Education*, 145 (17), 460–1.

332 Peter D. Pumfrey

Goodenough, F. L. (1926) *Measurement of Intelligence by Drawings*, New York, Harcourt Brace & World.

Instructional Objectives Exchange (1976) *Catalogue: Select Your Own Objectives-based Materials for Curriculum Design and Evaluation*, Los Angeles, Instructional Objectives Exchange.

Jencks, C. *et al.* (1975), *Inequality*, Peregrine.

Linden, K. W. and Linden, J. D. (1968) *Modern Mental Measurement: a Historical Perspective* (Guidance monograph series, Series III Testing), Boston, Houghton Mifflin.

Magnusson, D. (1967) *Test Theory*, Palo Alto, Addison-Wesley.

Naylor, J. G. (1973) 'Some Psycholinguistic Disabilities of Poor Readers: their Diagnosis and Remediation', unpublished M. Ed. thesis, University of Manchester Department of Education.

Pumfrey, P. D. (1974) 'Promoting more sophisticated use of reading tests: a national survey', *Reading*, 8 (1), 5–13.

Pumfrey, P. D. (1975) 'Season of birth, special educational treatment and selection procedures within an LEA', *Research in Education*, 14, 55–76.

Pumfrey, P. D. (1976) *Reading: Tests and Assessment Techniques* (UKRA Monograph Series), Hodder & Stoughton Educational.

Pumfrey, P. D. (1977) *Measuring Reading Abilities: Concepts, Sources and Applications*, Hodder & Stoughton Educational.

Scottish Council for Research in Education (1976) *Manual for the Burt Reading Test* (Scottish Council for Research in Education Publication no. 66), Hodder & Stoughton Educational (first published in 1974).

Shearer, E. and Apps, R. (1975) 'A re-standardisation of the Burt-Vernon and Schonell graded word reading tests', *Educational Research*, 18 (1), 67–73.

Start, K. B. and Wells, B. K. (1972) *The Trend of Reading Standards*, Slough, NFER.

Turner, J. and Moyle, D. (1972) *The Assessment of Reading Skills*, United Kingdom Reading Association Bibliography, no. 2, Sunderland, UKRA (2nd ed., 1976).

Wedell, K. and Raybould, E. C. (eds) (1976) *The Early Identification of Educationally 'At Risk' Children* (*Educational Review* Occasional Publications, no. 6, University of Birmingham School of Education).

5. 2   Standards of reading: a critical review of some recent studies

Elizabeth Burke and D. G. Lewis

Introduction

Standards of reading attainment in our schools are of central concern at the present time. The Committee of Inquiry into Reading and the Use of English (the Bullock Committee) has recently reported, and large-scale researches financed by the Schools Council are at present in progress in the Universities of Manchester, Nottingham and Sheffield. There is also the SSRC-financed project into the teaching of reading in Scottish schools.

In addition, a number of individual research studies are being undertaken in this area. The results that emerge may well suggest revision of our present methods of teaching reading, of the curriculum of the primary school and its time allocation to the development of reading skills, and of our training of teachers for remedial education.

Much of the evidence collated by the Bullock Committee is concerned with present practices in schools and with the opinions of teachers, administrators, reading specialists, child psychologists and others on what changes, if any, should be made. Surveys of existing practice and of informed opinion are of value. But of at least equal worth is the evidence of planned research. It is important too, not only that the implications of such research be understood but that its limitation be appreciated. A number of relevant research studies have been published in recent years. A critical review of those that seem of major importance may then be

Source: *Educational Research*, 17 (3), 1975, pp. 163–74.

helpful. The studies selected for this review fall under one of two heads:

(i) studies that are essentially normative, being concerned with standards of attainment,

and

(ii) studies that intend to reveal what concomitant variables (or combination of such variables)—and, in particular, variables in the 'school' or 'teacher' categories—are associated with high standards.

Only studies that come under at least one of these heads are included, and again any aspects of the selected studies not falling under these heads are excluded. Each study is subjected to a critical analysis, such an analysis being necessarily selective and concentrating on those points of omission or of misrepresentation which are most likely to mislead.

A fundamental question to be answered at the outset of any research is the choice of criteria. How, in any investigation in this field, is reading to be assessed? It is desirable that any proposed measure be objective (i.e. uninfluenced by the observer or process of measurement), reliable (in that it is repeatable and not subject to short-term fluctuation) and valid (agreeing reasonably well with other superficially equally plausible measures). Many investigators choose a group test of reading comprehension. Here the test items may require the selection of a word, from a given set of options, to 'complete' an incomplete sentence. Again, at a more advanced level, one could aim at the comprehension of a larger unit such as a paragraph of connected sentences. Other measures could focus on the speed at which a child can read, or on accuracy of pronunciation, or on whether he reads with expression. We could also depart from the purely cognitive and attempt to assess the interest in reading which a child has acquired (by noting the proportion of his 'free' time he chooses to devote to reading possibly). The point here is not that an investigator should attempt to include all, or even most, kinds of possible criteria, but rather that he should be aware that the initial problem is one of selection, and that other criteria of success are possible, and that any single criterion study is necessarily limited from the outset. Indeed we could go further and argue for a multi-criterion designed research whenever possible, if only to probe the extent to which the pattern of results differs for each of the separate criteria (Lewis, 1972).

A second basic issue—and one of equal importance to the choice of criteria—is one of sampling. This is because we are seldom concerned with the obtained results as end in themselves. Rather, we wish to generalize to other groups, to a (relatively large) population of which the group tested is representative. We have to concern ourselves then with such questions as whether the pupils tested in the study have been sampled directly, or whether the sampling was of more than one stage. Was it, for example, a two-stage or a three-stage process, 'areas', 'schools within areas' and 'pupils within schools'? Again if 'schools' have been built into the design as a sampling unit, have certain categories of schools been excluded, for example, independent schools and schools for special categories of children such as the maladjusted? When the design has been decided, it follows that every stage of the sampling process should be reflected in the subsequent analysis of results (Lindquist, 1956, pp. 2–5; Lewis, 1968, pp. 88–95), otherwise an inappropriate estimate of statistical error becomes inevitable.

A further point, not always appreciated, is that the selection of a sample inevitably implies a definition of a population. Here we have to consider two inter-related questions—whether the sample is likely to be representative of this population, and whether this population corresponds to any actual existing population of pupils or schools. These two questions correspond to the distinction between the internal and external validity of an experiment (Campbell, 1951; Campbell and Stanley, 1963). The former is essentially the control exercised over extraneous variables and the latter the extent to which we can generalize to practical situations. Ideally, designs should be strong in both. Given the limitations of time and finance, however, we have usually to steer a middle course between the Scylla of excessive control and the Charybdis of rampaging statistical error. Considerations such as these should always precede our evaluation of the results.

In the present case we have chosen to focus on six major studies on reading standards. After the aims, criteria and sampling procedures of the selected studies have been described, the findings, as well as the interpretations of the researcher, are critically appraised. An overall evaluation is added. A concluding discussion seeks to bring together some of the main issues brought out in the separate studies. The paper is intended as a contribution to the continuing debate as to how best to ensure standards of literacy in our schools.

The Morris study (1966)

(a) *Aims*. The two major aims of this study were (1) to compare the reading attainments of primary school children in Kent with those of children in the country as a whole, and (2) to relate these attainments, as well as preceding progress, to methods of teaching, type of school organization and the non-verbal ability of the pupils concerned.

(b) *Criteria*. Two tests of reading comprehension were used for both the aims stated above, namely the Watts Vernon (WV) and National Survey Form Six (NS6) tests. Each had been used in previous surveys and was of the 'incomplete sentence' type. The WV test, originally designed for a national survey of reading standards in 1948, has 35 items and a time limit of 10 minutes, while the NS6 test, constructed in 1954, with 60 items and a time limit of 20 minutes, provided more scope for the abler pupils.

In addition, for the longitudinal study necessary to assess progress, Watts' Sentence Reading Test (SR1) was used together with other measures.

(c) *Sampling*. The sampling unit was that of 'schools', 52 schools being selected, all part of the sample taking part in an earlier 1954 survey (Morris, 1959) and having pupils who since January 1955 still had eight terms of primary schooling to come. Thirty-nine schools were junior with infants and 13 junior without infants. Scores from 2,353 fourth-year pupils, presumably all in the schools concerned (absentees on the day of testing apart), were obtained.

For the study of reading progress, scores from 1,848 pupils from the same 52 schools were obtained over the period 1955–7. In addition twelve 'extreme' schools—three 'good', three 'poor', three 'improving' and three 'deteriorating' in respect of their pupils' reading attainment—were selected for special study.

(d) *Results*. A comparison of the mean scores of the Kent children on both the WV and NS6 tests with the national means (the Kent mean being adjusted to allow for age differences) provided the county authority with the assurance that the superiority of their reading standards found in the 1954 survey was being maintained (and possibly even increased). In deriving national means some extrapolation was necessary, but the amount was not excessive. More important than such prestige comparisons, however—the results of which should obviously be set alongside corresponding differences in the socioeconomic conditions of the homes—would seem to be the finding that the reading standards in the schools themselves were being maintained.

Of far more potential interest however are the results pertaining to the second aim of the study, namely the link with other concomitant variables, and for this purpose the schools were grouped on the basis of the commencing method of teaching reading, phonic or whole-word. The pattern of the SR1 mean scores suggested a better rate of improvement for the whole-word method, the difference being statistically significant however only after adjusting for school differences in non-verbal ability. Morris appears to argue (op. cit., p. 32) that the lack of significance between the two school groups in respect of non-verbal ability precludes a finding in favour of either method. But if the analysis of covariance is to be legitimately applied, in removing *chance* differences in non-verbal ability between the groups, it is this lack of significance that is vital. The evidence should not be discounted for this reason. The findings of course relate to two hypothetical 'populations' of schools of which the actual groups compared can be considered random samples.

Morris also investigates the effect of the type of organization, junior with infant schools versus junior without infants, but this variable is largely confounded with that of methods. There are in fact only three schools in one cross-classification. Obviously little of relevance can be extracted from this situation.

Finally, as regards the special sample of 'extreme' schools, the explanations suggested for these conditions—staff changes, influence of the staff and headteacher, etc.—should be viewed with reserve in that the design suffers from a fundamental defect of omission, the lack of control group of 'non-extreme' schools. It is possible for instance that the influence of the headteacher would have been equally dominant here.

(e) *Evaluation*. The finding that during the period of the investigation reading standards in Kent primary schools were maintained is clearly acceptable. The study is less successful in realizing its other aim of linking success in reading with method of teaching and type of school organization. No conclusion can be made here.

The National Child Development study (Kellmer Pringle, Butler and Davie, 1966)

(a) *Aims*. The general aim of this study was that of compiling normative data about the educational, behavioural, emotional, physical and social development of a large group of British children. As part of this aim, norms for reading attainments were included. It was also intended to concentrate upon the incidence and associating conditions of handicaps.

(b) *Criteria*. The Southgate Reading Test (Southgate, 1962) was used as a measure of word recognition. For each item children have to select from a number of options the word which corresponds to a picture in the test booklet. The test has a low ceiling for seven-year-olds, being unable to extend the above-average reader, and is more successful in differentiating among the backward.

As a second general measure of reading attainment the number of the reading primer then being used by each child was noted. While recognizing the variation in the level of difficulty between books in the various reading schemes, it was nevertheless considered that meaningful distinctions could be made on this basis.

(c) *Sampling*. The theoretically available sample consisted of the surviving children of the Perinatal Mortality Survey (Butler and Bonham, 1963), i.e. all children born in England, Wales and Scotland during the period 3–9 March 1958. Only children living in England, and in respect of whom information was received by mid-August 1965, were included in the sample however. The authors report some evidence of bias in that these early returns had a slight under-representation from the clerical and semi-skilled manual occupational categories. Data from 7,985 seven-year-old children were analysed.

(d) *Results*. The statistical analysis is largely confined to the reporting of descriptive statistics though some hypothesis testing also appears. Thus the null hypothesis of no sex difference in mean score on the Southgate Test is rejected, the difference in favour of girls being significant at the one per cent level. This result is confirmed too from a study of the reading primers used. More boys were still on Book 1 (for non-readers) and also on Books 2 and 3 (where the reading was mainly mechanical, with help from the teacher required frequently), while more girls were on Book 4 (an indication of true reading ability). The percentages of non-readers were 11.2 for the boys and 5.9 for the girls, the combined figure being 9.8 while the percentages of poor readers (Books 2 and 3) were 42.0 for boys and 31.2 for girls, the combined figure being 37.3. By comparing these findings with corresponding results from an earlier survey of Kent children (Morris, 1959), it is tentatively concluded that the number of poor readers and non-readers transferring to junior classes dropped during the years 1956–65. Apart from the inherent unreliability of the criterion employed, it is doubtful however if even a tentative conclusion based upon a comparison of two surveys, one national and the other of an untypical county, and separated by a time span of over ten years, can be justified.

Of the various concomitant variables included in the study the one of major educational importance is undoubtedly that of *length of schooling*. The research is advantageously designed to isolate this variable in contrast to many investigations where it is confounded with age. Two groups are isolated, one of 'early starters' aged from 4.6 to 4.11 on starting school in January 1963, the other of 'late starters', aged from 5.0 to 5.5 on starting school in the summer term of 1963. A comparison of the proportion of 'good' readers—scoring highly on the Southgate Test—in the two groups showed a clear and statistically significant advantage for the early starters. The authors also take account of *father's occupation*, and show that the advantage of early starting obtains for each occupational group. They claim too that the advantage is independent of occupational group (op. cit., p. 124). This however is not so. The breakdown for each group is shwon in Table 5.2.1, where the figures in the last column give the difference between the row differences ('early' minus 'late' starting) for the preceding two

Table 5.2.1 The proportion of good and other readers for early and late starting children in each father's occupational group

Occupational group	Early (E) or late (L) start	Good readers	Other readers	Difference $(a + d) -$ $(b + c)$
Professional	E	58.0 (a)	42.0 (b)	
and technical	L	47.8 (c)	52.3 (d)	20.5
Other	E	61.9	38.1	
non-manual	L	51.2	48.8	21.4
Skilled	E	39.2	60.8	
manual	L	36.7	67.3	9.0
Partly-skilled	E	33.1	66.9	
manual	L	28.2	71.8	9.8
Unskilled	E	25.7	74.3	
manual	L	22.5	77.5	6.4

Source: Kellmer Pringle, Butler and Davie, 1966, p. 122, Table 61.

columns (i.e. for the 'good' and 'other' readers). In other words the last column assesses the *interaction* between early versus late starting and reading, and we see that the extent of the interaction differs from group to group. The children of professional and other non-manual parents who have the advantage of an early start maintain this advantage to an appreciable greater extent than do the children of parents of manual occupations. There is a strong indication in other words, of a second-order interaction, that between reading, early or late starting *and* occupational group. The educational implications are of obvious importance.

(e) *Evaluation.* The study especially when supplemented by the inclusion of the 'late returns' provides valuable baseline data for future surveys. On the other hand, an attempted link up with a previous survey is best ignored. It is unfortunate that in the analysis of the interrelations of variables a second-order interaction involving length of schooling and parental occupation has been overlooked.

The Inner London Education Authority literacy survey (1969)

(a) *Aims*. The declared aims of this survey include (i) discovering the extent of children's reading difficulties sufficiently early to take any necessary remedial action in the primary school, and (ii) comparing reading standards in London with those nationally.

(b) *Criteria*. A group test of reading comprehension devised by the NFER for their streaming project (Barker Lunn, 1970) was used. The test is of the sentence completion type and has norms derived from a sample of 3,000 children in each year group.

(c) *Sampling*. All the junior schools of the Authority were asked to give the test in October 1968 to all their pupils born between 2 September 1959 and 1 September 1960. Test scores from some 96 per cent of the schools were obtained. With pupils from special schools excluded the number of pupils involved was 31,308.

(d) *Results*. The mean standarized score of the sample was 94.4, and this being relative to a 'national' mean of 100 and standard deviation of 15 shows the London eight-year-olds to be on average some six months behind in reading comprehension. Again, defining, 'poor' readers as those with a score less than 80, some 17 per cent of the sample (20.9 per cent of the boys and 11.8 per cent of the girls) are poor readers. This compares with 8.6 per cent of children nationally. Two very reasonable comments are made here. It is pointed out that nearly 17 per cent of the sample are immigrants, and overall the reading standards of immigrant children are lower than those of non-immigrants, the proportion of poor readers among immigrants being in fact almost double that for the non-immigrants. It is also pointed out that the intelligence of the London eight-year-olds may well be below that of eight-year-olds in the country as a whole.

The report goes on to illustrate the influence of *parental occupation* by showing that the proportion of good readers decreases markedly as one proceeds from children of professional parents to those of lower occupational status. It deals similarly with such variables as the *cultural stimulus of the home* (as assessed by the teacher), *parental interest in the child's education* (also as assessed by the teacher), *family size*, and *birth order*, the procedure in each case being that of simply reporting the proportion of poor readers and also that of 'good readers'—good readers being arbitrarily defined as those with a score of 115 or more—in each of the various levels of the variables concerned. The presentation is commendably clear throughout. Nothing more ambitious is attempted.

(e) *Evaluation*. The survey provides valuable evidence of reading standards in London primary schools, the very high proportion of respondents being greatly to the credit of the teachers concerned. As comparisons with national standards depend upon the norms of one test compiled from a standardization sample of only 3,000 eight-year-olds (a so-called 'national' sample) something less than complete assurance is advisable here.

The Clark study (1970)

(a) *Aims*. The aims of this investigation are three-fold:

(i) determining the general reading standards of primary-school children in the county of Dunbarton, Scotland;

(ii) making a study of all found to be backward readers (backwardness in this respect being defined as a reading quotient not exceeding 85); and

(iii) making a further, more intensive study of those backward readers who were average in intelligence.

(b) *Criteria*. The Schonell Graded Word Reading Test (Schonell and Schonell, 1960) was used to determine general reading standards. This is essentially a test of word recognition, the numbers of words correctly pronounced being converted to a reading age for accuracy in the reading of isolated words out of context. The English Picture Vocabulary Test (EPVT) (Brimer and Dunn, 1963) was used as a supplementary measure. This is intended to assess levels of listening vocabulary, and each item consists of four pictures, the child having to identify the one associated with the word spoken by the tester.

For the second of the aims of this study as stated above the Southgate Reading Test (Southgate, 1962) was used, and the Neale Analysis of Reading Ability (Neale, 1966) was administered to all selected for the more intensive study of reading backwardness in the final stage.

(c) *Sampling*. The sampling was in three stages according to those of the research. For the initial stage, all Dunbartonshire children whose date of birth fell between 1 April and 31 August 1959, and who were still attending a school in that county in June 1966, were tested. By restricting the dates of birth in this way all the sample had completed two years of schooling at the time of testing. 791 boys and 753 girls were tested.

The stage two sample consisted of all the stage one sample whose (Schonell) reading quotient did not exceed 85 (apart from the very few who had left the county during the interviewing year). This sample of eight-year-olds consisted of 138 boys and 92 girls. The sample was selected by intelligence only in so far as intelligence was correlated with reading. The mean WISC IQ was 89.8.

For the stage three sample, selection in respect of WISC IQ was deliberate. An experimental group of 46 boys and 23 girls (now as nine-year-olds) was selected and all with at least one IQ not less than 90 (all three of full-scale, verbal and performance IQ being considered) and with a 'poor' Southgate Reading score (21 or less). A corresponding control group was selected on the same basis regarding IQ but with a 'good' Southgate Reading score (22 or more).

(d) *Results*. The mean standardized scores obtained by the stage one sample on the Schonell test, 106.8 for boys and 108.3 for girls, were both above the mean of the standardization sample (100). This however should not be taken as evidence of a rise in reading standards partly because the norms may now be out of date and partly because on the similarly standardized EPVT means nearer to 100 were obtained (and as a measure of comprehension this second test seems the more relevant). Equally, of course, no hypothesis of decline can be sustained. Mean reading scores for different levels of drawing and right–left differentiation are recorded—with no connection between the variables being apparent—though coefficients of correlation based on individual measures are not reported. But the finding of main interest is undoubtedly that some 15 per cent of all Dunbartonshire seven-year-olds are backward readers to the extent that their (Schonell) reading quotient does not exceed 85. It is these backward readers who comprise the stage two sample.

The author finds that as much as 44 per cent of the stage two sample have WISC IQs under 90, and that if the *verbal* subscale IQ of 90 is taken instead this percentage figure rises to 51. Clearly then IQ emerges here as a variable of major importance. Other variables may of course have an even greater educational significance and the search for them should be carried out painstakingly. The results too should be co-ordinated preferably by a regression analysis where the relative importance of these other variables as *accompanying* predictors could be ascertained. Clark's analysis however is insufficiently detailed, being confined to a consideration of each predictor in isolation. At the same time what has been done in the analysis of results from the stage one and stage two samples impresses as sound even if the maximum information has not been squeezed out of the data. It is when we turn to stage three that this verdict has to be revised.

Despite the dominant role clearly played by intelligence, Clark decided to restrict her further, more detailed study of backward readers to those 'within the normal range' of intelligence. At the same time a second (control) group was selected, of similar intelligence but of higher reading attainment (though still part of the stage two sample of backward readers). The criterion for eligibility for 'normal' intelligence is a curious one. It is that *any one* of the three WISC IQs—full-scale, verbal and performance— be 90 or more. There are two objections to this. One is that the three IQs are not parallel measures of the same trait, or combinations of traits, and the other is that the one-in-three procedure capitalizes on chance errors of measurement—many whose 'true' IQ (of whatever variety) is below 90 qualify for 'normalcy' in this way, and this is. particularly so when the additional criterion of a very low reading level is also applied (as it is for the experimental group). Intelligence in fact has not been controlled between the experimental and control groups, despite the application to both of the same selection procedure as is seen from Table 5.2.2.

Table 5.2.2 Mean WISC IQ of the experimental and control groups of backward readers of normal intelligence

	Experimental group	Control group
Boys	94.4	98.6
Girls	91.4	92.0

Source: Clark, 1970, p. 137, Table g.

A further criticism is that even if the scores had been equalized in respect of IQ the fact that the experimental group is an extreme selection of backward readers means that in any subsequent testing its mean score on reading—or on any correlated measure—can be expected to regress upwards, towards the population mean, i.e. towards the mean score of all the backward readers if they had been included in the testing (see McNemar, 1962, pp. 161–2). There is in other words, a built-in bias for the experimental group's results to be inflated. Actually, group comparisons do not seem to have been followed up in full, the author's main interest appearing to be in individual case studies. Nevertheless, the defect in design needs pointing out.

(e) *Evaluation*. The normative aims of the study have been pursued with commendable thoroughness and some useful information on several psychological variables has been gained. The intensive study is less successful. It is unfortunate that advice from a statistician was not obtained at the planning stage.

The Start and Wells study (1972)

(a) *Aims*. The primary aim of the study is that of assessing the attainment in reading comprehension of English children at two age levels, those of eleven and fifteen years, and so making possible comparisons with previous surveys and providing a baseline for the future. A further aim is that of making comparisons among sub-groups, such as boys and girls and pupils from different types of schools. This however is conceived as of secondary importance, and might well have been an afterthought.

(b) *Criteria*. Again the Watts–Vernon (WV) and National Survey Form Six (NS6) were used as measures of reading comprehension, the former having been used in national surveys since 1948 and the latter since 1955

(c) *Sampling*. The sampling was performed in two stages—schools and pupils, and that of schools was stratified both by *school type* (the strata being grammar, modern, technical, comprehensive and direct grant for the senior sample, and junior without infants and junior with infants for the junior sample) and *school size* (large, medium, and small). The actual selection was made randomly by computer from lists supplied by the Department of Education and Science. Within each of the co-operating schools, pupils were selected on the basis of their date of birth in any month. Two equivalent samples of junior schools were selected, one for each of the tests, while at the senior level only one sample was selected, the schools being asked to administer the WV to half their pupil sample and the NS6 to the other.

The proportion of schools declining to co-operate was disturbingly high, only 73 per cent of the primary schools agreeing to take part. Again, due largely to a protracted postal strike, only 53 per cent of the secondary schools were able to return data. Further data relating to the WV test was lost (some 9 per cent of the design sample) through an office mishap. The final yield was 73 WV schools (1,660 pupils) and 69 NS6 schools (1,470 pupils) at the junior level, and 135 schools (1,844 pupils) for the WV test and 161 schools (2,194 pupils) for the NS6 test at the senior.

(d) *Results*. The test mean scores for the present and previous national surveys were age corrected—to remove the effect of (slight) age differences between the various year groups—and for the junior level these were found to be as shown in Table 5.2.3. For neither test is the difference between the 1970 mean and the mean immediately preceding significant at the 5 per cent level, though for the WV test the difference only narrowly fails to attain significance at this level. Start and Wells point out that if the means had been corrected to the mid-point of the mean ages for the 1964 and 1970 surveys, the differences would then (just) become significant at 5 per cent. Numerically the difference corresponds to a reading age of 4.38 months. For the more reliable NS6 test the difference between the last two mean scores corresponds to a difference of only 0.24 months. The mean scores for the surveys at the senior level are as shown in Table 5.2.4. Both the slight rise in the 1971 NS6 mean and the slight drop in the 1971 WV mean are statistically insignificant.

Table 5.2.3 Mean scores for pupils aged 11 years 0 months

A   The Watts–Vernon (WV) test (maintained schools only)

Date of survey	1948	1952	1956	1964	1970
Mean score	11.59	12.42	13.30	15.00	14.19

B   The National Survey Form Six (NS6) test (maintained schools only)

Date of survey	1955	1960	1970
Mean score	28.77[a]	29.48	29.38

Source: Start and Wells, 1972.
[a] Estimated from the obtained mean applying to England and Wales.

Table 5.2.4 Mean scores for pupils aged 15 years 0 months

A   The Watts–Vernon (WV) test (maintained and direct grant schools)

Date of Survey	1948	1952	1956	1961	1971
Mean score	20.79	21.25	21.71	23.85[a]	23.46

B   The National Survey Form (NS6) test (maintained schools only)

Date of survey	1955	1960	1971
Mean score	42.38[b]	44.51	44.65

Source: Start and Wells, 1972.
[a] Estimated from the obtained mean applying to secondary modern and comprehensive school pupils only, being the mean of the *two* estimates quoted by Start and Wells.
[b] Estimated from the obtained mean applying to England and Wales.

What the authors emphasize however are not the differences between the 1971 mean scores and those immediately preceding but differences from 'expected' or 'anticipated' mean scores resulting from extrapolation of earlier increases. Thus, for the eleven-year-olds' performances on the WV test an 'anticipated' mean of 16.30 is forthcoming if the almost linear trend from 1948 to 1964 were continued to 1970 and it is the 'drop' from this extrapolated figure, i.e. $16.30 - 14.19 = 2.11$ points of score and equivalent to over 12 months of reading age, which is hailed as a cause for concern. (A similar 'drop' in the eleven-year-olds' performance on the NS6 test is equivalent to over 5 months of reading age.) Such differences between obtained and 'anticipated' means lead the authors to 'face up to the distinct possibility that the 1970/71 scores are in fact depressed'.

Now despite the cautious phraseology—in the realm of statistical estimation nothing can be ruled out with complete certainty—and the qualifications subsequently made, this conclusion merits a firm rejection as blatant nonsense. The only valid conclusion is that the null hypothesis of no real change in mean attainment since the preceding survey has to be retained. In particular it is wrong to describe a position of no change as one of decrease merely because a forecasted increase has not occurred. And the description is especially unfortunate when there is no rational basis for the forecast. This last point is taken up again later.

There are moreover two further reasons why the pessimism of the authors is misplaced. Both are discussed in the report but are discounted as of little weight. One concerns the ageing of the tests. At the time of the investigation the WV test was twenty three years old and the NS6 was sixteen years old, and both showing signs of being dated. The authors draw attention to certain items which would obviously not find a place in a newly constructed test, and point to the possibility of the pupils of the latest survey being at some disadvantage relative to those tested earlier. This possibility is discounted however since the 'ageing' was twice as long for the period 1948–64 (when the previous survey was undertaken) as for the period 1964–70, and that it would therefore be necessary to postulate 'extreme change' in the latter period. But the effect could very reasonably be expected to become more intense, for a given time span, the more distant the date of the test. An age increase of three years could have little effect on the footballing skill of a player in his middle twenties while the same increase in his early thirties could be catastrophic. Familiarity with language, and within a particular social climate, may well be subject to a threshold effect in much the same manner. Again the depression of test score induced by ageing could follow a logarithmic rather than a linear trend. But concrete evidence on this point would be welcome. An estimate of the effects of dating could be obtained by separating off the obviously out-dated items and comparing the change of score on the 'out-dated' and 'less out-dated' sections of the tests. Perhaps the authors could be persuaded to publish a research note on this?

A second reason why a pessimistic interpretation of the findings is to be deplored derives from the 'immigrant corrections'. The proportion of immigrants (almost all low scorers on the tests) had increased substantially since the previous surveys, and the authors estimate that if the West Indian, Indian and Pakistani children had not participated, the mean score of the junior group would have increased by 0.15 points on the WV test and by 0.18 points on the NS6 test. For the senior group the immigrant corrections would have been higher, approximately 0.3 on the WV test and 0.8 on the NS6. These corrections were not in fact applied as it is possible they are over-corrections, since *some* immigrant children had taken part in the previous surveys. But why could not corresponding corrections have been applied to these results also? A second reason advanced for not applying these corrections to the 1970–1 data is that the immigrants are now better taught, and so presumably are less deserving of treatment as a special sub-group. But this is a *non sequitur*. Comparisons, if they are to be meaningful, must be between like and like. It is worthy of note that if the above immigrant corrections had been applied, the drop in the junior WV mean (Table 5.2.3) would not have been significant even if corrections to the age midpoint had been applied.

Comparisons of the proportion of illiterates and semi-literates (based on the 1938 criteria reference levels for reading ages of seven and nine years) would need similar qualifications, and especially with respect to the vastly increased numbers of immigrants in the 1970–1 survey. Apart from this it needs to be pointed out that the standard errors of percentages derived from small and extreme subgroups are very considerably greater than for the overall group means, and would inevitably cloud into statistical insignificance the differences reported. The reporting of figures showing the change in such percentages without reference to the increased statistical errors involved can only be deplored.

(e) *Evaluation*. The high proportion of schools in the design sample refusing to co-operate renders suspect the application of the findings to the country as a whole. It is unfortunate, too, that an unjustified inference of decline in standards could well be made because of the incorrect basis of comparison adopted and other reasons.

The Cockburn study (1973)

(a) *Aims*. The main aim is that of determining the extent of reading backwardness among seven-year-old children in Angus, Scotland, and of relating the findings to those of previous annual surveys. It was also intended to assess the reading attainments of a subgroup who had been identified as backward readers three years ago.

(b) *Criteria*. The Vernon Graded Word Reading Tests had been used for all annual surveys since 1963. This is an individually administered test of word recognition and has Scottish norms. For the assessments of those previously identified as backward readers the National Survey Form Six (NS6) test was used.

(c) *Sampling.* All seven-year-old children attending schools in Angus in each of the years 1963 to 1972 were tested. (Testing had been undertaken in 1962 but a different test was then used.) The testing was undertaken in all cases by the class teacher, so any absentees were presumably tested on their return to school. Some 1,600 children were involved in all in 1972.

In addition a survey was made in 1969 which included all the seven-year-olds tested in 1966, and who were then found to be backward readers. 117 children were in this category.

(d) *Results.* The percentage of seven-year-olds classified as backward readers by their reading age, as determined by the Vernon test, being at least one year below their chronological age, was found for each of the years 1963–72. The results are shown in Table 5.2.5. We see that the percentage of backward readers rises sharply in the years 1968 to 1970 and this is only partially offset in 1971 and 1972. Cockburn comments that the poor results of 1968–70 were not confined to a small number of schools, or to any

Table 5.2.5 Percentage of backward readers in the Angus Annual Reading Surveys

Year of survey	1963	1964	1965	1966	1967
Percentage	9.9	10.4	8.6	8.4	11.0
Year of survey	1968	1969	1970	1971	1972
Percentage	13.5	14.6	15.0	12.9	12.7

Source: Cockburn, 1973.

one type of school, but were general, affecting town and rural schools alike. The difference between the percentages for 1968 and 1966 (selected for this purpose presumably because it is the lowest) was found to be significant at the 1 per cent level. Apart from this being an *a posteriori* comparison, and therefore suspect when tested by the same procedures as for planned comparisons (Edwards, 1966, pp. 329–30; Lewis, 1968, pp. 49–52; Snedecor and Cochran, 1967, pp. 268–71), it is debatable whether any differences between years should be tested for statistical significance at all. What, after all, is the 'population' with respect to what generalization is desired? This does not detract of course from the value of the data both intrinsically and as a basis for possible changes in educational practice.

In the survey of ten- and eleven-year-old children, only 88 of the

117 backward seven-year-olds had remained in the county and of these all but eight were still backward readers. They were joined in this respect by another 43 who had not been identified as backward readers at the age of seven.

(e) *Evaluation*. This is a valuable contribution to our knowledge of reading standards and is precisely the kind of exercise, involving the co-operation and participation of teachers, that needs to be repeated in other parts of the country. An increase in the proportion of backward readers in Angus since 1967 has been established. No information is provided as to whether this is due primarily to population changes in the county or to different conditions in the schools.

Concluding discussion

All the studies reviewed in this article are essentially normative in that they seek to ascertain standards, regional or national. At the same time some are also concerned (and possibly to at least an equal extent) with a probing for variables of an organizational or psychological kind associated with relatively high attainment (or, negatively, with a relative absence of low attainment) in reading. We see too that almost all employ either a single criterion or two criteria of the same type, and that even when two or more essentially different measures of reading are employed, these are treated separately, and not in combination. In other words all the studies are uni-criterion in design. Conclusions from even the most ambitious study—ambitious as far as geographical coverage or intensity of sampling is concerned—must therefore be modest. This is not to deny the relevance of the type of criteria chosen. The tests of reading comprehension and, in the case of younger children, word recognition might well impress as reasonable, and set against the total complex of reading skill could emerge with respectably moderate validities. At the same time the confinement to the cognitive is worthy of note and should perhaps be contemplated with at least a modicum of unease.

Turning now to sampling methods—the second basic issue mentioned in the introduction—we see that the studies divide into three groups of two. In the ILEA and Cockburn studies practically the whole of the defined population is sampled, with the need to generalize the resulting statistics consequently removed. In a second group, consisting of the studies of Kellmer Pringle *et al.* and Clark, the child is the sampling unit, while in the third group of studies, those of Morris, and Start and Wells, the initial unit of sampling is the school. Insufficient information is provided to be sure that for this last group account of the two stage sampling has been taken in extracting the estimates of statistical error.

Another fundamental difference among the studies is that of the geographical coverage attempted, and here the division is between the two national surveys on the one hand and the four regional (or county) surveys on the other. Yet another distinction is whether or not the findings are placed in relation to those of previous surveys, in a time sequence, so that a rise or decline in standards may be inferred. A common problem here—and one discussed with reference to the Start and Wells study—is that of the ageing of the tests. The best solution would seem to be for a test suspected of ageing to be used only alongside a new replacement test on the next survey, the replacement test then taking over (until it in turn becomes 'aged') on subsequent surveys. Resorting to subdivisions of the test, to 'aged' or 'dated' and 'less dated' sections as suggested in the criticism of the Start and Wells study, is obviously very much a second best.

The Start and Wells study can be placed in a category of its own if only because it is both a national survey and one which places its findings in a temporal sequence. Again it is the only study reviewed that deals with standards of reading in secondary schools. Attention has been drawn to its defects and in particular to the use of a forecasted increased score as a baseline for assessment. It is interesting to speculate why such a baseline was chosen. It may well be part of the same climate of thought that exalts economic growth—as assessed by a percentage increase in gross national product—above all else. In the present context such thinking would lead to an expectation of increased performance in tests of the comprehension of incomplete sentences even though the validity of such tests becomes increasingly imperfect for older children. It is at least arguable that the benefits of any increased 'input'—in the form of more enlightened teaching for instance—should be expected in this particular way. A more comprehensive approach to the basic problem of criteria together with an increased use of regional (or local authority) surveys would seem to provide the most promising lines of advance at present.

References

Barker Lunn, J. C. (1970) *Streaming in the Primary School*, Slough, NFER.

Brimer, M. A. and Dunn, L. M. (1963) *English Picture Vocabulary Tests*, Bristol, Educational Evaluation Enterprises.

Butler, N. R. and Bonham, D. G. (1963) *Perinatal Mortality*, Edinburgh, Livingstone.

Campbell, D. (1951). 'Facts relevant to the validity of experiments in social settings', *Psychol. Bull.*, 54, 297–312.

Campbell, D. and Stanley, J. (1963) 'Experimental and quasi-experimental designs for research on teaching', in N. Gage (ed.), *Handbook of Research on Teaching*, Chicago, Rand McNally, ch. 5.

Clark, M. M. (1970) *Reading Difficulties in Schools*, Penguin Papers in Education.

Cockburn, J. M. (1973) 'Annual surveys of reading disability in a Scottish county', *Brit. J. Educ. Psychol.*, 43 (2), 188–91.

Edwards, A. L. (1966) *Statistical Methods for the Behavioral Sciences*, N.Y., Holt, Rinehart & Winston.

Inner London Education Authority (1969) 'Literacy Survey: Summary of Interim Results of the Study of Pupils' Reading Standards', cyclostyled report from the Education Officer, The County Hall, London.

Kellmer Pringle, M. L., Butler, N. R. and Davie, R. (1966). *11,000 Seven-Year-Olds: First Report of the National Child Development Study (1958 Cohort)*, Longmans.

Lewis, D. G. (1968) *Experimental Design in Education*, University of London Press.

Lewis, D. G. (1972) 'Research Methods in Education: the Basic Concepts of Design', London, Thames Polytechnic address (available on request from the Department of Education, University of Manchester).

Lindquist, E. F. (1956) *Design and Analysis of Experiments in Psychology and Education*, Boston, Houghton Mifflin.

McNemar, Q. (1962) *Psychological Statistics* (3rd ed.), New York and London, Wiley.

Morris, J. M. (1959) *Reading in the Primary School*, Newnes.

Morris, J. M. (1966) *Standards and Progress in Reading*, Slough, NFER.

Neale, M. D. (1966) *Neale Analysis of Reading Ability*, Macmillan.

Schonell, F. J. and Schonell, F. E. (1960) *Diagnostic and Attainment Testing*, Edinburgh, Oliver & Boyd.

Snedecor, G. W. and Cochran, W. G. (1967) *Statistical Methods*, Iowa State University Press.

Southgate, V. (1962) *The Southgate Group Reading Tests: a Manual of Instructions*, University of London Press.

Start, K. B. and Wells, B. K. (1972) *The Trend of Reading Standards*, Slough, NFER.

5. 3 A critical review: informal reading inventories

John Pikulski

Problems in evaluating reading performance and achievement continue to plague reading specialists and researchers. The United States has always been a very 'test conscious' nation and this emphasis has not diminished.

Evaluation of reading in this country surged ahead in the 1920s and 1930s with the advent of group standardized reading tests. However, limitations in these standardized measures were rapidly recognized, and the search for more complete and more diagnostic measures of reading was begun. Beldin (1970) concisely traces the rise of informal diagnostic procedures. For example, he notes that in a 1923 book by Wheat, the general concept of informal diagnosis is outlined rather well. Wheat recommended spending the reading periods of the first week of each school year in 'testing' the oral and silent reading skills of the children by having them try to read from several books which vary in level of difficulty—the core of informal diagnosis.

There was then a lull in the development of strategies for use of informal diagnostic procedures until the mid-1930s. In his 1936 book, Betts began to give some general consideration to evaluation based on samples taken from instructional materials. By 1941, he was using the term 'subjective reading inventory' and was using the informal approach on a regular basis at the Penn State Clinic. In 1942, Killgallon completed a doctoral dissertation which is usually cited as the first attempt to empirically validate some of the concepts involved in informal evaluation. Beldin (1970) also summarizes the major studies that have dealt with attempts to validate informal diagnostic procedures.

Source: *Reading Teacher*, 28 (3), 1974, pp. 141–51.

The concept of informal diagnosis continues to receive widespread attention as a means of evaluating the reading performance of children. Nevertheless, in spite of widespread recognition, decades of discussion and a few research attempts to determine the most appropriate procedures and criteria to use with informal reading inventories, there are still several very vexing problems regarding the use of informal reading inventories. The purpose of this paper is to review and explore some of these areas and to invite greater activity aimed at approaching a solution to these problems.

William Powell (1971) summarized what may be a very valuable distinction in this area: 'The strength of the IRI is not as a test instrument, but as a strategy for studying the behavior of the learner in a reading situation and as a basis for instant diagnosis in the teaching environment.'

Far too many teachers and reading specialists continue to think of the IRI as a 'test' that appears in printed and mimeographed form and that is based on materials different from those that are being considered for instruction. They attempt to avoid what should be the ongoing activity of continuously constructing and revising informal reading inventories. There have been several well-received attempts to 'standardize' or package informal reading inventories. Using a published inventory such as that by McCracken (1966), Silvaroli (1965) or Smith (1959) certainly simplifies the task of testing a child. However, it may give rise to some very difficult questions that will be pointed out below.

There appear to be two major ways in which IRIs have been used. First, they have been used in reading clinics and by school reading specialists to diagnose individual children; set independent, instructional, and frustration levels for them; and to design a plan for the remediation of any difficulties found. In this framework, since the examiner sees children who are receiving instruction with materials that are different from case to case, it has not been feasible to construct or have available IRIs that fit each child's instructional program. In this situation, one or two mimeographed or printed informal reading inventories are used on a recurring basis.

The second major strategy involves the classroom use of informal reading inventories, based on potential instructional materials. A primary reason for use of this strategy has been appropriately to 'group' children, and also to gain some insight into specific strengths and weaknesses, both of the child and the program. They have also been used to assess growth, and to set independent, instructional and frustration levels. With this approach, it is reasonable to use a teacher-constructed informal inventory that samples the material that is under consideration for instructional use or to use an IRI that a publisher includes with his instructional materials. In both cases, the IRI is simply a sampling of the materials that will later be used for teaching.

Many of the problems to be discussed in this paper are much easier to work out when informal procedures are used in a classroom context. They are far more challenging when they are applied to informal reading inventories that are used as clinical instruments on a recurring basis. In the latter situation, questions of reliability and validity deserve attention. However, as this happens, do these inventories remain 'informal' or do they become another standardized diagnostic reading test? Perhaps the primary strength of an IRI, that of close correspondence between the test material and the teaching material, is lost. Some reading specialists would maintain that unless there is this correspondence, the diagnostic instrument is not an IRI.

Lowell (1970) in a very critical article about informal reading inventories states that 'despite the value placed on the concept of informal analysis the practice of using informal reading inventories by classroom teachers is not widespread' (p. 120). In the pages that follow, he makes interpretations based on evidence presented in studies by Emans (1965), Ladd (1961) and Milsap (1962) which generally have suggested that teachers are inaccurate and incapable of adequately administering and interpreting the results of informal reading inventories. Ladd, for example, found that even after thirty hours of training, teachers still failed to record 33 to 37 per cent of the errors. Some counterbalancing positive evidence is supplied by Kelly (1970) who reports very satisfactory, practical application of information from informal reading inventories, if the teachers received an inservice training program early in the school year. He also reported that 95 per cent of the teachers trained under these conditions used IRIs to place children in reading groups.

Some teachers are reluctant to try reading inventories because they are often represented as a highly formalized and very precise technique. However, if the IRI is viewed as a sampling procedure designed to give a teacher some direction with regard to instructional strategies, it may be that a very high degree of precision is unnecessary. This would be the case if the teacher continued to evaluate the child's performance during instructional periods and altered her diagnostic impressions. It is difficult to argue against the idea that diagnosis should be a continuous process, and that extant measures of reading provide data that are meaningful only within the context of an instructional program.

More information needs to be collected regarding the practicality of using informal procedures. How widely are they used and how accurate are or need teachers be in recording and interpreting results?

Reliability and validity

The central concepts that are generally considered with regard to any evaluation instrument are validity and reliability. Reliability is a measure of the consistency of an evaluation instrument, while validity is a reflection of the extent to which the test measures what it purports to measure. Full consideration of the several forms of reliability and validity is impossible in the context of this report. In addition, validity is difficult to assess without reference to the purpose for which and the population with which the measure is being employed. Classroom use of informal reading inventories that are based on materials that are being considered for instruction probably does not need to be subjected to most traditional evaluation procedures by which reliability and validity are judged. There *is* a strong case for 'face validity.' The adequacy of the sampling of the materials and skills would probably be the main validity question. Testing is generally a sampling of behavior. In classroom use of informal inventories, the sample used in the test comes directly from the material that will be used in teaching. Testing procedures closely approximate, but do not duplicate, the procedures that are most frequently used for teaching reading.

On the other hand, it should be possible to expose informal reading inventories that are being used on a recurring basis to many formal evaluations of reliability and validity. Some questions that might be pursued include: Do two examiners observing and recording the same reading performance obtain similar results? If alternate IRI forms are used, is the performance of one child similar on the two instruments? If it is assumed that the several levels of an IRI become progressively more difficult, do a group of children perform increasingly more poorly as the assumed difficulty increases? The final question is probably the most important: Do the results of an informal reading inventory predict whether or not a child will be successful with particular classroom reading materials? Will the instructional level established by an IRI predict the level of book in which the child can profit from instruction? There have been some research attempts to deal with almost all of the above with some tests resembling IRIs, but there is a serious need for additional evidence in this area. As noted earlier, some would maintain that if reliability and validity measures are carried out the material so studied is no longer an 'informal' inventory. However, it seems unjustifiable to recurringly use an IRI not taken from the materials planned for instruction without raising reliability and validity questions.

Establishing 'levels'

One of the main purposes of an IRI is to set 'functional reading levels' for a child. Betts is usually credited with suggesting that a child does not have a reading level, but instead that he has three reading levels—an independent level, an instructional level and a frustration level. There are two ways to describe each of these levels—descriptively and quantitatively.

Descriptively we talk about an *independent level* as the highest level of difficulty of a book that a child can cope with on his own. He can sustain an almost perfect performance. He has almost no difficulty with word recognition, understands the passage, can remember most of its contents and answer questions about it. *Quantitatively* the independent level is defined as the highest level of material with which a child can sustain approximately 99 per cent word recognition and can answer 90 per cent of the comprehension questions that an examiner asks.

At the other end of the spectrum is the *frustration level*, the point at which the material becomes so difficult that the child can no longer cope with it. The word recognition demands *or* the level of understanding required by the comprehension questions exceed the skills that the reader possesses. *Quantitatively* the frustration level is defined as the lowest level of reading material at which the child makes more than 10 per cent of errors in word recognition (less than 90 per cent accuracy) or where he can answer less than half of the comprehension questions he's asked.

Finally, there is the *instructional level*, which is probably the level of greatest interest to the teacher. Descriptively, this is the level of material where the child encounters some difficulty, but where the difficulty is not so great that the child will not be able to successfully deal with it if given help from a teacher. *Quantitatively* the instructional level is the highest level at which the child is able to correctly deal with 95 to 98 per cent of the word recognition demands and can answer 75 to 90 per cent of the questions he is asked.

A number of questions and objections have been raised with regard to the concepts involved in functional reading levels. Most of these deal with the quantitative aspects, but at least one objection has been raised regarding the qualitative descriptions.

George Spache (1963), for example, takes issue with the concept of independent level as described above. He writes, 'A pupil's independent reading level need not be limited to material graded at or below his instructional level. Rather, pupils should be encouraged to read from books available at all levels up to the limits of their independent level. It is not essential that pupils read only very easy materials for understanding or enjoyment' (p. 20). Thus, according to Spache, a comprehension score of 85 per cent is generally recommended for an instructional level; but a score of only 60 per cent is required for an independent level. Spache maintains that his concept of an independent level emphasizes the role that interest plays in making a book readable.

While most reading teachers would support the position that a reader's independent reading level is lower, consisting of easier materials, there would be almost universal agreement that readers who are highly motivated to read something can enjoy that material, even if the word recognition and comprehension challenges are very significant. However, we need evidence to show that children who are guided to read at the more traditional independent level read more, enjoy it more, develop long-term reading habits to a greater extent, and in general have a more positive attitude toward reading.

As noted, most of the questions, however, have focused upon the quantitative aspects of IRI reading levels.

Evaluating validity

The IRI shares a problem with most other evaluation instruments in reading. The child's independent, instructional and frustration levels are usually expressed in grade or reader level scores. For example, a child's independent level may be the third reader level, his instructional level may be fourth and his frustration level, sixth.

The above means, among other things, that he should be able to work effectively, with a teacher's help, using a third reader level book. However, even a very inexperienced teacher knows that the skill demands made even by basal readers, which are highly controlled, vary considerably from one series to the next. Again, there is no problem when the evaluation has been made sampling from the third reader level book that is being considered for instructional use. But it seems quite unsafe to assume that a child designated as reading at the third grade level as determined by an IRI based on one series of books will be able to read a third grade level book from another series, the one that he might meet in classroom instruction. One has only to compare the same reader level books from more than one series or even various editions of basal readers done by the same company, to become impressed with the nature of the problem. For example, those produced in the 1970s are generally more challenging than those produced in the mid-1950s and 1960s. If, as is sometimes recommended, the recurringly used IRI is based upon outdated material in order to be sure the child is not familiar with it, and if the child is going to be receiving instruction with a different basal series or even a non-basal approach, the problem becomes increasingly compounded, and the need to establish validity becomes a matter of critical importance. The problem becomes more acute when trade books, magazine and newspaper articles, books in content areas and instructional materials other than basals are being chosen on the basis of IRI results.

The child who has been taught using a non-basal approach is frequently particularly penalized when evaluated with an IRI which generally follows basal reader procedures. He is not 'test-wise' with respect to the procedures. Some of these children show improvement in performance as the testing proceeds even though the material is supposedly becoming more difficult. They seem to 'catch on' quickly to what is expected.

Many of the above problems can be avoided by simply emphasizing areas of strength and weakness demonstrated by the reader in an IRI performance and de-emphasizing the setting of levels. Many reading clinicians do an outstanding job in this respect. They use the IRI as a criterion referenced test. However, the grade level designations for independent, instructional and frustration levels are widely used and appear to have some utility. It will help considerably (1) if teachers are carefully alerted to the difficulties and limitations involved in the grade level designations, (2) if researchers move toward attempting to provide a clearer method of designating level of functioning, and (3) if attempts are used to locally validate recurringly used IRIs.

Using quantitative criteria

Two criteria are used in setting functional reading levels: the word recognition in context score and the comprehension score. The first number, the word recognition score, is derived by having the child read a paragraph or paragraphs of material. The examiner makes an effort to record all 'errors' that the child makes in reading. A percentage score is then derived by dividing the number of 'errors' or 'miscues' by the total number of words in the passage and subtracting from 100. Even the term 'errors' has been challenged. Ken Goodman, based on his linguistic analysis of children's errors in oral reading, suggests that the term 'miscue' is much better than 'error.'

The first question, of course, is: What constitutes an error? In the early work by Betts (1936) and Killgallon (1942), repetitions were counted as errors: most current writers do not suggest that repetitions be counted. Some include self-corrections while others do not. There is, however, more agreement than disagreement about what should and what should not be counted as an error.

A much more difficult problem is: Should all errors be counted equally or should they be weighed in some way? For example, look at the following two readings of the sentence: The boy sits on the chair and waits for his mother.

Child 1: The boy is sitting on a chair waiting for his mother.

Child 2: The [hesitation] boy s-s-s [examiner must give the word sits] on the [hesitation] champ and [hesitation] water for his mother.

In the first, the child read fluently and with meaning. The substitutions and insertions did very little to change the meaning of the sentence. He made four scoreable errors. The second child read in a word-by-word fashion, needed examiner help with one word and substituted *champ* for *chair* and *water* for *waits*. A very substantial amount of difficulty with word recognition is suggested and the child received very little meaning from the sentence. Yet, the first child made four scoreable errors and the second made only three. Quantitatively, the second child did better according to conventional IRI scoring systems.

It should be strongly emphasized that users of informal reading inventories *do* make interpretations beyond the quantitative information and take symptoms and qualitative information into consideration. If errors similar to those above were made by the two children in completing the reading of a passage so that both achieved a score of 88 per cent, it is conceivable that a reading diagnostician might conclude that the first child was 'independent' with respect to that material while the second was 'frustrated.' In most courses which prepare teachers to use informal reading inventories, students are cautioned to go beyond the numerical data. This points out why the following statement is heard so frequently: 'An informal reading inventory is no better than the person using it.'

Research such as that conducted by Weber (1970) and Goodman (1965) might be translated into a set of specified guidelines for interpreting the extent to which different types of errors should be considered diagnostically significant. A recently published manual by Yetta Goodman and Carolyn Burke (1972) provides some valuable clues as to how this can be done. They suggest, for example, that nine questions be asked by the diagnostician regarding oral reading miscues:

Dialect: Is a dialect variation involved in the miscue?

Intonation: Is a shift in intonation involved in the miscue?

Graphic similarity: How much does the miscue look like what was expected?

Sound similarity: How much does the miscue sound like what was expected?

Grammatical function: Is the grammatical function of the miscue the same as the grammatical function of the word in the text?

Correction: Is the miscue corrected?

Grammatical acceptability: Does the miscue occur in a structure which is grammatically acceptable?

Semantic acceptability: Does the miscue occur in a structure which is semantically acceptable?

Meaning change: Does the miscue result in a change of meaning?

Each of the reader's miscues is categorized according to this scheme. For example, if the sentence: 'I looked up and *had* my first view of a lion' were read: 'I looked up and *heard* my first view of a lion,' the substitution would not be considered the result of dialect, there was no shift in intonation, there was a strong graphic similarity, a moderate amount of sound similarity, the two words serve the same grammatical function, the child did not correct the error, it was grammatically acceptable but not semantically acceptable and there was a meaning change. By analyzing each of the child's miscues in this fashion a detailed analysis of his word recognition strategies can be made and his strengths and weaknesses evaluated. From this type of evaluation, the authors maintain that lessons which use the reader's strengths to help overcome his weaknesses can be devised and used. Throughout this manual are provocative but helpful suggestions; for example, 'often substitutions of words like *a* for *the*, *by* for *at*, *in* for *into*, do not cause a change in meaning. The story context is the determining factor in how extensive the change has been. Substitutions like *daddy* for *father*, *James* for *Jimmy* cause no change in meaning. These types of habitual association miscues are generally produced by proficient readers and are not reading problems' (pp. 101–2). The important point is that if numerical criteria are going to be used, efforts should be made to refine existing procedures so that the interpretation of results would be somewhat less reliant on the judgment of the examiner.

There are striking similarities as well as differences between the IRI and *Reading Miscue Inventory*. The latter may, however, have some valuable suggestions to make with regard to the weighting of oral reading errors or miscues. The oral Miscue Inventory is based on extensive research and a well-defined linguistic theory of reading. It may be that most teachers would find it difficult to use in its present form and that there are too many and overlapping categories, so that it probably needs simplification in order to come into widespread use. However, it certainly deserves attention from reading specialists and researchers.

There are also considerations that need to be made regarding the quantitative aspects of comprehension. Generally, in IRI procedure, a child is asked to read two selections at each grade level. One is read orally and one read silently. Comprehension questions are asked after each selection is read. A percentage score is then calculated for each, and the two are then averaged. This seems acceptable when the two scores are similar, but many questions arise when the two are dissimilar. Consider the scores in the Table actually attained by a sixth grade student. The word recognition was relatively perfect throughout. If the criteria for IRI levels were

Grade level	Oral comprehension	Silent comprehension	Average
Fourth	60	80	70
Fifth	80	90	85
Sixth	50	85	68
Seventh	50	80	65

applied strictly, and *once again it is not suggested that diagnosticians are encouraged to do this*, this youngster would have no independent level established, her instructional level would be fifth and her frustration level would remain unestablished. However, even the novice examiner would almost certainly conclude that so literal an application of the criteria would be inappropriate since comprehension of silently read material approximates much more closely the type of reading demands that are placed on a sixth grade child. Is there a point then at which the averaging of comprehension scores is no longer appropriate? Is there a point, for example, at first grade level where comprehension of orally read material should be considered *more* important? Unquestionably, the adequate examiner takes such questions into consideration when formulating diagnostic decisions; however, once again, might it not be possible to refine IRI methodology to a greater extent so that less reliance is placed on examiner judgment?

The question of questions

There is also the question of what types of questions should be asked of the child, since this is an important contributor to scores. Johnson and Kress (1965) in an unusually comprehensive and lucid discussion of IRI procedures suggest the use of four types of questions: factual recall, inferential, vocabulary and background of experience. Valmont (1972), on the other hand, in an article in the *Reading Teacher* suggests the categories of main ideas, seeing cause and effect relationships, and several other specific comprehension skill areas. It has also been argued that taxonomies such as that offered by Bloom (1956) and modified by Sanders (1966) would work better.

Two points seem important here. First, the problem is not unique to informal reading evaluation; it is shared by other approaches to evaluation and by the area of reading instruction. Simons (1971) does an excellent job of describing some of the difficulties that remain in conceptualizing and evaluating reading comprehension. Also, this seems a far less perplexing question for those who use IRIs as a classroom technique. They should employ in the IRI questions which are like those that they employ in their classroom instruction. The question is more serious for the clinic evaluator or diagnostician who evaluates children from a variety of classrooms.

There is yet another problem with respect to questions which revolve around the concept of reading-dependent questions. Tuinman (1971) has made a strong plea for using only those questions that can be answered on the basis of reference to information contained in the selections read. This would largely eliminate vocabulary questions like: What is a beach? What is a ticket? What is a lunch basket? What is a mongrel? It would also eliminate background of experience questions like: Where do birds who do not stay in the north go in the wintertime? What do insects do in the winter? Although vocabulary and background of experience are factors which unquestionably contribute to a good reading performance, should they not be kept separate from questions which can be answered only with reference to information contained in the selection read?

Content area considerations

One often finds quite inconsistent scores in selections, especially beyond sixth reader level. Comprehension scores such as those in the Table do occur.

Grade level	Oral comprehension	Silent comprehension	Average
Sixth	80	100	90
Seventh	60	50	55
Eighth	70	90	80

Repeatedly-used selections vary as to subject area. Usually, science, social studies and fiction are included. When this is the case, the child who is generally interested in geography, and who ènjoys this area, frequently does well in answering comprehension questions based upon a selection which taps geographical concepts and vocabulary. He may do very poorly with a science selection carrying the same grade level designation. Talking about grade level scores may be particularly useless beyond sixth.

Criteria for selecting levels

William Powell has been particularly prominent in challenging one of the numerical criteria for setting an instructional level: the 95 per cent score for word recognition which is usually attributed to Betts. Where did he get it? Critics talk about pulling numbers from the air. Powell (1971) has suggested that different criteria are called for at various grade levels. He suggests that at grades one and two, word recognition scores between 85 and 98 per cent signify an instructional level; whereas, at third through fifth grade, 91 to 98 per cent is the appropriate range and that at sixth grade, 95 to 98 per cent is acceptable.

After noting that there is a dearth of experimental evidence to support the Betts criteria, he conducted the following study. He began by adopting the rationale that if a child's comprehension score remained above 70 to 75 per cent, the word recognition scores achieved at those levels were 'tolerable.' He selected groups of children in grades one through six who were average in ability and achievement. The comprehension scores of each child were surveyed, and the highest level at which the child was able to attain 70 per cent comprehension was identified. Scores in word recognition were then surveyed at and below that level to determine the lowest word recognition score achieved. This score was recorded for each child, and the mean was calculated. Mean scores were calculated for each grade level with the results as in the Table.

Grade	Per cent
First	83
Second	87
Third	91
Fourth	92
Fifth	92
Sixth	94

Although the results of the study have been available since 1968, there are few published attempts to verify or refute them. Therefore, two exploratory studies were undertaken at the University of Delaware. Both focused on second graders, since the Betts and Powell criteria were most disparate at that level. The first, conducted by Bassett and Hutchison (1972), used 'average' second graders. Using an informal reading inventory similar to Powell's, they administered it to twenty-eight subjects, the exact number of subjects used by Powell at that level. Using the same calculation procedure employed by Powell they obtained the following results:

School A	94.9 per cent
School B	96.7 per cent
Total Population	95.8 per cent

In spite of every effort to follow Powell's procedure, the results were supportive of the original Betts criterion and in fact exceeded it.

There was one very important population characteristic that is different in the two studies. The children in Powell's study had been taught to read using a popular basal reader series, while those in the Bassett–Hutchison study had been instructed using programed reading. The investigators concluded, and Powell concurred (personal communication, 1970), that the strong emphasis on phonics probably created the high word recognition scores relative to the comprehension. Thus, it appears that the method used for teaching reading will influence the configuration of scores.

A second phase was undertaken by the author using a sample of second grade children who had been referred to a clinic for evaluation. When the same procedure was applied to this group, the resultant word recognition score was 83.8, a sharp contrast to the score found by Bassett and Hutchison, in spite of the fact that the informal testing materials were the same. The results of this second investigation are almost identical to those found by Powell. As with so many studies, these two suggest the need for more exploration. They are helpful in trying to identify some of the factors that will influence the scores.

Powell has offered a challenge to the frequently employed criteria for establishing a child's instructional level. He does not challenge the utility of informal reading procedures, but seeks only to refine or verify the utility of our present practices. Preliminary work at the University of Delaware has suggested that the method used for teaching the child to read, and whether the child is an achieving or non-achieving reader may influence the balance of word recognition and comprehension scores. Perhaps the weighting of scores in terms of *type of word recognition errors* will need to be developed before the numerical criteria can be adequately specified.

The problems raised in this paper can be solved. Pointing to difficulties in no way suggests that informal reading inventory procedures are not useful. As a matter of fact, it is probably because they have proven so useful and because they have been placed into the hands of extremely competent professionals who compensated for many of the limitations noted, that research has been so limited. The purpose here was simply to point out some pitfalls that should be guarded against and to suggest the need for more study to make the IRI an even more useful instrument.

Classroom use of informal reading inventories based on instructional materials seems strongly indicated, since this procedure provides the closest match between testing and teaching. This alone compensates for some of the imprecision and uncertainty that exist with regard to informal procedures. On the other hand, there are very important methodological questions that deserve closer scrutiny by examiners who use informal reading inventories on a recurring basis.

References

Bassett, D. and Hutchison, M. L. (1972) 'Criteria for Instructional Levels for Second Graders', unpublished manuscript, University of Delaware.
Beldin, H. L. (1970) 'Informal reading testing: historical review and review of the research', in W. Durr (ed.), *Reading Difficulties: Diagnosis, Correction and Remediation*, Newark, Del., International Reading Association.
Betts, E. A. (1936) *The Prevention and Correction of Reading Difficulties*, Evanston, Ill., Row Peterson.
Betts, E. A. (1941) 'Reading problems at the intermediate grade level', *Elementary School Journal*, 40, 737–46.
Bloom, B. (ed.) (1956) *Taxonomy of Educational Objectives. Handbook I: Cognitive Domain*, N.Y., David McKay.
Cooper, J. L. (1952) 'The Effect of Adjustment of Basal Reading Materials in Reading Achievement', unpublished doctoral dissertation, Boston University.
Emans, R. (1965) 'Teacher evaluation of reading skills and individualized reading', *Elementary English*, 42, 258.
Goodman, K. S. (1965) 'A linguistic study of cues and miscues in reading', *Elementary English*, 42, 639–43.
Goodman, Y. and Burke, C. (1972) *Reading Miscue Inventory*, N.Y., Macmillan.
Johnson, M. S. and Kress, R. A. (1965) *Informal Reading Inventories*, Newark, Del., International Reading Association.
Kelly, D. (1970) 'Using an informal reading inventory to place children in

instructional materials', in W. Durr (ed.) *Reading Difficulties: Diagnosis, Correction and Remediation*.

Killgallon, P. A. (1942) 'A Study of Relationships among Certain Pupil Adjustments in Language Situations', unpublished doctoral dissertation, Pennsylvania State University.

Ladd, E. M. (1961) 'A Comparison of Two Types of Training with Reference to Developing Skill in Diagnostic Oral Reading Testing', unpublished doctoral dissertation, Florida State University.

Lowell, R. E. (1970) 'Problems in identifying reading levels with informal reading inventories', in W. Durr (ed.), *Reading Difficulties: Diagnosis, Correction and Remediation*.

McCracken, R. A. (1966) *Standard Reading Inventory*, Klamath Falls, Oreg., Klamath Printing.

Milsap, L. N. (1962) 'A Study of Teachers' Awareness of Frustration Reading Level among Their Pupils in Basal Readers', unpublished doctoral dissertation, University of Oregon.

Pikulski, J. (1972) 'Criteria for Instructional Levels for Disabled Readers', unpublished manuscript, University of Delaware.

Powell, W. (1971) 'Validity of the I.R.I. reading levels', *Elementary English*, 48, 637–42.

Sanders, N. M. (1966) *Classroom Questions: What Kinds?* N.Y., Harper & Row.

Silvaroli, N. (1965) *Classroom Reading Inventory*, Duburque, Iowa, William C. Brown.

Simons, H. (1971) 'Reading comprehension: the need for a new perspective', *Reading Research Quarterly*, 6, 338–63.

Smith, N. B. (1959) *Graded Selections for Informal Reading Diagnosis*, New York University Press.

Spache, G. D. (1963) *Diagnostic Reading Scales*, Monterey, Cal., California Test Bureau.

Tuinman, J. J. (1971) 'Asking reading-dependent questions', *Journal of Reading*, 14 (February), 289–92, 336.

Valmont, W. J. (1972) 'Creating questions for informal reading inventories', *Reading Teacher*, 25 (March), 509–12.

Weber, R. M. (1970) 'A linguistic analysis of first grade reading errors', *Reading Research Quarterly*, 5, 427–55.

Wheat, H. G. (1923) *The Teaching of Reading*, Boston, Ginn.

Section 6 Reading and Responsibility

Whatever the theories held about the reading process, and whatever the methods and materials available, the essential factors affecting the success or failure in reading instruction are the teacher and the school. Who takes the responsibility for providing the child with the skills needed in a literate society is a problem tackled by Michael Marland (6.1): 'we have introduced compulsory education up to the age of sixteen while shifting the curriculum to more independent learning, to more problem-solving, and have not realised that the entire scheme depends on a high level of literacy.'

He outlines what he sees as the major problems facing the development of literacy: the fragmented school; culture–class conflict; the retreat from print and the growth of the project system. Each of these problems prevents the pupil from realizing the experiences afforded by reading, and prevents teachers from contributing to such reading development. Marland's major message is that we are all of us learning to read all our lives, and that *every* teacher is responsible for knowing about and nurturing reading in the curriculum: 'Only if we can create a coherent school team—specifically teaching reading, giving experience of reading, and making reading available—are we going to begin to tackle the problem.'

Training and preparing teachers for reading is, as Alan Robinson (6.2) states, a world problem. We need to be concerned about the shortage of qualified teachers, and the quality and relevance of teacher-training programmes (cf. Unesco report, 1.1). Like Marland (6.1), Robinson emphasizes that all teachers are involved in the teaching of reading in one way or another. And preparing the classroom teacher for the teaching of reading and writing must be a continual rather than a once-off programme: 'It would seem that if we are to develop more expert classroom teachers of reading and writing, the pre-service programme must be the first, very powerful, step in a never-ending continuum which also includes on-the-job in-service activities for teachers throughout their total teaching careers.' Robinson impresses upon us the need to see the extent of the problem and to share in the responsibility for preparing classroom teachers to teach reading effectively.

Both the teacher and the school are directly involved in the teaching of reading. But fundamental questions are: To whom are they responsible; for what and to what extent are they accountable?

Tackling the issue of accountability is like opening Pandora's box. Peter Pumfrey (6.3) examines the notion of accountability, its realization in educational practice, and its implications. The notion of accountability is, in theory, generally accepted, but in practice accountability raises a host of disparate views:

> While all parties to the educational venture may agree in principle that 'accountability' is desirable, disagreement frequently appears when the notion is put into practice. Some teachers of reading see accountability as essential if reading standards are to be maintained or raised. Others see current and proposed innovations in this field, with their emphasis on the testing of measurable objectives, as reducing even further the limited time available for teaching reading.

Reviewing the ways in which accountability procedures have been introduced, Pumfrey points out the potential limitations of such practices. However, given the disadvantages inherent in past and present attempts to build a system of accountability into the educational system, Pumfrey concludes his article on an optimistic note: 'Accountability can lead to opportunities for the teacher. It encourages innovation in the conceptualization, assessment, monitoring, diagnosis and teaching of reading. As a stimulus to the development of professional awareness and competence, its arrival can be welcomed.'

6. 1 Responsibility for reading in the secondary school

Michael Marland

The nation is concerned about reading standards, and we know that the nation feels that they have fallen. But the Bullock report, after re-analysing the data, came to the journalists' most boring conclusion of the year—that actually we can't tell whether reading standards are marginally up or marginally down. However, the bombshell in the report, surprisingly missed by the journalists, is that in any case the lowest attainers on the kinds of scales used are more homogeneously working class than ever they have been; and that after a quarter of a century of egalitarian education we have managed to pack the bottom end of the reading scales more solidly with the children of the lower socio-economic families than ever before.

Yet even that is not really what worries us most. The Bullock Report made it quite clear that, whatever such standards may say, reading ability is insufficient for the needs of people personally, for their needs as learners, for their needs as members of the public. We have done a very weird thing in this country: we have introduced compulsory education up to the age of sixteen while shifting the curriculum to more independent learning, to more problem-solving, and have not realised that the entire scheme depends on a high level of literacy. However optimistic we may sometimes feel, the difference between our aspirations and our achievement is too great to allow us a very happy professional career. I would like to try and look in some detail at the reading of non-fiction in secondary schools.

Source: *School Librarian*, 25 (2), 1977, pp. 101–9.

The problems for reading

I think that there are four problems. The first I call the fragmented
school. The cardinal strength of the comprehensive school is its
variety; the cardinal weakness, however, is fragmentation. You can
see it in a hundred and one ways. Read *The Creighton Report*,
Hunter Davies's book, and that description of the art department.
Now, you and I know a dozen such stories of the fragmentation of
the comprehensive school—each department developing its own
specialism, which, in the sixties, pushed the curriculum to levels we
had never envisaged in the fifties as possible; but like all good
things this had its bad effects, isolation and fragmentation. The
challenge, now that we have settled for comprehensive education, is
to achieve the *coherent* school.

The second problem is, I believe, a product of the sociologists'
talk of culture–class conflict. You've all come across the idea. Very
crudely, it says that poetry is a middle-class occupation, and
therefore it doesn't do working-class children any good to
introduce it to them: it's merely imposing middle-class values on
them. Now I won't pursue this (except to say that I have never
known poetry to be a typical middle-class occupation). In schools I
find that exactly the opposite is true. On the whole, when teaching
purely middle-class groups, there are complicated attitudes which
prevent various forms of literature being taken straight; attitudes
which you do not get with people who do not suffer that particular
brand of middle-class complication. You can show, in my
inner-city school (as I do every Christmas to my religious studies
class), slides of the Christmas story through great art—providing
you don't tell them it's 'great art'! The pupils take it for what it is,
because of its power. 'Oh!' they say, 'chipped out of marble!' So,
it's marvellous. And it *is* marvellous. You show that to some
middle-class pupils, and to them it has associations of churchify-
ing, and respectability, and all kinds of complicated things—a
sort of filter between them and the experience. The same is true of
books. One never, in an inner-city area, says, 'This is a great writer,
or a good writer.' Let the story do the work: 'trust the tale and not
the teller,' as Lawrence put it. But—apart from these personal
experiences—my own reading of the sociologists is that such people
as Michael F. D. Young and Nell Keddie have based their research
on very limited samples of the curriculum. For all they write,
commerce and the crafts, for instance, never come into schools; it's
only the humanities that they research into. The best research on
this in my opinion is that by Robert Witkins, republished in
Eggleston's volume on research in the comprehensive school. That
shows exactly what is found by those of us working with deprived
children: there is not in fact really a class–culture conflict. That

which you offer in a school is taken by the pupils if it has validity in its own right.

The third problem, as I see it, is what I call a retreat from print. This I find the most frightening of all. Word has gone round that the textbooks have been badly written. So what you in fact do is to try and buy a simpler book—and you find the pupils can't read that either. So you tear the pages out and put them on the electronic stencil-scanner, which by some miraculous method is meant to make them easier to read. You then distribute them. When you find they still can't read the text, you give out sheets you typed yourself very late last night (not terribly well) on a rather tatty portable. When you find they can't read *that* (a) you hate the class and (b) you give up altogether. You can see this happening, time and time again. A reading assignment is given; the teacher then finds it hasn't been understood; he then *circumnavigates* the print by putting it in his own words. I do it myself. One feels this lovely warm glow—'I've made it clear!' I learnt my lesson from one of my housecraft teachers: she said, 'I would never answer a question till the pupil has his finger on the place in the sentence where he found it difficult and had lost the meaning.' But what most of us do is simply say, 'Oh, it's like this,' and explain it, thereby teaching (a) that reading is not necessary and (b) that reading is far too difficult—both extremely bad lessons to teach. You can see this happening in lesson after lesson.

Fourth is the growth of the project system. Now in this university [Oxford] the highest academic accolade is given to somebody who can see a problem that requires investigation, then defines that problem, and can trace the sources of information to help him investigate it; who, having traced the sources, can gut the books to get the relevant data; can then (almost the hardest intellectual feat of all) re-organise that information in the correct sequence and then write it up. Now, if you can do that, Oxford gives you a DPhil. We, in our wisdom, call that 'the project method' and we have used it for the least able and the least well-motivated people in schools. I am not saying we shouldn't do it; all I am saying is that we ought to realise what we have done. I am not denigrating the project system: I am denigrating people like me, who have elevated it to the status of prime teaching method without the concomitant, which is suitable teaching to support it.

The conditions for effective reading

You will notice that I am not speaking about fiction, because on the whole I think that we are here rather more successful. Before we look at the responsibility for reading there are three cardinal conditions to be discussed. The first is the *teaching* of reading; the second is the *experience* of reading; the third is the *availability* of reading material. I suggest that if we ask most of our secondary schools what things are like under these three headings, the answer will be that very little is done. There is rather little teaching of reading, rather little experience of reading, and rather limited availability of books.

My main thesis is that a school needs a coherent plan—in two ways. First, it needs a coherent plan across the three elements (availability, teaching and experience). Second, it requires a coherent plan across and among all those at work in the school. I would suggest that in most schools neither of these two conditions is actually met. The Bullock Report is hated by heads because it puts literacy in the head's in-tray. (You know, the art of being a head is to get stuff out of your in-tray into your out-tray as quickly as possible. Good heads do it by break, and others try to do it before they go home at night. The trouble with the Bullock Report is that a head can't do that: it's the only book on language which has 'head' in the index!) There are recommendations in our field: recommendations 138 and 139, which say that every school should have a language-across-the-curriculum policy and, as part of this, every teacher should understand the reading process and how reading can be developed in his or her own area. This is an extremely difficult challenge to meet. The place of the librarian in these two recommendations is something on which I would think a professional association could well spend a great deal of time.

The teaching of reading

Now, the three elements. I'll take teaching first, and start with the point that in secondary schools there is very little teaching of reading. If you put on one side the basic teaching of reading for so-called primary skills, there is a very weird paradox in our educational system. Almost all the subsequent teaching of reading is in the field of English, and it's based on narrative material, with some poetry and some drama; whereas almost all the reading for learning is based on non-narrative material. You've only got to *say* that to realise that it's highly eccentric: it would be sensible only if the skills were obviously transferable. Word-recognition skills may be transferable, but we know that these don't carry you very far. We know that the nature of these contrasted kinds of writing is startlingly different. If you look at any word-count on different categories of writing, you will be amazed at the extent of the differences. Take a simple one, like the frequency of 'I', and compare it with the frequency of 'the'. Narrative, as you might imagine, has 'I' predominating, non-narrative has 'the'. If you take sentence length, narrative has a tiny average compared with non-narrative. If you take the connectives, you'll find that not only Is a different range used in non-narrative, but there are actually different balances within the various specialist fields: history uses a different balance from mathematics, and science is different again. The whole structure of narrative and non-narrative is entirely different. It is not surprising that our pupils find such immense difficulty in the bulk of their reading. I would suggest that in secondary schools we have not devoted anywhere near enough time to this. We have little knowledge of pupils' actual reading abilities.

More specifically, I think it's very difficult to know particular difficulties that pupils are having unless you are working on a one-to-one basis, or unless you analyse in some methodical way the kinds of difficulties that arise. We tend to lump everything together: 'a good reader' or 'a bad reader'. Worse still, we tend to divide humanity into readers and non-readers. As professionals, a moment's thought reminds us that that's not so. The most important sentence, I think, in the Bullock Report is an old, old, old quotation from I. A. Richards: 'We are all of us learning to read all our lives.' Throughout education we need to be aware constantly of learning to read, and therefore of teaching to read. And second, I think it means that the hierarchy of skills cannot in fact be given age locations. You can't say that young children learn the primary skills and finish with them: even the youngest of children have to have the higher skills taught simultaneously. Even when they're mainly battling with word recognition, they're also thinking about inference, evaluation and so forth: as someone rather neatly put it, 'reading the lines, between the lines and beyond the lines'. That is perhaps the best easy definition of the hierarchy of reading skills. But it also means that every secondary teacher needs to be reasonably conversant with the basic phonic analysis skills and to be aware that pupils—even reasonably able ones—are going to have some difficulty in those basic skills even at age fourteen to sixteen. It particularly means that a school has to ask itself who teaches reading, what is being taught to whom, and in what context.

Two teaching strategies

Could I at this point make a distinction, which I find helpful, between disseminated and specific teaching? When you go to a head and say, 'What do you think about careers education?' and he says, 'Oh, it's terribly important. We don't leave it to specialists; we all teach careers education here'—I call that the disseminated approach. Its advantages are that that which is taught is taught in context with a real situation, and given relevance. You go to another head: 'Oh, careers! Desperately important,' he says: 'can't leave it to everybody. No, no, no! We have a department of careers education—Monday 3, Tuesday 5, along the corridor there.' Advantage? Well, at least that head can sleep at nights. He knows somebody at the school knows something about careers education, and every pupil is getting at least a dose. Disadvantage? So terribly cut off, isolated; and every other teacher steps back with a sort of professional modesty and says, 'Well, we've got a Department of that: we'll leave it to him.' I suggest the same is true of the teaching of reading. Neither way alone is sufficient. The first, on its own, entails the risk that nothing is ever actually explained to a pupil, because in the middle of a science experiment that involves reading a certain paragraph you can't really stop the Bunsen burners to explain what that particular paragraph is doing: you can only take a short cut for the moment. The risk of the other road, the specific one, is a risk which the Americans have discovered. It is that of an isolated, de-contextualised, artifical kind of exercise, lacking any real purpose. Both these extremes have disadvantages and we need a mixture of both.

Now what do I mean by the teaching of reading skills? (I am leaving out the basic skills of word recognition.) You're no doubt all familiar with the notion, nicely phrased by an American who calls reading a 'psycho-linguistic guessing game,' that the basic belief, held by some teachers—that the worst thing you can do in reading is to guess—is fundamentally wrong, because in fact that's the highest thing you can do in reading—reading being a constant process of guessing. Another such belief is that you always read from left to right, which is how we have to teach beginners: too many of us teachers get hooked at that stage, and we drum into our pupils that reading is a left-to-right thing. We talk about 'regressive' eye-movements. 'Regressive' technically means the eye going back; but of course it has pejorative associations, and regressive eye-movements became a very bad thing in the teaching of reading, because you must keep moving. In fact proper tests have shown that the good reader *does* use regressive eye-movements: he is constantly leaping ahead, making a guess, leaping further ahead, and back-checking to make sure of his guess—as it were, refining his guess down to the real intended meaning.

What I'm suggesting is that we should look at these as skills to be taught. Take the meaning of words. How does a pupil work out a word he doesn't know? What do we do as teachers? We tend to do one of two things: either explain it, and once again feel that we've earned our living today; or we say, 'Look it up in a dictionary.'

That is arguably better, but there's an even better thing to do! How about training the pupil to work out the meaning as far as he can from the context? There's nothing wrong with having only a rough meaning—that's how half of us read half the time. It's a very important skill. How does a pupil acquire this? Some teachers just say, 'Give him plenty of contextual work and it will grow.' I believe we must have some specific teaching. First of all we teach him the syntactic contextual clues—we don't use this jargon at all, of course: that's just our own little check list. Take this sentence—I quote from an actual history book used by twelve-year-olds—'In the crowded hovels of the poor, lacking privacy, sanitation and water supply. . .' The pupil doesn't know the word 'hovels': he doesn't have to give up; he doesn't have to ask Sir, or even go to a dictionary. He can work it out by the position. It's not something you *do*, it's some sort of *thing* . . . and then he can work out from its position enough of the meaning to get it. There are various markers that we need to point out; for instance a word coming after 'the' or 'a' must be a certain kind of word. There are semantic clues: italics, bold type, brackets. Second-year pupils reading a play never read, 'Joe, angrily, get out!' because they've been taught what italics are used for—taught it by year after year of English teachers saying, 'No, Mary, you don't *read* "angrily", that's what you *do*.' But nobody may give them a similar explanation of other typographical uses. Now you may say, 'Right, we pick them up.' *We* pick them up—we've picked them up over the years—but the evidence shows that the majority of young people do not just 'pick them up'. My suggestion is that these are ways, very obvious ways, of working out the meaning of words or conventions, that should be taught. On the one hand it should be taught *specifically*, that is to say a teacher should have it on a syllabus somewhere and at some point should show it with examples. Also it should be taught in a *disseminated* way: every teacher in the school should consciously know about this, know it's being taught. Too often my colleagues think that 'reading difficulties' mean 'inability to read certain words': my view is that there is more of a difficulty in reading a *sentence*.

Then there is the question of the 'signal words'. It was Coleridge who wrote, 'A close reasoner and a good writer in general may be known by his pertinent use of connectives.' Now we English teachers are dab hands at adjectives and adverbs: we are really having a life-long love-affair with them. However, those are not the key words of the language of exposition, argument and non-narrative. The history teacher may define a word like 'franchise'; he is unlikely to define a word like 'development', which actually is one of those crucial words without which you can't understand history. He is even less likely to explain a word like 'since'. Take the little word 'if'. I have three quotations from one extremely good topic book on the American War of Independence. It sells very widely, it's beautifully designed and written, but, I think, very difficult to read. (1) 'If the range was close, the guns fired grape-shot or canister.' (2) 'If the Americans were going to fight against a great power like Britain, Congress had to set about raising an army.' (3) 'If British soldiers had suffered much, the Loyalists had suffered more.' Those sentences depend on that word 'if'; if you are not used to construing the sense of that 'if' you can't make sense of them. Take the last one. British soldiers *had* suffered much: it's *not* a conditional in the simple sense at all. Take the middle one: the Americans *were* going to fight. They were fighting. Now I would suggest that this needs teaching every bit as much as some of the other things we teach in language. The signal words are the ones which cause a great deal of difficulty.

Paragraphs, relationships and study skills

Let us move on via signal words to the structure of paragraphs. We are very good at teaching the structure of narrative, and it is exciting to hear very ordinary kinds of teenage pupils discussing with perception and intelligence a passage from a novel read with real understanding. But there's another sort of structure and logic in the non-narrative paragraph. It's rather nicely put in a book called *The Labyrinth of Language*:

> Problems of clarifying meaning are constantly with us . . . If we find it hard to understand well, the fault is not altogether that of the writer or speaker. Even at its most lucid, discourse is inescapably linear, doling out scraps of meaning in a fragile thread. But significant thought is seldom linear. Cross-references and overlapping relationships must be left for the good reader to tease out for himself.

The art of reading is to reconstruct the three-dimensional structure that lies behind the linear discourse. This means looking at the structure of paragraphs. Many will have a main idea with supporting examples. Some will be mere lists, some will have chronological order, some will have comparison, contrast, some cause and effect, and so on. The reader's job is to reconstruct the relationships. *The teacher's job is to help him do so*, partly by specific teaching and partly 'in context'.

I shall finish the teaching section by going on to 'study skills'. I think that we are very bad at teaching these in the secondary school. We have our introductory lesson in the library in year one, hoping it will carry on for the rest of the time, but we know very well it won't. We know that when it comes to fourth-year projects it will be 'ask Miss' to find out what's in the library. I believe that this skill should be taught again, both specifically and in a disseminated way. It should be a working rule that nobody sets any project without teaching the particular skills required for it—particular classification numbers and so forth—and taking particular examples to explain them. A third-year religious studies text-book had at the end of a chapter: 'Things to do—write a report on Judaism.' Now have you ever tried to write a report on Judaism? I came across a teacher who had prepared her own guide—how to focus your question down, what kinds of things to find out, the sources (cuttings, the local newspaper, TV, books), the relevant classification numbers: so that instead of the Dewey system being taught 'once off' it's actually reinforced and explained when required *at the point of need.*

Reading (beyond the basics) cannot be allowed to develop wholly spontaneously, and virtually every teacher, including the librarian, is a teacher of reading.

The experience of reading

My first point here is that there is very little experience of reading in the secondary school—or junior school, for that matter. You may think I'm just being polemical, but I'm not. The research done for the Schools Council project Effective Use of Reading, which is not yet published, is really quite devastating. Top juniors spend most of their time writing, and secondary pupils spend most of their time listening. One particular eleven-year-old was observed by the researchers, on a 35-minute 'reading comprehension test'. The teachers had said, 'This is a reading lesson—35 minutes of reading.' But the pupil, timed, spent only a minute and three-quarters reading: the rest was writing answers to the comprehension exercise in rough, and then copying them out 'in best'.

The second frightening fact is that, whereas one might have thought that we teachers fell into the trap of expecting too much from reading, the teachers when actually questioned didn't even expect the pupils to get anything much from their reading. What the Americans call pre-reading study strategies seem to me quite valuable: that is, you ought to say to the class, 'Why are we setting this? And what are the problems to look out for?' and *help* the pupil into the text.

The third worrying aspect is the continuity of reading. Now reading, if it's anything, is an affair of length. I've quoted one figure: $1\frac{3}{4}$ minutes out of 35. The same research has produced some even more worrying figures on continuity. Social studies, you would perhaps have thought, was one of the fields in which you had a lot of continuous reading. Sixty of the pupils sampled spent only between one and fifteen seconds reading in one burst; only 3 per cent worked in bursts of more than a minute.

I'm trying to suggest that there is less experience of reading than we would like to think. Now, what do I recommend? I believe that we have hardly learnt to handle the so-called project method. We have nowhere near learnt how to devise the best sort of topic, how to help pupils to focus it, how to relate it to specific materials, and how to go to the right kind of sources. Again research has shown that most of the indexing systems made available in libraries are not used by the children. If the librarian is not there only the encyclopaedia is looked at. We know that *within* books they do very badly indeed. The Open University did an interesting bit of research, supposed to be on note-making. They set up a time-lapse camera on a sixth-former who had a particular task; they wanted to see how she set about making notes. The film ran out before she got to the bit of the book that she wanted, because she started at page one and just kept going. Knowing how to use a book is extremely difficult, but the art is not taught. We tend to presume that slow, steady reading is the best kind but research has shown that flexible reading skills are vital. The art of reading is knowing when to read fast, when to read slowly, when to re-read, and so forth. This is barely taught at all. I would suggest that one major task for in-service training is to sharpen our project methods.

Availability of books

I come lastly to my third element, and I fear that in too many schools there is also very little availability. There are six aspects of availability. The first is *quantity*: the problem of sheer shortage of books. I worked out a few months ago that we spend as a nation one penny per pupil per hour on learning materials of all sorts. Now you try and entertain a youngster for a penny for an hour! On the Bullock Committee we were amazed by the paucity of book stocks in some libraries; I am also amazed by the high rate of losses.

Second is the problem of *suitability*. Are the stocks of our school libraries suitable for our pupils? I don't think they are. This is usually not the librarian's fault: it's the vestigial remains of an old tradition. I remember my own schooldays (at a very distinguished seat of learning): you weren't allowed into the library until you were fifteen. Only the post-adolescent was worth educating. Consequently it was basically a sixth-form library. And isn't it still true that the majority of teachers recommend to librarians books suitable at the top end? Someone has worked out that for independent study pupils need a book of a reading age two years younger. It's an artificial figure, but I think the thesis is right. Now a library is by definition for independent study, and I believe that most secondary school libraries do not have nearly enough simple, straightforward books.

This brings me to my third heading, *liaison*. Draw a flow-chart to show the structure of your school: where would you put the librarian? Only if you've got a position on that flow-chart have you in fact got power. How many librarians are represented on the central planning body, either directly or by an immediate superior? Do they even know who their immediate superior is? Liaison is a major problem. Make a simple experiment: go to a typical classroom and take up the textbook in use. At the end of a chapter, where it has those 'things to do', it has half a dozen titles for recommended reading. Go along to the library catalogue and check: you can bet your last five-pound note they're not there! Nobody ever lent the librarian that textbook; the librarian probably hasn't even got a syllabus for that subject. There is a continuum that needs to be established between the textbook, the topic book, the book recommended by the department for the library, and the librarian's extension of that into the wider field of reading.

The fourth aspect of availability is the *use* of the library. How many people work in schools where the library is in fact a classroom, not used as a library in any meaningful sense at all? The fifth aspect is *other outlets* for books—other than the library, I mean. When librarians start bookshops, I think that's splendid. When schools start bookshops, and librarians get guilty, or worried, and there's a great split, I find that very worrying. I think that every school should have a bookshop and it should be related to the library stock. The two are not in competition; they're complementary. The sixth and last aspect is that there should be what I call a *focus* on books—an advertising of books: outstations of the library, display cabinets and book-jackets in remote parts of the school.

I have mentioned these six aspects of availability because I believe that so much of the use of libraries is desultory. It's a great tradition that we have in this country: it has perhaps become a victim of its own success. Libraries have been established, but the rest of the staff leave them to the specialist.

Reading and the coherent school

The great challenge in the secondary field is to make the

comprehensive school coherent. This requires a new team-work. Norman Beswick, in *Resource-based Learning*, speaks of the team-work of the media resources producer, the librarian and the teacher. I'd like to speak of an even wider team-work—that of teacher and teacher. We have institutionalised, in three separate associations, three specialisms: UKRA essentially 'basic' reading, NATE basically reading as literature, SLA separate again; and very few people who are members of all three. Not as bad as in America, where the teachers of reading won't talk to the teachers of English; but separation is institutionalised all through our profession: remedial *departments*, English *departments*. We require a new teamwork between these specialists, across the subjects. The librarian must be familiar with the research on reading; and whereas there must be somebody in a school who knows each specialism properly, all of us must know a little bit about each. Only if we can create a coherent school team—specifically teaching reading, giving experience of reading, and making reading available—are we going to begin to tackle the problem.

6. 2 The preparation of teachers and specialists

H. Alan Robinson

The training of teachers is a world problem. There appear to be two main reasons for this; one is a shortage of qualified teachers. The other concerns the quality and relevance of teacher-training programmes.

Shortage of qualified teachers. The need for teachers exists in every country of the world. In some areas, about one-third of those children ready for schooling have no teachers, qualified or otherwise. In other places, particularly in rural areas, children must be 'taught' by other children who have had as little as eight years of schooling. Even in some countries with highly developed educational systems in operation for many years, teacher shortages force the hiring of teachers who do not meet the standards of certification.

The words 'shortage of qualified teachers' mean very different things in different places. A qualified teacher is some 'developing' countries would not be considered qualified in others. Whatever 'qualified' may mean in a specific nation or area, teacher shortages do exist.

Quality and relevance of teacher-preparation programmes. Although the stages of development of programmes are different throughout the world, each country is confronted by this problem. In some cases the important problem is that there is no programme at all; children become teachers after eight to thirteen years of schooling without any special training. In other instances, teacher education programmes exist but are so general in nature that student teachers are not trained to deal with the particular needs of their specific pupils.

Source: R. Staiger (ed.), *The Teaching of Reading*, Paris, Unesco, 1973, pp. 127–41.

In all cases, regardless of the excellence of the training programme at an academic level, teacher trainers and others from many walks of life are questioning the relevance of traditional curricula to the demands of society. This concern is visible everywhere. People seem to agree that teacher-training programmes must be designed to facilitate changes which will directly serve the immediate needs of society.

An instructional philosophy

Since there are so many needs facing all nations in the general preparation of classroom teachers, one might raise the question whether this chapter is necessary and/or timely. The responses to such a question, taken from questionnaire returns, a review of the relevant literature, and personal interviews, are largely affirmative. Several educators in developing countries join in the consensus but feel that they are not at all ready to undertake such training. One questionnaire respondent said, 'For those of us working in a developing country, such services you have asked about must remain luxuries.'

The greatest number of educators in those countries polled are very much in agreement about the need. They state that there is a need for more concentration on methods of teaching reading and writing adapted to the needs of a variety of types of learners. Chinna Chacko of India speaks for her country and others when she says, 'The teaching of reading is unknown in this part of the world.' Most other sources show that when reading skills *are* taught, little is done beyond the first year or two of school.

A few educators suggest that there is richness in the concept of 'language teaching' where all language skills are taught in a unit. These educators do not like the idea of separating the teaching of reading or writing as a separate 'subject', as they call it. These voices come from the so-called 'developed' countries as well as those called 'developing'. And their point is well taken, for no efforts directed toward the teaching of reading apart from other language skills have been successful.

Yet, too often 'the general teaching of language' has ineffective results for a number of learners. This is true of developed as well as developing countries. When the complex process of using a language for effective communication is not specifically and carefully taught, most learners do not become fully literate. Aside from specific instruction in many skills throughout the grades in the lower school, language skills need to be developed throughout the total school programme.

In order to achieve full literacy, teacher-preparation programmes must, therefore, emphasize methodology; specific skills in comprehension as well as word recognition must be developed. Developing countries cannot be satisfied with increasing the quantity of education; in many developed countries with compulsory education through high school (and the United States is a prime example) there are too many illiterates and semi-literates. Increasing the quality by planning the development of specific reading and writing skills throughout the curriculum, and by matching methodology and learner, will accomplish more than merely increasing the time spent in school. Both quantity and quality are essentials, but quantity is useless by itself.

In order to help teachers-in-training to produce literate pupils, the trainers of teachers must assist their students in developing a philosophy of education, and then a philosophy for the teaching of reading and writing. Too often reading and writing is taught, when it is specifically taught, as a prescription. Teachers, because they have no conceptual framework from which to draw, do exactly what one book, or one series of books, or one inspector or supervisor, tells them to do. Sometimes the advice may be appropriate; at times it is limited. If teachers-in-training were given a good background in psychology, sociology, linguistics, learning theory and methodology in the teaching of reading and writing, they could be helped to develop broad instructional philosophies. They could, with assistance, learn to use what they have learned in adapting instruction to the specific needs of the learners in their classrooms.

Learning by prescription only works for those who happen to fit the prescription. An instructional philosophy must include relevance for the learner at any learning level. A teacher well prepared in the teaching of a particular system of reading and writing may fail completely because the instruction has no personal relevance to the learner. Nakorn Pongnoi (1969), in speaking of adult hill tribers in Thailand, says,

> It would be useless to gather them all into a classroom and start teaching them the alphabet or fundamentals of Thai patriotism. That can come later. First, these people must be introduced to learning in ways immediately interesting and useful to them.

Few pupils will learn well as long as goals are distant and abstract. Reading and writing must be immediately meaningful to learners whether they are six or sixty. The content, what people read and write about, cannot be separated from the reading or writing act.

Many educators who know that reading and writing skills must be immediately functional are concerned with 'higher values'. They feel that an instructional philosophy based only on immediate needs will not enrich the life of the learner. Eikichi Kurasawa (1968) of Japan states,

> The subject of language must serve life. On the other hand, in order to elevate one's own life, it is necessary to cut oneself off from one's life. This means that we must do certain things which do not directly relate to our daily lives, such as the study of culture and classical literature. How should such a contradiction of practicality be integrated?

There is no certain answer to that question, raised by educators throughout the world, but the answer must lie somewhere in a flexible instructional philosophy based on a concern for individual needs. Many pupils will never become engaged in learning unless the learning tasks are related to their immediate needs. The hope is that once they are engaged in learning and achieve success and competence they will be able to focus on more distant and abstract goals. Even if they do not, however, they are entitled to an education which will permit them to use reading and writing to help themselves live useful and enjoyable lives.

As Jean Robertson (1969) of Canada has said,

> Teacher-education programs have little relevance if planned apart from personal, student needs and the national needs of the country in which students study . . . To develop literacy programs and to extend them to ensure a functional level of literacy, which is sufficient to allow the individual if necessary on his own to extend his range of knowledge, necessitates educational planning of which teacher education is . . . an integral part. The particular plan adopted should be integrated with the general and specialized national needs, should prevent drop-outs, should include women and girls, and should teach relevant content and if necessary use methods which may represent radical deviations from the traditional.

Teacher attitudes

A person's attitudes are shaped by the environment in which he lives; therefore, different nations or regions often have different attitudes towards life and learning. Positive attitudes toward learning achievement need to be nurtured in both developing and developed countries.

An American educator, Malcolm Douglass (1969), after a first-hand survey of Norwegian education, suggests several reasons for the low incidence of 'reading problems' in Norway (compared with the United States)—school entrance at an older age, lighter schedule in lower school, same teacher for several years, heterogeneous grouping. And then he adds,

Coupled with all this is the absence of a concept pervasive in American education: the idea of failure. That a child might fail to learn to read, or indeed that he might fail in any other aspect of the primary school curriculum, is not considered as a viable possibility. . . . It is part of their [Norwegians'] national character to respect the independence and the autonomy of the individual—young and old. They are, as well, optimistic about individual development. They expect success, and they learn from their earliest years to find value in the performance of others. Parents consistently praise their children and are loath to find fault with their performance, in school or out. Teachers function within this frame of values, of course. The result can perhaps be best described as a positive example of the self-fulfilling prophecy. If one expects success, the chances for success are enhanced; expectations of failure appear to breed failure with monotonous regularity.

Perhaps if teacher trainers could place a great deal of emphasis on developing such positive attitudes among teachers-in-training, this one factor alone would make a large difference in the educational success of pupils. Obviously, it is easier to say that this should be done than to do it. Probably the best way to help teachers have positive attitudes toward their pupils is for the trainers of teachers to develop such attitudes about their own student teachers. The trainers of teachers should take time to study each student teacher so that he gets to know him well, both his weaknesses and his strengths. The teacher should try to understand his weaknesses and the reasons for them. He should then design a programme for him that will attempt to remedy the weaknesses and ensure success in teaching.

The same technique can be used to help the teacher of reading, whether he is teaching reading in the classroom as part of his total programme or whether he is a reading specialist. Arthur Gates (1966) states that he has 'been told by hundreds of teachers that nothing in their training program compared in fruitfulness with several months devoted to internship in individual case-study work and individual instruction'. Aside from developing ability in reading instruction, the teacher who works with pupils intensively and individually gains respect for the learner and gains insights into the behaviour and learning styles of other pupils.

When teaching reading and writing in particular, the attitudes of teachers are most important. As Arthur Gates also indicates, 'Learning to read is conditioned by many influences.' Pupils are confronted by new learning tasks for which many of them have had little readiness. The successful teacher of reading will help the pupil learn rather than try to make him fit a particular method. The curriculum should be adjusted to the learner, not the learner to the curriculum. A good reading teacher is flexible.

Most successful teachers are honest in their approach to learners. They are critical when necessary, but they do not assault and damage the learner's confidence. They give praise whenever it should be given for they know that one successful step makes the next one easier. They are generally patient and kind, and most important, show a personal interest in each learner.

The reading specialist or supervisor or inspector whose primary job is to help teachers develop improved programmes in the teaching of reading (and often writing) must develop the same attitudes as teachers. A teacher is defeated, not helped, if a reading specialist comes in and takes over the classroom, showing pupils and teacher alike that he can do the job, but that the teacher cannot. A teacher is defeated, not helped, if the reading specialist, supervisor or inspector is always negative and never positive. And, to be sure, if the teacher loses hope and confidence, those who are really defeated are the pupils in the classroom.

In introducing the 1970 theme, 'The Qualities of a Teacher', of the World Confederation of Organizations of the Teaching Profession, Secretary-General William G. Carr (1969) said,

> Teachers need the accumulated knowledge of an encyclopedia, the financial skills of a banker, the adaptability of a chameleon, the courage of a persecuted saint, the subtlety of a serpent, the eyes of a hawk, the gentleness of a dove, the patience of Job, the strength of a lion, the hide of a rhinoceros, and the perseverance of the devil.

Reading and the classroom teacher

Since almost all classroom teachers use materials pupils must read, they are all involved in the teaching of reading and writing, in one way or another. In the lower grades more attention is usually placed on figuring out the words than in the upper grades. Even when the teacher of the lower grades is not teaching pupils how to read and spell in materials designed for that purpose, he should be helping pupils learn how to figure out the words in history books, arithmetic books and in other textbooks. And teachers of both lower and upper grades through high school and even into college should give guidance in the comprehension of what is read. The act of reading is meaningless if comprehension is not considered part of it. Comprehension skills must be taught: how to find the important details; how to get the main idea; how to make inferences. Such skills cannot be taught with one set of materials in the first or second year with the belief that they will be transferred automatically to everything else the pupils read or write at all grade levels.

Pre-service education

In spite of the importance of reading and writing, little attention seems to be paid to helping teachers-in-training learn how to teach specific skills of reading and writing. Of the responses received to the questionnaire mentioned earlier, nine countries reported offering separate courses in the teaching of reading as part of their pre-service programmes. Even in these countries, however, the courses are usually offered only in certain institutions and in some states, provinces or sections of a nation. The predominant way of communicating a limited amount of information about the teaching of reading and writing appears to be in a course or courses dealing with methods of teaching the language. This trend holds true, in the main, for both developed and developing countries. In a number of situations there are no special courses in language skills or reading; the little attention given to the teaching of reading and writing is done in a general 'teaching methods' course.

In most cases, it appears that student teachers are not involved in classroom experiences early enough, and that the student teachers are not given enough opportunity to work with many different kinds of learners and learning environments. It would seem more logical for teachers of methods of teaching writing and reading to play some role in supervising students during their apprenticeship periods. Mary Austin (1967) (who conducted two large studies of teacher training in reading in the United States), in reporting at an international symposium, implied that there should be a re-organization of the apprenticeship period which ought to begin earlier and cover a longer period of time. She also felt that more care needs to be taken in the selection of schools and teachers co-operating in apprenticeship programmes. She stated that, in the United States, in more than 50 per cent of the schools surveyed, the supervision of student teachers was not done by the content and methods teachers.

Because most children are taught by regular classroom teachers, not by reading specialists, the International Reading Association (1965) prepared a set of minimum standards for the classroom teacher. Obviously, each region or nation is not ready to meet these standards, but it is hoped that the standards may serve as a goal in some situations and as a foundation from which to build further in others. The minimum standards suggested by the International Reading Association are outlined here. They have been adapted in an attempt to ensure understanding of terms used in different ways throughout the educational world:

I.   Twelve to thirteen years of schooling resulting in a diploma or certificate from a secondary school; then, completion of four years of academic work at a college or university resulting in a bachelor's degree. During this four-year period the student should have apprenticeship or student-teaching experiences. In addition to reading courses, the four-year period should include courses in child development, educational psychology, educational measurement, and children's literature.

II.   A minimum of two courses in reading:

A. One or more courses for elementary teachers covering each of the following areas (one course may deal with a number of the areas):

General background. The nature of language, the relationship of reading to other language skills, definitions and descriptions of the reading act, and the nature and scope of a reading programme.

Reading skills and abilities. The preparatory or readiness steps for reading, word-recognition skills, vocabulary development, reading comprehension abilities, and oral reading.

Diagnosis and remedial teaching. Reading problems and how to diagnose them, adjusting instruction to fit individual needs within the classroom, methods of evaluation or measuring gains.

Organization of the reading programme. How to work with small groups and individuals within the classroom, how to vary approaches to reading instruction, how to plan reading lessons.

Materials. Knowledge and use of materials of instruction, how to select suitable reading materials, and knowledge of the literature read by children.

Application of reading skills. Teaching and guiding the application of reading skills in each subject, developing appreciation of literature, and encouraging the lifetime use of reading.

B. One or more courses for secondary teachers covering each of the following areas:

General background. The nature of language, the relationship of reading to other language skills, definitions and descriptions of the reading act, information about the teaching of reading in the elementary school, and the nature and scope of the reading programme in a secondary school.

Reading skills and abilities. Preparation or readiness for reading tasks at the secondary school level, word-recognition skills (for those students who will need this kind of help), vocabulary development, reading-comprehension abilities, adjustment of silent reading rates to the purpose of reading and to the difficulty of the material, and oral reading.

Diagnosis and remedial teaching. Reading problems and how to diagnose them, adjusting instruction to fit individual needs within the classroom, methods of evaluating or measuring gains.

Organization of the reading programme. Varied approaches to reading instruction at the secondary-school level.

Materials. Knowledge and use of materials of instruction, how to select suitable reading materials, and knowledge of the literature read by adolescents.

Application of reading skills. Teaching and guiding the application of reading skills in each subject, developing appreciations of literature, reading in a variety of mass media, and encouraging the lifetime use of reading.

C. It is recommended that the courses in both elementary and secondary reading include direct observation and participation experiences in elementary- and secondary-school classrooms. When such experiences are limited or impossible, the teachers-in-training should work on realistic problems in the college classroom. When possible, taped or filmed observations should be used.

III. Student teaching (apprenticeship) experiences in reading:

A. Colleges and universities should make every effort to place student teachers with co-operating teachers who demonstrate a good knowledge of the teaching of reading. In some instances, it may be necessary to prepare co-operating teachers in the use of good reading methods.

B. Elementary-school teachers-in-training, as well as secondary-school teachers-in-training, should have experience in the teaching of reading in a number of subject areas.

IV. In those areas where teachers are required to have additional preparation for permanent certification as a classroom teacher, it is recommended that this preparation include a graduate course in reading as part of the requirements. This course should include, among other topics, the following: important research findings that may affect reading instruction; advanced information on the psychology of reading; current issues and methods of teaching reading; extension of skills taught in the preservice programme.

At this time there appear to be no nations that have certification requirements which meet the minimum standards recommended by the International Reading Association. Of the nations responding to the questionnaire, none reported that one separate course in reading was required under any circumstances for the certification of teachers. A few provinces in Canada have such a requirement, and this is true of less than 15 per cent of the states in the United States. Several of the nations reporting (Canada, Denmark, Israel, New Zealand, Norway, and the Philippines) require either a separate course in reading or a course in language skills of elementary-school teachers who wish to be certified. Unfortunately, even such requirements result in very inadequate preparation for the classroom teacher in the teaching of reading and writing. Some nations, or parts of nations, are now moving towards the requirement of a single course in reading for certification; but, at this time, the movement can hardly be called a trend.

In-service education

On the other hand, there is a trend towards doing much more training in the teaching of reading for teachers who are already in service. Perhaps this trend is best described by a questionnaire respondent—a county inspector in England—who states,

> There has been some complaint among college leavers—and the schools which receive them—that some colleges of education do not pay sufficient attention to the teaching of the basic skills of reading. In general colleges are now aware of this and much more attention is being paid to the teaching of reading. Over the last few years, in-service courses in this subject organised by the various sources responsible for these—university, local authority, department of education, etc.—have become more frequent and are well attended.

Many countries and areas report that most of the in-service work takes the form of refresher courses held during vacation periods. These are usually voluntary and may be offered by reading specialists, university staff members, principals, supervisors or inspectors. A number of schools offer in-service work in reading at the close of the school day, although this time of day after working with children for many hours is not the best time for in-service work. Some schools and regions are attempting to make in-service training a part of the school day, when personnel and situations permit. Other forms of in-service training include a short course or a number of sessions just before school opens for the year, university courses at under-graduate and graduate levels, and a limited number of travel grants.

A trend toward conducting more in-service programmes in reading was reported by Australia, Brazil, Canada, Chile, Denmark, England, Finland, Guam, India, Israel, Japan, Nepal, New Zealand, Norway, Portugal, the Philippines and the United States. Such activity, of course, may also be going on in a number of other regions that either did not respond to the questionnaire or did not have the opportunity to publicize their programmes widely. The nature of the in-service programmes is wide and varied, usually dependent on a specific need. For example, in Israel intensive in-service training is given to the teachers of disadvantaged children whose schools have been designated N N (Need for Nurture) schools (Feitelson, 1969). In Brazil, in a national attack on illiteracy, lay teachers are invited to take intensive courses in three different stages at training centres in cities and villages of the interior (Lopes, 1967). In Chile and India, in-service work is offered when new methods and/or materials are to be introduced. In Austria, voluntary lectures on various aspects of reading are offered from time to time through the Children's Book Club. For teachers concerned with problem readers in their classrooms, in-service work is offered centring on diagnosis and remedial methods through the ministries or departments of education or the educational institutions in a number of countries. Often this work may be directed toward classroom teachers who are working with special groups of people such as the handicapped, those with exceptionally deprived backgrounds, etc.

There are times, particularly in developed countries, where the immediate needs might not always be quite as apparent as in developing countries, when much time and effort are put into in-service activities in reading with unsatisfactory results. Austin (1967) reported that the main type of in-service activity in reading in the United States in early 1960 consisted of workshops which were not always successful for three reasons: (a) they are usually scheduled at the end of a long hard day's work; (b) the content was unrelated to needs; (c) the leadership was poor. She suggested the need for in-service programmes in reading that are continuous, where the content is relevant, and where teachers are granted released time to attend the meetings.

Training methods

Whether the training is pre-service or in-service, a variety of training methods should be used. A most important consideration in using any combination of training methods is that the teacher become involved in using the techniques being taught, as soon as possible and under supervision until some degree of mastery is attained. Theory alone, or discussion of techniques alone, does not do much to change teaching behaviour (Sawyer and Taylor, 1968). More co-operation needs to be implemented among schools and colleges and universities for both pre-service and in-service programmes.

Aside from actual experiences in which teachers watch demonstration lessons and conduct them themselves, the tape recorder and television are useful training tools. If a teacher is able to hear the results of a lesson he taught, the content can also be evaluated by his supervisors and colleagues; he is usually helped to develop insights which help him improve in the next teaching situation. Although tape recorders are valuable, television adds another extremely useful dimension. In addition, a taped television lesson done by a master teacher gives everyone in the audience an ideal seat for the performance.

There is no one way to help all pupils learn to read and write. Approaches to instruction must differ according to the needs and learning styles of the children in the classroom. Allen (1969) found that the best ways to teach reading and writing to native Samoans included, not readers imported from other places, but teacher-constructed stories, manuals and workbooks based on the village life and recorded legends of Samoa. As teachers developed materials they became very sure that there was no one way of teaching, and as they grew to know more about the pupils, they were able to adjust instruction to the needs of particular children.

Although Feitelson (1969) reported earlier on some fine in-service activity in Need for Nurture schools in Israel, she feels that in-service work is certainly not enough. She suggested that the most hopeful approach for breaching cultural gaps between teachers and pupils is a well-planned pre-service programme with theory and intensive field experience. It would seem that if we are to develop more expert classroom teachers of reading and writing, the pre-service programme must be the first, very powerful, step in a never-ending continuum which also includes on-the-job in-service activities for teachers throughout their total teaching careers.

Reading specialists: teachers and clinicians

In a brochure stating minimum standards for reading specialists, the International Reading Association (1968) defines reading specialists as personnel (a) who work directly or indirectly with either those pupils who have failed to benefit from regular classroom instruction in reading or those pupils who could benefit from advanced training in reading skills and/or (b) who work with teachers, administrators, and other professionals to improve and co-ordinate the total reading programme of the school. In this section of the chapter we shall turn our attention to the special teacher of reading and the reading clinician.

The International Reading Association lists the following responsibilities for special teachers of reading:

1 To identify pupils needing diagnosis and/or remediation.
2 To plan a programme of remediation from data gathered through diagnosis.
3 To implement such a programme of remediation.
4 To evaluate pupil progress in remediation.
5 To interpret pupil needs and progress in remediation to the classroom teacher and the parents.
6 To plan and implement further work as necessary.

The reading clinician (working in a school, university, or private clinic) is expected to have the same responsibilities as the special teacher of reading except that he is able to treat the more difficult and severe cases of reading problems. The reading clinician may also provide internship training for prospective clinicians and/or special teachers of reading.

The International Reading Association lists the following qualifications for special teachers of reading:

To have completed a minimum of three years of successful classroom teaching in which the teaching of reading is an important responsibility for the position.

To have completed a planned programme for the master's degree from an accredited institution. The programme should include a minimum of four courses in reading with at least one course concerned with a survey of reading instruction, at least one in diagnosis and correction of reading disabilities, and one in clinical or laboratory practice under supervision. The rest of the programme should include courses from related areas, particularly measurement and/or evaluation, child and/or adolescent psychology, and literature for children and/or adolescents.

In addition to the above, the International Reading Association recommends an additional year of study for the reading clinician to include advanced courses in diagnosis and remediation of reading and learning problems, a course or courses in individual testing and advanced clinical or laboratory practicum in the diagnosis and remediation of reading difficulties, and field experiences under the direction of a qualified reading clinician.

The standards suggested by the International Reading Association are extremely valuable for use as minimal goals. At this time it would appear that there are very few places throughout the world where the standards are being met, or can be met. The information below describes what is now being done by those nations and areas which responded to the questionnaire, or about which such information was readily available through other sources. Perhaps the minimal standards and the examples of practice will help those nations or areas which now have no such positions to decide how to train and use special teachers of reading and reading clinicians in their own situations.

The most commonly used titles for the special teacher of reading are remedial teachers, remedial reading teachers and special reading teachers. In a few nations or areas, teachers of special education become special teachers of reading because so much of their work is directed towards reading instruction. Reading therapist is sometimes used in Norway and in the United States; reading adviser is used in New Zealand. Supernumerary teachers in some parts of Canada and Australia, as well as itinerant or peripatetic teachers in New Zealand, England, Finland and Wales, often serve as special teachers of reading. Very few people, except in the United States, appear to be called reading clinicians although a number seem to serve the function in clinics or special centres in Australia, Canada, New Zealand, Wales and the United States.

The training of reading teachers and clinicians seems to vary greatly, from no special training at all to the doctorate. In many places, from Austria where there are very few, to the United States where there are many, there seem to be no special requirements other than successful teaching experience and interest. A questionnaire respondent from Quebec, Canada, suggested that the few special teachers of reading they have were trained by 'empirical jam sessions'. On the other hand, in many areas special teachers of reading are required to have advanced degrees. In Canada, as in the United States, graduate programmes through the doctorate are offered in reading.

Most special teachers of reading and reading clinicians have no special certification, although frequently they may be certified in special education. Norway, for example, requires one to two years of additional training and awards a certificate in special education. Finland requires an additional year of training but awards no certificate. Special teachers of reading are certified by the ministries in Denmark, Turkey and Western Australia. Training for certification varies from completion of a formal degree to several weeks of training. Most often, whether certification is given or not, the special training includes several summer courses and some in-service experiences during the school year. As of 1968, twenty-three of the states in the United States required special certification, but most did not meet the minimal standards suggested by the International Reading Association (1965).

Some interesting trends have been reported. New Zealand has itinerant reading advisers at the elementary- and secondary-school levels in each board of education area, and the numbers are increasing. Remedial reading clinics also exist in most metropolitan areas of New Zealand. Chile reports a new special school for poor readers, and Wales now has a Remedial Teaching Centre. Turkey has begun a new programme and has seventeen special reading classes in its primary schools; Israel now has 100 remedial reading classes in 100 schools. A number of areas report an increase in itinerant special teachers of reading particularly where there are large populations of children in need of special help.

Reading specialists: consultants and supervisors

In the International Reading Association brochure (1965) concerning minimum standards of reading specialists, reading consultants and reading supervisors are described in the following way.

Reading consultant. A reading consultant works directly with teachers, administrators and other professionals within a school to develop and implement the reading programme under the direction of a supervisor with special training in reading. The reading consultant should survey and evaluate the present programme and make suggestions for needed changes. He should help to translate a philosophy of reading into a working programme consistent with the needs of the pupils, the teachers and the community. He should work with classroom teachers and others in improving the total reading programme. He should meet all of the qualifications suggested for the special teacher of reading, and should have an additional year of graduate work. This work should include an advanced course in the teaching of reading in the regular classroom, a course or courses in curriculum development and supervision, a course and/or experience in public relations, and field experiences under a qualified reading consultant or reading supervisor in a school setting.

Reading supervisor. A reading supervisor (sometimes called a director or co-ordinator of reading) provides leadership in all aspects of the reading programme in a school system. He should develop a system-wide reading philosophy and curriculum, and interpret this concept to the school administration, staff and public. He should exercise leadership with all personnel in carrying out good reading practices, and should evaluate reading personnel and personnel needs in all aspects of the school-wide reading programme. He should make recommendations to the administration regarding the reading budget. The reading supervisor should meet all qualifications suggested for the special teacher of reading and the reading consultant. In addition he should complete a course or courses in administrative procedures, and field experiences under a qualified reading supervisor.

In reality, the descriptions above must be looked upon as goals of the future, for very few areas throughout the world come anywhere near meeting the given standards. To some extent, Guam and Israel have comparable positions. Most of the positions, however, exist in the larger cities of the United States and Canada. In a number of instances, the reading consultant, or even the reading supervisor, serves as both a special teacher of reading and as an adviser to staff members. As education turns more towards serving the needs of the individual pupils in its charge, and as communication and communication media become more complex and more significant in our society, there will probably be an increase in the number of consultants and supervisors in reading and the language arts. It seems imperative that the expertise of the reading specialist focus on assisting the classroom teachers, rather than only on small groups of youngsters in need of remedial help. Improved classroom teaching of reading and writing cannot but help to raise the levels of literacy throughout the world.

Aides for teachers

An important trend, however slight, in some 'developed' countries is the emergence of teacher aide, who often helps in the teaching of reading and writing. Usually the teacher aide has less training than the teacher and sometimes no training in teaching at all. Most of the training is done on the job or in in-service activities after school and during vacation periods. It has been estimated that one in five of the elementary-school teachers in the United States have the part-time assistance of a teacher aide (McCreary, 1969). Many teacher aides serve voluntarily, but a large number are supported through local, state, federal or foundation funds. When aides are used to help teachers in the teaching of reading and writing, their major tasks appear to be reading aloud and telling stories to children, tutoring individual pupils and correcting workbooks.

University staff members and reading specialists in colleges, universities and school systems are being used throughout the United States to train teacher aides in the teaching of reading and writing. Some colleges actually offer courses for teacher aides and handbooks have been prepared for their use.

Teacher aides have many backgrounds, some with college work and others with just some secondary-school training. Most are women; there is a great need for men. In some places in the United States at present, training programmes are being set up for teacher aides to permit them to take advanced schooling in addition to the work they need for their jobs. Co-operative plans among schools and universities are being constructed so that a teacher aide might some day become a qualified teacher.

This plan of setting up co-operative educational advancement programmes for teacher aides seems particularly valuable not only for developed but for developing countries. Even if the classroom teachers in a nation or area are not well qualified, the use of a teacher aide, less qualified but none the less interested, will provide needed assistance for the pupils and the teacher. In addition, this on-the-job training may be the best preparation for the teacher aide who wishes to become a teacher.

Although teacher aides and plans for upgrading teacher aides are largely found only in the United States at present, some function in a few schools in Canada, England and New Zealand. New Zealand is the only nation, other than the United States, which reports the use of a limited number of teacher aides in reading who work in areas of deprivation. Canada reports the development of plans for more use of teacher aides in the future.

A concept that is beginning to be developed in the United States, and which is recommended for the future by Dobinson (1963) of England, is the use of differentiated instructional personnel. In such a plan, the talents of many people with varying educational and experiential backgrounds can be used. The teacher would not be expected to take care of every responsibility, but could delegate certain duties. In such situations teacher aides could be used for special duties in the teaching of reading and writing. However, retired teachers, university students and other people in the community with particular talents could be employed.

The use of differentiated instructional personnel is a valuable idea that can be most helpful in improving literacy throughout the world. Where severe teacher shortages exist, or where otherwise desirable, teacher aides and others in the community can be utilized very effectively, working under the supervision of a qualified classroom teacher. Passageways cut between rooms in old buildings permit aides and the master teacher to work with double the number of pupils a single teacher could handle. New buildings can be built (and have been in a few countries) so that one can easily move from room to room, and so that large rooms are also available when it is necessary or desirable to combine groups of children for a particular activity. This is a type of team teaching which include aides from many walks of life as important members of the team. Pupils are given the benefit of a teaching team qualified to give them individual attention, and certainly able to ensure that reading and writing instruction is directly related to their needs.

Concluding remarks

The preparation of teachers is a problem faced by all nations. The preparation of classroom teachers qualified to teach reading and writing and the development of reading specialists is a subject of growing concern. Undoubtedly, if universal literacy is to be achieved, it is essential that educators be developed who can match methodology to learning styles and to the needs of individuals. In addition, if learning how to read and write is to be lasting and meaningful, the materials used for instruction must be relevant to the needs and demands of individual learners.

Pre-service and in-service education for both classroom teachers of reading and writing and reading specialists must provide specific information about the reading and writing skills and attitudes to be developed as well as specific instructional procedures. Teacher training should emphasize the building of positive attitudes towards each individual learner; the expected goal should be success for each pupil. A teacher should be prepared to guide the learner towards this success by being aware of his weaknesses and strengths in reading and writing. The teacher should have enough knowledge about the skills and the learning styles of individual pupils to assist the learner to capitalize on his strengths and eliminate his weaknesses.

The minimum standards for classroom teachers of reading and reading specialists set by the International Reading Association are far from being met in all nations. There are, however, many in-service activities which appear to be directed towards helping more educators become knowledgeable in the teaching of reading. Many of the in-service programmes are directed towards assisting teachers to help pupils with reading problems due to lack of educational opportunity, insufficient education or ineffective education.

Pre-service education in the teaching of reading and writing is in the greatest need of development. Too many learners across the world are not being adequately guided towards the kind of literacy which is needed in our present societies. All nations have the obligation of training teachers and other instructional personnel, as quickly as possible, to become effective in the teaching of reading and writing. In-service programmes should be developed to help instructional personnel already at work in classrooms, school buildings and throughout the world. But our greatest, vital need is to prepare new teachers and other instructional personnel who will be knowledgeable about instruction in reading and writing, who will adjust methodology to individual differences, and who will shape the curriculum to meet the needs of their pupils.

Note

This paper was written with the indispensable collaboration of forty-three educators throughout the world who responded to an appeal for help. During the autumn of 1969, a questionnaire about the preparation of reading specialists was sent to 151 educational leaders throughout the world, excluding the United States where information was readily available. The questionnaire was designed by Shirley Aaronson, doctoral candidate in reading at Hofstra University. Eight questionnaires were returned unopened; of the forty-seven completed and returned, forty-three were usable. Although the 30 per cent usable return is small, it does represent a sampling of activities throughout the world in the training of reading teachers, and particularly of classroom teachers of the lower grade. The information received is used throughout this paper.

References

Allen, Darlene J. (1969) 'A primer for professors of reading', in A. J. Figurel (ed.), *Reading and Realism, Proceedings of the Thirteenth Annual Convention (1968) of the International Reading Association*, Newark, Del., IRA, 13 (1), pp. 481–5.

Austin, Mary C. (1967) 'Training teachers to teach reading', in John Downing and Amy L. Brown (eds), *Paper on the Past and Present Practices in the Teaching of Reading, Research and Theory in Reading, and Retardation in Reading, Proceedings of the Second International Reading Symposium, London, 1965*, Cassell, pp. 26–34.

Carr, William G. (1969) 'Introduction to the 1970 theme of WCOTP', *Echo* (Washington), July–October, 7.

Dobinson, Charles H. (1963) *Schooling, 1963–1970*, Harrap.

Douglass, Malcolm P. (1969) 'Beginning reading in Norway', *Reading Teacher*, 23, October, 20–2.

Feitelson, Dina (1969) 'Training teachers of disadvantaged children', in R. C. Staiger and O. Andersen (eds), *Reading: a Human Right and a Human Problem, Proceedings of the Second World Congress on Reading, Copenhagen, 1968*, Newark, Del., IRA, pp. 141–6.

Gates, Arthur I. (1966) 'Characteristics of successful teaching', in Alan Robinson (ed.), *Reading: Seventy-five Years of Progress* (Supplementary educational monograph, no. 96), University of Chicago Press, pp. 15–16.

International Reading Association (1965) *Minimum Standards: for Professional Preparation in Reading for Classroom Teachers*, Newark, Del.

International Reading Association (1968) *Reading Specialists: Roles, Responsibilities, and Qualifications*, Newark, Del.

Kurasawa, Eikichi (1968) *Reconstruction of Language Education: Examination of its Essential Qualities and Problems*, Tokyo, Meiji. (Published for the Association of Japanese Colleges for Language Education.) (Reviewed by I. K. Sakamoto in *Journal of Reading Behavior* (Athens, Ga.), 1, autumn 1969, 69.)

Lopes, Wanda R. P. (1967) 'Promoting literacy in Brazil', in Marion D. Jenkinson (ed.), *Reading Instruction: an International Forum, Proceedings of the First World Congress on Reading, Paris, 1966*, IRA, Newark, Del., pp. 254–66.

McCreary, Eugene (1969) 'Preparing paraprofessionals as reading aides', in Richard Molony (ed.), *Revitalizing Today's Reading Instruction, Proceedings of the Third Annual Conference of the California Reading Association, 1969*, pp. 50–4.

Pongnoi, Nakorn (1969) 'Reading centers in remote areas', in R. C. Staiger and O. Andersen (eds), *Reading: a Human Right and a Human Problem*, p. 115.

Robertson, Jean E. (1969) 'Teacher education: privileges and problems associated with reading programs in developing countries', in A. J. Figurel (ed.), *Reading and Realism, Proceedings of the Thirteenth Annual Convention (1968) of the IRA*, 13 (1), p. 885.

Sawyer, Ruth and Taylor, Lucille B. (1968) 'Evaluating teacher effectiveness in reading instruction', *Journal of Reading*, 11, March, 415–18, 484–8.

6. 3 Accountability: theoretical and practical issues related to reading

Peter D. Pumfrey

'Malpractice' case highlights growing US move for return to basics in teaching

Illiterate man sues school for $5m

From Michael Binyon   Washington, Feb 24

An 18-year-old school leaver in New York is suing his high school because he cannot read or write. Edward Donohue from Long Island cannot read a menu, the cleaning instructions on clothes labels or the documents needed to take a driving test. So he has sued Copiague Union Free School for $5m (about £2.9m) on the grounds of educational malpractice.

Mr Donohue and his family say his school failed in its basic duty to educate him properly and has left him 'unable to cope properly with the affairs of the world'.

His difficulty is not unique. A recent survey at the University of Texas indicated that as many as one in five American adults was 'functionally illiterate'—that is, without the minimum educational skills needed for everyday life.

The realization that many school leavers cannot write a correct sentence or even read properly, has so alarmed both teachers and parents in America that a strong 'back to the basics' movement has been sweeping the whole educational system.

Authorities in at least 20 states are now insisting on minimum standards before awarding a high school graduation diploma.

Many other states are also considering competency tests. Last month New York State began a new test of applied mathematics and reading skills for all those who expect to leave school in 1979.

Mr Donohue is not the first person to go to court and accuse the schools of not teaching properly. In 1973 a group of parents in New

Source: article commissioned for this volume. Mr Pumfrey is Senior Lecturer in Education, University of Manchester.

Jersey successfully sued the state because they said the schools were of such poor quality that their children had learnt almost nothing. This led to an important change in the financing of schools all over America. Several university students have also recently claimed a breach of contract because they were learning nothing, but so far none has yet succeeded.

Mr Donohue has set an important precedent at school level however, although people in his neighbourhood have written to newspapers bitterly criticizing his action.

It is being said that he was to blame for not working and his parents for not telling the school about his reading difficulties earlier. The school itself has refused to discuss the matter.

Mr Donohue attended local state schools, and although held back on several occasions, graduated from elementary, junior high and senior schools. His high school record reveals that he failed 7 of his 23 courses.

A diploma, which he says he cannot read, was apparently assured by the fact that during his final year he took three English courses and passed them with marks of 65, 65 and 68.

Mr Donohue said that being functionally illiterate posed continual, and often embarassing [sic] problems. He failed his driving test because he could not handle the written section and he had to bring job application forms home for his mother to fill out.

His personal relationships suffered because he could not discuss anything friends have read in books and newspapers and he was unable to sign a friend's autograph book.

At school, his attendance record was not very good. He says that he realized at an early age that he had reading difficulties and by the time he reached high school he regarded formal instruction as meaningless and often humiliating. It was only in his last year, he said, that he realized the school was as much at fault as himself.

The case will not be decided for some time, and on past precedent Mr Donohue will certainly not get his $5m.

But his case shows how the demand for accountability from schools has both aroused public support and spurred the schools themselves into trying to make sure others do not slip through the net.

The importance of this case is that it raises a host of questions concerning the accountability of teachers, schools and educational systems. The matter is unlikely to be decided for some time, 'but all over the country courts are becoming more receptive to the idea that schools may be held accountable' (Binyon, 1976). That this hearing is taking place in the USA and not (yet?) in Britain should not lead us to assume that similar pressures for accountability are not building up here.

Indeed, in a Consultative Document on education in England and Wales, the Government argues that standard procedures should be established for considering the dismissal of incompetent or inefficient teachers 'whose performance clearly falls below any acceptable level of efficiency' (DES, 1977a). Presumably a teacher whose pupils made no progress in their reading attainments might be expected to account for such a phenomenon. Already a situation has been reported in which the reading attainments of certain groups of pupils with reading difficulties in primary school showed no increase in their average reading age *after two years in the normal secondary school* (Tobin and Pumfrey, 1976). If these findings are valid, they raise important issues of accountability.

Current concern: contributory factors

Concern about reading standards has been a recurring theme in the history of education in Britain. Several major factors have contributed to the current public and professional interest in the concept of accountability in relation to pupils' standards of literacy in general and reading attainments in particular.

The first of these major factors is related to economic pressures. At present Britain is spending about 6 per cent of its gross national product on education, compared with 2 per cent during the 1930s. In 1975 the average annual costs (excluding buildings and equipment) of educating primary school pupils and secondary school pupils were £261 and £379 per annum (DES, 1977b). These costs have risen considerably since then, and are likely to increase further. Staff to pupil ratios are the highest yet known in the state system. In primary schools the national teacher to pupil ratio is 1:23.6. In secondary schools it is 1:16.7 (Chartered Institute of Public Finance and Accountancy, 1977). Yet with teachers trained for a longer period, there is no evidence to show that reading standards have risen as a consequence.

Increasingly it is believed that those accepting the tasks of educating the nation's children should be held fiscally and professionally accountable. This trend reflects a concern about the return to the nation from its investment in education. Standards of literacy are a focal point. Leader-writers in reputable papers have reflected this. Thus, for example, we find the statement of opinion that 'It is a crime to allow a child to finish school unable to read and write adequately' (*Observer*, 18 July 1976). One implication is that teachers bear considerable responsibility in this matter.

Second, concern was generated by the results of a national survey of reading comprehension commissioned by the DES and carried out by the NFER (Start and Wells, 1972). This concern contributed to the setting up by the Secretary of State for Education and Science of a Committee of Inquiry headed by Sir Alan Bullock, FRA. As a consequence of certain major recommendations in the Committee's Report, *A Language for Life*, LEAs are introducing various monitoring and screening surveys in addition to a national scheme to be introduced by the DES (DES, 1975).

Third, following a Government White Paper, *Educational Disadvantage and the Educational Needs of Immigrants*, it was recommended that a unit be established 'To promote the development of methods of assessing and monitoring achievement at school and to seek to identify the incidence of under-achievement' (DES, 1974). Thus, under the aegis of the DES, the Assessment of Performance Unit (APU) was born. The unit will implement the national system of monitoring recommended in the Bullock Report.

A fourth major factor helping to generate concern about accountability derives from the reorganisation of secondary education and from claims and counter-claims concerning the effects on children's attainments in the basic subject in particular.

Fifth, research studies at the primary level into teaching styles and pupil progress in certain aspects of reading comprehension carried out at the University of Lancaster and the rather less well controlled 'experiment' at the William Tyndale Junior School in London have received extensive and prolonged national coverage. In so far as children's attainments in reading were subject to intensive scrutiny in both situations, the great public interest in these topics derived partly from a widespread concern about the attainments and progress of pupils and the accountability of teachers.

All five contributory factors underline the fact that the literacy of its pupils is seen as one of a school's curricular imperatives. Together with numeracy, it 'must form part of the core of learning, the protected area of the curriculum' (DES, 1977a). No other curricular aim in the primary school should deflect teachers from both objectives. In the same Green Paper, paras 3.3 to 3.11 indicate current DES thinking concerning accountability. This can readily be related to reading and other aspects of literacy, as the following quotation shows. The 'growing recognition of the need for schools to demonstrate their accountability to the society which they serve requires a coherent and soundly based means of assessment for the educational system as a whole, for schools, and for individual pupils.'

Context and definition

Over the past five years, accountability has received increasing emphasis in discussions concerning education in Britain. However, it is not a novel concept. It is perhaps no more than a new flask with vintage contents. The notion of accountability is an example of the introduction of current business and management terminology into discussions on education. Its popularity suggests that the concept helps in the communication of some pressing concerns about education in general and reading standards in particular. Educational accountability has been defined as 'reporting the congruence between agreed upon goals and their realisation' (De Novellis and Lewis, 1976). To apply this apparently simple definition to the teaching and learning of reading is far from easy.

The teacher of reading who thinks about accountability in relation to his or her reading programme is concerned with the following questions (among others):

1 Who is to be held accountable for reading standards and to whom are they accountable?

2 For what are they accountable? How can this be defined and assessed?

3 Who will be responsible for the system of accountability and how will it be established?

1 The first question poses the problem of interdependence. The recognition by those involved of the reciprocal nature of accountability is vital. An (oversimplified) instance is that if teachers are responsible for ensuring that their pupils learn to read, parents should ensure that their children attend school. The way in which the nation views its educational system is a further aspect of interdependence between parties having legitimate interests in pupils' reading attainments. Here one is referring to government, to taxpayers, ratepayers, parents, teachers and pupils. One model of education is that of the factory with children having certain reading attainments, interests and attitudes as the input to the system. The output of the reading curriculum might be changes in these. Such products of the system can be quantified and their cost calculated. This 'consumer' model of education parallels an increased consciousness in society of the case for consumer protection. Manufacturers must not mislead buyers as to the performance or quality of their product. Some would argue that schools must not mislead as to the effectiveness with which they produce literate pupils. In this context a perennial concern with the increasing standards of reading needed by members of an industrialised democracy in a competitive world is crucial. It is a matter of concern to all members of society and is not the preserve of any one group.

2 These points raise professional questions concerning the measurement of reading abilities. It can be argued that reading is so complex that it is impossible to measure any significant component with any accuracy or to any purpose. A diametrically opposed position would be that many important aspects of reading

attainment can be adequately defined and, to advantage, measured by an informed selection from the vast range of reading tests and assessment techniques that is available (Pumfrey 1977a).

It is also essential that an acceptable means of monitoring attainments be devised and applied. If the teaching profession is to make its contribution to shaping national, local and classroom policy and practice, it is incumbent on teachers to be involved at all levels whenever such matters are discussed. The profession also needs to be better informed about current thinking on the developmental nature of reading acquisition, of the objectives that may be set and of the strengths and weaknesses of the variety of reading tests and measurement techniques that can be used to determine the extent to which objectives are being achieved (Pumfrey, 1977a, 1977b; Vincent and Cresswell, 1976).

This question also raises important considerations concerning the relationship between the means and the ends of the teaching and learning of reading. Should means and ends be reconciled, and, if so, how? There are some means of producing high reading standards that would *not* be acceptable to many individuals and groups in society because the psychological costs would outweigh the benefits; e.g. intensive and prolonged rote learning.

3 The third question brings into focus the means by which accountability for the reading programme evolves and is made explicit. Three distinctive modes of negotiation: the authoritarian, the laissez-faire and the democratic, are pertinent. The long abandoned 'payment by results' system is currently seen as an imposed and authoritarian approach, although it did have the approval of an elected Parliament (albeit with a severely restricted electorate). The laissez-faire approach is not readily found within the state system in its extreme form. Possibly some of the ill-understood misapplications of the 'play-way' approach in vogue in certain schools after the Second World War might have been an example. There is increasingly a tendency towards a more explicit, informed and democratic means of determining reciprocal account-abilities. Perhaps in 'performance contracting', a contemporary American equivalent to our defunct 'payment by results' system, we have an example of an empirically dominated consumer model of education. In its restricted field of application in the basic subjects, accountability is voluntarily and democratically negotiated between the interested parties.

However, it must be recognised that the material, human and emotional 'costs' of high and rising reading attainments can become too expensive to be borne. If the proportion of a school's resources, including both teacher and pupil time and effort devoted to this end, becomes such that other important aspects of pupils' development suffer, the situation must be reviewed and priorities re-negotiated. Although standards of reading and literacy are important, they must always be considered in relation to the overall balance of the curriculum. Such negotiations are continually taking place in education in response to changing perceptions concerning the present and future needs of our pupils and the resources available. The case for a democratic model of accountability that *denies* the value of accepting the maximisation of utility for society as a criterion of classroom accountability has been discussed and merits the profession's attention (Elliott, 1976).

While all parties to the educational venture may agree in principle that 'accountability' is desirable, disagreement frequently appears when the notion is put into practice. Some teachers of reading see accountability as essential if reading standards are to be maintained or raised. Others see current and proposed innovations in this field, with their emphasis on the testing of measurable objectives, as reducing even further the limited time available for teaching reading.

Approaches to accountability

The idea outlined earlier of education as a business has an appealing (and deceptive) simplicity. Using pupils' reading attainments and attitudes as one index of output, the cost-benefit ratio for systems, schools, classes and even individual teachers could be calculated. Between the start and end of children's formal education, schools are seen as directly producing changes in their pupils. Thus, for example, reading skills may be enhanced in many ways. In certain respects the changes can be seen *as analogous* to those effected by factories on the raw materials entering and the finished products leaving their premises. Such a model represents the 'commodity' concept of education. The major characteristics of such systems of accountability in relation to reading are:

1 their goals are specific and few in number;

2 the goals are operationally defined in terms of pupil behaviours that can be observed;

3 reinforcement is systematically provided to encourage achievement of the goals; and

4 the pupil's attainment on the prescribed criterion measures is the major focus of attention with little or no attention being paid to side-effects.

The dilemmas presented by such systems have been well outlined in an article, 'A place for payment by results?' (MacBeath, 1971). More recently, a trenchant article, 'Battery fed and factory tested', has indicated the dangers of what has been called a utilitarian model of accountability based on the idea of education as a business and schools as factories (Clegg, 1975). Such systems of accountability stemming from central government at a time of national economic difficulty can be construed as attempts to reduce expenditure on education and to increase institutional controls rather than to raise standards (Elliott, 1976). *Caveat emptor!*

'Payment by results'

An early application of such a system took place in Britain during the nineteenth century. In the Revised Code of 1862, the Education Department introduced a grant system related to the amount raised by local voluntary effort and the attendance of pupils under a certified teacher, but dependent also on the results of an examination in the 'three Rs'. The examination was carried out by a visiting inspector. The Revised Code specified the standards to be reached after each year of education. Thus the aims of elementary education were narrowly defined. A child completing his first year in Standard 1 was expected to be able to read 'a short paragraph from a book used in the school not confined to words of one syllable'. The Education Department wanted evidence that such objectives were being achieved in order to justify spending public money on education (Pidgeon, 1972). The test was a 'criterion-referenced' or 'mastery test', in current terminology (see my paper, 5.1 in this Reader). It was, admittedly, rather rough and ready and open to subjectivity in its administration and assessment. On the other hand, the criteria of success were explicit. Inter-individual differences were not the focus of concern; absolute standards were. Successful pupils earned a grant for the school. No pupil could be presented more than once at the same grade and could not proceed to the next grade until he had passed the previous one.

The nineteenth-century scheme fitted in with then current free-trade theories of supply and demand. The advocate of the system, Robert Lowe, said: 'Hitherto we have been living under a system of bounties and protection. Now we propose to have a little free trade'. In introducing the Revised Code on 13 February 1862, Lowe said: 'I cannot promise the House that this system will be an economical one; and I cannot promise that it will be an efficient one; but I can promise that it shall be either the one or the other. If it is not cheap it shall be efficient; if it is not efficient is shall be cheap' (Hansard, vol. 165, p. 229). It *did* effect economies but was severely criticised for many educationally undesirable consequences. The system was both mechanical and rigid. The shortcomings of the Revised Code were recognised before its introduction by educationists such as Kay-Shuttleworth and

Matthew Arnold. It led to the neglect of pupils least likely to produce money for the school by passing the prescribed examinations and to a narrowing of the curriculum. With its ending, there was no further national attempt at an annual, systematic and formal evaluation of reading standards.

Has the experience of a 'payment by results' system any message for us now in the ongoing 'Great Debate' initiated by the Prime Minister? While the social, economic and political changes that have taken place in our culture over the last century indicate the need for caution, some important points can be drawn in relation to current concern about our pupils' standards of reading. While the narrowness of the aims then set out and the subjectivity of the evaluation can be criticised from today's position, there is much to be said for the logic that was followed. After considering the aims of education, a means of evaluating the extent to which these were achieved was devised and an incentive scheme to encourage their achievement was built into the system. The 'payment by results' system operated for thirty-five years until it was disposed of in the Code of 1897. Indeed, even today, that logic still pervades our educational thinking and practice. We still direct a greater proportion of the resources of the educational system to those pupils likely to achieve examination success (Jencks *et al.*, 1975). Whether this policy is an appropriate one for a nation in our situation is controversial.

As a profession, teachers are both attracted to yet suspicious of simplistic systems of accountability. To ignore individual differences between pupils in potential to learn is the basis of one such approach to accountability. On the other hand such individual differences between pupils can be used as a defence by teachers against charges that their pupils' reading standards are unsatisfactory.

In the demonology of the teaching profession's folklore, the memory of the Revised Code of 1862 lingers on. It is the profession's emotional equivalent to the means test of the 1920s. Once again echoes of Lowe's cry, albeit in a different key, can be heard in the corridors of political power. The cry is 'accountability'. It must be dealt with constructively and not by a Luddite-like reaction. One promising sign in this direction is a two-year project on accountability in the middle years of schooling currently being undertaken by Sussex University. The research is supported by the Social Science Research Council with a grant of £42,858 and will involve about twenty schools that have shown particular interest. The work will include interviews with parents and other interested groups. A study of the uses of tests and records in the schools' accountability, both internal and external, will be made, as well as a study of how far schools are prepared to demonstrate their accountability to those other groups in society having a legitimate concern, and whether the proposals of schools meet the requirements of such groups. It will be interesting to see how satisfactorily the problems of accountability in relation to standards of attainment and progress in reading are resolved.

Performance contracting

A more sophisticated example of 'payment by results' has appeared in the USA. It is called 'performance contracting'. In terms of reading attainments, it has been suggested that every child should read at his own grade level (Lessinger, 1970). If schools cannot achieve this goal, and it is patently clear that so far they have not, then commercial firms should be allowed to compete. The arrangement would be that payment was dependent on individual pupils reaching predetermined levels of, say, reading, in a prescribed period. The first school systems to engage commercial firms on this basis were in Texas and Arkansas (Texarkana). Dorsett Educational Systems established six 'Rapid Learning Centers' in the schools involved, using their own specially devised audiovisual teaching system. The firm trained its own staff from applicants for teaching posts in Texarkana who had not been engaged because of lack of openings. The target population was potential 'dropouts'. These were operationally defined as 'students two or more grade levels behind in reading and mathematics tests and having an IQ above the special education level of 75'. The teachers received the same salary as those employed in schools. Additionally, they received overtime pay and bonuses for efficiency, but failure to produce results could lead to summary dismissal. Pupils were rewarded with Green Stamps for each lesson successfully completed. Transistor radios were given for each grade level of progress. A television set was to be awarded to the outstanding student.

It appears that initially the use of a piecework system with material rewards linked to the achievement of specified attainments in, for example, reading helped to capture the pupil's attention. Subsequently the intrinsic satisfactions provided by the pupils' success with the materials in the individualised programme became progressively more important motivators.

The dropout rate of those pupils on the programme fell to one-third of that of a control group. The assessment of reading gains was less clear cut, in part because some of the items in the reading tests had been used in the instructional materials.

A report prepared for the US Department of Health, Education and Welfare gives some important pointers to our deliberations on accountability in relation to standards of literacy. Of the project, the report says (Carpenter, Chalfant and Hall, 1971, p. 1):

> Historically, it pioneered the performance contracting technique; it aroused nationwide interest in and controversy about performance contracting; and it was the locale of the first scandal over 'teaching to the test' and the first dispute between a local education agency (LEA) and learning system contractor (LSC) over final payment.

Accountability poses many problems! However, lessons have been learned. The conclusions and implications from five cities' experience with performance contracting shows the strengths and weaknesses of this approach to accountability. The three major advantages are:

(a) performance contracting encourages the introduction of new techniques and concepts in education;

(b) it emphasises the accountability for improvement in pupils' attainment of administrators, contractors and teachers; and

(c) innovations that prove effective can be handed over to local education systems.

The three major disadvantages are:

(a) some performance contracting programmes have been too administratively complex, hence increasing unit costs;

(b) the area of application is severely restricted because of the need to operationally define goals and measure attainment; and

(c) unresolved problems on legal matters, teacher status and problems of test selection and administration have been raised (Carpenter and Hall, 1971).

A follow-up study of the five systems was cautiously optimistic (Hall *et al.*, 1972b). A handbook on educational performance contracting has been produced for the US Department of Health, Education and Welfare. While neither endorsing nor opposing performance contracting, it gives guidance to LEAs concerned with accountability on minimising problems arising over legal issues, programme management and the assessment of the efficacy of the scheme (Hall *et al.*, 1972a).

Although the performance contracts did not produce dramatic gains on standardised tests, in many instances gains were made. A gain score is the *difference* between a child's standardised normative test scores on the same (or a parallel) instrument *before* and *after* a period of teaching and/or learning. If the score on the second occasion is greater than on the first, the child has made an improvement in his attainment vis-à-vis his peers over the given period. Conversely, if his second standardised score is lower than his first, the difference is a negative one and the child has made less progress than his peers over the particular period. One result of the experiments was to focus interest on the many technical problems associated with the use of gain scores derived from normative standardised test. Some amplification of this issue is essential if an adequate consideration of point 2 in the earlier section on 'Context and Definition' is to be made.

Measurement considerations central to accountability

Standardised instruments incorporating age allowances have many attractions as indices of educational output, but they can be misused and misunderstood. The crux of the problem is that standardised reading tests are not primarily designed to assess the effects of short-term instruction in reading. They are intended mainly as predictive instruments. Thus, given a pupil's standardised reading test score at a given age it is possible to predict within limits his likely future relative attainments in the light of experience with previous groups. This is why normative tests can be used in the early identification of children likely to experience difficulties in reading at a later stage. Such reading tests are deliberately constructed so as to spread children out along an ability continuum. They were not designed to distinguish between the effects of 'good' teaching of reading as distinct from other variables known to be related to reading attainments such as socio-economic and cultural variables. Normative tests are also often inadequate when used with pupils at the lower end of the attainment range where such instruments are usually less reliable.

A central aspect of this problem is that the skills a performance contracting programme may teach can be different from those tested by available normative reading tests. If this is so, such tests are inadequate. For example, if a teaching programme concentrated on a narrow set of word attack skills, assuming that mastery of these would help the student to cope with more general reading comprehension skills, one might have reservations about a standardised test of reading comprehension providing valid data concerning the effectiveness of the teaching. Conversely, there is the problem that in defining narrow objectives that can be readily taught and measured one might miss out on broader important objectives. The summation of the various lists of sub-skills of reading that have been identified do not, even if individually mastered, necessarily lead to a universally accepted range of reading competencies. The whole is more than the sum of the parts we can specify at our present stage of understanding of the reading process. This suggests that the integration of a language experience approach and a skills analysis approach to the teaching of reading is a compromise with much to commend it. However, if the objectives of the reading programme are very broad and wide ranging, no single standardised normative reading test could sample adequately the content of a given school's reading programme. It has been suggested that by drawing selectively on the items of various standardised tests, this problem can be overcome. Unfortunately, by matching a reading programme's content in this way one has completely vitiated the one great strength of a standardised test—namely, the existence of norms.

All concerned with the teaching of reading wish to see pupils make progress, increasing their mastery and field of application. Often change is measured by a child's successive scores on the same test. A commonly used means of presenting children's scores on a reading test is by means of a deviation quotient. Such quotients assume that the skill being tested is normally distributed in the population of pupils for whom the test is intended. Thus, the score is expressed in terms of an arbitrary mean and standard deviation. If a score is presented as a deviation quotient, the *same* raw score at *different* ages gives the *same* quotient. The NFER Reading Test BD is standardised to give deviation quotients with a mean of 100 and a standard deviation of 15. Monthly age allowances are built into the conversion tables. Hence an eight-year-old child in a first or second year junior class getting thirteen items correct on the test will obtain a quotient of 100. An older child aged nine with the same score will have a lower quotient of 92. In successive administrations of the test, a child making the progress typical of his age group in the aspect of reading comprehension that the test measures will answer more items correctly on a later administration *but will obtain the same quotient*. Thus no change in quotient indicates progress. In contrast if one uses, say, the Schonell Graded Word Reading Test, increase in raw scores over time are converted to increasing reading ages. These provide a useful index of improvement but are less simple than at first appears, as account is not taken of the increase in spread of pupils' scores on the test with age (Pumfrey, 1977b). With ten words equivalent to one year's average improvement in word recognition, it is often not appreciated that a gain of five words at the six-year-old level is far greater than a gain of five words over the same time at the ten-year-old level.

A great deal of academic attention has been given to the conceptual and practical problems involved in measuring and interpreting change and progress in reading attainments using scores on normative tests. There are at least five different ways in which progress in reading can be assessed. All have varying strengths and weaknesses (Davis, 1970). An article entitled 'How we should measure "change"—or should we?' grapples with these complex problems and presents some partial solutions (Cronbach and Furby, 1970). The difficulties derive in part from certain assumptions underlying conventional test theory. A humorous and controversial criticism has been recently published (Lumsden, 1976). The problems of measurement brought to the fore by considerations of accountability are complex and important both in theory and in practice. The knowledge of and ability to understand these difficulties in relation to the measurement of reading standards, reading progress and the diagnosis and remediation of reading difficulties are a professional responsibility. If the teaching profession does not undertake responsibility in this area, it will be taken over by other agencies.

As standardised normative reading tests have certain weaknesses if used to assess the changes in skills taught to and learned by pupils, are 'mastery' or content-criterion-referenced tests more suitable? (The distinction between normative and mastery tests has been discussed in my article 5.1, 'Reading measurement and evaluation: some current concerns and promising developments'.) Various series of quite specific, measurable and (in theory) hierarchically related reading objectives have been produced by commercial firms. Mastery of these objectives is assumed to lead to competent reading. In the USA, the Center for the Study of Evaluation established the Instructional Objectives Exchange (IOX) in 1968. This functions as a clearing-house enabling the nations' schools to exchange instructional objects. Thus duplication of efforts is reduced and ideas disseminated more readily (IOX, 1976). The use of such objectives-based mastery tests has much to commend it—provided it is not taken to extremes. In the American studies of performance contracting the construction and use of such tests was attempted. The official report concluded that the technical and practical difficulties had not been anticipated. 'Much more work needs to be done on criterion-referenced tests before their results can be interpreted meaningfully' (Carpenter and Hall, 1971). This is still true today.

The system of accountability exemplified in the performance contracting approach shows clearly that those concerned with passing judgment on the efficacy of a reading programme—whether it is of an individual pupil, a class, a school, an LEA or a nation—must after agreeing objectives become involved in selecting and devising tests and assessment techniques that are able to assess the programme's results. The fear that the profession in Britain may be excluded from such deliberations has been expressed as follows (Clegg, 1975):

What I suspect will happen is this. A few compliant teachers will sit on some national committee, testing will be said to emanate from the teachers with the full support of the unions and the National Union of Teachers will be too busy with matters of status and salary to intervene . . . But most important of all, once the tests have been devised we shall teach to the tests and sack the teachers whose children can't manage them.

Both normative and mastery tests can be used to the advantage of all concerned with maintaining and improving the reading standards of our pupils. Clegg's prophecy seems unduly pessimistic. The work undertaken and commissioned by the Assessment of Performance Unit rejects the notion of rigid and uniform national tests of reading (Kay, 1975, 1976).

The Assessment of Performance Unit

The APU (currently headed by T. Marjoram, HMI) has been mentioned earlier. Its terms of reference are 'To promote the development of methods of assessing and monitoring the achievement of children at school, and to seek to identify the incidence of under-achievement.' As the concept of under-achievement with the implication that we know what could or ought to be achieved by pupils is highly complex and controversial, this remit is difficult. Professor Barry Supple chairs a Consultative Committee. Its composition was announced in February 1976 and includes members from local authorities, educational associations and the NFER, plus representatives of both employers and unions, and parents. These are precisely the parties referred to earlier in the section on 'Context and Definition' (p. 405). Are the teachers involved the 'compliant' ones referred to by Clegg? The function of the Committee is to discuss the work of the APU and make suggestions for its programme. Of the six 'broad lines of pupils' development which the curriculum exists to foster', reading, as one facet of the linguistic development which underpins and contributes to all subjects, is the concern of this paper. Building on the work of the Bullock Committee, a working group has been looking at children's writing, the uses to which it is put, the circumstances under which it is produced and the criteria by which it can be classified. This will enable a selection of types of reading representative of the range produced to be specified and sampled (Kay, 1976):

> a point has almost been reached when a research team can be called upon to develop the appropriate assessment techniques in accordance with the specifications laid down by the working group.

Similar work has gone on in the analysis of reading, especially in relation to the ways of categorising the different types of material pupils read; both in school and outside, and the different purposes for which they read them, with a view to sampling both of these for testing purposes.

The system of light sampling suggested in the Bullock Report for the assessment of reading standards means that only a small proportion of schools will be tested on a given occasion, but that other small samples will be monitored relatively frequently rather than, as previously, testing all pupils at specified ages at lengthy intervals (DES, 1975, paras 3.19 to 3.24). A pool of items will be developed and different selections from it will be taken to construct different tests of the same ability. The results of successive testings can be compared by virtue of the items being drawn from a common pool and having specified characteristics.

Some of the difficulties facing the APU in its attempt to monitor national standards are seen as so great that the APU is bound to fail. Political pressure for rapid results is one of the reasons why expedience may triumph over an adequate fulfilment of the unit's task, even in the field of reading (Leonard, 1977).

One aspect of the profession's accountability is to seek continuously to understand the nature and extent of individual differences in reading skills both between and within pupils, often referred to as inter-individual and intra-individual differences respectively. An understanding of both is necessary if our ability to help individuals and groups to optimise their reading attainments is to increase. This task is exceedingly complex, but a professional imperative. While normative objective tests of reading attainments optimise individual differences, mastery tests do not. Whereas the former must not be taught to pupils, the latter may. Thus mastery tests have a great appeal. For example, a teacher may consider it essential that all pupils recognise at sight the 100 words that make up 50 per cent of those in common use. She can then set about helping *all* her pupils to master this task and can readily test the progress her pupils are making (McNally and Murray, 1973). However, individual differences between pupils in any aspect of reading attainment will not disappear merely because we abandon the use of normative tests.

Children's reading behaviour is at once the inspiration and the cemetery of any theory of reading. Reading tests and assessment techniques are tools that help interested parties to evaluate and subsequently develop or to bury the notions of theorists and practitioners alike.

The remedial teaching of reading

When one thinks of reading and the teacher's responsibility, an outstanding example of accountability in action has been provided by the various LEA Remedial Education Services that were established in Britain during the late 1940s.

At that time considerable concern was being expressed nationally concerning the number of apparently able junior school pupils who were having difficulties with reading. Proponents of the establishment of Remedial Education Services claimed that it was possible both to identify and alleviate the reading difficulties of many such pupils. Teachers working for such services were keen that the efficacy of their work be monitored. LEAs saw such services as providing a cost-effective way of helping individual pupils and simultaneously stimulating interest in a general raising of reading standards. It was the presentation to LEAs of evidence based on objective tests and on the opinions of class- and head-teachers whose pupils benefited from the work of remedial teachers that led to the expansion of such services. It has been said that no other sector of education in this country has better exemplified accountability to its employers, its clients and the teaching profession.

Employing LEAs were not only told what they would get for their investments, but were given hard evidence of results. The vast majority of clients made marked short-term improvements in reading until the specialist support was withdrawn. The teaching profession became sensitised to the extent of reading failure and of ways in which help could be given. Additionally, the extension of the theory, practice and organisation of the remedial teaching of reading by members of remedial services led to many innovations in identification, diagnosis and the prescription of treatment. The pioneer work of L. B. Birch in Burton-on-Trent and of W. D. Wall (working under Schonell) in Birmingham provided demonstrations of what could be achieved in the remedial teaching of reading. Their objectives and teaching approaches were described in detail in the professional journals. The use of intelligence and reading tests in the identification of pupils in need of help and also in the evaluation of the efficacy of the teaching given was widely reported. An excellent account is available of the history and continuing evolution of the remedial teaching of reading, in which extensive quotations from the less accessible primary sources are given (Sampson, 1975).

The movement developed rapidly. Usually a psychologist was involved. Because of such staff's background in psychometrics and mental testing, most remedial education services kept comprehensive records based on valid tests of the progress of their pupils. Claims for the marked beneficial short-term effects of the remedial teaching of reading seemed well founded. However, when pupils who had been discharged from the care of a remedial service were followed up about two years later, it was often found that on average their reading attainments were no higher than those of a control group of poor readers who had not received remedial teaching of reading. It has been suggested that the situation is analogous to pulling a child out of a bog and hosing off the mud. He is then much cleaner than he was. If, however, he is thrown back into the situation from which he originally came, it is not surprising if his condition reverts. Accepting that argument by analogy is notoriously weak, the case for an ongoing programme of help for pupils experiencing difficulties with reading is strongly supported by a considerable body of research (Moseley, 1975; US Office of Education, 1976).

As a consequence of the remedial education services' willingness to assess and quantify their own effectiveness in the teaching of reading, there have been considerable changes in the work of these services. The feedback of information provided by the careful and systematic individual records of reading attainments that are kept, and of the ways in which these are analysed, is the outstanding example of how, *without once using the word 'accountability',* *these services are sensitive to the needs of their clients and* *answerable to all interested parties.*

The ultimate irony has been that because the poor long-term effects of the remedial teaching of reading were exposed by remedial services, some services were axed. In contrast, elsewhere, such evidence led to further innovations in the search for ways of improving reading attainments and to developments that anticipated many of the recommendations in the Bullock Report. Thus, series of in-service courses on the teaching of reading for *all* teachers were run by the staff of the Schools Psychological Services and Remedial Education Services in some authorities (e.g. Brannen, 1971; Platt, 1976). A host of innovations deriving from practitioners in the field have recently been published by the National Association for Remedial Education (Widlake, 1977). Accountability encourages innovation but avoids the danger of change for change's sake alone.

This is not to say that enough is being done, for example, in enabling teachers to acquire the knowledge and expertise required if reading tests are to make the contribution that they can towards improving accountability practice in classes, schools, LEAs and the nation. In 1973 a survey of courses run by Schools Psychological

Services and Remedial Education Services was carried out. The intention was to establish the extent to which in-service courses of instruction and training in the uses and limitations of reading tests had been run during the year. Of the 164 LEAs in England and Wales, 159 responded. The number of such courses was not impressive. The information available on reading tests and assessment techniques in pamphlet form was also limited and extremely variable in quality (Pumfrey, 1977b). The question of accountability arises at a different level. Subsequently there have been considerable efforts made to rectify deficiencies noted in the above survey (Makins, 1976; Marder, 1976).

The much wider picture of accountability and training for teachers by other educational bodies (including the Open University) in the teaching and testing of reading is beyond the scope of the present paper.

Records and accountability

Accountability demands records that have a content agreed by those having a legitimate claim to a voice in this matter, and systematic and, in so far as possible, unambiguous. The many possible different *interpretations* of the same data do not negate this requirement. With records, the questions of confidentiality and access immediately arise. There is considerable controversy as to what information should be recorded in a pupil's file and to whom it should be available. Some LEAs have a policy whereby parents have a right to see their child's school record file. This practice is by no means uniform throughout Britain, but may well become so. The advent of computerised systems of data storage and retrieval raises complicated ethical questions concerning accountability in our society.

A recent Green Paper indicated some key aspects of sound record-keeping. These are listed below and can readily be related to all aspects of a child's language development (DES, 1977a, p. 20):

> The keeping and transmission of records should be systematic and understandable; they should be subject to clearly understood and agreed controls on what information is kept and what is not; and on what is disseminated and to whom; and full regard must be paid to the rights of parents, as well as those of teachers and pupils, to know what material is included . . . There is a need for high standards of professional accuracy in record-keeping and for a reasonable consistency of practice between different areas of the country.

While the principles may be sound, translating them into practice will involve a great deal of negotiation between those involved.

Many teachers and schools evolve their own systems for recording pupils' reading attainments and progress. In LEAs where the Schools Psychological Service and the Remedial Education Service have, in co-operation with the schools, introduced an agreed basic screening and monitoring system, the notion of accountability has been implicit in what has been done. The latter procedure allows schools to develop their own system of screening and monitoring as they deem appropriate. It also allows LEA policy decision concerning, for example, allocating resources in relation to needs, to be examined more rationally on the basis of comparable data.

Ostensibly because the information may be misunderstood and/or misused, teachers rarely tell parents their child's reading age or quotient on a test. The information is usually kept either in class or in school records. The discussion of a pupil's progress in reading over a period is also (and perhaps legitimately) done in ambiguous ways.

The American Family Educational Right and Privacy Act 1974, coupled with the recent Buckley Amendment which allows students access to confidential records, has apparently led to many schools in the United States recording nothing that could be misinterpreted and lead to litigation. To move from this defensive posture to a more positive one required that the teaching profession educates its pupils' parents in the meaning of both mastery and normative reading tests. As scores on such tests are objective and descriptive, their value is enhanced.

The recording of pupils' reading attainments and progress is not generally well done within the state system. In contrast, that developed by schools for the children of members of the Armed Forces is far superior. Because of the frequent movement of families, the transfer of accurate and educationally useful information concerning children's school work to a receiving school must be done rapidly. Typically, the information reaches the receiving school before the pupil arrives. It is an example of sound practice epitomising one aspect of accountability.

Conclusion

Our children's reading attainments and progress are but one part of their development, albeit a vital one, because reading to learn evolves with learning to read. The ability to read is an amplifier of the child's power to understand, appreciate and control his environment. Our society reinforces high reading attainments and often punishes in subtle and sometimes not-so-subtle ways the child or adult who is not a competent reader. Nonetheless, the psychological costs of high reading attainments to the individual and to society can sometimes be too high if the resources required for their realisation are obtained at the expense of other activities for which a valid case can be made. Thus the ESN(S) child may benefit more from attention to the learning of social skills than by spending the time on reading. Up to a certain point, the more pupil and teacher time and energy is devoted to reading in its many guises, higher standards and greater progress are likely to occur. Beyond that point, a law of diminishing returns may set in for some pupils. For teachers of reading to be myopically concerned only with their pupils' standards and progress in this area would be the antithesis of professional accountability.

The call for 'equality of opportunity' in education has, from some quarters, been replaced by one for 'equality of outcome'. All children, it has been asserted, have a right to read at their grade level. Others argue that heterogeneity in, for example, reading standards is a more appropriate goal, provided that the higher achievements of some pupils are not purchased by the neglect of other individuals as in the 'payment by results' system. Those adopting this position recognise the great range of inter- and intra-individual differences in the abilities and attainment of children. There can be no easy, simple or definitive formulations of accountability for the teacher of reading. The best that can be done is to have agreed explicit objectives, an agreed process for establishing these with those involved and a means of monitoring and recording the progress of individual children. The data obtained should lead to a continuous process of modification of reading goals, the reading curriculum and means of assessing its effects on process and outcome.

Accountability can lead to opportunities for the teacher. It encourages innovation in the conceptualisation, assessment, monitoring, diagnosis and teaching of reading. As a stimulus to the development of professional awareness and competence, its arrival can be welcomed.

Acknowledgment

The author and the Open University are grateful to The Times for permission to reproduce the passage from *The Times* of 25 February 1977.

References

Bennett, N. (1976) *Teaching Styles and Pupil Progress*, Open Books.
Binyon, M. (1976) '"Illiterate" student loses fraud case against school', *Times Educational Supplement*, 27 August.

Brannen, B. (1971) 'The Evaluation of an In-service Course for Teachers in the Teaching of Reading', unpublished Diploma in Educational Guidance dissertation, Department of Education, University of Manchester.

Carpenter, P. and Hall, G. R. (1971) *Case Studies in Educational Performance Contracting: Conclusions and Implications* (prepared for the US Department of Health, Education and Welfare), Santa Monica, Rand.

Carpenter, P., Chalfant, A. W. and Hall, G. R. (1971) *Case Studies in Educational Performance Contracting, no. 3: Texarkana, Arkansas, Liberty-Eylan, Texas* (prepared for the US Department of Health, Education and Welfare), Santa Monica, Rand.

Clegg, A. (1975) 'Battery fed and factory tested', *Times Educational Supplement*, 11 July.

Chartered Institute of Public Finance and Accountancy (1977) *Education Estimates Statistics 1976–7*, CIPFA.

Cronbach, L. J. and Furby, L. (1970) 'How we should measure "change" —or should we?', *Psychological Bulletin*, 74, 68–80.

Davis, F. B. (1970) 'The assessment of change', in R. Farr (ed.), *Measurement and Evaluation of Reading*, N.Y., Harcourt, Brace & World.

De Novellis, R. L. and Lewis, A. J. (1976) 'Professional accountability in speech communication: promise, plaything or primrose path? ERIC-RCS Report', *Communication Education*, 25, January.

DES (1974) *Educational Disadvantage and the Educational Needs of Immigrants* (Observations on the Report on Education of the Select Committee on Race Relations and Immigration), Cmnd 5720, HMSO.

DES (1975) *A Language for Life* (Report of the Committee of Inquiry appointed by the Secretary of State for Education and Science under the Chairmanship of Sir Alan Bullock), HMSO.

DES and COI (1976) *Assessment of Performance Unit: an Introduction*, HMSO.

DES (1977a) *Education in Schools: a Consultative Document*, Cmnd 6869, HMSO.

DES (1977b) *Statistics of Education (1975): vol. 5, Finance and Awards*, HMSO.

Elliott, J. (1976) 'Preparing teachers for classroom accountability', *Education for Teaching*, 100, 49–71.

Hall, G. R. *et al.* (1972a) *A Guide to Educational Performance Contracting* (prepared for the US Department of Health, Education and Welfare), Santa Monica, Rand.

Hall, G. R. *et al.* (1972b) *The Evolution of Performance Contracting in Five School Districts, 1971–2* (a Working Note prepared for the US Department of Health, Education and Welfare), Santa Monica, Rand.

Instructional Objectives Exchange (1976) *Catalogue: Select Your Own Objectives-based Materials for Curriculum Design and Evaluation*, Los Angeles, Instructional Objectives Exchange.

Jencks, C. *et al.* (1975) *Inequality*, Peregrine.

Kay, B. W. (1975) 'Monitoring pupils' performance', *Trends in Education*, 2, 11–18.

Kay, B. W. (1976) 'Justified impatience: Brian Kay describes the progress made by the Assessment of Performance Unit in its first two years', *Times Educational Supplement*, 1 October.

Leonard, M. (1977) 'Art of the impossible?', *Times Educational Supplement*, 17 June.

Lessinger, L. M. (1970) *Every Kid a Winner: Accountability in Education*, N.Y., Simon & Schuster.

Lumsden, J. (1976) 'Test theory', in M. R. Rosenzweig and L. W. Porter (eds), *Annual Review of Psychology* (Palo Alto), 27, 251–80.

MacBeath, J. (1971) 'A place for payment by results?', *Times Educational Supplement*, 27 August.

McNally, J. and Murray, W. (1973) *Key Words to Literacy and the Teaching of Reading: a Basic Word List for Developing Early Reading and Writing Skills*, London, Schoolmaster Publishing Co.

Makins, V. (1976) 'Bullock plus one', *Times Educational Supplement*, 6 February.

Marder, J. V. (1976) A register of activities related to the recommendations of the Bullock Report and reported from teacher-training institutions in England and Wales; with a contribution from the New University of Ulster (University of Southampton Education Library).

Moseley, D. (1975) *Special Provision for Reading: When Will They Ever Learn?*, Slough, NFER.

Pidgeon, D. A. (1972) *Evaluation of Achievement*, Macmillan.

Platt, G. F. (1976) 'Some Effects of the In-service Training of Teachers in the Teaching of Reading', unpublished M.Ed. thesis, Department of Education, University of Manchester.

Pumfrey, P. D. (1977a) *Reading: Tests and Assessment Techniques* (2nd impression, with amendments), Hodder & Stoughton.

Pumfrey, P. D. (1977b) *Measuring Reading Abilities: Concepts, Sources and Applications*, Hodder & Stoughton.

Sampson, O. C. (1975) *Remedial Education*, Routledge & Kegan Paul.

Start, K. B. and Wells, B. K. (1972) *The Trend of Reading Standards*, Slough, NFER.

Tobin, D. and Pumfrey, P. D. (1976) 'Some long-term effects of the remedial teaching of reading', *Educational Review*, 29 (1), 1–12.

US Office of Education (1976) *A Study of Compensatory Reading Programmes*, Elementary and Secondary Programmes Division, Office of Planning, Budgeting and Evaluation, Washington, D.C., US Office of Education.

Vincent, D. and Cresswell, M. (1976) *Reading Tests in the Classroom*, Slough, NFER.

Widlake, P. (ed.) (1977) *Remedial Education: Programmes and Progress*, Longmans.

Section 7 Where to Next?

This volume on reading has covered a number of topics from different perspectives. The final two articles act as a postscript to the collection by looking at the directions in which future research might move. All concerned with the teaching of reading need to concern themselves not only with present theoretical formulations and current educational practice, but also with ways in which our understanding of process and practice can be improved.

Robert Calfee (7.1) concentrates his attention on the type of research being carried out and the need for research procedures which can analyse the effects of educational processes. We need, he points out, to find out what the reading process is; how to measure it; how to find out what happens in the classroom; how to identify and evaluate critical curriculum activities; and how to improve teacher training and teacher behaviour. Our research methodology needs to become more efficient, and more suitable for the complex dynamics of an educational system.

The last article, by Albert Harris (7.2), looks at the research 'fashions' and notes that only *some* significant studies have any substantial impact. He indicates that we need to improve the lines of communication between research and practitioner, and to ensure that published research is of value to those involved in applying theory to practice. Hopefully, this volume has gone some way towards fulfilling such needs.

7. 1 A proposal for practical (but good) research on reading

Robert C. Calfee

Introduction

. . . Our knowledge of the nature of the reading process and the acquisition of reading has increased noticeably over the past ten to twenty years, largely as a result of government funding of basic research on reading (Kling, 1971; Kavanaugh and Mattingly, 1972). To be sure, no adequate review of this progress is currently available, and the impact of these research findings on classroom practice has been minimal. As recently as this year (1974), a review of the psychology of reading introduces the area of research on reading acquisition (Gibson and Levin, 1975, p. 264):

> Despite all the current emphasis on literacy, the wealth of 'programs' commercially available, the 'learning specialists' who have set up in shopping centers and the arguments over phonics or whole word methods, it is the beginning phase of learning to read that we seem to know least about. All the talk is of what the teacher does or should do and not of what happens or should happen in the child. This is a very peculiar situation. There is presumably a learning process going on, but it is a rare psychologist who studies it.

Large amounts of money continue to be poured into the development and evaluation of competing reading curricula, with outcomes that are disappointing, to say the least (Bond and Dykstra, 1967; Corder, 1971). With few exceptions, these evaluation projects have fallen far short of minimum standards of experimental research in the behavioral sciences (Corder, 1971). There is little one can learn from 'bad' data. It is not surprising to find, on reanalysis, that the major outcome of the large First Grade

Source: *Research in the Teaching of English*, 10, 1976, pp. 41–50.

Cooperative Reading study was the discovery that children of high IQ were more successful in learning to read than children of low IQ (Lohnes and Gray, 1972).

There have been at least three recent major efforts to synthesize the research literature in reading for the purposes of establishing goals for future research—Carroll's (1971) monograph for the National Academy of Education, the Targeted Research Program (Blanton, 1973; Gephart, 1972), and the Miller Task Force on Linguistic Communication (1973). Most of these efforts were too diffuse. They tended to be more 'basic' than applied—most dealt little if at all with regular classrooms. And none eventuated in a very clear statement of priorities in reading research.

There is a general awareness that (a) reading is a complex concept, capable of several definitions, (b) little is known about the processes that underlie the acquisition of reading, and only a modest amount about the processes in skilled reading, (c) many children do not learn to read very well in our schools today—we know a fair amount about the kinds of students, schools, teachers and curriculum programs that are associated with reading failure, but we lack techniques for improving this state of affairs that consistently succeed in a variety of situations.

Definitions of reading

So what do we need to do? First, what shall we mean by reading? The Task Force on Linguistic Communication proposed what seems a reasonable breakdown into three components:

(1) Decoding
(2) Comprehension
(3) Application (functional literacy).

What is the general character of each of these components? What is known in each of these areas? What are current needs for knowledge and for action?

Decoding and related work attack skills are, in some respects, the best defined of the components. In principle, devising techniques for assessing and teaching the relations that comprise English letter-sound correspondences should be relatively simple. There is a general impression in some quarters that this job is complete. To the contrary, not a single commercial norm-referenced reading test directly assesses this component, and most other instruments measure it indirectly if at all. We know relatively little about the status of decoding skills in American school children today, and hence we should hesitate before deciding to assign low priority to investigation of it.

Comprehension is virtually whatever one thinks it to be—in the broadest sense, it is synonymous with thinking. Although comprehension is typically considered a central component in reading, this correspondence may be thwarting the efforts of reading researchers. Existing assessment instruments make no effort to separate out those elements that are unique to reading, and those that depend but little on reading. There is no question but that eventually a student has to 'get it all together,' so that reading becomes a kind of thinking. But when a student is beginning to learn to read, both for his sake and the instructor's, it would help greatly to know whether particular difficulties are uniquely tied to the printed page, or can be dealt with at the level of the spoken language. In any event, what we know about reading comprehension at the present time is thoroughly intertwined with what we know about thinking and language in general.

Functional literacy refers to a person's ability to use written and other kinds of information to realize practical goals. National Assessment (1973) has pioneered in this area. The program is not very analytic; it has not pushed to identify the elementary skills in a particular task. But the work is a refreshing departure from the classical 'academic comprehension' model.

What do we know about the state of affairs in our nation in each of these three areas? Relatively little. We know next to nothing about decoding competence. A direct measure of this set of skills would require a student to make a spoken response to a written word, and this cannot be done with group-administered, multiple-choice technology. Knowledge about the state of reading comprehension and functional literacy is an unsystematic glob in which verbal fluency, previous academic experience and training, and general thinking ability are all interwoven. And again, most of what is known comes from group-administered multiple-choice tests.

Assessment of minimal skills and knowledge

For these reasons, I think that the *top priority* for reading research should be given to the task of improving our systems of assessment. Until we have more adequate, 'cleaner' systems for measuring reading skills at different stages of the development of reading, we will be working in the dark. Let me reemphasize what is being said here—we do not need new tests; we need new ways of testing (Calfee, 1974a,b).

Tied to the assessment problem is another significant goal—the *identification of minimal sets of skills and knowledge necessary for acceptable reading competence at several stages of development in the reading process.* The idea here is to establish three or four 'test points' falling at major transition points in the acquisition of skilled reading. At each of these points, the effort should be to identify a small set of criterial competencies, comprising no more than five to seven categories within each stage. This is a 'thought' problem, requiring a melding of available research, current practice and common sense. Existing instructional programs and achievement test systems do not adequately specify skills or knowledge in any defensible fashion—'vocabulary knowledge,' 'word attack skills' and 'comprehension ability' are much too broad and ill-defined to be either teachable or testable. At the other extreme are compendia of behavioral objectives, lists of thousands of specific performance goals. The problem is that these are generally too specific. Without additional organization and assignment of priorities, behavioral objects constitute an intolerable burden for the teacher, who, being human, has an upper limit on memory of five to nine pieces of information.

It would seem reasonable to me to establish four test points, corresponding roughly to the developmental stage now identified with kindergarten, third grade, sixth grade and ninth grade. These test points range from a prereading stage to the final stage of skilled reading where a student has acquired strategies for scanning and analysis during reading. The variety of abilities changes from one level to the next—at the prereading stage we are concerned with cognitive and linguistic skills; later word attack and comprehension become key terms, albeit in need of tighter definition.

I would urge that emphasis be placed on identification of underlying competence, on domains of skill and knowledge, rather than specific performance objectives (Hively, 1975). It is more important that a child understand the major contrast in English between 'long' and 'short' vowel patterns than that he be able to pronounce a list of fifty words in which the contrast is reflected. Measurement of understanding requires decisions about what the test shall contain, I realize. But making a measurement is not the same as understanding what is being measured.

Development of appropriate instruments must await some agreement on what skills should be considered essential. Even then, the technical task is not trivial. Adequate tests would require that incidental factors such as instructions, clarity of materials, and minimization of extraneous factors be properly dealt with.

My particular concern is for the development of instruments that are usable by teachers in the classroom, as well as by those who have responsibility for program and curriculum evaluation. Many people are working on this problem, but the troops seem in considerable disarray. There is no agreement on whether we need to focus on the general development of specific instructions or on processes of instrumentation. Criteria for the development of measurement instruments are a mixed bag. Professional test developers are concerned about the reliability and validity of instruments, whereas the demands for rapid and efficient testing lead to 'quickie' instruments developed for specific purpose.

Development and validation of content-oriented classroom observation systems

To find out how reading is presently taught in regular classrooms, we need better ways of viewing the process of classroom instruction. I am in general agreement with the critical review of classroom observation systems by Dunkin and Biddle (1974, pp. 53–80), and will not go into detail here on the point. Whether for purposes of hypothesis generation or for describing the effects of program variations, there is an urgent need for a classroom observation system that focuses on the substance of instruction. We need a system (or collection of compatible systems, or format for creating systems) that is comprehensive—that covers the teacher, students, the content and character of what is being taught and learned. There is little reason to hope for new technology to do miracles; in my opinion, television provides a limited view of much that goes on in a classroom unless the teacher stands still, the students all stay in place, and the bulk of what transpires is either spoken (loudly and clearly) or is clearly apparent from the camera vantage. These conditions are not to be found in many typical classrooms.

I think the problem is solvable, if we provide teacher-observers with suitable means of recording what they see, and the freedom (indeed, the mandate) to become dynamic agents in the classroom, moving to the scene of the action. We have carried out some preliminary work with a system constructed along these lines (Calfee and Hoover, 1974); and while no formal results are available at present on the suitability or reliability of our systems, we feel encouraged.

Experiments in classroom on critical program factors

Next priority should go to the identification and evaluation of potentially critical program factors (by 'program' we mean curriculum and instructional activities) and to efficient experimental evaluation of these factors under natural classroom conditions (Calfee, 1974c). Current practices in program research have been severely criticized by numerous investigators (Cronbach, 1963). We need no more research in which method A is compared with method B. Such gross comparisons are unenlightening to the researcher and useless to the practitioner. For that matter, there is probably no need to develop new curricula or new programs. A great wealth of curricula, supplemental systems, teacher-training packages and so on already exists. The problem is that we don't know how to use what we have; we don't know what really makes a given program effective in the context in which it seems to be working; we don't know the boundary conditions.

I think we need more adequate programs for teacher training. There is a need for improvement in pre- and inservice programs and for systematic development of on-the-job training procedures. The study by Beall and Dominick (1973) of preservice training in reading instruction documents the distressing fact that most of the people who teach children to read have little or no training in how to perform this task.

Likely candidates for training include: (a) adequate knowledge of the content of reading instruction, (b) skills at collection of evidence for evaluating what a student knows and does not know, and (c) the development of skills in the art of classroom management.

Along with evidence of the effectiveness of training programs designed to enhance skills in these areas, we need data on the relative efficiency of various means of delivering such programs. The typical inservice training session may not be the best way to change teacher behavior. Lest I be misunderstood, let me hasten to say that I am impressed by many of the teachers whom I have met in classrooms. As Sarason (1971) points out in his book on the structure of the school and the problem of the change, there is much that researchers can learn from effective classroom teachers. Nevertheless I am convinced that the contrary is also true—teachers can learn from effective educational researchers.

Finally, there is need for a more systematic examination of the principal as a change agent. Studies of the role of the principal in reading might suggest that this person has no role at all. Such a finding would merit thoughtful reflection. The research might also reveal that the degree of knowledge and concern by the principal in specific content areas such as reading is directly related to the effectiveness of the reading program in the school.

Experimental research methodology. If reading research is to prove useful and relevant in the next decade, experimental methodology applied to practical questions in real-life settings must become the model. The methodology must become more efficient, more suited to the complex dynamics of an educational system.

Whether a research question is descriptive (what is happening) or prescriptive (what is the best course of action), methodology should yield outcomes that are *objective, generalizable*, and *multivariate*. In addition, for prescriptive research, the methodology should permit causal rather than correlational outcomes and hence should be *experimental*. *Objective* means that a set of results is reproducible within tolerable limits; we clearly understand what was done, and the conditions under which the evidence was obtained. *Generalizable* means that we can estimate the probable effects of contextual variations on a set of results; if a study is replicated in a different situation, we can predict how large a change in the results to expect. *Multivariate* means that we need to provide for identification and measurement of multiple aspects of the reader's responses. The input–output relations in reading are complex, and the measurement system must encompass this complexity. Finally, *experimental* means that the investigator maintains direct control over the various components in an environment that are likely to affect performance.

Much of the research on reading has been correlational in nature—the investigator obtains numerous measures of a system, and by examining covariation tries to gain an understanding of how the system works. However, correlation is not causality; it is not true that it gets cold at night because the stars come out. In an experiment, the investigator systematically varies selected factors and observes the outcome. Causal links can then be traced with more certainty.

Of the reading research that can in any way be construed as experimental, the bulk falls into one of two categories: (1) small-scale, tightly controlled, laboratory-like research, so remote from the classroom as to be of questionable applicability; (2) large-scale, poorly controlled, real-world research—one method is compared with another; no matter what the outcome, the results are uninterpretable. For example, consider the Government Accounting Office review of the 'Performance Contracting Experiment' (1973): (a) there may have been no difference in the way the experimental and control schools were treated; at least nobody checked to see if there was (also cf. Charters and Jones 1973); (b) the planned differences were multiply confounded, so even if the experiment had been conducted as planned, no one could say for sure what any differences between experimental and control groups might reflect; (c) the performance measures were not selected because they were appropriate to the nature of the program, but because they were conventionally acceptable. For all these reasons, the 'Performance Contracting Experiment' left the critical question unanswered.

The behavioral sciences possess a variety of procedures and analytic tools to meet the requirements stated above. To be sure, the researcher who has chosen to investigate the process of reading instruction may have to range over many disciplines to collect the necessary tools—he may borrow survey methods from sociology, factor analysis and multiple regression from test theory and educational psychology, fractional factorial designs from agriculture and industrial statistics. He will have to overcome the weakness of standardized, norm-referenced tests, the confounding present in method A/method B designs, and the rapture of high-speed digital computers. These temptations are the more dangerous because they cannot be entirely avoided. But whether the investigator's task is basic or applied research, powerful and informative methodological tools exist (Cronbach *et al.*, 1972; Finn, 1974; Glass and Stanley, 1970; Kerlinger, 1973; Snow, 1974; Wittrock and Wiley, 1970).

Procedures for efficient experimental investigation of complex systems have existed for some time, and have been employed in industrial research—these are called fractional factorial experimental designs. These procedures have seen little application in educational research, largely because of lack of familiarity, but also because of concern with complicated interactions. We have adapted these procedures to the study of a young child's thought process during reading (e.g. Lucas, 1974). They have proved successful in several other applications. At present we are documenting the design and analysis procedures as they apply to behavioral research problems. These same ideas are applicable to large-scale educational research, where the payoff should be even greater. In place of an experimental-control comparison focused on a single variable, one can examine a dozen or more relevant variables simultaneously for about the same cost as the simple design.

This approach has particular relevance for longitudinal study of reading acquisition—for a *case study*. The numerous calls for case-study investigations of reading spring from many causes, but it seems that (a) rigorous, generalizable research can be built around the case-study model, and (b) this paradigm will provide answers to significant questions that cannot otherwise be handled. In a great deal of educational research, 'individual differences' refers to statistical scatter in a collection of univariate measures. In English composition, the individual's style in approaching a variety of writing tasks would seem to be a fundamental question. Longitudinal data, obtained over periods of months and years, may be essential to accurate characterization of an individual.

A case study based on a single individual (this is often what people mean by 'case study') serves certain restricted purposes. Where the individual is of note *per se*, as in the case of biographical studies of a famous person, the rationale is clear cut. And where the phenomenon under investigation is relatively stable and unchanging from one individual to the next (as in psycho-physical investigations of sensory functioning), the 'N-1' case study serves quite adequately.

But for purposes of generalizability, case studies of the educational development of an individual require that several individuals be included in a study. In such a case, where a substantial investment in investigative time and effort is expended on each individual in a study, the investigator must select his subjects to yield the largest amount of useful information. Sampling designs are useful in this respect, and fractional designs are exceptionally efficient for this purpose. We are using this procedure now in studies of the acquisition of beginning reading. In this study, a relatively small number of students ($n < 50$) are intensively studied over one or more school years. The students are selected so that a large number of potentially significant sources of individual differences are controlled by the sampling design. This procedure provides the generalizability features of large-scale survey designs with the data-intensive features of a case study, and seems well suited to the needs of many other educational research questions.

Research consortia. Most well-controlled research on reading has been done in laboratories, not in real schools. And almost everyone shudders at the thought of experiments in real schools. But progress in reading research is probably going to require that we deal with this difficulty directly.

I believe that it is feasible to carry out reasonably controlled experimental investigations in real schools. Such efforts require certain conditions. Foremost, they require a mutual commitment by researcher and school community to 'live together' for a while. These efforts also require more thoughtful prior consideration of the question under study by the investigator, more advance planning of a substantive sort, a willingness by schools staff to change their way of doing things from time to time, and cooperation of staff and students in the data collection process.

A number of serious problems must be faced. There is a widespread scepticism among school people about the potential value of research and evaluation, and with some reason. Schools tend to be 'closed' to researchers. Too many principals and teachers have been stung by the 'fly-by-night' researcher who promises everything and delivers nothing. Too many schools have experienced evaluation as measuring the wrong things at the wrong times to no obvious end. Researchers and evaluators, in turn, have had to trust to the vagaries of fickle funding agencies, with random changes in level of support, duration, and requirements.

We have no easy answers to these problems. It does seem that 'strong' experimentally-oriented research should be part of large-scale innovative efforts. And it does seem that *evaluation* of innovative programs should be taken more seriously. Evaluation all too often is at the end of the line vis-à-vis planning, staffing and funding. Nothing is rendered and everything is expected. To facilitate such efforts, it would seem reasonable to organize consortia of schools and research groups, built upon a relatively long-term and collaborative commitment to the pursuit of specified research goals. These may strike you as fanciful ideas, but we seriously advise against collecting more numbers of questionable origin for doubtful purposes.

The broader context of reading failure. There is a fundamental concern that lurks in the shadows of any discussion of priorities in reading research, evaluation, and instruction. Development of reading skills is a very specific educational goal. Our present methods of measuring reading achievement show that existing instructional practice fails to teach many children to read well enough to meet their needs. However, it is equally clear that the problem is not strictly a function of reading programs in our schools, nor of shortcomings of students. It also has to do with the allocation of resources by the larger society. We know where the majority of reading problems are found—they occur in urban schools that serve poor families. It seems doubtful that different curricula, better trained teachers, or changes in classroom management routines will make much difference to the overloaded school in a disadvantaged neighborhood. We can try to improve the efficiency of the educational processess in various ways, but eventually we need to assign more resources to those places where greater need exists. Attention to the priorities discussed in this paper does not cope with the obstacles presented by inadequate resources. However, such a focus would permit us to be more effective in teaching children to read when and where resources are available.

Note: The preparation of this paper was supported by a grant from the Carnegie Corporation.

References

Beall, J. G. Jr. and Dominick, P. H. (1973) S.1318. A Bill to Amend the Elementary and Secondary Educational Act of 1965, to Authorize Reading Emphasis Programs to Improve Reading in the Primary

Grades, and for Other Purposes, *Congressional Record*, 22 March, SS5369–77.

Blanton, W. E. (1973) 'TRDPR as an answer to problems of reading behavior research and a basis for future directions' (guest editorial), *Reading Research Quarterly*, 8 (2).

Bond, G. L. and Dykstra, R. (1967) 'The cooperative research program in first-grade reading instruction', *Reading Research Quarterly*, 2.

Calfee, R. C. (1974a) 'Assessment of independent reading skills. Basic research and practical applications', in A. S. Reber and D. Scarborough (eds), *Contributions to Symposium on Reading*, sponsored by the Center for Research in Cognition and Affect of the City University of New York and the Eastern Verbal Investigators League (in press).

Calfee, R. C. (1974b) 'Sources of dependency in cognitive processes', To appear in *Cognition and Instruction* (10th Annual Carnegie-Mellon Symposium on Cognition).

Calfee, R. C. (1974c) The Design of Experiments and the Design of Curriculum, occasional paper for Stanford Evaluation Consortium.

Calfee, R. C. and Hoover, K. A. (1974) 'Reading and Mathematical Observation System: RAMOS', unpublished manuscript, Stanford University.

Carroll, J. B. (1971) *Report of the Committee on Reading of the National Academy of Education*.

Charters, W. W. Jr. and Jones, J. E. (1973) 'On the risk of appraising non-events in program evaluation', *Educational Researcher*, 2 (11), 5–7.

Corder, R. (1971) *The Information Base for Reading*, Final Report, project no. 0–9031, Office of Education.

Cronbach, L. J. (1963) 'Evaluation for course improvement', *Teachers College Record*, 64 (also in R. W. Heath (ed.), *New Curricula*, N.Y., Harper & Row, 1964, pp. 231–48).

Cronbach, L. J. *et al.* (1972) *The Dependability of Behavioral Measurements: Theory of Generalizability for Scores and Profiles*, N.Y., Wiley.

Dunkin, M. J. and Biddle, B. J. (1974) *The Study of Teaching*, N.Y., Holt, Rinehart & Winston, 1974.

Finn, J. D. (1974) *A General Model for Multivariate Analysis*, N.Y., Holt, Rinehart & Winston.

Gephart, W. J. (1972) 'A progress report and a directional question' (guest editorial), *Reading Research Quarterly*, 7 (4).

Gibson, E. J. and Levin, H. (1975) *The Psychology of Reading*, MIT Press.

Glass, G. V. and Stanley, J. C. (1970) 'Fundamentals of experimental design', chapter 19 in *Statistical Methods in Education and Psychology*, Englewood Cliffs, N.J., Prentice-Hall.

Hively, W. (ed.) (1975) *Domain-referenced Testing*, Englewood Cliffs, N.J., Educational Technology Press.

Kavanaugh, J. F. and Mattingly, I. (1972) *Language by Ear and by Eye*, MIT Press.

Kerlinger, F. N. (1973) 'Designs of research', part 4 in *Foundations of Behavioral Research*, N.Y., Holt, Rinehart & Winston.

Kling, M. (1971) *Models of Reading* (Report of the Targeted Research on Reading Committee).

Lohnes, P. R. and Gray, M. M. (1972) 'Intelligence and the cooperative reading studies', *Reading Research Quarterly*, spring.

Lucas, J. F. (1974) *A Stage Processing Model of Reading for Elementary School Pupils*, Technical Report, Children's Research Center, University of Illinois, Urbana.

Miller, G. A. (ed.) (1973) *Linguistic Communication: Perspectives for Research* (Report of the Study Group on Linguistic Communication to the National Institute of Education), Newark, Del., International Reading Association.

National Assessment of Educational Progress (1973) *Reading: Released Exercises*, Report 02-R-20, July.

Sarason, S. B. (1971) *The Culture of the School and the Problem of Change*, Boston, Allyn & Bacon.

Snow, R. E. (1974) 'Representative and quasi-representative designs for research on teaching', *Review of Educational Research*, 44 (3), 265–91.

United States General Accounting Office (1973) *Evaluation of the Office of Economic Opportunity's Performance Contracting Experiment*, B-130515.

Wittrock, M. C. and Wiley, D. E. (1970) *The Evaluation of Instruction: Issues and Problems*, N.Y., Holt, Rinehart & Winston.

7. 2 Practical applications of reading research

Albert J. Harris

Research in reading has been going on for nearly a century, and more research is done on reading than on any other curricular area; more than on all other curricular areas together. The most recent annual summary of reading research in *Reading Research Quarterly* covered 369 items, a tremendous number of reports. Yet reading research often fails to have the impact on practice that it might and should. New ideas in reading sometimes make great headway with no supporting research or with a very shaky and unconvincing research base.

There are three main reasons why reading research has not had a stronger influence on what goes on in schools. The first of these is the powerful impact of social forces such as the bandwagon effect, the pendulum swing, and the prevailing climate of opinion.

The bandwagon is well known in politics. In a time of widespread dissatisfaction a new slogan can quickly attract a small following, even if untried and untested. If these supporters are enthusiastic and make sufficient noise they can create the impression that a great and glorious change is getting started. Attention from the mass media can accelerate the process. A rush can develop to be among the first to join; as others observe the rapid growth of the movement they also may feel impelled to jump on the bandwagon.

Education has had its share of bandwagon effects. Within the past two decades there have been the rush to revise science teaching after Sputnik, the non-graded school, team teaching, the free school, and the open school, to name just a few. Most of these have not shown clear superiority over what had preceded them before

Source: *Reading Teacher*, 29, 1976, pp. 559–64.

they were recommended for widespread adoption. Tryout under favorable circumstances had demonstrated that they could work. But how they *would* work in more typical schools, with varying teachers and various groups of pupils, had usually not been determined. Salesmanship preceded research.

Given a bandwagon movement, it is almost inevitable that a pendulum swing will develop. The new idea becomes more and more popular, then doubts about it arise, and a trend away from it begins.

Many of the new movements which are current in education have persuasive rationales, but have little in the way of research support. In a just-released volume on new ways of dealing with individual differences, philosopher Michael Scriven (1975) asserts that such movements are packaged individualized learning systems, competency-based teacher training, behavioral objectives, criterion-referenced testing, resource centers, and responsive environments have been promoted primarily on the basis of novelty, the positive implications of the movement's name, pressure from sponsoring groups and individuals, government funds for experimental implementation, and endorsement by people with prestigious names, rather than on the basis of solid evaluative studies. He calls for an attitude of cool and skeptical caution regarding innovations until there is satisfactory evidence on what they can and cannot accomplish. He particularly deplores the pendulum swing.

> It is the metronome of mediocrity, the crude clock that marks our lost chances of progress, and, I think, of survival. Once we have wound up this great engine, with all the forces of fashion and faddism, it is no easy task to slow it down, to get its cadence into step with the instruments that measure quality. The clock ticks on, and movements come and go to its beat.

One effect of the pendulum swing is that often practice shifts from one undesirable overemphasis to an even more undesirable opposite. A change which may have originally been based on some valid research may be carried to an extreme far beyond what the research justified. Thus the idea that words can be recognized as wholes, which had a valid base in the early eye-movement and tachistoscope studies, was carried in some school systems to the extreme of forbidding teachers to teach phonics. Some of my students in the 1940s, when I would encourage them to include some phonics instruction in their reading activities, were afraid that if they did so, they would get in trouble with their school principals. Those who taught some phonics felt like educational bootleggers. During the 1960s the systematic teaching of decoding skills became fashionable again.

Another pendulum swing has taken place with regard to IQ tests. After World War I, group IQ tests came into very wide use in American schools. It was widely believed that the IQ was constant, mainly determined by heredity, and an excellent predictor of how much and how fast a child could learn. Gradually research revealed that the IQ was less constant, more modifiable by environment, and less accurate in predicting learning than had been supposed. But it took the social concerns about the disadvantaged which came to the fore in the 1960s to carry the pendulum swing to an undesirable extreme. In at least one great city, New York, the use of group IQ tests was forbidden in the schools even for purely research purposes such as the equation of experimental groups, and even when the results would not be communicated to school personnel nor entered on school records. This pendulum is still swinging, and it is risky to predict where it will be ten years from now.

A third aspect of the social forces that influence education is the powerful effect of the prevailing climate of opinion, the spirit of the times or *Zeitgeist*. Edwin G. Boring (1950), the historian of psychology, has pointed out that some psychological discoveries had no effect or influence for a generation or two, and then were recognized as having been major contributions. When research results run counter to the prevailing orthodoxy, they may be dismissed as invalid, or just ignored. When the pendulum swings and the climate of opinion shifts, the previously neglected results may be resurrected or rediscovered. Jeanne Chall (1967) has emphasized the importance of the climate of opinion on the reception of research on beginning reading.

These factors, the bandwagon effect, the pendulum swing, and the prevailing climate of opinion, determine to an unfortunately large degree whether or not particular research results will be accepted as guides to practice.

The second main factor limiting the impact of reading research on practice is that the lines of communication between researcher and practitioner are often down. Reading research is published in dozens of journals, few of which are read by reading practitioners. Because of space limitations and editorial preferences, published reports tend to be written in a compressed style that is difficult to read, and often employ technical jargon and statistical procedures that are unfamiliar to the practitioner. Even if a practitioner has had the technical training to be able to understand and appraise research reports, he or she usually does not have either the time or the library resources to keep abreast of research trends in this way.

A third factor which diminishes the potential effect of research on practice is that much of the published research on reading is of quite limited value. As Campbell and Stanley (1963) have pointed out, many research studies on the results of teaching have been quasi-experimental rather than truly experimental in design. Limitations of funding and resources have often resulted in small-scale studies, with unrepresentative populations, carried on for too short a time, with inadequate measures of results, and with less than ideal statistical treatment. Such studies are useful in training research workers but are not of much use in deciding important questions about practice. If so many published studies are inadequate, one can hardly blame the practitioner for looking elsewhere for guidance.

Up to here, this paper has discussed a number of reasons why research has not had more of an influence on reading practices. From here on, emphasis will be placed on what can be done to make the results of research more useful.

Current controversial issues

Teaching to the stronger modality

It has long been known that some learners do better with one method of instruction and others do better with a different method. This fact, often referred to as 'aptitude-treatment interaction,' focuses attention on finding which method is right for which child, rather than which is best for everyone. Wepman (1971) and many others have recommended that one should determine the child's strongest aptitude and teach by the method which stresses that aptitude. In both beginning reading and remedial instruction, this implies that pupils with stronger visual than auditory aptitudes should be taught by a primarily visual method, while those with stronger auditory aptitudes should be taught by a method stressing phonics. That seems very reasonable.

In beginning reading, the best study yet available, by Helen M. Robinson (1972b), found no relation between a child's stronger aptitude (visual or auditory) and success in learning to read by a particular method. Most children were high in both aptitudes or low in both. The minority who had discrepant aptitudes did not do better when the method matched their higher aptitude. Similar results were found by Barbara Bateman (1968). Perhaps with improved aptitude tests the results will be different. Meanwhile research does not support this particular application of the aptitude-treatment interaction idea. Research seems to support the use of a multisensory method from which the child can select whatever cues are most helpful to him in learning to identify written or printed words. In regard to remedial teaching there is insufficient research on this issue to decide the question.

Perceptual and perceptual-motor training

A related issue is the use of tests of special abilities at the preschool or first grade level and giving specific instruction to strengthen those abilities in which the child does poorly. A case in point is the use of Frostig Developmental Tests of Visual Perception and the Frostig–Horne teaching materials, which give practice in the five perceptual areas covered by the test. This had a tremendous bandwagon effect in the 1960s and is still quite widely used.

There has been a wealth of research on the Frostig program, and careful and authoritative reviews of this research have been prepared by Robinson (1972a) and by Wiederhold and Hammill (1971). These reviewers agree on the following conclusions: (1) the Frostig–Horne training program produces improved scores on the Frostig tests; (2) it sometimes but not always produces improved reading readiness scores; and (3) it usually fails to do better than, and sometimes does not do as well as, conventional readiness and beginning reading instruction in its effect on reading.

The Kephart approach was also widely adopted in the 1960s, particularly in classes for exceptional children. Kephart (1964) advocated a variety of activities to promote sensory-motor development and perceptual and motor integration. Klesius (1972) analyzed more than thirty studies on the Kephart approach. Of the eleven studies which met his standards for acceptable research, six did not favor the Kephart procedures.

Another careful review covering seventy-six studies on the Frostig and Kephart procedures was issued by Hammill, Goodman and Wiederhold (1974). They concluded as follows:

The readiness skills of children were improved in only a few instances. The effect of training on intelligence and academic achievement was not clearly demonstrated. Particularly disappointing were the findings which pertained to the effects of such training on perceptual-motor performance itself. We have little doubt that any interested person who reads the efficacy literature will conclude that the value of perceptual training, especially those programs often used in schools, has not been clearly established. If he concludes that such training lacks solid support, he may begin to question the purchase of attractively packaged materials which some companies offer teachers along with unsubstantiated claims concerning their merits, the practice of providing perceptual-motor training to all school children in the name of readiness training, and the assumption that a lack of perceptual-motor adequacy causes a considerable amount of academic failure.

If the Robinson, Klesius, and Hammill reviews were widely known, their effect on kindergarten and primary practices would be substantial. What they have shown is that perceptual and perceptual-motor practice that does not utilize verbal symbols is of doubtful value for reading.

Teaching reading skills or training deficient abilities

In the area of remedial reading one issue became a bone of contention during the 1960s. Many of the leaders of the learning disabilities movement taught that learning failures are due to the retarded or defective development of specific mental abilities. Train those abilities and the child will be able to learn. The Illinois Test of Psycholinguistic Abilities (ITPA) has twelve subtests and is the instrument most often used to identify specific abilities related to reading. However, a review of more than 200 references on the ITPA by John B. Carroll (1972) in the *Seventh Mental Measurements Yearbook* indicates that: there are only three main factors in the ITPA, namely expressive vocabulary, receptive vocabulary, and rote memory; the test is biased in favor of middle-class children; it has a quite high correlation with IQ; and there is no pattern of high or low scores that is characteristic of children with reading disabilities. It would seem that a program of training specific abilities based on the ITPA rests on fairly shaky ground. Furthermore, there is very little evidence as to the degree to which deficient abilities in children can be improved by special training.

The practical implications for the reading specialist and the classroom teacher trying to give individualized help to a poor reader, are that the limited time available can be spent more profitably in direct teaching of needed reading skills than in attempting to build up supposedly deficient abilities. The value of special abilities training in a self-contained class for learning disabilities is uncertain.

Making research accessible

It is a major service to the improvement of reading instruction when an expert on research makes an intensive, critical, and evaluative study of the work done on a significant problem and writes a critique which analyzes the results of the various studies, integrates them, and arrives at conclusions and recommendations. Several such reviews have been cited above. But all too often they do not reach the eyes of the practitioner.

Over a period of many years the *Reading Teacher* had a special feature in which recent research on a specific topic was succinctly reviewed in each issue. Agatha Townsend started this in the 1950s; Samuel Weintraub carried it on during the 1960s; and J. Wesley

Schneyer supervised it in 1970 and 1971. The last such feature was in the May 1971 issue. This feature brought the results of recent research to the attention of the majority of International Reading Association members, and nothing as satisfactory for that purpose has yet taken its place. Restoring this feature, perhaps in an improved form, would seem highly desirable. The annotated bibliographies which IRA publishes from time to time are also helpful, but probably do not reach enough people. The reviews of research in specific fields prepared by special committees of the National Conference on Research in English are also valuable but do not reach a wide enough audience. The same is true of the volumes on reading published every few years by the National Society for the Study of Education.

Much more ought to be done, and can be done, to bring distillations of the results of research in readable form to the attention of the reading practitioner.

Federal support has been given to some efforts to select reading programs that are worthy to be emulated and to make information about them available. A few years ago, the American Institutes for Research were funded to identify exemplary remedial reading programs and to make descriptions of these programs available. These descriptions were entered into the ERIC system in 1971 with the identification numbers ED 053 881 to ED 053 890.

Twelve of these programs were selected by the Right to Read Program of the US Office of Education for publication, now available as multimedia packages presenting case studies, program components, and procedures. [. . .] The criteria used in selecting these programs are given in full in chapter III of the final report from AIR (Bowers *et al.*, 1974) and should be crucial in helping one decide whether or not the selected programs are exemplary.

Additional programs are described in a catalog, *Effective Reading Programs: Summaries of 222 Selected Programs*, published by ERIC/RCS and available through the National Council of Teachers of English, 1111 Kenyon Road, Urbana, Illinois 61801.

According to John T. Guthrie, Director of Research for IRA, the Association is taking part in a major effort to determine what makes a compensatory program in reading superior or inferior. The Educational Testing Service has a grant of $2,500,000 to collect data on 700 schools, selected to be representative of schools with compensatory education programs. Two hundred of these schools have supplied test data as well as questionnaire data; thirty of the 200 were selected as representing the full range of achievement, from highest to lowest. Those thirty schools are being intensively studied, using interviews and classroom observations as well as the test and questionnaire data. The results should show which kinds of compensatory programs produce superior or inferior results, and the conditions necessary for superior reading results. The Educational Testing Service's report to the US Office of Education may not be made public. However, the data are also being released to IRA for use by a special committee chaired by William Eller, and statistical work is in process. The committee will make its own analysis and interpretation of the results and formulate a report which will be published by IRA. This large-scale, carefully planned, and well-funded project should be worth more than a score of small-scale studies in helping to identify practices that really work well in school settings.

References

Bateman, Barbara (1968) 'The efficacy of an auditory and a visual method on first-grade reading instruction with visual and auditory learning', in H. K. Smith (ed.), *Perception and Reading*, Newark, Del., International Reading Association, pp. 105–12.

Boring, Edwin G. (1950) *A History of Experimental Psychology*, 2nd ed., N.Y., Appleton-Century-Crofts.

Bowers, John E. *et al.* (1974) *Identifying, Validating and Multi-media Packaging of Effective Reading Programs*, Final Report, Palo Alto, Calif., American Institute for Research, December.

Campbell, Donald T. and Stanley, Julian C. (1963) 'Experimental and quasi-experimental designs for research on teaching', in N. L. Gage (ed.), *Handbook for Research on Teaching*, Chicago, Rand McNally, pp. 171–246.

Carroll, John B. (1972) 'Review of the ITPA', in O. K. Buros (ed.), *Seventh Mental Measurements Yearbook*, Highland Park, N.J., Gryphon Press, vol. 1, pp. 819–23.

Chall, Jeanne S. (1967) *Learning to Read: the Great Debate*, N.Y., McGraw-Hill.

Hammill, Donald D., Goodman, Libby and Wiederhold, J. Lee (1974) 'Visual-motor processes: can we train them?', *Reading Teacher*, 27 (5), February, 469–78.

Kephart, Newell C. (1964) 'Perceptual-motor aspects of learning disabilities', *Exceptional Children*, 31, December, 204–6.

Klesius, Stephen E. (1972) 'Perceptual-motor development and reading—a closer look', in R. C. Aukerman (ed.), *Some Persistent Questions on Beginning Reading*, Newark, Del., International Reading Association, pp. 151–9.

Robinson, Helen M. (1972a) 'Perceptual training—does it result in reading improvement?', in *Some Persistent Questions on Beginning Reading*, pp. 135–50.

Robinson, Helen M. (1972b) 'Visual and auditory modalities related to methods for beginning reading', *Reading Research Quarterly*, 8 (1), Fall, 7–39.

Scriven, Michael (1975) 'Problems and prospects for individualization', in

H. Talmadge (ed.), *Systems of Individualized Education*, Series on Contemporary Educational Issues, National Society for the Study of Education, Berkeley, Calif., McCutchan Publishing Corporation, pp. 199–210.

Wepman, Joseph M. (1971) 'Modalities and learning', in H. M. Robinson (ed.), *Coordinating Reading Instruction*, Glenview, Ill., Scott Foresman, pp. 55–60.

Wiederhold, J. L. and Hammill, D. D. (1971) 'Use of the Frostig–Horne visual perception program in the urban school', *Psychology in the Schools*, 8, July, 268–74.

Index